MAPPING
OUR
ANCESTORS

PHYLOGENETIC APPROACHES IN
ANTHROPOLOGY AND PREHISTORY

MAPPING
OUR
ANCESTORS

EDITORS

CARL P. LIPO
MICHAEL J. O'BRIEN
MARK COLLARD
STEPHEN J. SHENNAN

FOREWORD BY NILES ELDREDGE

ALDINETRANSACTION
A DIVISION OF TRANSACTION PUBLISHERS
NEW BRUNSWICK (U.S.A.) AND LONDON (U.K.)

Library of Congress Catalog Number: 2005050649
ISBN: 0-202-30750-6 (alk. paper)—ISBN 0-202-30751-4 (alk. paper)
Printed in the United States of America

Library of Congress Cataloging-in-Publication Data

Mapping our ancestors : phylogenetic approaches in anthropoloogy and
    prehistory / Carl P. Lipo... [et al.], editors ; foreword by Niles Eldredge.
        p. cm.
    Based on two symposia held during the 2003 Annual Meeting of the Society
for American Archaeology in Milwaukee, Wis.
    Includes bibliographical references and index.
    ISBN 0-202-30750-6 (alk. paper)—ISBN 0-202-30751-4 (alk. paper)
        1. Human evolution—Congresses. 2. Paleoanthropology—Congresses.
3. Anthropology, Prehistoric—Congresses. 4. Phylogeny—Congresses. 5.
Cladistic analysis—Congresses. I. Lipo, Carl P. II. Society for American
Archaeology. Meeting (68th : 2003 : Milwaukee, Wis.)

GN281.M336   2005
599.93'8—dc22   2005050649

Contents

Figures

Tables

Foreword

Niles Eldredge

One of my favorite papers in the literature devoted to phylogenetic analytic methods was a collaborative effort by a classicist, H. Donald Cameron, and an arachnid systematist, Norman I. Platnick (Platnick and Cameron 1977). Cameron was working in the spider collections at the University of Michigan Museum of Zoology as a devoted amateur. He noticed Platnick's publications and was struck by the similarity between the analytic techniques— "cladistics"—Platnick was using to reconstruct spider phylogenies, and the techniques of historical linguistics. Their joint paper traces the development of the logic of genealogical reconstruction to a third field: stemmatics, the study of the history of manuscripts. Cladistics—Willi Hennig's "phylogenetic systematics"—was identified by Platnick and Cameron as the same strategy to recapture and reconstruct genealogical pathways.

The logic, as has since become well known in evolutionary biology, and which is well represented and discussed in many papers in this volume, is simplicity itself: in any system based on transmissible information, any modification of that information will be passed along to future "generations" —or, more generally, future instantiations—in the same, or in progressively still further modified form. If there are bifurcations in the pattern of transmission, lineages will share only features held in common by their latest shared ancestor. Darwin (1859) realized these two important points, showing that the nested pattern of resemblance linking all life, already known to systematists before his time, would be the necessary, expected result of a genealogical process of "descent with modification"—the first use he made of his sole diagram of lineages acquiring novelties through time—that occasionally produced bifurcation (as there are patently more than one species of organisms on the planet at any one time).

Imagine a group of monks seated around a table, each making a copy of the same manuscript. Perhaps all the copies would be 100 percent true to the original; but monks, not being human Xerox®machines, would as likely make mistakes in their copying as be perfect—and their introduced errors would in most instances be different from each other's. (Though undoubtedly apocryphal, it has been said that the entire tradition of Saint James's remains ending up in Spain—the birth of the entire elaborate trans-European pilgrimages to Santiago de Campostela—arose from such a copying error, when someone mistook "Heirusalem" for "Hispania.") When the manuscripts were completed and disseminated to different outlying monasteries, there perhaps to be copied over again, the copying errors peculiar to each manuscript would be (more or less) faithfully rendered, and new ones introduced—leading to a hierarchically structured array of modifications (perpetuated errors).

Voila: Hennig's "heterobathmy of synapomorphy"—at once a highly descriptive and overbearingly pedantic phrase. The reconstruction of the past becomes a mapping exercise—trying to ascertain the true distribution of any particular character state. The potential sources of error—at least in biological systems for which cladistics was initially developed (i.e., sexually reproducing organisms with little or no exchange of genetic information across clades) are basically only two: convergence (or parallelism—i.e., two characters are taken to be the "same" when they are in fact separately evolved) and pure analytic error—where character states thought to be limited to a particular segment of a tree are in fact more widely distributed, meaning they in fact evolved earlier in the history of the system. Homoplasy is the blanket word for false signal—the noise in the system that must be ferreted out to come up with the "true" phylogeny.

Sounds simple. The logic is unassailable. But in practice conflicts nearly always show up even in the most linear, simple-bifurcating systems. And when the systems themselves are intrinsically more complex than the relatively simple case of a bunch of monks sitting around a table copying a manuscript, things rapidly become intractably messy. The problems, yet to be fully analyzed, all revolve around what used to be a relatively straightforward concept: "homology." In the earlier days of evolutionary biology, homology was "true" resemblance: the human eye is homologous with the eyes of vervet monkeys, eastern gray squirrels, and Australian lungfish—the vertebrate eye is manifestly evolved once (though independently lost in many unrelated lineages). In contrast, "analogy" is "false" similarity, albeit interesting: the independent development of features, superficially similar, evolved as adaptations to "solve" the same mechanical problem—but *not* inherited from a single common ancestor. Cephalopod eyes are rather like vertebrate eyes, but they evolved independently as did the really structurally different compound eyes of arthropods.

So, from the point of view of phylogenetic systematics, homology becomes a nested sequence of derived character states (synapomorphies): the vertebrate brain is homologous throughout the subphylum Vertebrata, but the derived condition of the brain in mammals is homologous within Mammalia; and the further derived condition in *Homo sapiens*, shared perhaps only with a few (extinct) species, is further restricted. Still sounds simple and fairly straightforward.

But problems arise. It has been relatively easy to ignore cases of rampant hybridization within eukaryotes, as restricted to certain notorious groups (zoologists are still fond of saying that hybridization is mainly a problem in plant evolution—and even there, restricted to certain groups, like the rose family). And algorithms have, in any case, long since been developed to detect hybridization. More difficult is the problem of horizontal transfer between "unrelated" groups of prokaryotes, and here, too, analytic protocols have been (relatively recently) developed to map such gene transfers. As several authors in this volume say, we should in principle be able to map the flow of information regardless of how complex that flow may turn out to have been.

Further muddying the waters, evolutionary developmental biology ("evo-devo") has recently mounted a fascinating challenge to the comfortable old concept of homology: it turns out that the regulation of the development of *both* vertebrate and arthropod eyes lies in undoubtedly homologous genetic mechanisms. In some profound sense, the traditional, easy distinction between homology and analogy has been shattered as new understandings of the nature of the genetic information that is actually transmitted—and modified in the evolutionary process—becomes better known. Scary stuff: when the conceptual underpinnings of homology are challenged in biology, we find ourselves in uncharted waters.

That said, how about other systems with histories of information transmission? As the chapters in this volume make clear, it has long made perfect sense to speak of "cultural evolution"—and indeed there is a huge literature on the subject going back at least to Herbert Spencer. Most analysts have readily seen the critical difference between cultural and biological information in both their respective natures and modes of transfer. Culture—whether material culture or the more exiguous canons of behavior not tied to physical objects—is taught/learned/copied/stolen. So (and, again, as many chapters in this volume make abundantly clear), horizontal transmission is expectedly rife in cultural evolution, and it may even predominate over the sort of vertical transmission that protocols like cladistics were originally developed to capture.

Indeed, the more linear and simply bifurcating the history of a cultural system, the more it approximates biological phylogenetic patterns, and the more effective cladistic and similar algorithms will likely be in recapturing the history of the system. This conclusion comes from comparing analyses of two different examples of musical instrument "evolution." The first system is Balto-Finnic and north Slavic psalteries, with their relatively simple morphology and apparent migratory history from lyre-like ancestors in the Mediterranean, up through to the present examples in contemporary Northern Europe (Temkin 2004). Even here, conflicts persist and the efficacy of phylogenetic methods is not 100 percent clear. But cladistics nonetheless sheds far more light on the history of the relatively simple psaltery system compared with preliminary analyses of a database I have recently compiled on cornet (so-

prano brasswind instruments) design history ("evolution"). Suffice it to say
that theft of idea is so pervasive in this system that most cladograms and
phenograms generated so far bear only a slight resemblance to what is otherwise known about the actual design history of these instruments.

But there is one further problem that deserves serious analysis—and once
again "homology" rears its increasingly ugly head. I have in mind here what I
call the "Hannah Principle" (for Bruce Hannah, former chairman of industrial
design at Pratt Institute, who first suggested the notion to me). Biological
evolution produces transformation series in homologous characters—a sequence of primitive to derived to even-more-derived states that phylogenetic
algorithms are designed to detect. Even when alternative character states are
not explicitly ordered in a data set, cladistic algorithms are nonetheless geared
to detect sequences of primitive to derived states: polarity in character states is
simply a given in both biological evolution and the algorithms developed to
reconstruct phylogenetic patterns. Advanced states are modifications of pre-
existing states.

And, often, cultural items—certainly parts of objects, as the bell of cor-
nets—can be said to change through time in the same way, where later states
are outgrowths, modifications, of previous states. But often in design history
such is not the case. Rather, humans invent alternative solutions to the same
problem—a sort of planned, deliberate convergence that nonetheless pur-
posefully does *not* end up in confusingly similar states. This is homoplasy of
a rather different sort. For example, patents might, at least temporarily, pro-
hibit (or at least inhibit) a certain innovation from being incorporated into the
products of competitors, in which case (as in the history of valves in brass
instruments) other makers simply come up with their own "improvements"
(whether in a mechanical sense these alternate states really in fact constitute
"improvements" is another matter). The history of the Périnet valve (Eldredge
2003) is a case in point: the temporal sequence of disparate designs is far more
a sequence of alternates—or even reactions against pre-existing configurations—than it is a simple derivation of progressively more advanced forms
from pre-existing, more "primitive" forms. In my opinion, this is the most
profound obstacle to applying phylogenetic analytic methods developed in
evolutionary biology to cultural systems yet to emerge.

The authors of the sixteen chapters of this book are aware of the potential
pitfalls. Together, they explore a range of techniques that can be brought to
bear on the difficult task of reconstructing pathways of historical cultural
change. Biological systems are turning out to be more complex than we used
to think, and cultural systems, at least potentially, present an order of magnitude of greater complexity than their biological counterparts. The explora-
tions in this book take us closer to developing realistic procedures for the
rigorous analysis of cultural evolutionary history.

Preface

Much of what we are comes from our ancestors. Through cultural and biological inheritance mechanisms, our genetic composition, instructions for constructing artifacts, the structure and content of languages, and rules for behavior are passed from parents to children and from individual to individual. In order to explain how cultural material, language, and biology came to be as they are, we need tools that can trace their development through time and across space. We need a means of determining phylogeny, reconstructions of historical relationships: a map of our ancestors. For this reason anthropologists are increasingly turning to quantitative phylogenetic methods. Cladistic methods in particular make it possible to trace patterns of inheritance, thus providing the basis for building evolutionary explanations. These methods depend on the transmission of information regardless of mode and, as such, are applicable to many anthropological questions. In this way, phylogenetic approaches have the potential for building bridges among the various subdisciplines of anthropology. This is an exciting prospect indeed.

The structure of *Mapping Our Ancestors* reflects our goal of developing a common understanding of the methods and conditions under which ancestral relations can be derived from a range of data of interest to anthropologists. Specifically, this volume explores the degree to which patterns of ancestry can be determined from artifactual, genetic, linguistic, and behavioral data and how processes such as selection, transmission, and geography impact the results of phylogenetic analyses. The volume is divided into four parts. The first addresses the basic methodological framework of phylogenetic methods and explores issues of their application to anthropological data. Topics covered in this part include the construction of measurement units, considerations in applying the methods to cultural data, confounding factors, and systems of graphical representation. The latter three parts focus on issues related to the determination of ancestry in biological, cultural, and linguistic samples, respectively.

The idea for this volume came from a British Academy–funded workshop organized by James Steele (University of Southampton) and José-Luis Lanata (University of Buenos Aires) at the University of Southampton in June 2002, entitled "Human Global Dispersals." This stimulating and productive sharing of ideas led to two sessions ("Theoretical and Methodological Fundamentals of Applying Phylogenetics to the Archaeological Record") at the 68th Annual Society for American Archaeology meetings in Milwaukee, Wisconsin, in 2003. These joint symposia were organized by Carl P. Lipo, Michael O'Brien, Stephen Shennan, and James Steele and included twenty-six papers. All of the presenters from this meeting were invited to contribute to this volume.

In bringing this book to fruition we want to acknowledge the contribution of others. First, many thanks to the British Academy, AHRB Centre for Evolutionary Analysis of Cultural Behavior (CEACB), the Institute of Archaeology, and the University College London Graduate School for the funding that made the original workshops possible and for several of the authors to attend the symposium that led directly to this volume. We express our gratitude to the United Kingdom Arts and Humanities Research Board for funding for the CEACB, which also made possible several of the UK-based projects presented here. We also thank our colleagues at our home institutions (California State University Long Beach, CEACB, University of Missouri, and University of British Columbia) for providing a stimulating environment. In addition, we are grateful to Dan Glover for all his work on the figures and tables. Finally, we thank our original series editor Monique Borgerhoff Mulder for her enthusiasm for this project and for her guidance and support throughout its development.

Part 1

Introduction

1

Cultural Phylogenies and Explanation: Why Historical Methods Matter

*Carl P. Lipo, Michael J. O'Brien, Mark Collard,
and Stephen J. Shennan*

Imagine finding a collection of things and having to figure out how each one got to be the way it is. In addition to learning about, say, the chemical and physical characteristics of the objects, resolving this issue would lead you to ask about their history. Are they related to one another? If so, are they equally related, or are some items related more closely and some more distantly? These are not easy questions to answer, but they are ones with which natural and social scientists wrestle on a regular basis. They also are central to the chapters in this book.

Interest in genealogical, or "phylogenetic," relationships has a long tradition in the natural sciences. Although efforts at explaining the natural world in phylogenetic terms can be traced to at least 350 B.C. and Aristotle's *Historia Animalium*, most of the major steps in developing a means of describing biological organisms in a way that reflects their affinities have occurred in the last 300 years. One of these was the publication in 1735 of Carolus Linnaeus's *Systema Naturae*. Linnaeus popularized what has become one of the core ideas of biological phylogenetics, namely that species can be grouped into a hierarchy of progressively more inclusive taxa. Further progress in building a robust set of methods for delineating phylogenetic relationships among organisms came in 1859 with the publication of Charles Darwin's *On the Origin of Species*. Although it was not immediately recognized, Darwin's theory directed biologists interested in relatedness to limit their descriptions to one form of similarity—the kind that results from heredity. Traits that two or more taxa share because they inherited them from a common ancestor are termed "homologies."

A robust numerical method that made use of this portion of Darwin's theory emerged in the twentieth century at the hands of Walter Zimmerman (1931) and especially Willi Hennig (1950, 1966). The key component of this method, termed "phylogenetic systematics," or more commonly "cladistics," is its focus on a subset of homologous traits, namely those that are considered to be "derived" rather than "ancestral." Derived traits are character states exhibited

Figure 1.1
Phylogenetic Trees Showing the Evolution of Six Taxa (after O'Brien et al. 2001)

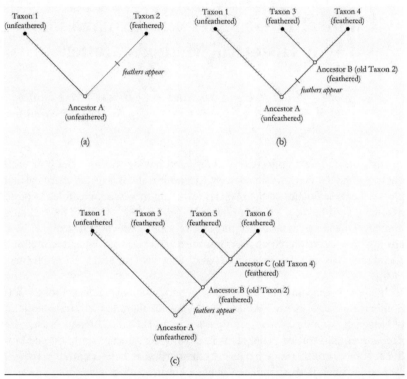

In (a) feathers appear during the evolution of Taxon 2 out of its ancestral taxon. The state "feathered" is termed an "apomorphy." In (b) Taxon 2 has produced two taxa, 3 and 4, both of which contain feathered specimens. The appearance of feathers in those sister taxa and in their common ancestor (B) makes it a "shared derived" character state, technically termed a "synapomorphy." In (c) one of the taxa that appeared in the previous generation (Taxon 4) gives rise to two new taxa, 5 and 6, both of which contain feathered specimens. If we focus attention only on these two new taxa, "feathered" is now an "ancestral" character state, technically termed a "plesiomorphy" (shared ancestral character states are termed "symplesiomorphies"). Note that it is shared by more taxa than just sister taxa 5 and 6 and their immediate common ancestor. But if we include Taxon 3 in our focus, having feathers is a synapomorphy because, following the definition, it occurs only in sister taxa and in their immediate common ancestor.

by a set of sister taxa and their immediate ancestor but no other taxon (figure 1.1). The final products of cladistic analyses are treelike structures called "phylogenetic trees," or "cladograms,"[1] that depict relationships among taxa.

In Figure 1.1(a) feathers appear during the evolution of Taxon 2 out of its ancestral taxon. The state "feathered" is termed an "apomorphy." In (b) Taxon 2 has produced two taxa, 3 and 4, both of which contain feathered specimens. The appearance of feathers in those sister taxa and in their common ancestor (B) makes it a "shared derived" character state, technically termed a "synapomorphy." In (c) one of the taxa that appeared in the previous generation (Taxon 4) gives rise to two new taxa, 5 and 6, both of which contain feathered specimens. If we focus attention only on these two new taxa, "feathered" is now an "ancestral" character state, technically termed a "plesiomorphy" (shared ancestral character states are termed "symplesiomorphies"). Note that it is shared by more taxa than just sister taxa 5 and 6 and their immediate common ancestor. But if we include Taxon 3 in our focus, having feathers is a synapomorphy because, following the definition, it occurs only in sister taxa and in their immediate common ancestor.

The principles that drive phylogenetic methods are not restricted to the study of biological entities. Indeed, phylogenetic methods are simply algorithms for building phylogenies once descriptions of taxa are made. The important point is that phylogenetic methods can be used to relate any set of features that change in nonrandom fashion over time, regardless of the mechanism or process.

In recent years, a growing number of social scientists have begun to use phylogenetic methods, especially cladistics, to address questions of cultural evolution. The datasets used in these studies come from a wide range of locations, including the Pacific (e.g., Gray and Jordan 2000; Hurles et al. 2003; Jordan 1999; Kirch and Green 1992, 2001), Africa (e.g., Foley 1987; Holden 2002; Holden and Mace 1997, 1999; Mace and Pagel 1994), Europe (e.g., Collard and Shennan, 2000; Gray and Atkinson 2003; Renfrew and Boyle 2000), Asia (e.g., Tehrani and Collard 2002), and North America (e.g., Lipo 2001; Lipo et al. 1997; O'Brien and Lyman 2003a; O'Brien et al. 2001, 2002).

The subject matter is similarly diverse. The growing literature on the use of phylogenetic methods in studies of material culture includes applications to stone tools (Foley 1987; Foley and Lahr 1997, 2003; O'Brien and Lyman 2003a, 2003b; O'Brien et al. 2001, 2002; Robson Brown 1995, 1996), baskets (e.g., Jordan and Shennan 2003), pottery (e.g., Collard and Shennan 2000), carpets (e.g., Tehrani and Collard 2002), written texts (e.g., Spencer et al. 2004) and even entire industries (e.g., Anderson 2003). The use of phylogenetic methods is also seeing a growing usage in sociocultural anthropology (e.g., Borgerhoff Mulder 2001; Borgerhoff Mulder et al. 2001; Holden and Mace 1997, 1999; Jones 2003; Mace and Pagel 1994; Sellen and Mace 1997), in historical linguistics (e.g., Gray and Atkinson 2003; Gray and Jordan 2000;

Holden 2002; Jordan 1999; Platnick and Cameron 1977; Rexová et al. 2003), and in multi-disciplinary studies (e.g., Hurles et al. 2003).

Adopting phylogenetic methods that have been developed primarily in biology and paleontology creates a set of theoretical, methodological, and empirical challenges as we attempt to apply the methods anthropologically. From a practical standpoint, do the methods accomplish what we want them to? From an epistemological standpoint, are they appropriate methods to use? And at the most fundamental level, are the products something that we as anthropologists need? Put simply, should we even care about phylogeny?

Phylogeny and Cultural Evolutionary Research

Let us return to the example we used in the opening paragraph: we have a collection of things and are interested in figuring out how each got to be the way it is. This is a phylogenetic problem. For the sake of argument, let us say that the things in the collection are artifacts recovered from an archaeological site. One means of creating a sequence is to examine artifact form. Analysis of form has long been used as a means of studying cultural continuity, the assumption being that artifact similarity often is a function of common ancestry (O'Brien and Lyman 1999). As Albert Spaulding (1955: 14) argued, variation in material culture "can be related to the proposition that cultural change is systematic rather than capricious and to the auxiliary proposition that an important basis for the systematic behavior of culture is its continuous transmission through the agency of person to person contact." Artifact variation, when described appropriately, can be explained as a function of descent with modification. Archaeologists such as A.V. Kidder (1932) and James Ford (1936) knew this, and it formed the basis of the approach that came to be known as culture history (Lyman et al. 1997).

The culture history approach to anthropology is broadly compatible with the biological model that views heritable change as descent with modification. Archaeologists have been modeling change in artifact form in this way since the birth of the discipline (e.g., Evans 1850; Petrie 1899). One example is E. B. Sayles's (1937) diagram (figure 1.2) showing the evolution of manos and metates from Snaketown, Arizona. In this figure, Sayles makes the claim that mano and metate forms have a single ancestor and diversify over time. This is descent with modification.

Another example is James Bennyhoff's (1994) map of the relations of Central Valley, California, projectile points, beads, and amulets (figures 1.3 and 1.4). Bennyhoff detailed change in these artifact classes through time and linked cases where he believed divergence occurred among artifacts (as with the amulets and beads) as well as convergence (as with the projectile points). These time-space charts are an embedded feature of archaeology and provide a framework for studying culture change. And for good reason: whenever our goals include explaining change through time, it is necessary to build models

Figure 1.2
Development of Manos and Metates at Snaketown, Arizona (after Sayles 1937)

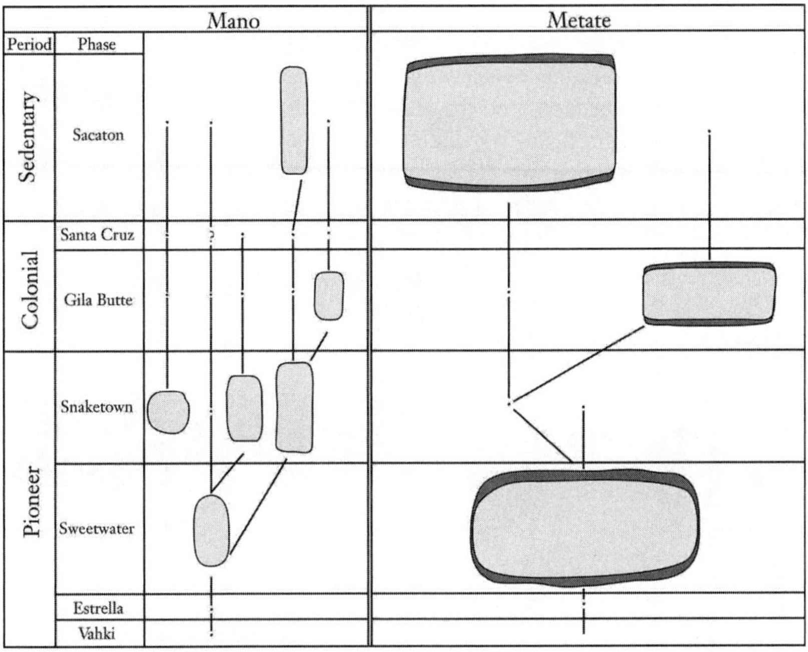

of relatedness. These models isolate characters suspected to be the result of inheritance as they vary through time and across space.

Accurately determining the degree to which the sharing of traits is a function of historical relatedness is vital in building evolutionary explanations. In order to explain the distribution of cultural traits across populations we must be able to identify those traits that are present as a result of historical contingency ("homologies") versus those that are a product of processes other than descent ("homoplasies"). Consider a case of explaining why projectile points found distributed in densely wooded upland environments are different from those found along oak-savannah valley bottoms.[2] We might find, for example, that some of the points in the uplands are slightly smaller than contemporaneous ones in the lowlands. A chi-square test might demonstrate statistical significance in the pattern, and we might therefore be tempted to explain the differences as a function of the different environments. Such an explanation is plausible but potentially wrong. It is possible that the lowland and highland groups may have inherited their preferences regarding projectile-point length from different common ancestors. If this were the case, it would be inappropriate to treat the groups as independent data points in a statistical analysis (Harvey and Pagel 1991). Reconstructing phylogeny is therefore a vital pre-

Figure 1.3
Historical Evolution of Beads and Amulets in the Central Valley, California (after Bennyhoff 1994)

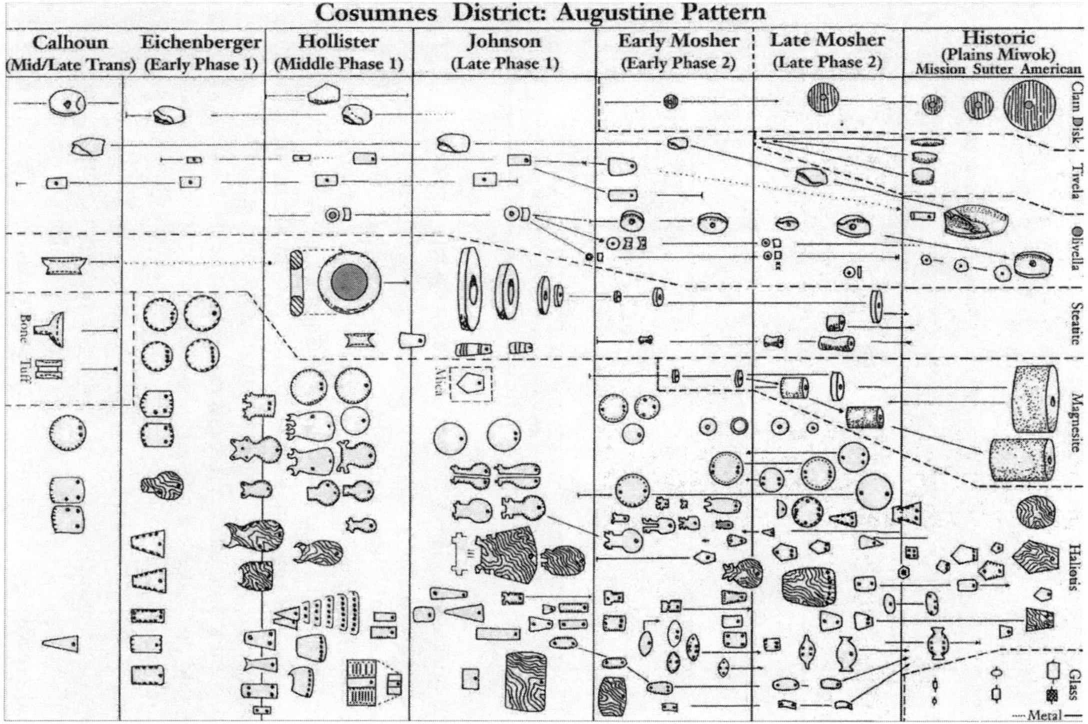

Figure 1.4
Historical Evolution of Projectile Points in the Central Valley, California (after Bennyhoff 1994)

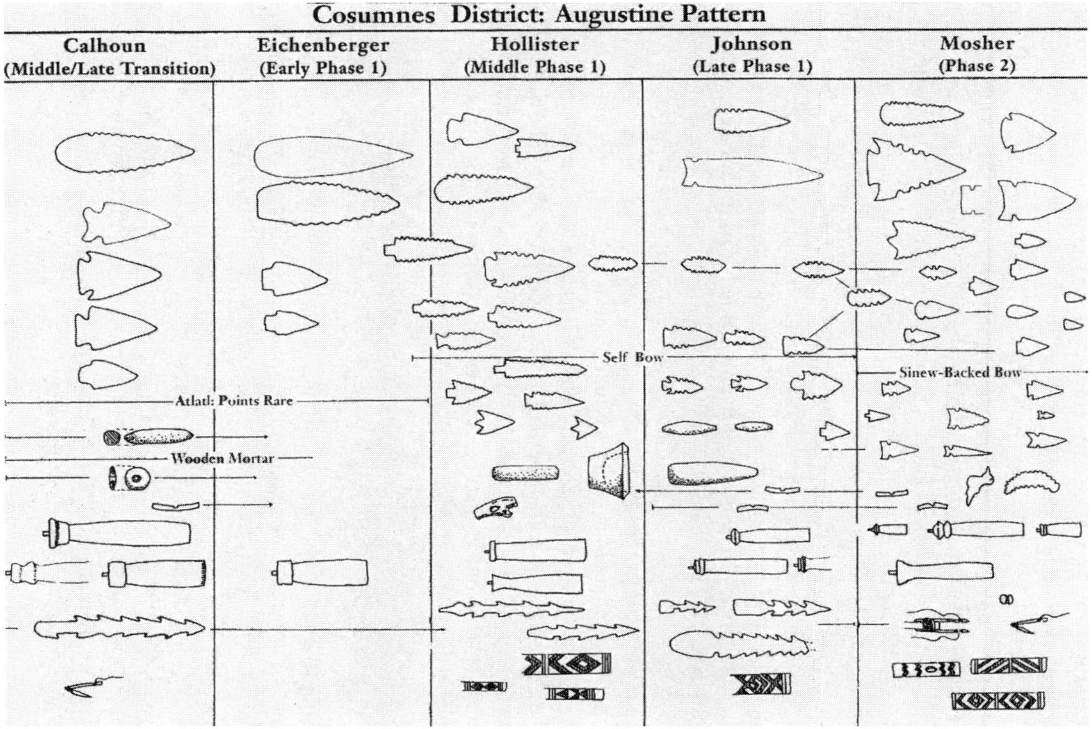

requisite when testing hypotheses about the role of environments in structuring variability in cultural behavior. As the zoologist Paul Harvey (1996: 257) has noted, "if we want to understand why different traits are more commonly represented in one community than another we shall frequently find phylogenetic information useful. It can only help, and it will produce statistically appropriate degrees of freedom."

Culture-historical time-space charts are definitely the sort of product we need. However, the means of generating them must be vastly improved. We must be able to build maps of relatedness in ways that are theoretically justified, reproducible, and quantitatively defensible. The majority of culture-historical depictions of patterns of descent are little more than intuitive claims about relationships based on experience and authority. Although these maps do a reasonable job of determining large-scale differences (for example, distinguishing between early and late manifestations), they are incapable of resolving small-scale differences. At best, they are nominal-level representations of relatedness. Here is a significant reason for us to care about phylogenetics: phylogenetic methods such as cladistics offer us a means of systematically deriving theoretically justifiable maps of relatedness using explicit algorithms in a way that is repeatable. These methods are integral to all forms of evolutionary explanations, whether biological or cultural, since the central tenet of evolution, descent with modification, requires us to track related entities as they change through time and across space. Without showing relatedness, explanations of change are simply chronological, not evolutionary, statements. Thus, phylogenetic methods are central to our quest for explaining the natural world.

Issues in Cultural Phylogenetics

Given the requirements of evolutionary studies, regardless of whether the subject matter is language, artifacts, or social institutions, we see phylogenetics as an important component. Critics, however, have not only raised a number of issues with respect to the appropriateness of various methods for unraveling cultural phylogenies but have also questioned whether cultural phylogenies can even be understood, regardless of the method used. If the criticisms are valid, they not only limit the applicability and effectiveness of various phylogenetic methods, they call into question the entire phylogenetic enterprise. We summarize some of these issues below, leaving it to various chapter authors to address them in more detail.

Culture versus Genes

Some researchers argue that phylogenetic methods are inappropriate for studying cultural evolution because they rest on a false analogy. This argument is not new (e.g., Brew 1946). It holds that cultural transmission is not analogous to genetic transmission—that unlike with genes, culture is not a transmission system in which physically identifiable entities are passed from person to person structurally intact (Atran 2001; Aunger 2000; Sperber 1996). As such, we cannot directly apply biological methods to cultural data. In an intuitive sense this argument appears defensible. Obviously the "things" that pass between people in a cultural-transmission system are not sharply defined objects. However, simply because we cannot see the transmitted "things" does not mean that we cannot see their effects.

Sometimes cultural transmission is said to take place via gene-like units called "memes" (Dawkins 1976). Although the concept of meme enables us to conceptualize a unit for measuring cultural transmission, we agree with Lake (1996) that much of the memetics literature creates confusion by conflating the physical expression with the content being transmitted (e.g., Blackmore 1999; Gabora 1996). The example of an image or string of words, copied and passed around while retaining its essential identity, is commonly used as a memetic example of cultural transmission. This image is inappropriate.

If physical expression is not part of the process of cultural transmission, then what does transmission consist of? What is passed on? In a word, information is passed on. Clearly, we are not the first to say this (e.g., Cloak 1973, 1975; Dawkins 1976). But in order to address the criticism that cultural evolution is at best analogous to genetic evolution (and then only vaguely so), we have to be clear that transmission is about the passage of information between individuals at whatever scale and using whatever physical means is available (chemical, molecular, sound, or light). Thus, there cannot be a single, physical entity in any system of information transmission. There are no "strings of words."

It is important to recognize that the lack of a single physical entity is true even in the case of genetic transmission, where there are numerous physical entities—DNA, transfer RNA, and many proteins—that carry and pass on information. As we have delved deeper into the mechanisms of genetic transmission, we have learned that DNA does not play an exclusive role in transmitting information between individuals. Similarly, in cultural transmission there are also a number of physical mechanisms that result in the transmission of information.

Even though we might not all agree on the mechanism or even on what is transmitted between individuals, we should be in general agreement that some information is passed on. Thus, the distinction between genetic transmission and cultural transmission is artificial. Both genes and culture are transmission systems. They differ mechanistically and also in terms of their dynamics, but this is irrelevant to their information-theoretic structure. They differ as well in the degree of average fidelity of transmission, but this is a quantitative, not a qualitative, difference.

This has important implications for the "analogy" argument and for the potential use of phylogenetic methods in the study of cultural inheritance. Using this model of transmission, we can see that the goal of phylogenetics is simply to build maps that allow us to track information across space and through time, regardless of the physical means by which this information is transmitted. All the methods require is that information be transmitted, by whatever means (O'Brien and Lyman 2003a). Thus the "analogy" argument that seeks to divide cultural from biological forms of evolution is spurious.

Homology and Homoplasy

Anthropologists have long been aware that care must be exercised in studying relatedness so as not to confuse similarity that results from shared ancestry from similarity that is a product of technological constraints, development, or from a common solution to an environmental condition (Cronk 1999). This means that as we try to explain the distribution of cultural material we must be able to distinguish homologous similarity from all other kinds of similarity (homoplasies). Biologists currently recognize several forms of homoplasy (Collard and Wood 2001; Lieberman et al. 1996; Lockwood and Fleagle 1999; Sanderson and Hufford 1996). Analogous and convergent homoplasies are caused by adaptation to similar environments (Simpson 1953). Analogies and convergences differ in that natural selection operates on different developmental processes in the former, but on the same developmental processes in the latter (Lieberman et al. 1996). Parallel homoplasies result from aspects of ontogeny (i.e., development) that limit phenotypic diversity, but which have no necessary connection with the demands of the environment (Wake 1991). A fourth type of homoplasy is reversal, in which, for example, a trait increases and then decreases (Simpson 1953). Most cases of reversal are probably due to natural selection, but the authors of a recent assessment of silenced-gene reactivation have suggested that reversal may also be neutral with regard to adaptation (Marshall et al. 1994). The last form of homoplasy that biologists recognize is homoiology. Homoiologies result from phenotypic similarities in the way that different genotypes interact with the environment (Lieberman et al. 1996).

Some of these forms of homoplasy probably do not need to be considered when dealing with artifacts and cultural practices, but others clearly do. Potential examples of the cultural equivalent of parallelism can be readily identified. For instance, painted designs will rarely be found on the interior of narrow-necked jars because of the mechanical constraint caused by neck restriction and physical inability to apply designs (Krause 1978). Evidence for convergence in cultural behavior is even more plentiful. For example, once considered to be strong indications of relatedness, things like pyramid construction and paramount chiefdoms have proven to be the result of convergence. Likewise, populations have repeatedly found baked clay to be a highly efficient solution to the creation of watertight and fire-resistant vessels. The common triangular shape of projectile points found worldwide represents another excellent case of convergence. The physics of flight and impact strongly favor a common solution to prey disablement. Thus projectile points used to tip arrows from prehistoric Afghanistan look remarkably like those from late-prehistoric eastern North American contexts. This similarity is once again not a product of common descent but of evolution "finding" the best configuration for stone projectile points launched from bows (see chapter 7 for additional discussion). Even forms of decoration can be highly convergent, as Meggers, Evans, and Estrada found in their comparison of Jomon and Ecuadorian ceramics (Meggers et al. 1965).

In culture as in biology, it appears that there may be a surprisingly small set of solutions to many problems that would initially appear to have many degrees of freedom. This means that as we try to explain the distribution of cultural material, we may find that much of what we think is homologous similarity may turn out to be cases of analogous or convergent similarity. Culture historians were sensitive to this issue and sought to minimize the chance of using homoplastic similarity by evaluating the complexity of a trait, the presence of a probable ancestral trait in the same geographic area, the quantity of other shared traits, and the geographic proximity of the localities (Steward 1929; see O'Brien and Lyman 2000a). Each criterion was thought to help minimize the likelihood that a trait independently appeared multiple times and in multiple places. Concern over confusing homologous and homoplastic variability is one reason why the use of adaptively neutral variants may produce more robust measures of inheritance than studies that make use of functional traits (Dunnell 1978; Lipo and Madsen 2000). Because they do not affect inclusive fitness, such variants are likely to reflect patterns of inheritance rather than adaptation to similar environmental conditions. However, even these procedures provide no guarantees. Each case must be evaluated for the possibility of homoplasy.

Cultural Phylogeny and Horizontal Transmission

Efforts to identify homologies in cultural materials are further complicated by the need to take into account a form of homoplasy not mentioned in the preceding section, namely homoplasy that results from "horizontal transmission," the transmission of information between contemporaneous entities. Critics argue that information about relatedness will be drowned out by noise as a result of borrowing and recent interaction, thus limiting the application of certain phylogenetic methods to cultural phenomena. Certainly, given the common perception that cultural transmission is reticulate as opposed to ever-branching, it is reasonable to argue that any method needs to be examined and justified before we uncritically assume that it will work as well for artifacts and languages as it does for biological data. In addition, we also have to recognize that despite the range of applications we can dream up for cladistics and other phylogenetic methods, the methods were originally designed to distinguish among patterns of inheritance over large amounts of time and space and within a transmission system that was assumed at the time to be strongly vertical.

Issues raised by horizontal transmission relative to cultural phenomena are essentially the same as those it raises in biology (O'Brien and Lyman 2003a). One must wonder whether a different set of methods would have emerged in biology had phylogeneticists had to deal from the start with the problem of tracing information flow in a system without a sharp distinction between vertical and horizontal transmission–that is, if "branching" were not a fairly reasonable assumption. In fact, phylogeneticists exploring the origins of life have encountered precisely this situation. Many biologists have been frustrated that during the earliest phases of evolution it appears that horizontal transmission "erased" all of the records of the oldest branches on the tree of life. But we need to remember that horizontal transmission is relatively common even today (Skála and Zrazvý 1994; Woese 2000).

In general, vertical transmission appears only in complex organisms with DNA transmission, where the system has evolved to conduct periodic, not continuous, transmission in an all-in-one exchange of information. This turns out to be fairly rare in biological systems. On a taxonomic basis, the vast majority of life over the last three billion years has not been organized along lines where mechanisms exist to constrain information flow to strict "vertical" lines. Constraining information during transmission is a derived trait. Terminal sequestration of the germ line is relatively recent and also taxonomically restricted (Buss 1987).

Managing cases in which information is not constrained in synchronous bundles is not an insurmountable task. It simply means that there is not necessarily going to be one "best" phylogeny for any specific transmission group, genetic or cultural. Rather, we are often going to end up with different phylogenies for different sets of traits, which may imply different sources and patterns of transmission. Some traits may coincide in terms of a phylogeny, which implies that they moved as a package, whereas other traits are likely to have followed unique pathways of descent. In addition, we have to allow for the possibility that the phylogenies of some traits will be best represented by treelike diagrams, whereas those of other traits will be more appropriately depicted by what John Terrell (2001) calls "maximally connected networks," or reticulated graphs (see chapters 5 and 6 for further discussion and examples).

Some of the concern that anthropologists have with the use of phylogenetic methods in the cultural case involves the origins of method as a means for measuring variability structured by vertical transmission. Cladistics is thus treated as applicable only in systems of biological reproduction. However, strict vertical transmission is not the general case, even in biology. An assumption that biological reproduction is a process of vertical transmission works well only in situations where there is terminal sequestration of the germ line and the lack of openness to horizontal transfer can be assumed. However, strictly speaking, nothing about tree analysis requires these assumptions. Cladistics works on any inherited information and can be used to determine the relative degree of horizontal and vertical transmission, as the chapters in this volume ably demonstrate.

What we do have to question is the nature of cultural transmission (e.g., periodic versus continuous transmission) and whether we should expect to be able derive a single tree that maps to a single phylogeny. This is an empirical issue that must be determined case by case. However, cultural phenomena are probably best represented by a general case in which transmission occurs simultaneously in vertical and horizontal dimensions and is not packaged into bundles bounded in time and space. The general case has important implications for our efforts to study historical relatedness among cultural phenomena. Most importantly, this means that when we study phylogenies in culture and language, our analyses will necessarily produce numerous trees. We should expect many trees for any population, each tracing the history of particular traits or sets of traits across sets of biological individuals. Richard Pocklington discusses this issue in chapter 2 of this volume.

Trees have to be evaluated first on formal and sampling criteria, then on correspondence. Trees are "correct" when the sampling strategy is good and the trees are built properly without violating the mathematical assumptions of the models used to build them. Differences among trees are data about different patterning of information flow, not an indication that one has not found the "one true phylogeny" among a series of taxa.

Foundation for the Volume

This volume brings together a number of scholars who have been working on the theoretical, methodological, and empirical issues involved in mapping patterns of cultural descent through the use of cladistics and other phylogenetic methods. Taken as a whole, the chapters provide a solid demonstration of the potential of phylogenetic methods for studying the evolutionary history of human populations using a variety of data sources. We hope the chapters provide a foundation for future work and offer inspiration to continue the application and development of methods for determining descent relationships and constructing evolutionary histories.

A few final points are worth noting. First, this is not a "how-to" manual on building phylogenetic trees, although methods play a major role in many of the chapters. There are a number of good books that cover the procedures and algorithms needed for building trees, including Felsenstein's (2004) *Inferring Phylogenies* and Hall's (2001) *Phylogenetic Trees Made Easy*. For a basic introduction to cladistics, we suggest Brooks and McLennan's (1991) *Phylogeny, Ecology, and Behavior* and Kitching et al.'s (1998) *Cladistics: The Theory and Practice of Parsimony Analysis.* Wiley et al.'s (1991) primer *The Compleat Cladist: A Primer of Phylogenetic Procedures* provides a good review of the basic principles and terms necessary for understanding cladistic methods. In addition, O'Brien and Lyman's (2003) *Cladistics in Archaeology* provides an introduction to the construction of phylogenies in the context of archaeological materials. We also need to make it clear that phylogenetic methods include more than cladistics. Several authors discuss related methods include material compositional analyses and seriation.

Second, although cladistics makes use of assumptions about branching to build maps of relatedness, and the final product of cladistics is a tree, the production of trees is not the central goal of this research. Instead, the research shares a simple commitment to determining evolutionary relationships. Trees are nothing more than hypotheses about relatedness that, once created, must subsequently be evaluated with external information. Hypotheses other than branching can potentially explain the generation of patterns of similarity, regardless of how it is measured. As Terrell (1988, 2001) and others have pointed out, geographical proximity and temporal differences are alternative hypotheses that can account for descriptions of material culture, linguistics, and genetics. Determining the "best" hypothesis is an empirical issue.

Third, there are numerous technical terms involved with phylogenetic methods. These terms are unavoidable, given that we must carefully specify the kinds of things being described and the manner in which they are described. Although technical terms such as "homoplasy," "synapomorphy," "phylogenesis," and "clade" are necessary for reasons of clarity and precision, the chapters have been written to make their presentations as clear and as jargon free as possible.

Notes

1.   Technically, a cladogram is an unrooted tree, although cladists tend to use the terms interchangeably. A cladogram becomes a tree when a starting point, or root, is identified. Most authors in this volume use the term "phylogenetic tree," indicating that the cladistic arrangement of their taxa has been rooted.
2.   This example is adapted from Harvey (1996).

Part 2

Fundamentals and Methods

2

What is a Culturally Transmitted Unit, and How Do We Find One?

Richard Pocklington

In recent years, considerable interest in anthropology and archaeology has focused on cultural transmission. The key concept in this area of thought is that culture is a process of social heredity that exists independently of, but parallel to, gene-based heredity (e.g., Boyd and Richerson 1985; Cavalli-Sforza and Feldman 1981; Durham 1991). To better understand the nature of the social-heredity system, some anthropologists and archaeologists have turned to phylogenetic theory, especially that which underpins cladistics. Here I show that although the path to assimilating theory and methods from the biological sciences into anthropology is not smooth, it is not impossible. The methodological tools that have been developed in contemporary evolutionary theory (primarily cladistic methods of phylogenetic reconstruction) may well prove useful to social scientists. Before such tools can be used fruitfully, however, methodological assumptions must be made explicit, as should the relationship between the concept of inheritance in cultural and genetic systems.

Any dataset can be fed into a cladistic algorithm to generate a treelike diagram of relationships among taxa. Such a result, however, provides no assurance that the material under investigation was generated by a process of descent with modification or that the branching pattern can be interpreted as anything other than a simple representation of overall similarity among the taxa. More than a tree-making algorithm is needed to do cultural phylogenetics. Later I will discuss two methodological tools that can be used to help assess the degree to which any particular dataset is amenable to phylogenetic analysis.

What is a Culturally Transmitted Unit?

Perhaps the best place to begin a discussion of cultural phylogeny is with the issue of units. This section probably deserves the slightly more complicated title, "What is a culturally transmitted unit (CTU), and why should we care?" I hope to answer both parts of the question. Much of the criticism leveled at cultural transmission theory has centered on our inability to identify a coherent culturally transmitted unit (Aunger 2000; Sperber 1996). Atran (2001: 356) claims that "there [is] no ready way of deciding what counts as a meme. There [is] no set of criteria for determining whether or not the chosen units or 'chunks' of information actually cut up culture at its natural joints." This is an insightful comment. In many cases, the abstraction of ethnographic or archaeological data into putative culturally transmitted units has been done with little reflection. The assumption that anything that one observes as data in a cultural system is itself reflective of a single unit of cultural transmission that has a distinct history and mode of transmission is a large leap of faith.

For example, Guglielmino et al. (1995) treat each category of behavior described in Murdock's (1967) *Ethnographic Atlas* as if it were a culturally transmitted unit. There is, however, no necessary one-to-one mapping between the observed categories of behavior that an ethnographer chooses to record and those elements of culture that have a transmission mode and that interact with human minds to give rise to behavior (Durham 1991). Therefore, it is inadvisable to attempt to trace the cultural genealogy of the behavioral outcome of a complex interacting socioeconomic process, such as "division of labor by sex," one of the categories used by Guglielmino et al. (1995). There is no known simple diffusing element that transforms a society without division of labor by sex into a society that has that trait. The observation that societies differ in their behavior in some identifiable aspect (such as persistent differences in the amount of work men and women do in any particular enterprise) is not enough evidence to suggest that the observed feature of the behavioral differences has its origin in an individual cultural feature that has a single identifiable history of transmission.

To be sure, some cultural elements may well travel between people and between cultures as coherent and consistent packages. Pocklington and Best (1997) have argued that the appropriate units of selection to use in modeling cultural adaptation will be the largest units that reliably and repeatably withstand transmission. Here I argue that it is worthwhile to investigate datasets to see if a particular set of cultural material can be adequately described as a culturally transmitted unit. Once we have found such cultural "particles," there are many ways in which they might be used.

When attempting to discern a pattern of relationship among a group of cultural elements, the first question we should ask is not, "What is the correct phylogenetic tree?" but rather, "Are the data best explained by a phylogenetic tree?" This question has assumed primacy from the dawn of tree-based models of culture history. While trees are currently a common starting point for analyses, the procedure is not a necessary one. Soon after Schleicher (1863) proposed his tree theory for the relationship among the Indo-European languages, Schmidt (1872) proposed an alternative, the wave theory.[1] Either model could have provided the framework for present-day analyses.

If we agree that the data *are* best explained by a treelike model, is there any *single* tree that best explains the data? The answer usually will be "no." For example, there is no single, universally accepted tree diagram that represents the entire Indo-European language phylum (Gray and Atkinson 2003), arguably the best understood language phylum and by far the one at which the most rigorous effort has been directed. This obviously does not mean that tree models are inappropriate for describing Indo-European language relationships (chapter 16, this volume). Rather, it means that one must recognize that in no case can we assume *a priori* that a given set of cultural materials is necessarily organized into a *single* set of hierarchical categories representing a series of historical bifurcations.

Three Primary Problems with the Genealogical Model

I see three problems or errors that can adversely affect our efforts to construct cultural phylogenies. One error that is relatively easy to make is to identify a basic element of behavior in one individual or group and associate it with a pseudo-ancestor that also shares the element. It may be this sort of simple error that is involved in attributing a particular historical origin to rationality (Derrida 1967). If rationality is something that emerges from the skull fully formed (the result of a cognitive module), then we must look into the deep genetic history of our species (or perhaps some higher taxonomic unit, such as family, class, or order) and not into the shallow genealogy of our culture to get at the root of its cause. We must recognize that many complex actions would be performed by any human who was confronted with particular circumstances (Cronk 1999; Flinn 1997). The construction of the phylogeny of material that is the result of universal human behavioral responses will produce tree diagrams that have nothing to do with historical contingencies and everything to do with the similarity of environmental circumstances under which cultural materials under scrutiny are found.

Evolutionary anthropology and archaeology should not be in conflict with evolutionary psychology. All social scientists should recognize that some complex human behavior is the result of relatively panhuman cognitive capacities reacting to similar circumstances in order to bring out behavioral responses, whereas other behavior is heavily influenced by historically contingent, culturally transmitted information (both recent and ancient). I argue that we must avoid what can only be called "cultural determinism," a system of thinking that demands that each and every aspect of human behavior be shaped and its expression controlled by the demands of the historically particular sociocultural situation in which humans live. Although this mode of thinking is popular, there is a dearth of evidence to support such a radical, culture-centered theory of human behavior.[2]

A second error is that the tales told about the history of cultural features do not reflect the true history of the material under investigation. One variant of this error is taking the point of codification of an element as the element's true point of origin. By identifying the codifier or translator and not the originator, we will be led astray in looking for other aspects of the pseudo-originator's culture and environment. This problem is never easy to solve, although by being on the lookout for data-acquisition biases we are better prepared to identify such issues when they do arise.

A third problem facing those who wish to apply phylogenetic theory to anthropology is the mistaken identification of a polygenetic element as having its origin in one particular lineage that contributed to its history. This issue has been a consistent problem since the dawn of philology (Lang 1885) and perhaps long before. For example, Christianity is often referred to as a descendant of Judaism (Armstrong 1993). However, the important influences on early Christianity by many other systems such as Mithraism, Persian Zoroastrianism, Roman Imperial cults, and Greek mystery religions are all well attested (Campbell 1955). This error is primarily one of confusion over the appropriate unit of historical analysis. Elements of Christianity are closely related to Judaism, but Christianity as a whole should be considered a polyphyletic amalgam. Once it formed a social entity with a defined boundary it may well have had a describable history, but at its point of origin it was only a social phenomenon that grew as the result of multiple threads of cultural input.

Focusing on the CTU is the appropriate response to this class of problem. Through the dissection of putative CTUs into their component portions and an examination of the transmission pathways of these subunits, we can help tune our phylogenetic model to an appropriate scale and thus avoid the folly of constructing phylogenies of things that do not replicate (see Dawkins [1976] on "replicators").

We should be aware that population genetics is not always an exemplary model system on which to base our methods. Populations, which are frequently shown as taxa at the termina of phylogenetic trees, are not often (but sometimes may be) homogeneous units that have clear patterns of descent and relationship. Thus we must recognize that a tree that represents the relationship among multiple human subpopulations (see, for example, Cavalli-Sforza et al. 1994) does not have the same meaning as a tree that represents relationships among various species of mammals (Eizirik et al. 2001). In the case of species, the tree represents a historical pattern of bifurcation (and bifurcation alone), as the species become reproductively isolated from one another and then continue on their separate evolutionary trajectories. A tree of populations is more an assessment of the proportion of similar gene frequencies and one potential representation of their (potentially historical) relationships. All trees representing the relationship on the basis of gene-frequency similarity could also be equally well explained through the use of a matrix showing relative rates of migration (Felsenstein 1982).

This should not be taken as a criticism of human population genetics. Interpreted correctly, population trees can be extremely useful. Moreover, the nonrecombining regions of genes, such as the mitochondria and the Y chromosome, do have true phylogenies that can accurately be reflected by trees even if whole human populations often do not. The combination of both classes of data (gene trees and trees built on the basis of population gene-frequency data) can be used to understand historical relationships among populations, even under circumstances where a single bifurcating branching pattern is not the best model for the history of the populations. The bottom line is that the tools of cladistics and numerical taxonomy are powerful, flexible, and of great utility to anyone who seeks to investigate issues of genealogy, no matter what the subject material. However, each method must be used with full awareness of what it can and cannot do.

Why the Largest Unit?

Much of the problem in determining what a CTU is revolves around the issue of scale. Although Dennett (1995) has claimed that "memes" are the smallest elements that replicate with reliability and fecundity, I have argued (Pocklington 2001; Pocklington and Best 1997) that the largest units of socially transmitted information that reliably and repeatedly withstand transmission make the best candidates for CTUs. Whether or not these units should be called memes is merely a semantic distinction, which at this early point in the development of evolutionary anthropology and archaeology is not yet particularly relevant. The utility of the term "meme" is already widespread among educated laypersons interested in anthropology and genetics. Conversely, much of what passes for memetics has been of limited interest within academic circles, and thus while the term carries some advantages in its ability to aid in the communication of information, it may actively inhibit our ability to communicate with other specialists who have already decided that the notion is bankrupt.

There are two reasons for favoring the largest discernible units as our primary (but not only) building blocks in the theory of cultural reproduction. First, the smallest units we can discern—phonemes, for example—are less likely to be able to accumulate adaptations, as they do not have sufficient subcomponents that can vary and thus provide grist for the mill of selection. They are, therefore, less amenable both to phylogenetic methods and to the adaptationist thinking that has so greatly enriched evolutionary biology in the last few decades.

Second, when multiple discernible units follow parallel transmission pathways over substantial periods of time, they are placed in a situation in which their replication does not leave room for any conflict of interest among the subcomponents (Bull 1994). The parallel transmission of once-unrelated components is a force that I believe has led, through symbiosis, to the cooperation behind the generation of larger-level structures such as cells, organisms, and social groups (Maynard Smith and Szathmáry 1997). When multiple replicators are all placed in a situation in which their fate is common, there are substantial benefits to interacting in a synergistic fashion. From an evolutionary perspective, it is parallel transmission of any sort that is the force that initiates the process by which multiple isolated elements begin to cooperate with one another and create larger-scale structural integrity (Ewald 1987).

The Polygenesis Problem

Kroeber (1931) knew that a culture complex can be polyphyletic. He proposed a model in which cultures would be treated more like faunal assemblages or ecosystems and that the equivalent of a biological species would be a cultural "trait." As he put it, although cultures have sometimes been compared to organisms, they are obvious composites—more or less fused aggregates of elements of various origin, ancient and recent, native and foreign. They therefore are more similar to faunas and floras, which also are composites, or aggregates, of constituent animal or plant species, themselves often of quite diverse origin in space and time.

Kroeber (1948) later claimed that culture was like a tree whose branches grew back together as easily and as frequently as they separated. He did not point out that each branch is composed of fibers that themselves have single origins. Unfortunately, the definition of the "trait" was never fully developed (Lyman and O'Brien 2003), and Kroeber's skepticism toward the drawing out of cultural phylogenies, not his approach to the solution of such a difficult problem, has made its way down to us.

This problem of polygenesis, as it was named in folklore research at the end of the nineteenth century (Lang 1885), has been presented as if it were an impossible hurdle for cultural phylogenetics (e.g., Moore 1994b). Nothing could be farther from the truth. As it stands, the problem is merely one of perception and scale, not at all a fundamental problem with phylogenetic methods or their potential application to cultural systems. Instead, we should see that the problem of polygenesis is a simple error in reference frame. If the object under study is itself composed of multiple subcomponents that fall together in order to form the amalgamation under study, then the proper application of phylogenetic thinking must be removed at least one level. Thus if social groups, as Kroeber (1931) supposed, are themselves polyphyletic amalgams of many independent bits and pieces (a claim that has still not been sufficiently demonstrated such that in all cases we can dismiss society-level phylogenies as useless), then the solution is that societies must be disassembled into some smaller set of units, which themselves may be tested to see if they have sufficient coherency to function as culturally transmitted units. It is for this reason that the issue of scale is key to developing evolutionary models of culture.

Key Properties of a Culturally Transmitted Unit

The ideal culturally transmitted unit has two important properties. First, it is a single cultural object that, when it passes within social arenas, maintains sufficient coherency that it can be recognized as clearly homologous. It cannot, at least within recent time, be a result of the interaction of multiple cultural features, although the social repercussions of the cultural pattern may well be the relatively predictable consequences of the cultural pattern under study and the socioeconomic circumstances into which it is assimilated. Second, in order for phylogenetic theory to be of value in the study of such culturally transmitted units, the material under investigation must itself be the result of a process of descent with modification. Nonhomogeneous replicators that do not leave behind descendants that can be organized into hierarchically organized clusters are much less likely to be subject to natural selection. If so, then evolutionary theory is of limited (if any) explanatory value in these cases.

To the end of exploring particular cultural patterns that may be amenable to evolutionary treatment, I have devised two sets of tests that can be applied to a wide variety of datasets. Data that withstand these two tests are particularly likely to be amenable to phylogenetic treatment. A tree generated representing their history can be assumed to represent a historical trajectory and not only overall similarity.

Cultural-Unit Transmission Integrity Assay

In order to examine the degree to which a set of cultural materials may be fairly considered to act as culturally transmitted units, we can test them for transmission coherency, or the degree to which variation in expression of the materials is geographically correlated.[3] Given that the cultural feature under investigation consists of discernible subunits, if the units are dispersed over the landscape as intact culturally transmitted elements, there will be high correlations between dissimilarity matrices generated by data drawn from each of the different subunits. Close correlations between dissimilarity matrices constructed on the basis of two different subunits within the larger cultural feature provide evidence for the internal coherence of the transmission pattern of the subunits.

Given three populations, each which reports the presence of a cultural trait (A, B, C) with three discernible subunits (i, ii, iii) (figure 2.1), if traits A and B are both most similar for each subunit ($AB_{i, ii, iii} < AC_{i, ii, iii} | BC_{i, ii, iii}$), with C more different from A or B than A is from B for each of the three subunits, this suggests that the trait exhibits substantial cross-cultural internal coherency. If, on the other hand, we find that for the first subunit (i) A and B are similar and C is different ($AB_i < AC_i | BC_i$), but for the second subunit (ii) A and C show more similarities ($AC_{ii} < AB_{ii} | BC_{ii}$) and for the third subunit (iii) B and C are most similar ($BC_{iii} < AC_{iii} | AB_{iii}$), then the patterns of similarity would be maximally uncorrelated. In this case, the feature of interest shows minimal cross-cultural internal coherency.

Figure 2.1
Traits and Subcomponents in Maximally Concordant and
Maximally Discordant Arrangements

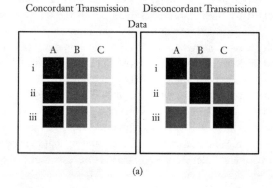

(a)

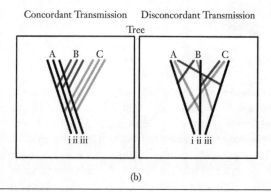

(b)

(a) the data matrix (each trait color coded, similar color implies similar trait value) for traits A, B, and C that have been divided into measurable subcomponents i, ii, and iii; (b) simple trees representing the most-parsimonious transmission pattern for each subcomponent. The left-hand box, representing maximally concordant transmission, suggests that the cultural unit (i, ii, iii combined) is a useful CTU. The right-hand box demonstrates the alternative case. Phylogenetic analysis of the composite CTU (i, ii, iii combined) is not recommended in this case.

I recommend using the Mantel matrix correspondence test (Smouse and Long 1992) to assess a dataset for such correlations. Given that the data are represented as sets of dissimilarity matrices, we have the problem that each distance in the matrix cannot be considered as an independent data point for statistical analyses (Smouse et al. 1986). The Mantel test allows us to estimate a correlation between pairs of distance matrices even though the entries in the matrix are not themselves independent data points.

One might object that these strong intra-unit correlations are representations of functional relationships, and that if populations A and B both have a particular variant of subunit i, then they will also have similar variants of subunits ii and iii. In this case we have a classic phylogenetic problem—the difficulty in assessing homology in situations where functional constraints may cause similarity among populations independent of shared history.

Another simple test may be used to help assess the likelihood that the pattern of variation observed is a result of historical distribution and not of functional constraints. Given that we already have a matrix representing the dissimilarity between observed varieties of cultural features in a sample of populations, we can observe the correlation between cultural dissimilarity and geographic proximity. A significant correlation between geographic distance and cultural dissimilarity provides some evidence that the pattern of variation observed cannot be ascribed solely to functional similarities and suggests that some type of diffusion process is at work. Chapters 4 and 10 in this volume provide examples of how this kind of analysis can be accomplished.

Assessment of Hierarchical Cluster Structure

Once a set of cultural structures is represented as a set of vectors in some N-dimensional space, we can begin constructing lower-dimensional projections of that high-dimensional space into some simpler space, usually in two or three dimensions at the most (as in classic multidimensional scaling). In doing so, we inevitably add some level of distortion to the actual appearance of the N-dimensional vector description. This is unavoidable, but we can work to counteract its effects. The creation of a tree is in some sense the process of collapsing a set of taxa, each of which has been scored for a number of characters, into a two-dimensional diagram. One of the assumptions of the process is that such a diagram of sequential bifurcations is a fair portrayal of the texture of the overall space. The following test is meant as a preliminary step through which we assess the overall character of the vector space before we use the clustering algorithm to produce a tree.

Once the data are represented as a set of vectors, each representing one of the taxa and having a length of one (with each of the many components of the vector representing the manifestation of one of the characters that have been discerned to be important), we can make use of a neighbor-joining algorithm to begin clustering the various taxa into groups (figure 2.2). The nearest-neighbor method works as follows. A single point is chosen from the dataset and assigned membership to cluster one. Each point in the dataset is then selected and compared against all existing clusters. If it is within some distance, r, of any other cluster, it is assigned to that cluster; otherwise it is assigned to a new cluster. The method is quick and efficient but can be sensitive to the order in which the data are entered.

For any given hypersphere radius, r, there will be some number of nonoverlapping clusters into which the points are partitioned (figure 2.2a). As

Figure 2.2
Four Steps in the Assessment of Hierarchical Cluster Structure Test

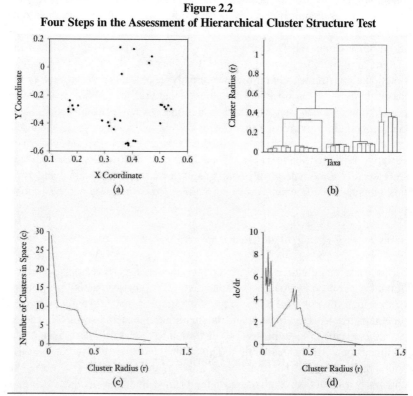

(a) 30 data points representing a population of observed cultural features; (b) a nearest-neighbor tree linking all 30 observations; (c) a plot of the total number of clusters in the space (starting with 30, each point in its own cluster, and ending with 1, where all points are in a single cluster); (d) the dc/dr vs. r plot showing two peaks, the first representing the distance at which most of the points found within the clusters are agglomerated, and the second representing the radius at which each of the five clusters begins to cluster. The rightmost cluster in the tree in (c) represents the clustering of the topmost group of points. They cluster with one another at approximately the same radius at which the tighter groups are beginning to cluster with one another.

the radius of the hypersphere increases, the total number of clusters will decrease. This assay is meant to determine how important each incremental increase of the hypersphere radius is in determining the number of clusters found in the total dataset.

In order to estimate the overall character of the vector space, we cluster all the taxa using the nearest-neighbor method one hundred times, varying the value of r between zero and one (figure 2.2b). After each clustering we note how many clusters have been produced. This provides us with a plot of c (number of clusters) against r (figure 2.2c). When $r = 0$, $c = N$, as each post is found in its own 0-radius hypersphere. When $r = 1$, then $c = 1$, as all posts in the space are found in a single cluster that encompasses the entire space. As r increases, c decreases monotonically, as fewer of the larger clusters are needed to contain all the points in the space. We can plot c against r and find some decreasing function that summarizes, in a very general manner, the character of the distribution of the points in the overall space.

This representation of c against r is not as informative as that of the rate of change of c with respect to r against r (dc/dr). The dc/dr against r plot (figure 2.2d) assesses the degree to which each incremental increase in the radius of the hypercones affects the number of categories found in the space. When dc/dr is low, then an increase in the radius of the hypercones has a small effect on the total number of clusters. This happens when increasing the radius of the hypersphere merely encompasses more empty space. When dc/dr is high, then an increase in the radius of the hyperspheres has a large effect on the total number of clusters. This occurs when an increase in the hypersphere results in the amalgamation of previously distinct clusters into metaclusters.

When we examine the dc/dr against r plot, we observe just how the use of a clustering algorithm works on the taxa in the space described by the data. A dataset with a single sharp peak is one in which the data fall into categories, but these categories are not themselves organized into supercategories, and so on, forming a hierarchical clustering scheme. A dataset showing multiple peaks demonstrates that the elements in the space described fall into clearly hierarchically organized categories.

Regarding Character Choice

Both methods depend on an appropriate choice of characters through which dissimilarity matrices representing the cultural objects can be constructed. An eighteenth-century parable seems appropriate to mention here. Biologists and natural historians (who, despite the protestations of Foucault [1966], represent a coherent intellectual lineage) spent more than a century discussing the concept of "character." Deciding on the appropriateness of a character involves all sorts of information that is, in each case, local to the particular taxonomic area in which one works. The development of what was called comparative anatomy in the early eighteenth century had a profound effect on taxonomic practice, disrupting many of the taxonomic categories that had been put in place in the previous century. The discovery of the linked physiological systems found within animals made it clear that certain superficial characters were likely repercussions of factors that were linked within a single being (Cuvier 1829). Thus many externally observed characters were found to be poor units for use in classification, a result both of convergence and of what we can call the predictable and multiple effects on the outward appearance of organismal form caused by single fundamental changes (at the genetic level) within the organism.

Taxonomic algorithms work best on datasets of completely functionally uncorrelated characters, where all of the correlation among characters in the cultural area is caused by historical connections among the taxa under study (see also chapter 6 in this volume for more discussion). Such data are difficult to find, and we should not under any circumstances model the development of an evolutionary anthropology or archaeology on contemporary molecular phylogenetics. The availability of large numbers of characters that are easily tested for independence—neutral molecular markers—is an amazing discovery in biological systems, yet there is nothing like a cultural genome that has been discovered (and perhaps never will be). Anthropology, then, has much to learn from earlier phases (a hundred years ago or more) of biological taxonomic theory, which finds the science in a state much more similar to our current situation than we are to molecular biology. In-depth knowledge of the particular features of a specific dataset is an important prerequisite to wise character choice for phylogenetic analysis (see also chapter 7, this volume).

We are stymied, however, by our lack of basic taxonomic knowledge of the parts that make up the things that we identify as societies. Good intuition regarding the function and organization of elements within a social matrix helps us make valid judgments of the representation scheme that will be used for any particular cultural dataset. This, in turn, will enrich our overall view of the taxonomy and provide a more robust test for function (Felsenstein 1985). These functional relations can then be used to improve our understanding of what is and is not functionally related within a social system. This is not a new problem; Driver and Kroeber (1932) clearly outlined this particular conundrum. What is new is the diverse assortment of computational tools available to the anthropologist.

Advances in cultural phylogenetics are likely to be achieved through the close collaboration between regional and technological specialists and those trained in the use of phylogenetic theory. Neither group alone has the skills and knowledge needed to adapt the powerful phylogenetic algorithms of evolutionary theory to the complex and fascinating realm of cross-cultural analysis. If the phylogenetic method works, we will see some of our favorite functional relationships and most trusted historical categories disrupted and replaced. So be it.

Notes

1. It is unclear whether at that point in the history of European scholarship the difference among a tree of language, a tree of genetic history, and a tree of cultural history was distinct or even distinguishable.
2. This makes the spread of such a culturally transmitted pattern particularly interesting from the memetic standpoint, as some characteristics of what has come to be referred to as textualism must be behind its rapid spread through certain areas of the academy.
3. For more details on the method and its application to a particular dataset, see Pocklington and Durham (2005).

3

Cultural Traits and Linguistic Trees: Phylogenetic Signal in East Africa

Jennifer W. Moylan, Monique Borgerhoff Mulder,
Corine M. Graham, Charles L. Nunn,
and N. Thomas Håkansson

In recent years there have emerged exciting multidisciplinary strands in the revival of history within anthropology. These strands combine macrolevel comparison with the analysis of long-term evolution, suggestive of a neo-Boasian paradigm. Most prominent have been investigations into human population movements, tackled either through analyses of the concordance between genetic and linguistic variation (e.g., Cavalli-Sforza et al. 1988, 1992; Chen et al. 1995) or through phylogenetic analyses of language itself (e.g., Gray and Atkinson 2003; Gray and Jordan 2000; Holden 2002). These studies use language to shed light on human population history, such as the spread of Austronesian-speaking peoples across the Pacific. Although analyses of the historical relationships among societies on the basis of cultural traits such as language are controversial (Bateman et al. 1990; Terrell 1988; Terrell et al. 1997) and not necessarily well replicated across different continents (Nettle and Harriss 2003), these macroevolutionary studies of culture have generated data to test specific hypotheses for regional patterns of human history (e.g., Bellwood 1998; Gray and Jordan 2000), stimulating highly interdisciplinary work (e.g., Diamond and Bellwood 2003; Hurles et al. 2003).

Increasingly, sociocultural traits—institutions, beliefs, and behavioral regularities—are being brought into systematic historical examination (e.g., Barth 1987; Jones 2003; Rodseth 1998). One line of investigation lies in determining whether cultural trait distributions are best explained by so-called "branching" or "blending" models (Bellwood 1996a; Boyd et al. 1997; Collard and Shennan 2000; Durham 1992; Moore 1994b; Terrell et al. 1997; chapter 12,

33

this volume). Another line of enquiry lies in quantitatively analyzing socio-cultural traits in the context of linguistic (e.g., Guglielmino et al. 1995) and genetic (e.g., Jones 2003; Pocklington 1996) variation.

Among sociocultural anthropologists the interest typically lies in deter-mining whether there are certain core institutions that characterize human populations and social groups across their history. In Africa, for example, there is considerable ethnohistorical research to suggest that such traditions persist through the successive migrations, splits, and expansions of different popula-tions (Kopytoff 1987; Vansina 1990). Many ethnographies stress how com-munities in the same social and ecological environment retain core institutions regarding property control and political organization that they appear to have inherited from their parent cultures (e.g., Spear's [1997] comparison of the Chaga and the Masai on Mt. Meru). In a similar vein, histories of single popu-lations that expand into new ecological niches demonstrate strong adherence to ancestral institutions despite changed day-to-day challenges (Edgerton 1971), as when formerly agro-pastoral groups apply rules developed for the intergenerational transmission of livestock to land (e.g., Håkansson [1988] for the Gusi).

Unlike the situation in archaeology (e.g., Neiman 1995; O'Brien and Lyman 2000b; Shennan and Wilkinson 2001), cultural anthropologists lack the time-series data with which to model cultural-trait evolution. Accordingly, their most widely used method focuses on analyzing the congruence among ge-netic, linguistic, geographic, and cultural traits, predicting different patterns of similarity to result from different hypothesized transmission modes (Guglielmino et al. 1995; also chapter 2, this volume). With demic expan-sions, cultural similarities stem from shared history, and cultural traits are likely to be more similar among populations with recent common ancestors (as assessed on genetic or linguistic data) than among populations with more distant common ancestors. With independent innovation, similarities occur between cultural traits and ecological (or other hypothesized) factors; with cultural diffusion, traits are shared as a function of geographic proximity.

Studies using this approach have produced suggestive findings (see be-low), but they face difficult problems when attempting to discern patterns in real-world datasets (Borgerhoff Molder, 2005). First, because of the tendency for daughter populations to settle in habitats ecologically similar to those they left (habitat selection or phylogenetic niche conservatism [Grafen 1989]), the pattern indicative of ecological adaptation can be difficult to distinguish from demic expansion. Second, and similarly, when demic expansions occur and daughter populations settle geographically close to their parent popula-tion, cultural diffusion can be difficult to disentangle from demic expansion. Third, the potential for cultural diffusion can be difficult to ascertain on the basis of the current location of each population, given the mobility of popula-tions and ethnicities over time. With such mobility, a population may have enjoyed (or endured) an array of different neighbors during its history than it does now. Fourth, given the inevitable colinearities among history, geography, and ecology, often more than one model is supported at the same time. Finally, with some hypothesized models of transmission admitting of a greater number of supportive patterns than others, it is probably unwise to consider certain hypotheses excluded, when the rationale for preferring one model over another is not statistical. For instance, Hewlett et al.'s (2002: 321) study of cultural traits in Africa concluded that "the impact of ecology is limited." However, results are biased toward this conclusion, given that there is only one way of supporting the ecological model, in contrast to three ways of supporting the models for both cultural and demic diffusion.

In summary, because of the inherent intercorrelation among the available indices of history (language or genes), the potentially transient measure of the potential for borrowing (based on current locations of populations), and the relatively crude statistical methods so far used, it has proved difficult to take the current (albeit promising) approach much beyond the level of pattern matching—that is, to disentangle the processes that account for variation in cultural traits. Fruitful advances lie in three areas. First, multivariate tests are needed to deal with the high intercorrelation among indices of vertical, horizontal, and ecological processes (Chakraborty et al. 1976; Nettle and Harriss 2003; Sokal 1988; also see chapter 2, this volume). Thus, correlations between cultural traits and geography, for example, can be examined holding historical relationships constant, and vice versa, using Mantel tests (e.g., Dow and Cheverud 1985; Pocklington 1996; Smouse and Long 1992; Sokal 1988). The advantage of this approach is that it allows for rigorous statistical treatment; the disadvantage is that no explicit evolutionary model is tested. Second, to take us from pattern matching to model testing, properly specified models need to be developed, potentially through simulation approaches, in order to set up reasonable expectations for how to gauge the relative support for different modes of transmission (Nunn et al. n.d.). Third, there are tools in biology that are particularly appropriate for detecting phylogenetic signal in discretely valued or continuous traits (e.g., Abouheif 1999; Blomberg et al. 2003; Freckleton et al. 2002; Maddison and Slatkin 1991). With these methods it is possible to determine which traits are the most strongly shared between parent and daughter populations and thereby derive inferences about modes of transmission.

Here we explore the last of the three approaches, specifically by applying two phylogenetic methods to detect the linguistic signal in cultural traits. Although this method focuses on only one aspect of transmission, we explore it for three reasons. First, we wish to introduce anthropologists to a relatively straightforward method that might usefully be applied to a suite of different traits, across distinct cultural domains, in different parts of the world, and at different scales (local to global). Second, we wish to probe the common wis-

dom that certain cultural domains show exceedingly high cultural conservatism. Third, many evolutionary biologists believe that phylogeny-based comparative methods are appropriate only when traits exhibit phylogenetic signal
(see Abouheif 1999; Freckleton et al. 2002; Losos 1999; Rhendt et al. 2004).

We stress three points. First, because we use a language tree to identify the
historical relationships among societies, we employ the term "linguistic" rather
than "phylogenetic" signal to denote an association between cultural traits
and the language tree. Second, demonstration of linguistic signal is merely
suggestive of the mode of transmission of traits between populations; this is
because of the interdependencies among history, geography, and ecology discussed above. Third, showing how traits might be transmitted between populations does not bear directly on how traits are transmitted *within* populations.

Continuity and Change in Cultural Traits

Anthropologists have long noted that family and kinship are particularly
conservative cultural domains (Jones 2003), and indeed there is now some
quantitative evidence to support this contention. The principal finding of
Guglielmino et al.'s (1995) African study is that family-kinship variables are
patterned more by the process of demic expansion than by cultural diffusion
or independent innovation. Other studies reach the same result, both in Africa
(e.g., Hewlett et al. 2002; Pocklington 1996) and elsewhere (e.g., Burton et al.
1996; Jones 2003). Measures of political complexity above the community
level also show evidence of demic processes in both Hewlett et al.'s and
Pocklington's studies, although there is no clear support for this in Guglielmino
et al.'s analysis. All other traits investigated show some consistency with either the horizontal-transmission model (particularly in Pocklington 1996), or
the independent-innovation model, although few consistent results emerge,
and many variables show no clear pattern.

What might render certain domains of sociocultural life particularly conservative (or nonlabile)? There are several expectations, all rather problematic. First, in nonhumans it is well recognized that behavioral characters show
less phylogenetic signal than life-history characters. Although this is generally true (e.g., Blomberg et al. 2003; Gittleman et al. 1996; Harvey and Nee
1997), it renders little analytical leverage with respect to the relative lability
of different cultural traits *across* human populations, all of which have behavioral aspects.

A second expectation is based on the conventional evolutionary view that
the most accurate phylogenetic trees are built on adaptively neutral traits
(Harvey and Purvis 1991; see also chapter 7, this volume). Under this view,
those traits whose distinct forms do not respond to different ecological influences in adaptive ways are the most likely to show strong linguistic signal—
to be carried with language-bearing populations across different environments
and therefore appear conservative (Neiman 1995). This view is problematic on

several counts. It begs the question of how we determine function in the first place. It also ignores the possibility that an apparently functionless trait can serve a function (for example as an ethnic marker), precisely because it is arbitrary and symbolic (Bettinger et al. 1996). In addition, traits that might be expected to be highly functional (relating to the making of a living or raising of a family) could show strong linguistic signal or not, depending on whether these traits were tracking a changing or a constant environment. More generally, we suspect it is inadvisable to use intuitive judgments about function (or the lack of it) to generate expectations about which traits might show linguistic signal.

A third set of expectations lies in the intuitions of sociocultural anthropologists and cultural evolutionary theorists who make explicit the notion that cultural traits are embedded in social processes (Kopytoff 1987), cultural values (secondary-value selection [see Durham 1991]), and transmission biases (Boyd and Richerson 1985). From the strictly sociocultural perspective, change and continuity in such "traits" (a term not in general use because of its atomistic implications [de Munck and Korotayev 2000; Holy 1987]) occur within institutions that both reproduce hierarchy (Giddens 1984) and respond to competition (Barth 1966). Thus, analyses like those of Vansina (1990) and Kopytoff (1987) investigate the subtle dynamics whereby core traditions (including social organization, notions of hierarchy, and ideologies) articulate across internal frontiers within Africa as a consequence of successive migrations, splits, and expansions of different populations, thereby modifying core traditions but failing to switch them into unrecognizable forms.

To recast this perspective within the terminology of the culture-trait approach, we can think of cultural groups as having variously permeable skins affecting the coherence of traits over time. In a broad discussion of the permeability of such skins, Boyd et al. (1997; see also Durham 1992) propose that coherence is most likely where traits are unified by meaning, by markers of group identity, by co-adapted trait complexes, or by well-integrated symbolic systems (such as language or power). This view is supported by the existence of shared core traditions, particularly regarding descent and marriage (for example, Tylor's [1889] trait adhesions), and by the protocultures that have been suggested for a number of different regions of the world (reviewed in Durham 1990), including Africa (Vansina 1990). Compelling as these accounts of cultural cores are, they generate few specific suggestions as to which kinds of traits are most likely to adhere to the core.

This brief overview suggests that there are few robust predictions regarding the extent to which parent populations transmit traits to their daughter populations. For this reason we propose a largely inductive approach to the question of which traits show strong effects of phylogeny on their distribution. We use a phylogenetic method on the assumption that a single tree adequately captures the history of a population's full array of traits. We recognize that this assumption is controversial (Borgerhoff Mulder 2001; Boyd et al. 1997) and that there is a critical need to evaluate the consequences of violations of this assumption for comparative methods (Nunn et al. n.d.).

With respect to the decision as to which phylogeny to use, we base ours on language. We follow Mace and Pagel (1994; see also Borgerhoff Mulder et al. 2001; Cowlishaw and Mace 1996; Sellen and Mace 1999) in positing that a language phylogeny best captures the cultural history of a population. We feel confident about this claim for Africa, where a strong case can be made that linguistic evidence forms the most comprehensive and dense documentation of a group's social history (Ehret 1998, 2001), and where genetic differences between human populations correspond broadly to language distances (Poloni et al. 1997). We note too that recent data on neutral genetic markers indicate a vast amount of gene flow between neighboring populations, such that much interesting fine-grained human history has been blurred if not erased from contemporary genetic study. In their review of this material, Harpending and Eller (2004) conclude that language may in fact be a better key to human history than genes.

Methods

We use our own codings of variation in cultural traits in thirty-five East African societies for which good ethnographic descriptions are available (Borgerhoff Mulder et al. 2001). With this sample we capitalize on the uncommonly systematic ethnographic work conducted in British East Africa between the 1920s and late 1950s (Murdock 1951) that focused on a tight range of issues such as traditional systems of lineal descent, kinship, marriage, jural rights, social control, and economy. Codes were originally developed to test hypotheses about cultural variation and to be sensitive to the specifics of East Africa. Two coders who were familiar with the literature were consistent in coding decisions (94 percent) and resolved differences with reference to decision rules. Details on the quality and comparative nature of the data are presented in Borgerhoff Mulder et al. (2001), and table 3.1 presents the raw data.

We developed a phylogenetic tree based on Ruhlen (1991), updating it in light of relevant new linguistic, ethnohistorical, and archaeological data (Borgerhoff Mulder et al. 2001). Recent modifications to the Bantu tree were incorporated (Ehret 2001; C. Ehret pers. comm.) to produce the tree shown in figure 3.1.

To determine the degree to which cultural traits share a common history based on linguistic phylogeny, we applied two tests of phylogenetic independence available for discretely coded data. First, we used a method developed by Abouheif (1999) that measures the degree of nonrandomness in a series of values, such as traits along the tips of a phylogeny, using Sokal and Rohlf's (1995) runs test. A randomization procedure addresses the arbitrariness of the species' order in a binary tree (Abouheif 2003). To implement the runs test, we

Table 3.1
Data Coding

Group	Language	Mean annual rainfall	Predominantly important productive resource	All stock per capita ratio	Population density per sq. kilometer	Lineage exogamic preferences	Organizing principles of local communities	Centralization	Existence of age organizations	Primary corporate groups	Nature of land ownership for average member	Warfare	Political relationships between clans/sections/phratries	Ideology	Primary residential groups	Does married daughter generally give birth to first child at her natal home?	Prevailing pattern of residence	Inheritance of positions of authority to sons	Relationship between full brothers	Normal time sons can first leave home	Free sexual access to wives of brothers	Gerontocracy	Dependence of sons on inherited resources	Does daughter retain jural membership of her natal lineage after her marriage?	Relationship between mother's brother and sister's son	Are the maternal origins of lineage segments observed?	Is genitor or pater relationship stressed in widow inheritance/levirate?	Do daughters receive livestock and/or land from their parents?
Baggara	2	2	2	2	99	0	2	2	0	S	0	3	0	1	CJ	0	1	10	2	99	99	99	0	2	4	0	99	2
Datooga	2	2	2	3	99	1	2	1	1	S	0	3	2	0	CJ	0	2	12	2	1	1	2	0	2	4	0	2	2
Jie	2	2	2	99	1	1	3	0	1	L	0	3	2	0	CJ	0	2	9	2	3	99	1	0	2	4	99	2	2
Murle	1	1	1	3	1	1	2	0	1	S	0	1	1	0	SN	99	2	12	99	1	0	2	1	2	4	0	2	0
Rendille	2	1	1	3	99	1	2	0	1	S	0	1	1	0	CJ	0	0	12	2	1	0	2	0	2	4	0	2	0
Samburu	2	2	1	3	99	1	2	0	1	S	0	3	2	0	SN	0	2	12	2	1	99	2	0	2	4	0	2	0
Somali	1	1	1	3	99	1	3	0	0	L	0	3	2	0	SN	0	0	9	2	1	99	2	0	2	99	0	2	2
Turkana	2	2	1	3	1	0	2	0	1	L	0	3	1	0	SN	0	0	11	2	1	0	2	0	2	4	0	2	0
Arusha	2	3	3	1	2	1	2	0	1	S	1	2	1	0	SN	0	0	11	2	1	0	2	0	2	4	0	2	0
Gusii	3	3	3	2	2	1	2	0	1	S	1	2	2	0	SN	0	0	11	2	1	0	2	0	2	4	0	2	2
Gikuyu	3	3	3	2	2	1	2	2	1	S	2	2	2	0	SN	0	0	11	2	2	0	2	1	2	4	0	2	2
Kipsigis	2	3	3	2	2	1	2	0	1	S	1	2	1	0	SN	0	0	11	2	1	0	2	0	2	4	0	2	1
Luo	2	2	3	2	2	1	2	0	1	S	1	2	2	0	SN	0	0	10	2	1	99	2	0	2	99	0	2	2
Shambaa	3	3	3	1	99	1	2	3	0	S	2	2	0	0	SN	0	0	11	2	0	99	2	1	2	4	1	2	2
Temi Sonjo	3	3	3	1	2	1	2	0	0	S	1	2	2	0	SN	0	0	11	2	1	0	2	1	2	4	0	2	1
Taita	3	3	3	2	2	1	2	0	0	S	1	2	2	0	SN	0	0	11	2	1	0	2	0	2	4	0	2	2
Vugusu	3	3	3	2	2	0	2	0	1	S	1	2	2	0	SN	0	0	11	2	1	0	2	0	2	4	0	2	0
Logooli	3	3	3	2	99	0	2	0	0	S	1	2	2	0	SN	0	0	11	2	1	99	2	0	2	4	99	2	0
Nyoro-Toro	3	3	3	1	2	0	2	3	0	S	2	2	0	0	SN	0	0	10	2	1	0	2	0	2	4	0	2	0
Soga	3	3	3	1	2	1	2	3	0	L	2	2	2	0	SN	0	0	11	2	0	99	2	0	2	4	99	2	0
Gisu	3	3	3	1	1	0	2	0	1	L	1	2	2	0	SN	0	0	11	2	1	99	2	1	2	4	0	2	0
Sebei	2	2	3	2	2	0	2	0	1	L	0	2	2	0	SN	0	0	11	2	1	0	2	0	2	4	0	2	0
Ganda	3	3	3	1	2	1	2	3	0	L	2	2	2	0	CJ	99	0	10	2	0	99	2	0	2	4	0	2	0
Karamojong	2	2	2	99	1	1	3	0	1	L	0	3	99	0	CJ	0	0	10	99	3	99	1	0	2	99	99	2	2
Alur	2	3	2	3	2	1	2	3	0	JL	0	2	2	0	SN	0	0	10	1	0	0	2	0	2	4	0	2	0
Acholi	2	3	2	3	2	1	2	2	0	JL	0	2	2	0	CJ	0	0	10	1	0	0	2	0	2	4	0	2	0
Dinka	2	3	2	99	1	1	2	2	1	JL	0	2	2	0	CJ	99	0	12	1	99	99	1	0	2	99	0	2	0
Nyamwezi	3	2	2	99	99	0	2	3	0	JL	2	2	2	0	SN	0	0	11	1	0	99	2	0	2	4	99	2	1
Gogo	3	2	2	3	99	1	2	0	1	L	1	2	2	0	SN	0	0	10	0	1	99	2	0	2	4	0	2	2
Kuria	3	3	2	99	99	0	2	2	0	JL	0	3	2	0	SN	99	0	12	1	0	99	2	0	2	4	0	2	0
OromoGalla	1	1	2	99	99	0	3	2	1	S	0	3	2	0	SN	0	0	10	1	0	0	2	0	2	4	0	2	0
Dassenech	1	1	2	3	99	1	2	1	1	JL	0	3	2	0	SN	0	0	10	1	1	0	2	0	2	4	0	2	0
Teso	2	2	2	2	99	0	2	1	1	JL	0	3	1	0	SN	99	0	11	1	0	99	2	0	99	99	0	2	0
Chaga	3	3	3	2	2	1	3	2	1	S	2	3	2	1	SN	0	0	12	1	2	0	2	2	0	4	0	2	2
Sukuma	3	3	2	2	2	1	2	2	1	JL	0	3	2	0	SN	0	0	12	1	1	99	2	0	2	99	0	2	2

Legend

- **Language:** 3: Bantu; 2: Nilotic; 1: Afro-Asiatic
- **Mean annual rainfall:** 3: >1000mm; 2: <1000mm; 1: <500mm
- **Predominantly important productive resource:** 3: cultivation; 2: livestock with cultivation; 1: livestock
- **All stock per capita ratio:** 3: high; 2: medium; 1: low
- **Population density per sq. kilometer:** 2: >100 km; 1: <100/km
- **Lineage exogamic preferences:** 1: preferred lineage exogamy; 0: preferred lineage endogamy
- **Organizing principles of local communities:** 3: extended families, neighborhood organizations or age structures; 2: lineage structures; 1: central political interests
- **Centralization:** 3: complex chiefdom & state; 2: simple chiefdom; 1: segmentary with weak leadership; 0: segmentary with strong leadership
- **Existence of age organizations:** 1: age grades and/or sets; 0: none
- **Primary corporate groups:** JL: joint families/lineage segment; S: stem families
- **Nature of land ownership for average member:** 2: strong corporate; 1: weak corporate; 0: no corporate
- **Warfare:** 3: offensive; 2: indeterminate; 1: defensive
- **Political relationships between clans/sections/phratries:** 2: hostile and competitive; 1: variable and indeterminate; 0: friendly
- **Ideology:** 1: rank recognized; 0: emphasis on egalitarianism
- **Primary residential groups:** CJ: corporate-joint; SN: stem-nuclear
- **Does married daughter generally give birth to first child at her natal home?:** 1: returns; 0: does not return
- **Prevailing pattern of residence:** 2: avuncu/matrilocal common; 1: avuncu/matrilocal very occasionally; 0: virilocal/patrilocal
- **Inheritance of positions of authority to sons:** 12: elder marked; 11: elder moderate; 10: equal; 9: younger
- **Relationship between full brothers:** 2: warm; 1: variable; 0: poor
- **Normal time sons can first leave home:** 3: after father's death; 2: between marriage and father's death; 1: at father's death; 0: at or before marriage
- **Free sexual access to wives of brothers:** 1: allowed; 0: not allowed
- **Gerontocracy:** 2: father usually wins; 1: son usually wins
- **Dependence of sons on inherited resources:** 2: crucial; 1: important; 0: limited
- **Does daughter retain jural membership of her natal lineage after her marriage?:** 2: natal lineage; 1: indeterminate shift; 0: husband's lineage
- **Relationship between mother's brother and sister's son:** 4: potentially warm and supportive; 1: cold
- **Are the maternal origins of lineage segments observed?:** 1: recognized by name or as structural bifurcations; 0: not recognized
- **Is genitor or pater relationship stressed in widow inheritance/levirate?:** 3: pater stressed; 2: pater stressed; 1: genitor stressed
- **Do daughters receive livestock and/or land from their parents?:** 2: yes if unmarried; 1: yes; 0: never

Table 3.1 (cont.)

Group	Who goes through initiation, female (1: neighbors, 2: age set, 3: alone or kin)	Who goes through initiation, male (1: neighbors, 2: age set, 3: alone or kin)	Details of operation, female (1: genital operations, 2: other operations, 3: no operations)	Details of operation, male	Women's status (1: low, with exceptions, 3: high)	Religion (1: traditional/animistic, 2: Islam, 3: Christianity)	Premarital sex (0: permitted, 1: common, 2: forbidden)	Adultery frequency (1: rare, 2: common, 3: extensive)	Freedom of choice in marriage (wife first marriage) (1: free/parental influence, 2: parental dictate)	Freedom of choice in marriage (male first marriage) (1: free/parental influence, 2: parental dictate)	Characteristic relationship between husband and his wife's kin (1: cold, 2: potentially warm, 3: supportive)	Do levirate or widow-inheritance marriages occur? (0: none, 1: unofficial, 2: official, 3: obligatory)	Divorce after kids (1: unknown, 2: rare, 3: common, 4: extensive)	Fate of bridewealth if husband retains children (1: returned under various conditions, 2: never retained)	Is bridewealth variable? (0: fixed, 1: negotiable or status dependent)	Who contributes to and who receives bridewealth payment? (1: parents only, 2: close kin, 3: distant kin)	Timing of bridewealth payment (0: all at once, 1: after 5 years, 2: continuing)	Brideservice (0: no, 1: yes)	Total bridewealth (1: low and medium, 2: high)	Primary principle for distribution of major resource type among paradhouses (1: joint, 2: unequal, 3: equal)	Co-wife residential arrangements (1: same house or compound, 2: nearby or distant)	Håkansson DCI index (1: centralized, 2: intermediate, 3: decentralized)	Co-wife rivalry (2: good, 3: average, 4: bad)	Co-wife status (0: None, 1: nominal, 2: marked)	Incidence of polygyny (1: >20%, 2: <20%)	Can daughter filiate children permanently to own natal lineage? (0: no filiation, 2: filiation)	Can livestock and/or land be inherited by a daughter's children? (0: never, 1: yes if mother unmarried, 2: yes)	Do sons-in-law receive livestock and/or land from their wife's parents? (0: never, 1: with residence, 2: yes)
Baggara	99	99	1	1	2	2	99	99	1	2	3	0	3	2	1	1	0	99	99	99	2	99	2	0	1	2	2	1
Datooga	99	2	3	2	2	2	2	1	2	1	2	2	2	1	0	3	2	0	99	2	2	2	2	0	2	0	0	2
Jie	1	1	2	2	1	2	2	3	1	1	2	3	0	99	0	3	1	1	3	2	99	3	2	0	2	2	2	2
Murle	88	88	3	2	2	2	0	99	2	1	2	3	0	99	1	3	2	0	3	99	2	3	99	0	1	2	2	1
Rendille	3	3	2	2	1	2	99	2	2	99	2	2	0	2	0	3	0	1	3	1	2	3	4	0	1	0	0	1
Samburu	3	3	2	2	2	2	1	2	2	99	2	3	2	2	0	3	0	0	2	1	2	3	4	0	2	0	0	1
Somali	-	-	1	2	1	2	99	-	99	99	2	99	0	2	0	3	0	0	2	2	2	99	4	2	2	2	2	0
Turkana	-	2	2	2	2	2	99	2	99	99	2	3	2	2	0	3	0	1	2	1	2	3	4	0	2	0	0	2
Arusha	-	2	2	2	2	2	-	2	2	2	3	2	2	2	0	2	2	0	2	2	1	2	4	1	2	2	2	0
Gusii	2	2	1	2	2	2	1	2	2	2	2	2	2	2	1	2	0	0	2	2	1	2	4	1	1	0	0	2
Gikuyu	2	2	1	2	2	2	1	2	2	2	3	2	2	2	2	2	2	1	2	2	1	2	4	1	2	2	2	0
Kipsigis	99	2	3	2	2	2	99	99	99	99	3	2	2	2	0	2	2	0	2	2	1	3	2	0	2	0	0	2
Luo	88	2	2	2	2	2	99	2	99	99	3	99	2	2	1	2	0	0	2	2	1	3	4	1	1	0	0	1
Shambaa	99	2	3	2	2	2	99	2	2	2	2	3	2	2	0	2	0	0	2	99	2	3	4	2	2	2	2	1
Temi Sonjo	99	2	2	2	2	2	99	99	99	99	3	3	0	2	0	2	2	1	2	99	2	3	4	1	2	0	0	0
Taita	88	2	3	2	2	2	99	2	99	99	3	3	0	2	0	2	0	0	2	99	2	3	4	99	2	99	99	1
Vugusu	88	2	3	2	2	2	99	2	99	99	3	2	2	2	0	2	0	0	2	99	2	3	4	2	2	0	0	0
Logooli	88	2	3	2	2	2	99	2	99	99	3	2	2	2	0	2	0	0	2	99	2	3	4	2	2	0	0	0
Nyoro-Toro	88	88	3	3	2	2	0	99	2	99	3	3	3	99	1	1	0	0	99	99	3	99	3	2	2	0	0	2
Soga	-	2	3	3	2	2	-	99	2	2	3	2	3	99	1	1	0	1	2	99	2	99	3	2	2	2	2	2
Gisu	88	2	3	3	2	2	2	2	2	2	3	2	2	2	1	2	0	0	2	99	2	99	3	2	2	0	0	2
Sebei	-	3	3	3	2	2	2	2	2	2	3	3	2	2	1	2	0	0	2	99	4	3	3	2	2	0	0	2
Ganda	88	88	3	3	2	2	2	99	99	99	3	2	2	99	1	1	0	0	99	99	99	99	3	1	2	99	99	99
Karamojong	-	-	3	3	2	2	-	99	1	1	3	3	2	2	0	2	2	1	3	99	99	99	3	0	1	0	0	99
Alur	88	88	3	3	2	2	2	2	2	2	3	3	2	2	1	1	0	0	99	99	2	99	3	2	2	99	99	99
Acholi	-	-	3	3	2	2	2	2	2	2	3	3	2	2	1	2	0	0	2	99	2	99	4	2	1	0	0	0
Dinka	88	88	3	3	2	2	2	99	2	2	3	3	0	2	0	2	2	0	3	99	2	99	3	2	2	99	99	99
Nyamwezi	-	2	3	3	2	2	2	2	2	2	3	2	2	2	0	2	0	0	2	99	2	99	4	2	2	2	2	2
Gogo	3	3	3	3	2	2	2	2	2	2	3	3	0	2	0	2	2	0	3	99	2	99	3	2	2	0	0	2
Kuria	3	3	3	3	2	2	0	2	2	2	3	2	2	2	0	2	2	0	2	2	2	3	3	2	1	2	2	0
OromoGalla	-	3	1	3	2	2	99	2	2	2	3	3	99	2	0	2	2	0	2	99	2	99	4	2	1	0	0	2
Dassenech	-	-	3	3	2	2	0	2	2	2	3	2	99	99	0	3	2	0	2	99	2	99	4	2	1	2	2	0
Teso	3	3	1	3	2	2	99	2	99	99	3	3	99	99	0	99	2	0	2	99	2	99	99	99	2	99	99	2
Chaga	88	88	3	3	2	3	0	2	2	2	3	2	99	2	0	3	2	0	3	2	2	3	99	99	2	2	2	99
Sukuma	3	2	3	3	2	3	0	2	99	99	3	2	99	2	0	3	2	99	3	2	2	3	3	2	1	99	99	99

Note: Values of 88 and 99 denote inappropriate categories or missing values.

used the program Phylogenetic Independence 2.0 (Reeve and Abouheif 1999), which can incorporate the polytomies (i.e., internal nodes of a cladogram that have more than two immediate descendents) present in the linguistic tree shown in figure 3.1. Societies with missing data were eliminated prior to running the test. Statistical significance was assessed using simulations to generate a null distribution ($n = 1000$ simulations), as described in Abouheif (1999). A trait was judged as exhibiting significant linguistic signal when fewer than 5 percent of the simulated datasets were less than the observed value in a one-tailed test.

Second, we use a method developed by Maddison and Slatkin (1991), which we call the "steps test." The assumption underlying this test is that a trait that exhibits less change (fewer steps) is more conservative, that is, shows more linguistic signal. We ran this test using MacClade 4.05 (Maddison and Maddison 2000). To use this method, we mapped each trait onto the phylogeny shown in figure 3.1 and calculated the number of steps. We then shuffled the data on the tips of the tree 4,999 times, calculating the number of steps for

Figure 3.1
A Linguistic Phylogeny for 35 East African Populations

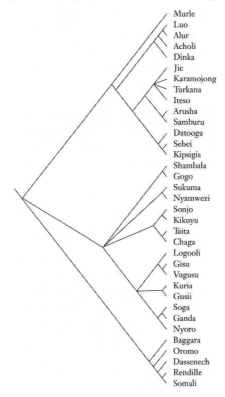

each shuffled dataset. Statistically significant linguistic signal was detected when the observed dataset had fewer steps than expected under the null hypothesis of no phylogenetic signal, which was generated by randomizing (shuffling) the data among the tips of the tree. Specifically, we calculated the percentage of times that the shuffled dataset had a number of steps equal to or less than the value for the real dataset, using this value as the p-value in a one-tailed test. For traits with more than two character states, some traits were treated as ordered and others were treated as unordered. Societies with missing data were not included in the analysis. P-values that were less than or equal to 0.05 were considered statistically significant.

Sequential Bonferroni corrections to the critical p-value were made to accommodate the fact that so many traits were under consideration (Rice 1989), both across the full set of tests ($n = 56$) and within categories (n varies from 3 to 8). Tests were ranked according to their p-values and were considered as significant only if $p \pounds \mu/n$ (for the first test) or ($p \pounds \mu/n - 1$) (for the second test, if the first was significant; see table 3.1, footnotes d, e).

As a test of the general approach, we first examined whether language codes were significantly correlated with the language tree. This was the case with both methods (table 3.1), indicating that they have sufficient statistical power for investigating linguistic signal with our dataset of thirty-five societies, fifty-six traits, and four polytomies.

Results

We present the results of our tests in table 3.2, breaking down the traits into *a priori* categories that match as closely as possible those of previous studies. The principal finding is that for only 18 of 55 traits is there direct evidence of linguistic signature, defined here as showing a significant association ($p < 0.05$) with language in one or both methods. For two thirds of the traits we are unable to reject the null hypothesis of no association between cultural and linguistic similarity. In the categories relating to the domain of family and kinship (residence patterns, agnatic relations, matrilineal biases, polygyny, bridewealth, and marriage-affinity), only 8 of 36 traits are significant, spread across each of the categories. Traits relating to politics show higher levels of linguistic signal (5 of 9), as do traits associated with rituals, beliefs, and attitudes (3 of 6) and ecology (2 of 4). Note, however, that sequential Bonferroni corrections within each category render all tests nonsignificant, with the exception of language, centralization, organizing principles of local communities, details of pubertal operations–male, details of pubertal operation–female (runs test only), and premarital sex (steps test only, table 3.2, *d*). There is considerable consistency between the methods, with both providing generally congruent results, although raw p-values are usually more likely to be significant in the runs than the steps test.

Discussion

We start by discussing the methodological issues surrounding comparison of the runs test (Abouheif 1999) to the steps test (Maddison and Slatkin 1991), and then turn to substantive matters, focusing first on how the evidence for linguistic signal in this study compares with that of other studies, then on the distinct patterns for different cultural traits, and finally on the troublesome concept of phylogenetic inertia. We consider as significant only results meeting the critical *p*-value prior to correction. Although the Bonferroni correction is statistically appropriate, these analyses are part of a largely inductive investigation into the prevalence of linguistic signal; any indications of such signal merit discussion. We stress, however, that by using uncorrected *p*-values we are largely de-emphasizing our principal conclusion—that linguistic signal is rather weak in these data, particularly in the domain of family and kinship.

Runs versus Steps Test

Our analyses revealed that for the same dataset, the runs test was usually more likely to find a significant association between a trait and the linguistic tree than was the steps test. Three factors may account for the discrepancy. First, it may reflect a real difference in statistical power, with the runs test better able to detect statistically significant differences. One reason for this may be that the number of steps for a tree exhibits a narrower distribution than statistics for the runs test, making it difficult to detect significant differences given the number of societies and transitions in the dataset. Second, some of the significant results from the runs test may be "false positives" (Type I errors), in which the null hypothesis of no significant pattern is falsely rejected. Third, it may be easier to detect significance for variables with more states, and there may be differences in the methods in how they detect signal for characters with multiple states. Until computer simulations have been conducted, as they have in testing the assumptions of independent contrasts (e.g., Harvey and Rambaut 1998; Martins and Garland 1991; Purvis et al. 1994), it is impossible to know which of these explanations is most likely. In general, continuous traits provide increased statistical power in comparative tests and should be used when data are available (see Garland et al. 1993).

Relatively Weak Evidence for Linguistic Signal

In this East African sample we find only one third of the traits studied to be highly conserved, and this only without Bonferroni corrections. Although there are no other data sets for which linguistic signature has been determined using phylogenetic tests such as those of Abouheif (1999) and Maddison and Slatkin (1991), results presented in Gugliemino et al. (1995) and Hewlett et al. (2002) provide somewhat comparable measures. In a study of 47 cultural traits across 277 African societies, and using the conventional significance level ($p < 0.05$), Gugliemino et al. (1995) found that 39 of 47 (83%) of their traits are significantly associated with their nine-category language variable; they also conclude that family-kinship traits are particularly conservative, although they draw this conclusion through a somewhat idiosyncratic interpretation of p-value counts and levels.

Hewlett et al.'s (2002) study investigated 109 traits (semes) in thirty-six African societies. According to their scheme for distinguishing why societies share semes, of the forty-five semes with distinguishable models, twenty (44%) show data patterns consistent with demic diffusion. This may be a high estimate, however, because of the potential (in their schema) for genetically similar but linguistically dissimilar societies to support the demic model if such societies share semes. Furthermore, the data patterns for another 73 (67%) of all 109 semes had multiple confounds or were otherwise ambiguous. As such it may be more accurate to conclude that only 20 of 109 (18%) of semes clearly supported the demic model. In these cases, however, we simply do not know whether or not semes showed linguistic associations, so this may be a serious underestimate of linguistic signature. Like Guglielmino et al. (1995), Hewlett et al.'s (2002) study draws the conclusion that traits related to family-kinship and stratification are particularly likely to be spread through the demic processes indicated by linguistic and/or genetic similarity, although in practice the models for the different kinds of traits are not distinguished statistically.

Our results show that linguistic signature is considerably less marked (18 of 55 traits, or 33%) than suggested in Guglielmino et al. (1995), the study offering the more certain and comparable estimates of linguistic signature. Given the simplicity of the methods used here, and the availability of extensive classifications of African languages from which linguistic trees can be built, it would be useful to extend our methodology to make directly comparable studies across different subareas of Africa or indeed across the whole continent (and other continents), with specific hypotheses for how linguistic signatures might vary at different scales of analysis and in different world areas (Nettle and Harriss 2003).

Regarding scales of analysis, there is no a priori reason to believe that the dynamics of trait transmission would be the same at different geographic scales. Indeed, the differences between our study and those reviewed above may reflect differences in scale, insofar as the distances between our sampled societies are small compared to those in the pan-African samples, and there is plenty of opportunity for horizontal transmission (Borgerhoff Mulder et al. 2005). Furthermore, at a local level, migration and interpersonal interactions may permit gene flow and linguistic exchange among groups, albeit accentuating sharp distinctions among others (e.g., McElreath et al. 2003; Turchin 2003). Temporal scale can also be important, with ecological patterns of variability predominating at some scales and disappearing at others. Thus in con-

Table 3.2

Linguistic Signals as Analyzed by Reeve and Abouheif's Runs Test and Maddison and Slatkin's Steps Test

Trait	Societies	N discrete character states [a]	Runs test [b, d]	N steps	Steps test [c, d]	Notes on character states
Language	35	3	**0.001**	2	**0.000**	Afro-Asiatic; Nilotic; Bantu
Ecology						
Mean annual rainfall	33	3 *	0.053	13	0.095	<500mm; <1000mm; >1000mm
Predominantly important productive resource	35	3 *	0.136	12	**0.045**	Livestock; livestock with cultivation; cultivation
All stock-per-capita ratio	27	3 *	**0.023**	12	**0.050**	Low; medium; high
Population density per square kilometer	21	2	0.098	6	0.452	<100 km; >100 km
Politics						
Lineage exogamic preferences	35	2	**0.014**	2	0.088	Preferred lineage endogamy; preferred lineage exogamy
Organizing principles of local communities	35	3 *	**0.001**	7	**0.001**	Central political interests; lineage structures; extended families, neighborhood organizations or age structures
Centralization	35	4 *	**0.001**	13	**0.000**	Segmentary with weak leadership; segmentary with strong leadership; simple chiefdom; complex chiefdom and state
Existence of age organizations	35	2	**0.028**	8	**0.045**	Age grades and/or sets; none
Primary corporate groups	34	2	0.241	9	0.186	Stem families; joint families/lineage segment
Nature of land ownership for average member	34	3 *	0.115	13	1.000	No corporate; weak corporate; strong corporate
Warfare	35	3 *	0.219	20	0.979	Defensive; indeterminate; offensive
Political relationships between clans/ sections/ phratries	34	3 *	0.356	13	0.247	Hostile and competitive; variable and indeterminate; friendly
Ideology	35	2	**0.021**	9	0.254	Emphasis on egalitarianism; rank recognized
Residence patterns						
Primary residential groups	35	2	**0.049**	7	0.327	Stem-nuclear; corporate-joint
Does married daughter generally give birth to first child at her natal home?	33	2	0.453	10	0.786	Returns; does not return
Prevailing pattern of residence	34	3 *	0.240	15	0.564	Viri/patrilocal; avuncu/matrilocal very occasionally; avuncu/matrilocal common
Agnatic relations						
Inheritance of positions of authority to sons	35	4 *	0.259	23	0.642	Younger; equal; elder moderate; elder marked
Relationship between full brothers	32	3 *	0.126	17	1.000	Poor; variable; warm
Normal time sons can first leave home	32	4 *	0.288	14	0.571	At or before marriage; between marriage and father's death; at father's death; after father's death
Free sexual access to wives of brothers	26	2	0.201	7	1.000	Not allowed; allowed
Gerontocracy	31	2	0.469	11	0.875	Son usually wins; father usually wins
Dependence of sons on inherited resources	33	3 *	**0.014**	15	0.069	Limited; important; critical

Table 3.2 (cont.)

Trait	Societies	N discrete character states [a]	Runs test [b,d]	N steps	Steps test [c,d]	Notes on character states
Matrilineal biases						
Does daughter retain jural membership of her natal lineage after her marriage?	32	3*	0.493	17	0.313	Husband's lineage; intermediate shift; natal lineage
Relationship between mother's brother and sister's son	32	2	**0.032**	4	0.059	Cold; potentially warm or supportive
Are the maternal origins of lineage segments observed?	32	2	0.071	9	0.183	Not recognized; recognized by name or as structural bifurcations
Is genitor or pater relationship stressed in widow inheritance/levirate?	33	3*	0.222	8	0.448	Genitor stressed; mixed; pater stressed
Do daughters receive livestock and/or land from their parents?	32	3*	0.382	22	0.927	Never; yes if unmarried; yes
Do sons-in-law receive livestock and/or land from their wives' parents?	29	3*	0.424	14	0.421	Never; with conditions; yes
Can livestock and/or land be inherited by a daughter's children?	31	3*	0.283	20	0.774	Never; yes if mother unmarried; yes
Can daughter filiate children permanently to own natal lineage?	30	2	**0.008**	5	**0.014**	No filiation; filiation
Polygyny						
Incidence of polygyny	35	2	**0.014**	8	**0.037**	<20%; > 20%
Co-wife status	31	3*	0.500	19	0.976	None; nominal; marked
Co-wife rivalry	32	3*	0.331	17	0.497	Good; average; bad
Håkansson's DCI index	27	3*	0.110	12	0.100	Centralized; intermediate; decentralized
Co-wife residential arrangements	33	2	0.454	11	0.637	Same house or compound; nearby or distant
Primary principle for distribution of major resource type among yards/houses	21	2	0.316	5	0.317	Equal; unequal
Bridewealth						
Total bridewealth	28	2	0.082	5	**0.044**	Low and medium; high
Brideservice	32	2	0.207	7	0.676	No; yes
Timing of bridewealth payment	31	3*	0.208	17	0.212	All at once; after 5 years and/or 2 children; continuing
Who contributes to and who receives bridewealth payment?	33	3*	0.058	16	0.267	Parents only; close kin; distant kin
Is bridewealth variable?	35	2	0.512	2	1.000	Fixed; negotiable or status dependent
Fate of bridewealth if husband retains children	27	2	0.139	6	0.648	Never returned; returned under various conditions

Table 3.2 (cont.)

Trait	Societies	N discrete character states [a]	Runs test [b,d]	N steps	Steps test [c,d]	Notes on character states
Marriage affinity						
Divorce after kids	33	4*	0.090	15	0.285	Unknown; rare; common; extensive
Do leviratic or widow-inheritance marriages occur?	30	4*	0.402	27	0.379	None; unofficial; official; obligatory
Characteristic relationship between husband and his wife's kin	32	3*	0.200	19	0.495	Cold; potentially warm; supportive
Freedom of choice in marriage (male first mg)	29	2	0.370	7	0.391	Free/parental influence; parental dictate
Freedom of choice in marriage (wife first mg)	28	2	0.467	9	0.819	Free/parental influence; parental dictate
Adultery frequency	32	3*	**0.049**	8	0.117	Rare; common; extensive
Premarital sex	25	3*	**0.009**	7	**0.004**	Forbidden; permitted; common
Rituals, beliefs, attitudes						
Religion	35	3	**0.018**	8	0.060	Traditional/animistic; Islam; Christianity
Women's status	34	2	0.124	12	0.912	Low, with exceptions; high
Details of operation, male	35	3	**0.002**	8	**0.007**	Genital operations; other operations; no operations
Details of operation, female	35	3	**0.002**	11	**0.020**	Genital operations; other operations; no operations
Who goes through initiation together, male	26	3	0.495	12	0.850	Neighbors; age set; alone or kin
Who goes through initiation together, female	16	3	0.181	6	0.329	Neighbors; age set; alone or kin

a * denotes ordered categories.

b P-value for comparison of real data to runs average (Abouheif 1999; see text).

c P-value for steps test (Maddison and Slatkin 1991; see text).

d Sequential Bonferroni corrections rendered all tests nonsignificant, with the exception of language.

e Sequential Bonferroni corrections within each category rendered all tests nonsignificant, with the exception of language, premarital sex for circumcised individuals, details of pubertal operations (males), and details of pubertal operations (females).

sidering the whole of the lower Paleolithic, Foley and Lahr (2003) suggest that the best predictor of artifact shape is the shape of earlier artifacts in the same region, thereby demonstrating fidelity of form that defies the scale of ecological variation. At shorter time scales, however, they find ecological variation to be much more important.

Specific Patterns in the East African Data

We grouped cultural traits into *a priori* categories that match as closely as possible those of previous studies. Because the ethnographies were coded with different analytical goals in mind, the categories are unfortunately uneven in size. Generally, traits relating to family and kinship show lower linguistic signal (8 of 36 traits, or 22%) than do traits relating to politics (5 of 9 traits, or 56%), rituals, beliefs and attitudes (3 of 6 traits, or 50%) and ecology (2 of 4 traits, or 50%). The specifics of each trait deserve detailed discussion elsewhere (Håkansson 2005). Here, we address only the general pattern, recognizing we provide no statistical test of these differences.

In line with previous work (Guglielmino et al. 1995; Hewlett et al. 2002; Jones 2003), we had expected most variables associated with family and kinship to show marked linguistic signal. In fact, evidence for linguistic signal is limited (8 of 36 traits in the categories of residence patterns, agnatic relations, matrilineal biases, polygyny, bridewealth and marriage-affinity; see table 3.2). Traits that show linguistic signal (in the uncorrected tests) are residential groups, the mother's brother's–sister's son relationship, filiation of children to the mother's lineage, incidence of polygyny, total bridewealth, adultery frequency, and premarital sexual access.

Although some of these traits (e.g., lineage filiation rules) might be part of a society's "core traditions" (see below), others (e.g., size of bridewealth or the nature of residential groupings) are known to be highly responsive to current social and ecological conditions (Borgerhoff Mulder 1995; Goldschmidt 1974; Håkansson 1989,1990; Schneider 1964). As such, we expected them to be less likely to show linguistic signal, but this is not the case. In some instances this may be a result of functional relations among traits. For example, bridewealth and polygyny co-occur worldwide (Hartung 1982; Spencer 1997) and in this sample (Borgerhoff Mulder et al. 2001). The implications of functional relationships are discussed in the following section.

The more evident linguistic signal in cultural traits associated with politics (5 of 9)—namely lineage exogamy, the organizing principles of local communities, centralization, age-based organizations, and egalitarianism—is more consistent with previous work (Hewlett et al. 2002; Pocklington 1996) and with Vansina's (1990) and Kopytoff's (1987) identification of core traditions that embody principles of social organization, hierarchy, and ideology. Given the strong expectation that global and regional world systems transform local sociopolitical relations (Feierman 1990; Wolf 1982), it is somewhat remarkable that these features still bear an apparent signature of the population's deeper history.

Traits categorized as associated with rituals, beliefs, and attitudes also show considerable conservatism (3 of 6), namely religion and the details of male and female pubertal rituals. Considering pubertal rituals, the conservatism might appear to reflect the fact that such ceremonies are often deeply embedded in cultural norms and concepts of identity. Among the Kipsigis, for instance, the very name "Kipsigis" implies being born again as a circumcised individual and, accordingly, as a true Kipsigis. However, this interpretation cannot be entirely correct, since there are well-attested cases of circumcision ceremonies being borrowed across ethnic lines (LeVine and Sangree 1962), and linguistic evidence that the age organizations that are often associated with pubertal ceremonies were repeatedly borrowed between protolinguistic units in Africa over the last 5000 years, reflecting periods of proximity, expansion, and political submission (Ehret 1971, 2001). In short, despite the strong phylogenetic signature to pubertal ceremonies in this data set, it would be difficult to generalize this finding across other contexts or different scales of analysis. We can conclude the same for religion, which in this sample shows a clear linguistic signature, even though it is commonly viewed as a trait subject to strong diffusionary effects, as for example with the spread of Islam across many parts of West Africa (Trimingham 1970) and East Africa (Ensminger 1997).

The apparently highly conserved nature of traits associated with ecology (2 of 4 traits), namely per-capita stock ratios and the principal productive resource (with rainfall bordering on significance), most probably reflects the underlying confounding effects of daughter populations settling in areas ecologically similar to those of their parent population, a phenomenon known as phylogenetic niche conservatism (Grafen 1989). This raises the pervasive question of the extent to which traits exhibit linguistic signature because of faithful transmission between parent and daughter populations, phylogenetic niche conservatism, and/or correlated evolution, such as bridewealth with polygyny. The latter two processes will generate spurious correlations with language. We return to this issue in the next section.

More generally, our results are consistent with ethnohistorical studies of East Africa. Detailed analyses have shown that when daughter groups move into new ecological zones, these groups tend to retain their social institutions, at least over the period of a few centuries. Thus the Maa-speaking Arusha on Mt. Meru in Tanzania, former pastoralists who migrated to the mountain during the nineteenthth century, now focus on irrigation agriculture yet retain many aspects of the basic family type and residential organization characteristic of the pastoral Maasai. Similarly, their neighbors, Meru people originally from Chaga, also retain the ancestral social organization of nineteenth-century Chaga (Spear 1997). As a result, these two communities have very different core institutions concerned with property control, resource access, and local leadership, each derived from its parent culture, despite almost identical present economic pursuits and a shared environment. There are many other examples of formerly agro-pastoral groups such as the Gusii (Håkansson 1988), the Nandi (Obler 1985), the Kuria (Tobisson 1986), and the Kipsigis (Borgerhoff Mulder 1989) that, despite shifts to greater agricultural production, persist in applying to land inheritance the rules for livestock inheritance.

Against this background, our finding that only a few family and kinship traits show linguistic signal becomes all the more puzzling. One possibility is that these traits are more labile than the traits we classify as political. Another possibility is that the types of structural continuities reported for the Chaga, Gusii, and Nandi (see above) persist for only a few generations and are therefore lost in broader phylogenetic analysis. Yet another possibility is that ethnographers and historians are biased toward looking for similarities and continuities between parent and daughter populations rather than on reporting borrowings and innovation. Accordingly, ethnographers may find stronger traces of history than will those using more objective quantitative approaches, at least in some domains.

Phylogenetic Inertia

It is important to stress that demonstrations of phylogenetic conservatism, here through linguistic signal, do not directly identify the mechanisms of trait transmission. Highly conserved cultural traits might reflect demic processes, with linguistically related populations preserving shared ancestral traits. Alternatively, when daughter populations share their parent-population traits, this may reflect a tendency for fissioning populations either to move into habitats similar to their source populations (phylogenetic niche conservatism, see above) or to establish themselves in contact with the same neighbors as their source populations, thus exposing themselves to similar diffusionary influences. Indeed, linguistic and cultural traits may be conditioned by same kinds of isolating factors, whether these are geographic or cultural boundaries (resulting from social conformity, imitation, ethnocentric biases, or other processes [Nettle 2005]). Further, if several traits show linguistic signature, this may reflect functional relations among these traits rather than demic processes carrying each trait independently. In short, ecological adaptation, cultural diffusion, and correlated evolution may well be confounded in the linguistic signal, as suggested at various junctures earlier in the discussion. Ultimately, we need methods that not only parse out the effects of geography and history (for example, with Mantel tests) but test hypotheses for correlated trait evolution while controlling for both historical and geographic distance.

Far more important than simply identifying cases of apparent trait inertia or conservatism is the specification of the mechanisms that underlie trait stability. In biology these might include low genetic variation, genetic or ecological constraints, or stabilizing selection (Blomberg and Garland 2002; Harvey and Pagel 1991). When considering *cultural* traits it is equally important to identify the mechanisms that account for the apparent persistence and change in traits over time, even though this can be very difficult.

The dynamics underlying behavioral and institutional transitions can be studied from various perspectives. Sociocultural anthropologists emphasize how cultural changes are embedded in social and political institutions that are themselves shaped by broader political economic and global dynamics (Barth 1966; Wolf 1982), dynamics that often reproduce inequality (Giddens 1984; North 1990). Evolutionary anthropologists see the apparent erasure of history as reflecting adaptive processes, as populations move to live in new ecological and political niches, and/or become exposed to the cultural practices of new neighbors (Boone and Smith 1998; Rogers and Cashdan 1997). Cultural evolutionists view changes in behavior and social institutions as a tradeoff between trial-and-error learning and culturally transmitted norms; in this view, norms can reduce the costs in arriving at locally adaptive behavior (Boyd and Richerson 1985; Henrich and Gil-White 2001); they are more efficient in terms of accumulating the critical knowledge for dealing with rarely encountered contingencies (Boyd and Richerson 1995; Richerson and Boyd 2000); and they are valuable in reducing the ambiguities and transaction costs inherent in generating collective action (Alvard 2003; McElreath, et al. 2003; Paciotti and Borgerhoff Mulder 2004; see also the work of neo-institutional economists such as Giddens [1984] and North [1990]).

Clearly, the more specific dynamics underlying institutional change and stability lie far beyond the remit of this chapter, and they are not at all well understood. We have provided a simple analytical tool for structuring empirical investigation into which features of societies tend to be most labile, a critical first step to any of the enterprises outlined above.

Summary and Conclusions

Three things stand out from these analyses. First, at the local level we do not find strong evidence for linguistic signal in traits relating to family and kinship; this runs counter to the suggestion of a faithfully transmitted family-kinship core (Guglielmino et al. 1995; Jones 2003). Second, traits associated with politics and ritual show stronger linguistic signal; this is more consistent with continent-wide quantitative studies (Hewlett et al. 2002; Pocklington 1996) and observations on core cultural traditions identified by historians (e.g., Kopytoff 1987). Third, traits associated with making a living show considerable linguistic signal and probably reflect daughter populations settling in an environment similar to that of their parent populations.

It would be rash to generalize too far from limited results such as these, at least until we have a much broader set of comparable studies based either on linguistic signal (as here), or (more indirectly) on cladistic studies of cultural traits themselves, such as projectile points (O'Brien and Lyman 2004, also chapters 11 and 12, this volume), pottery (Collard and Shennan 2000, also chapters 13 and 14, this volume), carpets (Tehrani and Collard 2002), or baskets (Jordan and Shennan 2003, also chapter 4, this volume). Here, we end by emphasizing two points. First, patterns of interaction among cultural, genetic, and linguistic evolution are likely to depend on the scale of the study. Second, simple phylogenetic methods such as those used here have the potential to lend rigor to cultural continuity models used in interpretations of prehistory (Huffman 1984; Schmidt 1978) and, as this study shows, can produce somewhat unexpected results.

Lastly, as regards the rashness of generalization, we should stress that very different processes responsible for cultural diversity characterize different parts of the world. Thus the well-attested demic expansions across Polynesia (Gray and Jordan 2000), central Africa (Holden 2002), and Eurasia (Renfrew 1992) may be very specific to particular zones (Nettle and Harriss 2003), perhaps ultimately because of geographic considerations (Diamond 1997). Here, we have tried to present a simple tool for examining one component of this complex story at a very local scale.

Acknowledgments

We thank Mark Grote, Richard McElreath, Mary Towner, and Bruce Winterhalder for helpful comments and discussion on the use of phylogenies in the study of human culture, and the editors for advice and cooperation. We have special thanks for Camilla Power and Elena Mouriki for codes on puberty rituals. Our work is supported by National Science Foundation grants BCS-0132927 and 0323793.

4

Branching versus Blending in Macroscale Cultural Evolution: A Comparative Study

Mark Collard, Stephen J. Shennan, and Jamshid J. Tehrani

The processes responsible for producing similarities and differences among cultures have been the focus of much debate in recent years, as has the corollary issue of linking cultural data with the patterns recorded by linguists and biologists working with human populations (e.g., Ammerman and Cavalli-Sforza 1984; Bateman et al. 1990; Bellwood 1996b, 2001; Bellwood and Renfrew 2003; Boyd and Richerson 1985; Boyd et al. 1997; Brace and Hinton 1981; Cavalli-Sforza and Cavalli-Sforza 1995; Cavalli-Sforza and Feldman 1981; Collard and Shennan 2000; Durham 1990, 1991, 1992; Goodenough 1999; Guglielmino et al. 1995; Henrich 2001; Hewlett et al. 2002; Hurles et al. 2003; Jordan and Shennan 2003; Kirch and Green 1987, 2001; Laland et al. 1995; Lumsden and Wilson 1981; Mesoudi et al. 2004; Moore 1994a, 1994b, 2001; O'Brien 1996; O'Brien and Lyman 2000a; Renfrew 1987, 1992, 2000b, 2001; Romney 1957; Shennan 1991, 2000, 2001, 2002; Smith 2001; Tehrani and Collard 2002; Terrell 1987, 1988; Terrell et al. 1997, 2001; Vogt 1964; Whaley 2001; Zvelebil 1995). To date, this debate has concentrated on two competing hypotheses, which have been termed the "branching" hypothesis (also known as the "genetic," "demic diffusion," and "phylogenesis" hypothesis) and the "blending" hypothesis (also known as the "cultural diffusion" and "ethnogenesis" hypothesis) (Bellwood 1996a; Collard and Shennan 2000; Guglielmino et al. 1995; Hewlett et al. 2002; Kirch and Green 1987; Moore 1994a, 1994b, 2001; Romney 1957; Tehrani and Collard 2002; Vogt 1964).

According to the branching hypothesis, similarities and differences among cultures are the result of a combination of predominantly within-group information transmission and population fissioning. The strong version of the hypothesis suggests that "transmission isolating mechanisms" (TRIMS) (Durham

1992) impede the transmission of cultural elements among contemporaneous communities. TRIMS are akin to the barriers to hybridization that separate species and include language differences, ethnocentrism, and intercommunity violence (Durham 1992). The branching hypothesis predicts that similarities and differences among cultures can be best represented by the type of tree diagram that is used in biology to depict the relationships among species. The hypothesis also predicts that there will be a close association between cultural variation and linguistic, morphological, and genetic patterning (e.g., Ammerman and Cavalli-Sforza 1984; Bellwood 1995, 1996b, 2001; Cavalli-Sforza and Cavalli-Sforza 1995; Cavalli-Sforza et al. 1988, 1994; Chikhi et al. 1998, 2002; Diamond and Bellwood 2003; Kirch and Green 1987, 2001; Renfrew 1987, 1992, 2000b, 2001; Sokal et al. 1989, 1991).

In contrast, supporters of the blending hypothesis (e.g., Dewar 1995; Moore 1994a, 1994b, 2001; Terrell 1987, 1988, 2001; Terrell et al. 1997, 2001) believe that it is unrealistic "to think that history is patterned like the nodes and branches of a comparative, phylogenetic, or cladistic tree" (Terrell et al. 1997: 184). They argue instead that human biological, linguistic, and cultural evolution are best characterized as "a constant flow of people, and hence their genes, language, and culture, across the fuzzy boundaries of tribes and nations, spreading within a region such as the Plains or the Southeast within a few generations, and across the continent in a few more" (Moore 2001: 51). That is, according to the blending hypothesis the patterns of similarity and difference among cultural assemblages are a consequence primarily of individuals in different groups copying each other's practices, exchanging ideas and objects, and marrying one another. The blending hypothesis predicts that similarities and differences among cultures can best be represented by a maximally connected network, or reticulated graph (Terrell 2001). It also predicts that there will be a close relationship between cultural patterns and the frequency and intensity of contact among populations, the usual proxy of which is geographic propinquity.

Recently it has been asserted that blending has been the major process in the ethnohistorical period and is likely to have always been more significant than branching in cultural macroevolution (e.g., Dewar 1995; Moore 1994a, 1994b, 2001; Terrell 1987, 1988, 2001; Terrell et al. 1997, 2001). In our view, this claim is problematic. Most contributions to the branching/blending debate have focused on macroscale cultural evolution in specific regions of the world often over relatively short spans of time (e.g., carpets made by Turkmen tribes between the eighteenth and twentieth centuries) rather than dealing with this form of cultural evolution as a general phenomenon (Borgerhoff Mulder 2001; Collard and Shennan 2000; Dewar 1995; Guglielmino et al. 1995; Hewlett et al. 2002; Jordan and Shennan 2003; Kirch and Green 1987; Moore and Romney 1994, 1996; Roberts et al. 1995; Tehrani and Collard 2002; Terrell et al. 1997, 2001; Welsch 1996; Welsch et al. 1992). A few papers have addressed the debate's key issues in universal terms (e.g., Moore, 1994a, 1994b, 2001; Terrell 1987, 1988, 2001), but the evidence discussed in these works is anecdotal. As such, we contend it is currently unclear whether cultural macroevolution is dominated by blending or by branching.

Here we discuss a study that goes some way toward rectifying this situation. In the study we assessed how treelike cultural datasets are compared to biological datasets. Essentially, we fitted the biologists' tree model to a group of cultural datasets and to a group of biological datasets that have been used to reconstruct the relationships of species and higher-level taxa. We then compared the average fit between the cultural datasets and the model with the average fit between the biological datasets and the model. Given that the biological datasets can be assumed to have been structured by speciation—a branching process—our assumption was that if the blending hypothesis is correct and macroscale cultural evolution is dominated by blending processes, the fit between the tree model and the cultural datasets should be significantly worse than the fit between the tree model and the biological datasets. Conversely, if the blending hypothesis is incorrect and cultural macroevolution is dominated by branching processes, the fit between the model and the cultural datasets should be no worse than the fit between the model and the biological datasets.

Materials and Methods

Our first step was to obtain biological and cultural datasets suitable for phylogenetic analysis. Acquiring the biological datasets was straightforward, as they are readily available in the literature, and many of them can be downloaded from on-line databases such as TreeBASE (Sanderson et al. 1994). Accordingly, we assembled a set of twenty-one biological datasets. We selected only datasets that have been used to reconstruct the relationships of species and higher-level taxa, assuming that the taxa have been structured by the branching process of speciation. Datasets pertaining to simple organisms (e.g., viruses, bacteria) and subspecies of complex organisms were avoided on the grounds that they may have been affected by blending processes (Mesoudi et al. 2004). An effort was made to include a broad range of taxa and characters. Thus, the biological datasets included DNA data for lizards, lagomorphs, and carnivores; morphological data for fossil hominids, seals, and ungulates; and behavioral data for bees, seabirds, and primates.

Currently, cultural datasets suitable for phylogenetic analysis are much less easy to come by than their biological counterparts. We had three datasets in our possession from previous work we had conducted on this topic (Collard and Shennan 2000; Jordan and Shennan 2002; Tehrani and Collard 2002). To these we were able to add three datasets from the literature (Jorgenson 1969; O'Brien et al. 2001; Welsch et al. 1992). In addition, Katerina Rexová of Charles University, Czech Republic, kindly provided us with data from her recent analysis of the relationships among Indo-European languages (Rexová et al. 2002). This gave us a total of seven cultural datasets with which to work. Details of the biological and cultural datasets are provided in table 4.1.

Thereafter, we used PAUP* (Swofford 1998) to evaluate how well the most parsimonious tree explains the distribution of similarities and differences within

Table 4.1
Datasets Used in Analyses

Dataset	Source
Australasian teal mtDNA	Kennedy and Spencer (2000) [a, b]
Corbiculate bee behavior	Noll (2002)
Pelecaniforme bird behavior	Kennedy et al. (1996)
Anoles lizard morphology	Guyer and Savage (1986) [a]
Primate behavior	DiFiore and Rendall (1994)
Strepsirhine morphology	Yoder (1994)
Hominid morphology	Lieberman et al. (1996)
Platyrrhine morphology	Horowitz et al. (1998) [c]
Ungulate morphology	O'Leary and Geisler (1999) [a, d]
Phalacrocoracid bird mtDNA	Kennedy et al. (2000) [e]
Phocid seal morphology	Bininda-Edwards and Russell (1996) [a]
Hawaiian fruitfly mtDNA	Baker and DeSalle (1997) [a, f]
Hominoid craniodental morphology	Collard and Wood (2000) [g]
Carnivore mtDNA	Wayne et al. (1997) [a]
Mammal mtDNA (with emphasis on Malagasy primates)	Yang and Yoder (2003) [h]
Carnivore mtDNA (with emphasis on Malagasy taxa)	Yoder et al. (2003) [h]
Mammal mtDNA	Yoder and Yang (2000) [h]
Insectivore mtDNA	Stanhope et al. (1998) [a, i]
Lagomorph mtDNA	Halanych and Robinson (1999)[j]
Hominoid soft-tissue morphology	Gibbs et al. (2002)
Anolis lizard mtDNA	Jackman et al. (1999) [a, k]
Indo-European lexical items	Rexová et al. (2002) [l]
Neolithic pottery	Collard and Shennan (2000)
California Indian basketry	Jordan and Shennan (2003)
North American projectile points	O'Brien et al. (2001)
Salish cultural practices	Jorgensen (1969)
New Guinea material culture	Welsch et al. (1992)
Turkmen weaving designs	Tehrani and Collard (2002)

a Downloaded from TreeBASE.
b Data for ATPase 6, ATPase 8, and 12S genes.
c Craniodental data.
d Data from runs 5 and 6.
e Data for 12S, ATPase 6, and ATPase 8 genes; provided by Martyn Kennedy, Department of Zoology, University of Otago, New Zealand.
f Data from "all genes" analysis.
g Qualitative dataset.
h Downloaded from the Web site of Anne Yoder, Yale University.
i Data for 12S-16S genes.
j Data for 12S gene.
k Data for ND2 gene and tRNA.
l Provided by Katerina Rexová of Charles University, Czech Republic.

each dataset. In all the analyses, the characters were treated as unordered, and the most parsimonious tree was identified by means of the heuristic-search routine. The goodness-of-fit measure we used was Farris's (1989a, 1989b) "retention index" (RI). Equivalent to Archie's (1989) "homoplasy excess ratio maximum index" (Farris 1989b, 1991), the RI is a measure of the number of homoplastic changes (see chapter 1, this volume) a phylogenetic tree requires that are independent of its length. The RI is a useful goodness-of-fit measure when comparing diverse datasets because it is unaffected by either the number of taxa or the number of characters. The RIs for the twenty-one biological datasets and the seven cultural datasets are presented in table 4.2. Also shown in table 4.2 are RIs associated with most parsimonious phylogenetic trees derived from two cultural datasets that we were unable to include in our PAUP* analyses (Gray and Jordan 2000; Holden 2002). The RI for the Austronesian language dataset was kindly provided by Russell Gray of the University of Auckland. The RI for the Bantu dataset was obtained from the results section of Holden (2002).

In the next stage of the study, we compared the RIs of the twenty-one biological datasets with the RIs of the nine cultural datasets with a view to determining whether or not they are significantly different. This was accomplished with the Wilcoxon rank-sum test, which was implemented in the manner described by Swinscow (1977). The Wilcoxon rank-sum test employs the same statistic and yields the same results as the Mann-Whitney U-test (Sokal and Rohlf 1995).

Results

The RIs associated with the most parsimonious trees derived from the biological and cultural datasets (table 4.2) suggest that the fit between the tree model and the cultural datasets is little different from the fit between the model and the biological datasets. Not only are the averages similar, but the ranges are comparable. The mean, minimum, and maximum biological RIs are 0.60, 0.35, and 0.94, respectively. The corresponding figures for the cultural RIs are 0.60, 0.17, and 0.93. Thus, descriptive statistics do not support the hypothesis that blending is more important than branching in macroscale cultural evolution. On average, the cultural datasets appear to be no more reticulate than the biological datasets.

The results of the Wilcoxon rank-sum test are in line with the descriptive statistics. The sum of the ranks for the biological RIs is 321, and the sum of the ranks for the cultural RIs is 118. Since the 5-percent-level critical point of a nine versus twenty-one cases test is 95 (Swinscow 1977), and this is less than the sum of the ranks for the smaller set of RIs, the biological and cultural RIs are not significantly different according to the Wilcoxon rank-sum test. Thus, once again, the hypothesis that blending is more important than branching in cultural macroevolution is not supported.

Table 4.2

Goodness-of-Fit Values Associated with Most-Parsimonious Phylogenetic Trees
Derived from 21 Biological and Nine Cultural Datasets

Datatset	RI[a]
Australasian teal mtDNA	0.94
Corbiculate bee behavior	0.94
Pelecaniforme bird behavior	0.84
Anoles lizard morphology	0.78
Primate behavior	0.73
Strepsirhine primate morphology	0.72
Hominid morphology	0.71
Platyrrhine morphology	0.70
Ungulate morphology	0.69
Phalacrocoracid bird mtDNA	0.65
Phocid seal morphology	0.60
Hawaiian fruitfly mtDNA	0.50
Hominoid craniodental morphology	0.49
Carnivore mtDNA	0.48
Mammal mtDNA (with emphasis on Malagasy primates)	0.47
Carnivore mtDNA (with emphasis on Malagasy taxa)	0.47
Mammal mtDNA	0.44
Insectivore mtDNA	0.44
Lagomorph mtDNA	0.39
Hominoid soft-tissue morphology	0.38
Anolis lizard mtDNA	0.35
Indo-European lexical items	0.93
Neolithic pottery	0.72
California Indian basketry	0.71
North American projectile points	0.70
Salish cultural practices	0.63
Bantu lexical items	0.59
New Guinea material culture	0.52
Turkmen weaving designs	0.44
Austronesian lexical items	0.17

a RI = retention index; a maximum RI of 1 indicates that the tree requires no homoplastic change, and the level of homoplasy increases as the index approaches 0.

Discussion

The failure of our analyses to support the claim that blending has always been the dominant macroscale cultural evolutionary process is in line with most region-specific quantitative studies that have been published to date (Borgerhoff Mulder 2001; Collard and Shennan 2000; Guglielmino et al. 1995; Hewlett et al. 2002; Jordan and Shennan 2003; Moore and Romney 1994, 1996; Roberts et al. 1995; Tehrani and Collard 2002). Several of these studies have focused on cultural variation among villages on the northern coast of New Guinea, using geographic distance and linguistic affinity as proxies for blending and branching, respectively. Using regression and correspondence analysis of presence/absence data, Welsch et al. (1992; see also Welsch 1996) found that similarities and differences among sets of material culture from the villages were strongly associated with geographic propinquity and unrelated to the linguistic relations of the villages. In contrast, correspondence and hierarchical log-linear analyses of frequency data carried out by Moore and colleagues (Moore and Romney 1994; Roberts et al. 1995) indicated that geography and language have equally strong effects on the variation in material culture among the villages. Moore and Romney (1996) obtained the same result in a reanalysis of Welsch et al.'s presence/absence data using correspondence analysis, thereby accounting for one potential explanation for the difference in findings, namely the use of different data sets. Recent work by Shennan and Collard (2005) confirms Moore and Romney's assessment that a combination of both branching and blending was operating in this case.

Three quantitative studies (Borgerhoff Mulder 2001; Guglielmino et al. 1995; Hewlett et al. 2002) have examined cultural macroevolution in African societies. The study by Guglielmino et al. (1995) explored the roles of branching, blending, and local adaptation in the evolution of forty-seven cultural traits among 277 African societies. The traits were divided into six categories ("family and kinship," "economy," "social stratification," "labor division by sex," "house," and "various other"), and then correlation and clustering analyses were undertaken to determine which of three models best explained the distribution of the traits in each category: demic diffusion, environmental adaptation, or cultural diffusion. Guglielmino et al. found that the "family and kinship" traits were best explained by the demic-diffusion model, whereas the "labor division by sex" and "various other" traits were best explained by the cultural-diffusion model. The distributions of the traits in the other three categories were found to be affected by demic diffusion, environmental adaptation, and cultural diffusion.

Hewlett et al. (2000) investigated the processes responsible for the distribution of 109 cultural attributes among thirty-six African ethnic groups. Using measures of genetic, linguistic, and cultural distance, together with an index of geographic clustering, they tested the same explanatory models as Guglielmino et al. (1995)—demic diffusion, environmental adaptation, and cultural diffusion. They found that 32 percent of the cultural attributes could not be linked with an explanatory model and that the distributions of another

27 percent of the cultural attributes were compatible with two of the models. Of the remaining cultural attributes, 18 percent were compatible with demic diffusion, 11 percent were compatible with cultural diffusion, and just 4 percent were compatible with local invention.

Borgerhoff Mulder (2001) examined correlations among cultural traits associated with kinship and marriage patterns in thirty-five East African societies. She found that when phylogenetic relationships were taken into account the data supported roughly half the number of statistically significant correlations returned by analyses of phylogenetically uncorrected data. These results failed to support Borgerhoff Mulder's preferred hypothesis, which is that adaptation to local environments plus diffusion between neighboring populations erase any phylogenetic signature. Were that the case, the correlations between different traits in the phylogenetically controlled analysis would have returned similar results to a conventional statistical analysis of the raw data. This was not the case. However, Borgerhoff Mulder's results also do not lend unqualified support to the branching hypothesis either, in that a high proportion of correlations remained unaffected by phylogenetic correction. In these cases, the trace of descent is obscured either by a relatively fast rate of cultural evolution and adaptation or by the mixing and merging of cultural groups that has been reported in ethnographic and historical sources on East African societies. Thus, the three African studies provide evidence for the operation of both branching and blending processes (see chapter 3, this volume).

Four other quantitative contributions to the branching/blending debate have been published—those by Chakraborty et al. (1976), Collard and Shennan (2000), Jordan and Shennan (2002), and Tehrani and Collard (2002). The study by Chakraborty et al. used regression analysis to examine the relationships among genetic variability, geographic distance, degree of Caucasoid admixture, and cultural and linguistic dissimilarity in seven Chilean Indian populations. The analyses returned significant correlations between geographic distance and genetic distance, geographic distance and cultural dissimilarity, and genetic distance and cultural dissimilarity. Linguistic dissimilarity and degree of Caucasoid admixture were not significantly correlated with the other variables or with each other. Thus, Chakraborty et al.'s analyses supported the blending hypothesis.

Collard and Shennan (2000) used cladistics to examine the evolution of assemblages of pottery from Neolithic sites in the Merzbach Valley, Germany. Their first set of analyses focused on assemblages from four settlements that have evidence for occupation throughout the whole of the ten-phase period. They conjectured that if the branching hypothesis is correct, analyses of the assemblages should divide them into the same groups in consecutive phases. On the other hand, if the blending hypothesis is accurate, the analyses should separate the settlements into different groups in consecutive phases. The results were not wholly compatible with either hypothesis. Rather, they indicated that branching and blending both were involved in the generation of the pottery assemblages.

Collard and Shennan's second set of analyses focused on three instances in which a new pottery assemblage appears. They reasoned that if the branching hypothesis is correct, then the newly founded assemblages should have a single parent assemblage in the preceding phase. Conversely, if the blending hypothesis is accurate, then the newly founded assemblages should have multiple parents in the preceding phase. This set of analyses supported the branching hypothesis rather than the blending hypothesis. Overall, therefore, Collard and Shennan's analyses of the Merzbach Valley early Neolithic pottery supported the branching hypothesis more strongly than the blending hypothesis.

Tehrani and Collard's (2002) study examined decorated textiles produced by Turkmen groups between the eighteenth and twentieth centuries. Two sets of cladistic analyses were carried out. The first focused on the period before the Turkmen were incorporated into the Russian Empire. These analyses indicated that in the pre-colonial period the evolution of Turkmen textile designs was dominated by branching. A randomization procedure (the permutation tail probability test) suggested that the data contained a phylogenetic signal, and parsimony analysis indicated that the data fit the tree model associated with cultural branching reasonably well. The fit between the model and data was not perfect, indicating that blending played a role in the evolution of Turkmen culture. However, goodness-of-fit statistics and a second randomization procedure (bootstrapping) suggested that blending was markedly less important than branching. According to the goodness-of-fit statistics, about 70 percent of the similarities among the assemblages were homologous, and approximately 30 percent were homoplastic. This is compatible with borrowing being responsible for a third of interassemblage resemblances.

Tehrani and Collard's second set of analyses dealt with the weavings produced while the Turkmen were ruled by the Russians. These analyses suggested that the changes experienced by the Turkmen after their incorporation into the Russian Empire led to a greater role for blending in Turkmen cultural evolution. Branching remained the dominant cultural evolutionary process, but the importance of blending increased. The goodness-of-fit statistics indicated that roughly 60 percent of the interassemblage resemblances are homologous, and roughly 40 percent are homoplastic. This is consistent with more intertribal borrowing of designs and motifs. Tehrani and Collard concluded that the two sets of analyses supported the branching hypothesis more strongly than the blending hypothesis.

Contrasting findings were obtained by Jordan and Shennan (2003), who used cladistics to examine variation in California Indian basketry in relation to linguistic affinity and geographic proximity. Jordan and Shennan carried out three sets of cladistic analyses. In the first, they used the permutation tail probability test to determine whether or not their basketry datasets (coiled baskets, twined baskets, all baskets) contain a phylogenetic signal. Analysis suggested that a significant phylogenetic signal was present in all three datasets. In the second set of analyses, Jordan and Shennan used a goodness-of-fit statistic (the consistency index) to assess the fit between the datasets and the bifurcating-tree model. Analysis suggested that the phylogenetic signal detected by the permutation tail probability test was weak. The fit between the datasets and the bifurcating-tree model was weak in all three analyses. In the third set of analyses, Jordan and Shennan used a statistical test developed by Kishino and Hasegawa (1989) to assess the fit between the datasets and trees reflecting linguistic relationships, geographic distance, ecological similarity, and adjacency (presence of shared borders). This test enabled them to distinguish between two different potential sources of homoplasy—independent invention and blending.

In the analysis of the complete sample of baskets, the fit between the dataset and the adjacency tree was considerably better than the fit between the dataset and the other trees. This suggested that blending had a larger impact on the distribution of similarities and differences among the basketry assemblages than branching or adaptation to local environments. In the analysis of only coiled baskets, blending was also found to play a more significant role than branching or adaptation to local environments. The analysis of the twined baskets contrasted with the preceding analyses in that the language tree fitted the dataset better than the other trees. This suggested that branching was more important in generating the twined baskets than blending or adaptation to local environments. Jordan and Shennan concluded on the basis of these results, and results of a range of multivariate analyses, that the variation observed among Californian Indian baskets is best explained by blending rather than branching, or rather that linguistic affiliation has not provided a strong canalizing force on the distribution of basketry attributes, which appears to be mainly determined by geographical proximity and therefore, presumably, frequency of interaction.

Overall, the suggestion that blending has always been a more important cultural macroevolutionary process than branching is not supported by the region-specific quantitative studies that have been published to date. Blending seems to have been the dominant process in the evolution of the Chilean and Californian datasets, but branching was at least as important as blending in generating the other datasets.

Conclusions

The results of the comparative study described here do not support the recent claim that blending, or ethnogenetic, processes such as trade and exchange have always been more important in macroscale cultural evolution than the branching, or phylogenetic, process of within-group information trans mission plus population fissioning. Collectively, the cultural datasets in our sample do not differ significantly from the biological datasets in terms of how treelike they are. The claim that blending has always been more important than branching in cultural macroevolution is also not supported by the region-specific quantitative assessments of cultural evolution that have been published to date. Blending processes clearly structure some datasets, but branching processes are equally clearly responsible for structuring other datasets. It appears, therefore, that branching cannot be discounted as a macroscale cultural evolutionary process. This in turn suggests that rather than deciding how cultural macroevolution has proceeded *a priori* (e.g., Moore 1994a, 1994b; Terrell 1988, 2001; Terrell et al. 1997, 2001), researchers need to ascertain which model or combination of models is relevant in a particular case and why.

Acknowledgments

We thank Martyn Kennedy, Katerina Rexová, and Anne Yoder for making their data available. We also thank Samantha Banks for assisting with the analysis of the Salish data set and Russell Gray for providing us with the RI for the Austronesian language dataset. We are indebted to John Bodley, Barry Hewlett, Stephen Lycett, Alex Mesoudi, and Mike O'Brien for providing useful comments and suggestions. Lastly, we would like to express our gratitude to the United Kingdom's Arts and Humanities Research Board for its on-going support of our work on cultural evolution.

5

Seriation and Cladistics: The Difference between Anagenetic and Cladogenetic Evolution

R. Lee Lyman and Michael J. O'Brien

We have argued in numerous venues that a significant step in archaeological research involves the construction of evolutionary histories of cultural phenomena (Lyman and O'Brien 1998; O'Brien and Lyman 2000a, 2000b, 2002a, 2003a). These histories can concern artifacts of any scale, from design motifs on ceramic vessels, to projectile-point shapes, to architectural forms, to tool kits. A critical aspect of constructing these histories involves ascertaining the *mode* of evolution, by which we mean the form of the evolutionary history of a lineage. Did the members of the lineage change in a linear fashion (perhaps projectile points got consistently longer over time)? Did the members diversify over time (did the projectile points in one population get longer whereas those in another population got shorter)? Was there hybridization (did a population with long, narrow points exchange ideas with a population having short, wide points so as to produce a new kind of point)? Was there a combination of these modes of change?

The evolution of a lineage is historical in the particularistic sense of being contingency bound (Simpson 1963, 1970)—minimally, the gene pool has unique spatial and temporal coordinates (Cooper 2002; Gould 1986). This does not mean, however, that determining the evolutionary history of some set of phenomena is less of a scientific endeavor than, say, calculating the atomic weight of an element (Lyman and O'Brien 2004). Indeed, it is precisely the theoretically driven nature of research on particularistic evolutionary histories that makes those histories empirically testable. The use of a theory with empirical implications is arguably a necessary condition of any science (Moore 2002).

In part because of the linear cultural-evolutionary models they have adopted, archaeologists have long examined culture change as if it were a linear progression of (typically, artifact) forms within a lineage (Lyman and O'Brien 1997). Contributing to the general feeling that prehistoric cultural evolution was generally linear were some of the chronometric methods developed by archaeologists early in the history of the discipline (O'Brien and Lyman 1999). In particular, various techniques by which the seriation method is operationalized produce linear orderings of phenomena that have the appearance of a linear mode of evolution.

This is, in part, a result of how change is graphed and the scale of the graphed units, but it is also in part a function of how change is viewed on a graph displaying a seriated ordering of artifacts. In particular, it involves an implicit view of evolution as occurring at the scale of a "culture" or some unit more inclusive than the classes of artifacts graphed. Many such units have been called "traditions," each of which is defined as "a socially transmitted form unit (or a series of systematically related form units) which persists in time" (Thompson 1956: 38). A tradition is equivalent to a biological lineage, or line of heritable continuity, but note that the definition of tradition specifies no scale. Contributing to conceptual and analytical difficulty is the fact that although we often speak of the evolution of culture, the unit that we call "a culture" in fact has no good, generally agreed-on definition within anthropology.

We explore here what we take to be two critical issues in the study of cultural phylogenies. First, we briefly expand on the immediately preceding statements and argue that the scale at which evolution occurs is an important consideration—a point emphasized in several other chapters of this book (e.g., chapters 10 and 11). Second, we show that our perceptions of evolutionary mode depend on the analytical technique, particularly the graphing technique, used to monitor evolutionary change and the scale of the units used to track evolution (see chapter 6, this volume). We conclude that evolution occurs at many and varied scales within cultural phenomena and that archaeologists interested in writing the phylogenetic histories of artifacts must be aware that the scale of units chosen for analysis and the graphic technique used to plot change both influence our perceptions of evolutionary mode.

Evolutionary Modes and Biological Methods

Evolution in the organic world is viewed as typically having two modes, each of which creates a particular phylogenetic pattern. The mode can be either "anagenetic" or "cladogenetic." Prior to about 1970, the former was characterized as linear (phyletic) evolution, in which the parental taxon becomes (evolves into) a daughter taxon. An important characteristic of anagenetic evolution is that the parental taxon goes extinct when the daughter taxon appears. In modern biology, most biologists relegate anagenesis to the production of intraspecific, small-scale changes that organisms go through as they pass from one generation to the next, though a few biologists believe that anagenesis can and does sometimes produce new species (e.g., Gingerich 1985; see Barnosky 1987).

Cladogenetic evolution is branching evolution; the Greek word *klados* means "branch." Cladogenesis occurs if the parental taxon goes extinct simultaneously with the appearance of two (or more) distinct daughter taxa. Importantly, cladogenesis can also occur when a parental taxon gives rise to a daughter taxon and then coexists with it. This is the mode of evolution that Niles Eldredge and Stephen Jay Gould (1972) had in mind when they coined the term *punctuated equilibrium*, a theory of both tempo (rate) *and* mode. Most biologists today believe that cladogenesis is (and was in the past) largely responsible for the creation of new species.

There is a third mode of evolution that is sometimes identified, generally referred to as "reticulation." It involves hybridization—the interbreeding of two distinct taxa, usually species—and the subsequent interbreeding of the hybrid offspring with at least one parent such that a new descendant population representing a new taxon is eventually produced (Levin 2002). Thus, one of the parental taxa, or at least a population thereof, effectively goes extinct (Rhymer and Simberloff 1996). Keep in mind the scale at which hybridization is generally viewed—at the species or a higher, more-inclusive taxonomic level.

Methods for monitoring organic evolution among both living and fossil organisms include what are referred to as "evolutionary taxonomy" and "cladistics" (Mayr 1969; Mayr and Ashlock 1991). Application of these methods hinges on two key aspects of Darwin's (1859) "descent with modification." The first is the process of transmission, which produces descent and ensures heritable continuity between ancestor and descendant. In biological evolution, genes are transmitted; in cultural evolution, packages of information are transmitted (Lyman and O'Brien 2003a). The second aspect involves the modification of descendants relative to their ancestors. That is, replication need not be and typically is not, carried out with perfect fidelity. Descendants are different, if only slightly, from their parents, and they are successively more different from their ancestors as their remoteness from those ancestors increases. Importantly, evolution is not just descent, nor is it just modification; it is, in fact, descent *with* modification.

The important analytical operation to monitoring descent with modification involves classification of the evolving and evolved phenomena of interest, whether organisms or something else. Classification involves an analytical choice of characters and character states (or what an archaeologist might term attributes) of phenomena based on the analytical question being posed (Lyman and O'Brien 2002; O'Brien and Lyman 2002b). The character states chosen should reflect descent with modification; their underlying genes or packets of information should have been transmitted (with greater or lesser fidelity) from parent to offspring, from ancestor to descendant (O'Brien et al. 2002). This means the chosen character states should be what are generally referred to as "homologues"—character states that are held in common by sister taxa precisely because the taxa are sisters. Evolutionary taxonomists and archaeologists have, to greater or lesser degrees, recognized this requirement for over a half century (Lyman 2001; Lyman and O'Brien 2003b), though archaeologists have struggled with determining which characters are homologues and which are not.

Evolutionary taxonomists consider all kinds of homologous characters in attempting to sort out phylogenetic history. They use what are called "shared ancestral characters," or those that are shared by a taxon and at least two generations of its descendants (figure 1.1). They also examine what are called "shared derived characters," which are shared only by a taxon and its immediate daughters (figure 1.1). Finally, they consider "unique characters" in order to determine the degree of morphological divergence among related and even unrelated taxa.

In contrast, cladists argue that only shared derived characters should be used when attempting to determine the phylogenetic relations of taxa. The reason to use only this particular subset of homologous characters (or character states) is that an ancestral trait is of no value in determining specific relationship. All animals with a backbone, for example, have the ancestral trait "vertebrae," but that homologue does not tell us whether Taxon A is more closely related to Taxon B or to Taxon C. Only shared derived character states allow us to make that determination. Cladistics is now the dominant method in biology for constructing phylogenetic hypotheses. We believe it can be equally usefully applied to cultural phenomena (e.g., Foley 1987; Foley and Lahr 1997; Gray and Atkinson 2003; Gray and Jordan 2000; Holden 2002; Holden and Mace 1997, 1999; Jordan and Shennan 2003; Mace and Pagel 1994; O'Brien and Lyman 2003a, 2003b; O'Brien et al. 2001, 2002; Rexová et al. 2003; Tehrani and Collard 2002).

Ontology of a Culture and the Scale of Evolution

Given the many discussions of what "culture" is that have appeared in the last fifty years (e.g., Keesing 1974; Kroeber and Kluckhohn 1952; Sahlins 1999; Shweder 2002), it is perhaps not too surprising that it is difficult to agree on what *a* culture is. In what we take to be an astute observation, George Murdock (1971: 19) noted that, to him, it was "distressingly obvious that culture, social system, and all comparable supra-individual concepts . . . are illusory conceptual abstractions inferred from observations of the very real phenomena of individuals interacting with one another." Such things as cultures and societies had, in Murdock's view, become "reified abstractions."

Twenty-five years later, Palmer et al. (1997: 296–297) reiterated Murdock's observation and added that whereas "conceptualizing and talking about people in terms of discrete categories referred to as 'cultures' or 'societies' is certainly a great convenience," the reification of these units is "scientifically unacceptable." They concluded that humans have a genetically programmed tendency that they termed "categorical perception," which causes us to unconsciously perceive individual phenomena and to group those individuals into categories. It is the unconscious nature of this grouping process that causes us to believe that we perceive discrete, well-bounded groups within a series of continuously varying phenomena. Human races are perhaps a prime example.

We believe the categorical-perception problem is well described by the differences between classes and groups as we and others have discussed them (Dunnell 1971; Lyman and O'Brien 2002; O'Brien and Lyman 2002b). Classes are ideational units with, ideally, explicit definitive criteria that have been chosen for their analytical and theoretical relevance. Because the criteria consist of character states, they are at a less-inclusive scale than the phenomena being classified. This is not trivial because it underscores the point that the phenomena being classified must all be of the same scale (e.g., set of artifacts, artifact, character, character state). Artifacts are classified based on their attributes; tool kits on the artifact types they include; site types on the architectural features they contain and the human behaviors that are inferred to have taken place; and so on. Groups are sets of empirical phenomena. The setness of each group rests on the criteria used to specify membership; the discreteness of each group rests on the distinctive and unique criteria of each group.

In our view, a culture is a particular kind of ideational unit that, unfortunately, at best has fuzzy definitive criteria, and thus its empirical members to greater or lesser extents are fluid and permeable. Each culture is not always equally distinct from every other culture because each has flexible boundaries (Palmer et al. 1997; Sahlins 1999). One might protest that a culture is manifest in a set of people who share a particular set of information that they acquired via enculturation (to put a modern spin on E. B. Tylor's [1871] seminal definition), but this leaves unspecified the definitive set of information making up the culture as well as the proportion of that information that must be shared by the society's members in order to be included within the bounds of one culture and excluded from a similar culture (Shweder 2002). Interestingly, most anthropologists during the first half of the twentieth century viewed cultures as having fuzzy, fluid boundaries precisely because of the interaction between them (Sahlins 1999).

It is difficult to identify a culture as a discrete unit with clear boundaries in an ethnographic setting. As with the spatial boundaries of culture areas, the definitive criteria and thus the boundaries of a culture must be specified by the anthropologist. Therefore, it is fallacious to argue that one cannot study the evolutionary history of a culture because cultural evolution is reticulate. Such an argument presumes that there is a clear boundary around each culture, just as the biological-species concept of a reproductively isolated population specifies boundary lines across which gene flow either does not occur or is extremely limited.

There were those during the first half of the twentieth century who contrasted a culture with a biological species in order to emphasize that species had impermeable (to gene flow) boundaries whereas individual cultures did not have impermeable (to information flow) boundaries (e.g., Boas 1904; Gladwin 1936; Kroeber 1931; Steward 1944). We agree with this early assessment of fuzzily defined and bounded cultures, but we also know that the boundaries of biological species are not nearly as impermeable to gene flow as once thought (Arnold 1997). Biologists have, nevertheless, not stopped attempting to unravel phylogenetic history.

We think it is realistic to conceptualize cultural evolution as occurring at a less-inclusive scale than a culture. As archaeologists, we study the evolution of particular artifacts and thus of technologies—stone tools, ceramic vessels, and the like. There are different mechanical requirements and constraints for subtractive technologies such as stone working than there are for additive technologies such as building composite tools and for technologies that modify the chemical and/or molecular structure of raw material, such as pot making. As a result, we find it quite likely that each technology evolves largely, if not completely, independently of other technologies (Hunt et al. 2001). This shifts the scale of analysis from the evolution of a culture to the evolution of a technological lineage. This scale shift does not preclude the hybridization mode, but it does negate the argument that "cultural evolution" is reticulate and reduces it to the less-pernicious "cultures interact in various ways." This means that phylogenetic signals may be muted, but it is improbable that they will always be imperceptible (O'Brien and Lyman 2003a).

But why should hybridization be such a bogeyman? Reticulate evolution, when detected using particular methods (e.g., Skála and Zrzavý 1994), may become a critically important part of writing an evolutionary history of a technological lineage (O'Brien and Lyman 2003a). Archaeologists have long struggled with the topic of cultural contact and have regularly attempted to develop methods for tracking the history of such contacts (e.g., Lathrap 1956; Thompson 1958). One early effort along these lines was James Ford's (1952) work. The basis for his effort was percentage stratigraphy and frequency seriation (Lyman et al. 1998; O'Brien and Lyman 1998), and his interpretations of the mode of cultural evolution rested in part on how he graphed change. Ford used what we call a centered-bar graph, which shows changes in the relative (proportional) frequency of each of several classes of artifacts over time. This brings us, finally, to the central issue of our discussion—the influence of scale and graphing method on our perceptions of evolutionary mode among artifacts.

Archaeology and Seriation

Seriation has a long history of use in archaeology. At least since John Evans (1850) ordered ancient British coins in the mid-nineteenth century, antiquarians and archaeologists have used character states to sort artifacts into what were believed to be chronologically ordered series. Augustus Pitt Rivers ordered an impressive array of archaeological and ethnographic artifacts, including throwing sticks, boomerangs, and spears from Melanesia (Pitt Rivers 1874a, 1875). Similarly, Sir William Flinders Petrie (1899, 1901) ordered a variety of ancient Egyptian artifacts that came from tombs along the Nile. We have referred collectively to such orderings as "phyletic seriations" (Lyman et al. 1997; O'Brien and Lyman 1999) to keep them distinct from the technique of "frequency seriation," invented by A. L. Kroeber (1916b), and from the distinctive "occurrence seriation," first described in the 1950s and early 1960s (Dempsey and Baumhoff 1963; Rowe 1959). Americanist archaeologists such as A. V. Kidder (1917) ordered artifacts using phyletic seriation before Kroeber's seminal frequency seriation, and some, such as E. B. Sayles (1937), continued to use the older technique well after Kroeber's work (figure 1.4).

As archaeological chronometers, all three seriation techniques (phyletic, frequency, and occurrence) rest on an assumption of historical continuity. That is, they assume that the degree of formal similarity between two phenomena is related directly to the degree of their temporal propinquity. The assumption of historical continuity in turn rests on an assumption of heritable continuity. In other words, the formal similarity of two phenomena is assumed to be a direct result of a genetic-like connection between them effected by cultural transmission. When the seriated phenomena are artifacts, the units of cultural transmission and heritability are packages of information—cultural replicators analogous to biological replicators (Dawkins 1976; Hull 1988).

Terms such as "replicator" and "meme" (Dawkins 1976) commonly occur in modern discussions of cultural evolution, but they were not coined until the last quarter of the twentieth century. Thus, Pitt Rivers, Petrie, and Kidder never used them when discussing their phyletic orderings of artifacts, though Pitt Rivers (1875) was explicit about "ideas in the mind" underlying artifact forms (a fair if general gloss of the meme concept) and that transmission of those ideas results in historical and heritable continuity and thus cultural traditions. It is clear that Pitt Rivers (1891: 116) had Darwin's (1859) descent with modification in mind when he pointed out that "knowledge of the facts of evolution, and of the processes of gradual development, is the one great knowledge that we have to inculcate, whether in natural history or in the arts and institutions of mankind."

Pitt Rivers was influenced by Tylor's (1871) unilinear cultural evolution, but he attempted to go beyond a simple rephrasing of Tylor's tenets and to link them to those of Darwin: "Human ideas as represented by the various products of human industry, are capable of classification into genera, species and varieties in the same manner as the products of the vegetable and animal kingdoms. . . . If, therefore, we can obtain a sufficient number of objects to represent the succession of ideas, it will be found that they are capable of being arranged in museums upon a similar plan" (Pitt Rivers 1874b:xi–xii; see also Pitt Rivers 1875).

Phyletic seriation is an important method of ordering phenomena, and from an evolutionary standpoint it can be used to illustrate all three modes of evolution (cladogenesis, anagenesis, and reticulation), as we show below. We use the terms for evolutionary modes to refer to the same sorts of patterns and processes in cultural change, noting that in the latter, as in biology, the distinction between cladogenesis and anagenesis often reduces to a matter of the scale of the units being used to measure change and of the graphic method of building phylogenetic hypotheses. In the following we focus first on phyletic seriation and then on frequency seriation. We illustrate how these two forms of seriation differ in terms of the scale of the units typically used in each, and how graphs displaying each influence whether one sees cladogenetic, anagenetic, or reticulate evolutionary modes.

Phyletic Seriation—The Scale of Character State of a Discrete Object

An example of a phyletic seriation is Kidder's (1917) ordering of decorative motifs on southwestern pottery shown in figure 5.1. Stratigraphic information told him which end of the sequence was older and which was younger. The character used to produce the ordering is found in the upper left portion of the motif. This character shifts in state from what might be described as a rectangle nearly filled with adjoining black rectangles in number 1, to about a third filled with two sets of adjoining black rectangles in number 2, to an empty rectangle in number 3, to more open space in number 4, to, finally, a nearly empty triangle in number 5. These descriptions are cumbersome at best, and we would need considerably more care in writing the character-state definitions were these to be reliable. If we were to transfer these data to a phylogenetic tree, the only possible result is what is shown in figure 5.2.

Another example of phyletic seriation is Pitt Rivers's evolutionary history of paddles from New Ireland, part of the Bismarck Archipelago. His depiction was anagenetic. We have modified it in figure 5.3 by adding arrows to show his proposed developmental sequence. If we were to transfer these data to a phylogenetic tree, the only possible result is shown in figure 5.4. But suppose we have additional phylogenetic information that allows us to create a cladogenetic ordering like that shown in figure 5.5. Notice that the sequence in figure 5.5 is the same as in figure 5.4, where the paddles are arranged anagenetically, but in figure 5.5 we are illustrating cladogenesis—the *mode* of evolution rather than the sequence. The differences between figures 5.4 and 5.5 tell us that analytically the cladogenetic evolution of taxa and the temporal sequence

Figure 5.1
A. V. Kidder's Phyletic Seriation of Ceramic Design Motifs from Pecos Pueblo, New Mexico (Modified from Kidder 1917)

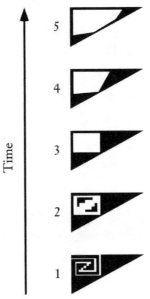

Figure 5.2
A Phylogenetic Tree of A. V. Kidder's Ceramic Design Motifs in Figure 5.1

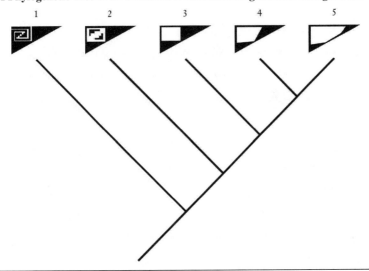

Note that the sequence of branching can be read as the same temporal sequence shown in figure 5.1.

Figure 5.3
A. H. Pitt Rivers's Evolutionary History of Paddles from New Ireland, Bismarck Archipelago (modified from Pitt Rivers 1875)

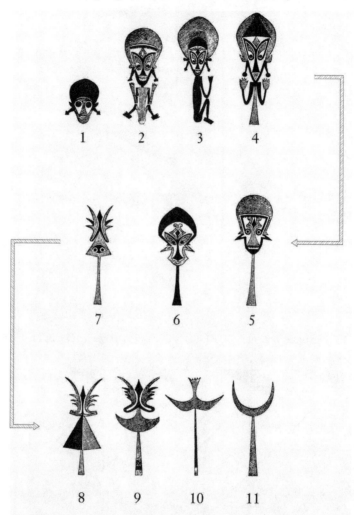

of the appearance of taxa are two different things. Thus, we cannot determine from figure 5.5 alone whether paddle form 3 or 5 appeared first.

Pitt Rivers did not suggest a cladogenetic arrangement of paddles—we made one up strictly as an example—but other prehistorians *did* propose that the cladogenetic mode occurred during the evolution of artifacts in phyletic seriations. An example is Petrie's arrangement of ceramic vessels from Egypt, part of which is shown in figure 5.6. Interestingly, Petrie (1899) referred to portions of his temporal sequence as "genealogies." The "genealogy" shown

Figure 5.4
A Phylogenetic Tree of A. H. Pitt Rivers's New Ireland Paddles in Figure 5.3

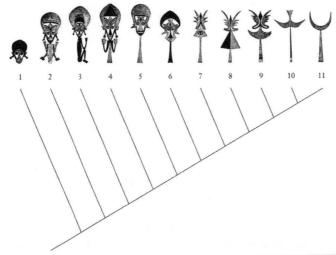

Note that the sequence of branching can be read as the same temporal sequence shown in figure 5.3.

Figure 5.5
A Fictional Phylogenetic Tree Emphasizing the Cladogenetic Mode of Evolution among A. H. Pitt River's New Ireland Paddles

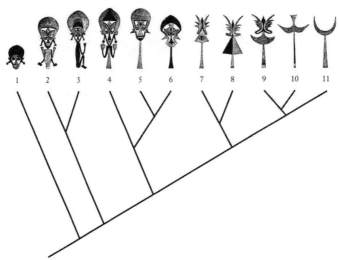

Note that the sequence of branching cannot be read as a temporal sequence like that in figure 5.3.

in figure 5.6 contains instances of both anagenesis and cladogenesis as modes of evolution. In terms of the latter, the jar form in period 38 gives rise to two forms—those in periods 48 and 49. Similarly, the form in time period 48 gives rise to two forms, as does the jar in period 70. In most other cases, the evolutionary mode is anagenetic, but in two places the mode of evolution is reticulate. The jar in period 38 is a hybrid of jars in periods 34 and 36, and the form in period 70 is a hybrid of two forms in period 60.

Petrie offered no clue as to how or why he distinguished instances of cladogenesis, anagenesis, or reticulation. We suspect that his basic method involved two steps. First, he ordered classes of vessels in what he believed was a temporal sequence according to an assumption of historical and heritable continuity. His temporal ordering was on a relative scale, and in some cases more than one form of vessels occurred during one time period. During the second step, we suspect Petrie judged whether a class of vessel displayed character states of one or two temporally contiguous earlier classes; if the former, anagenesis was

Figure 5.6
W. M. Flinders Petrie's Genealogy of Ceramic-Vessel Forms Recovered from Egyptian Burials (after Petrie 1899)

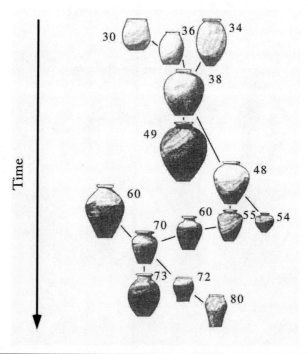

Numbers refer to temporal periods. Note that all three modes of evolution—anagenetic, cladogenetic, and reticulate—are indicated.

suggested, and if the latter, hybridization was suggested. A similar judgment accompanied inspection of classes that occurred later in the sequence.

Temporal propinquity and the ratio of shared to unique character states probably implicitly guided whether Petrie saw anagenesis, cladogenesis, or hybridization. We have modeled how Petrie's thinking might have looked in figure 5.7. Each capital letter denotes a particular character state, and the position of the letter in a list of states denotes a particular character. For example, assume that the last letter in a list represents the character "rim form:" F means an inverted-rim character state, H a vertical rim, and Z a lipped rim (compare figures 5.6 and 5.7). The scale of the evolutionary mode here concerns how the characters of vessels, not vessels themselves, change states over time. The form of recombination (note the word choice) of sets of particular character states on a discrete vessel suggests the evolutionary mode. It is important to emphasize that Petrie did not make explicit the definitions of his vessel classes, and thus it is unclear which character states he considered. We suspect that he used character states that represented both shared derived and shared ancestral character states, meaning that what he did was more akin to modern evolutionary taxonomy than to modern cladistics.

Figure 5.7
A Fictional Partial Genealogy of Ceramic-Vessel Class Definitions Based on
W. M. Flinders Petrie's Genealogy in Figure 5.6.

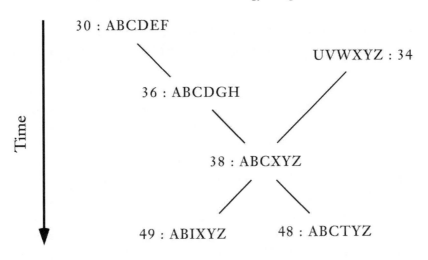

Numbers refer to temporal periods. Each capital letter represents a unique character state; the position of a letter in each class definition (list of letters) represents a particular character. Note that the class in period 38 is a hybrid of the classes in periods 36 and 34.

Frequency Seriation—Evolution at the Scale of Classes of Discrete Objects

As an archaeological chronometer, frequency seriation typically concerns discrete objects, though it could be used with any scale of item. In the discussion that follows, we consider classes of discrete objects in order to make our point that the scale of the units used to track evolution and how evolutionary change is graphed influence our interpretations of evolutionary mode. Frequency seriation assumes that each historical class occurs during only one span of time and that it has a frequency distribution that is unimodal relative to the frequencies of other classes. Thus, a dozen collections of artifacts, say, each with various classes of artifacts and sharing some classes, can be ordered such that each class displays a single continuous occurrence through the ordering and a unimodal frequency distribution. That the ordering reflects the passage of time is an inference and must be tested with independent chronological data. In the following, we presume for sake of discussion that the fictional frequency seriation in fact does reflect the passage of time.

An example of thirteen seriated collections with four classes is shown in figure 5.8. Notice that not only does each of the four classes occur during only one span of time and each displays a unimodal frequency distribution, but classes overlap in the sense that they occur in multiple assemblages that are adjacent to one another in the ordering. Simply put, overlapping is the basis for the underpinning assumption of historical continuity between assemblages affected by heritable continuity (O'Brien and Lyman 1999). Assume that each of the classes in figure 5.8 is defined by three characters, each having two possible states, A and B, and that the position in the list of character states defining a class specifies the character (first position is first character, second position is second character, and so on). Eight classes are possible (AAA, AAB, ABB, BBB, BBA, BAA, ABA, BAB). In the following discussion, we presume that the four classes represented in the collections in figure 5.8 are the first four listed.

Virtually all published frequency seriations made up of centered-bar graphs like that in figure 5.8 lack the definitions of the classes as part of the graph. If we were to inspect figure 5.8 without the class definitions clearly indicated, the evolutionary mode(s) represented by the graph would be obscure. On the one hand, that graph might be considered to show a cladogenetic mode, given that the oldest class could be interpreted as having diverged into the second class to appear in the sequence. The class definitions suggest such a cladogenetic event is likely because the two classes differ in terms of only one character (BBB versus ABB). We could show this with diagonal lines running from an early type to a later type; we might call such lines "phylogenetic-divergence" lines.

On the other hand, we might step back (lower the magnification power) and argue that the change from type BBB to AAA represents an anagenetic mode. Basically the same temporal information as is found in figure 5.8 is available

Figure 5.8
A Fictional Example of a Frequency Seriation of 13 Assemblages (Rows)
Containing Four Types (Columns) Plotted in a Centered-Bar Graph

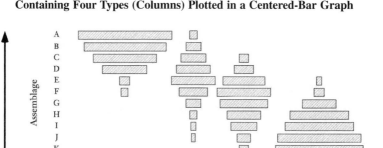

Note that class definitions typically are not included in such graphs.

in the ordering Class 1 (BBB), Class 2 (ABB), Class 3 (AAB), Class 4 (AAA). This listing, if graphed as in figure 5.7, would make the evolutionary mode appear anagenetic when in fact all we have done is alter the means of graphic representation and shifted the scale from frequencies of classes (in figure 5.8) to class definitions (lists of character states in figure 5.7).

Notice that in altering the scale of the evolutionary unit to frequencies of specimens within classes of discrete objects we have, in effect, masked the changes in character states displayed by those discrete objects (figure 5.7). Nothing about the mode of artifact evolution actually changed; only the scale of the classificatory unit and the means of graphing were changed, which is our main point. Thus one might find it rather perplexing that James Ford, who popularized centered-bar graphs like that in figure 5.8 (Lyman et al. 1998; O'Brien and Lyman 1998), would publish the model of change in artifacts shown in figure 5.9. The latter figure is in fact how Ford thought of change in artifact lineages—anagenetically—whereas graphs like that in figure 5.8 allowed him to monitor change over time.

Importantly, Ford had a particular analytical goal in mind when he used centered-bar graphs. He typically was concerned with what change within artifact lineages indicated about the passage of time and less often with evolutionary mode, at least in the sense that we have defined it here. In what we consider one of only two studies in which he specifically sought to detect evolutionary mode, Ford (1952) used centered-bar graphs to assist with chronological ordering of archaeological manifestations, but he also superimposed

Figure 5.9
James A. Ford's View of Culture Change as Exemplified in Pottery

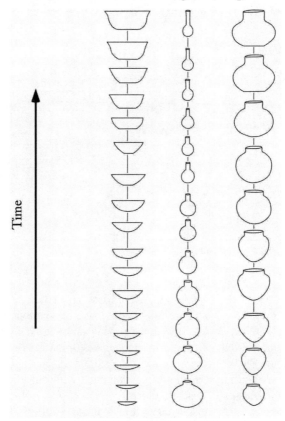

Note that within each lineage change is anagenetic. Compare with figure 5.6.

the vessel classes on those graphs. This resulted in a hybrid graph that combined features from figures 5.8 and 5.9, but it was the vessel classes, not the relative frequencies of those classes, that allowed him to infer evolutionary mode. Perhaps without knowing it, he was mimicking Petrie's procedure as we have modeled it in figure 5.7. The fact that different columns of centered bars contained from one to several classes of vessel and represented different geographic areas allowed Ford to track both the diffusion and the evolutionary mode of vessel forms across space and time. Ford's (1969) final monograph-length study of pottery evolution omitted the centered-bar-graph portion of the illustrations and focused only on simple phyletic seriations, arranged so as to imply diffusion and divergence (cladogenesis) across space and time.

Phyletic Seriation—Scale and Mode

In the two studies just mentioned, Ford (1952, 1969) clearly had questions of evolutionary mode in mind, though he did not phrase them in explicit evolutionary terms. The fact that he used a form of phyletic seriation to study artifact phylogeny and evolutionary mode is, we think, significant. It harks back more than fifty years to earlier phyletic seriations such as that by Petrie (figure 5.6). This seems to be the basic method many individuals used to track phylogenetic histories of artifacts. For example, numerous examples of arti-fact phylogeny are found in the work of Bashford Dean, curator of fishes at the American Museum of Natural History and honorary curator of arms and armor at New York's Metropolitan Museum of Art. In 1915 Dean published figure 5.10 in an article geared to changing how museums labeled exhibits. Dean's complaint was that museums for the most part did a terrible job of educating their visitors. Museums tended to fall into one of two camps: those that let objects speak for themselves and those that drowned the visitor in verbiage. Dean believed that visitors were confused by disassociated objects and that what was needed was a "plan" to bring together in the visitor's mind what he or she saw in the display cases. In Dean's view, one way to pull this off was to choose a category of items familiar to the visitor and to arrange the items so as "to show the changes which have taken place during the centuries," with "the first form begat[ting] the second, perhaps in a vaguely evolutionary way" (Dean 1915: 173).

There was nothing "vaguely evolutionary" about what Dean proposed (Coen 2002). His scheme was anchored in a diagram—shown in the lower left of figure 5.10—that illustrated the "characteristic parts" of a class of object. Those nine "characteristic parts" of helmets are the characters we believe Dean used to help construct his phylogeny. The larger diagram illustrates how and when those parts came into being and how once they came into being they changed states. Note, for example, that the earliest helmets do not have visors. Those come in later, at different times and in different branches. The same pattern exists with respect to crests. Once those characters come in, they change states rapidly. Dean followed the lead of paleontological practice and marked off temporal horizons for his helmets. The result, in Dean's words, was an illustration of, in this case, helmets "evolving." Significantly, Dean (1915: 174) noted that the graph displayed a chronological order of helmet parts— our characters and character states.

Dean's diagram not only epitomizes how important classification is to phy-logenetic research but also highlights differences in the kinds of trees that can be used to illustrate phylogenetic relations. Notice that Dean labeled most of the branches on his phylogenetic tree. The labels refer to general kinds of helmets, with individual "taxa" represented by the small drawings. Dean's diagram shows both anagenesis and cladogenesis. This is a very different kind

Figure 5.10
Bashford Dean's Model of Phylogenetic Evolution in Helmets

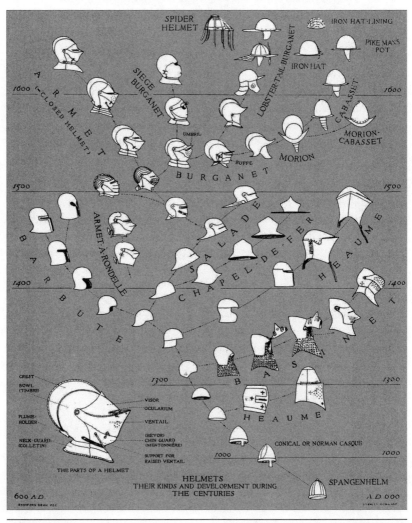

Note the designation of critical characters in the lower left and that both anagenetic and cladogenetic modes are shown (after Dean 1915).

of arrangement than would be shown in a cladistically derived phylogenetic tree built using only shared derived characters and character states. We show one in figure 5.11 strictly as an example. Note that all taxa are shown at the branch tips. Some taxa might be directly ancestral to other taxa, but it is unlikely that we will ever be able to verify such a relationship using strict cladistic methods. Thus, our tree shows all taxa as "terminal taxa."

Although Dean published only one drawing of an artifact phylogeny, he drew numerous other phylogenetic orderings of various kinds of artifacts. For example, he modeled an overall phylogeny of swords and the evolution of various sword subgroups, but the individual phylogenies were presented only in general form in one of Dean's figures, here reproduced as figure 5.12. Dean also took some of the individual subgroups—cinquedeas (figure 5.13) and rapiers and court swords (figure 5.14)—and traced their phylogenies at a detailed scale. In biological terms, the subgroups are individual "clades"—all descendant taxa of one ancestral taxon plus that common ancestor—in the overall "sword" phylogenetic tree. Importantly, the ordering is based on phyletic seriation, not on cladistics, just as was Petrie's ordering of Egyptian pottery in figure 5.6. We suspect that were we to build classes similar to Dean's and to build a phylogenetic tree cladistically, the sequence of taxa and the order of branching would pretty much mirror Dean's arrangement. This is because he had good chronological control of the artifacts he was concerned with, and he noticed which characters changed states over time.

Dean's graphs are phylogenetic trees, but not necessarily ones with single roots. Dean's trees show real ancestors, which cladistically derived trees cannot, and many of Dean's taxa are not terminal taxa, such as are produced by a

Figure 5.11
A Fictional Phylogenetic Tree Emphasizing the Cladogenetic Mode of Evolution among Some of Bashford Dean's Helmets (see Figure 5.10)

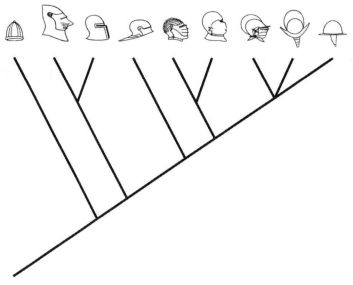

Note that the sequence of branching cannot be read as a temporal sequence such as can be done in figure 5.10.

Figure 5.12
Bashford Dean's General Model of Phylogenetic Evolution in Swords

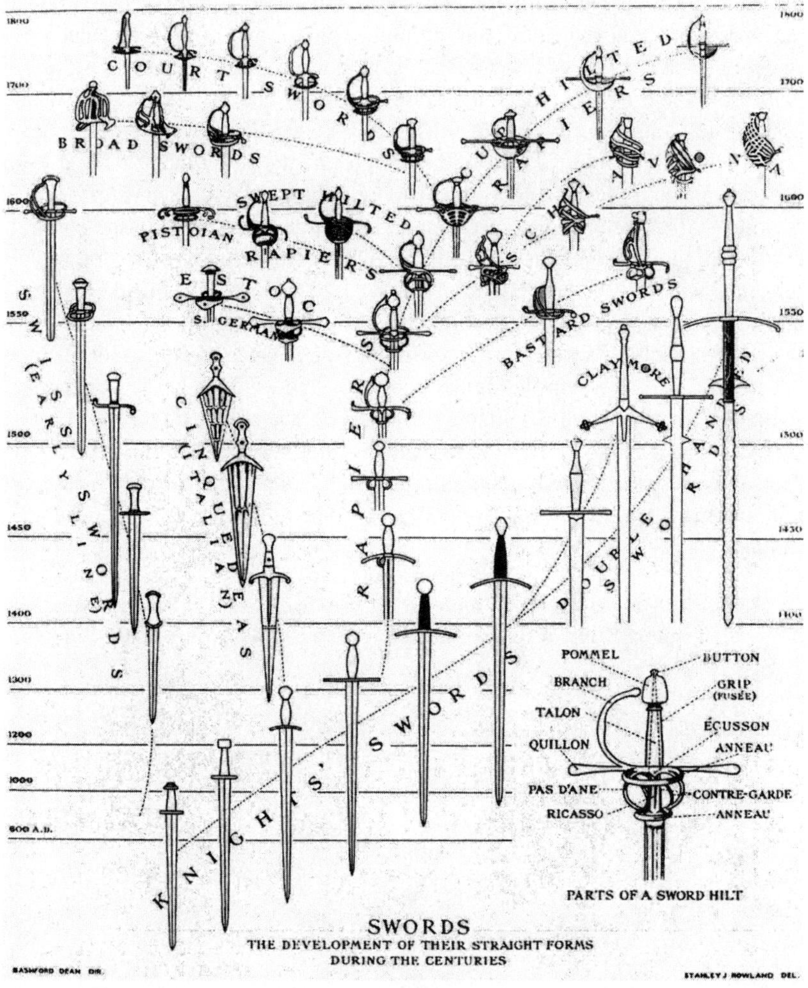

Note the designation of critical characters in the lower right and that both anagenetic and cladogenetic modes are shown. (Not previously published.)

cladistic analysis. The important thing to realize in the context of our discussion here is that figures 5.10 and 5.12–5.14 show both anagenetic and cladogenetic evolutionary modes. None of Dean's sixteen drawings of artifact phylogenies that we have inspected includes instances of reticulate evolution. We suspect this is because when he was constructing the graphs, during the second decade of the twentieth century, many biological evolutionists

Figure 5.13
Bashford Dean's Detailed Model of Phylogenetic Evolution in Cinquedeas

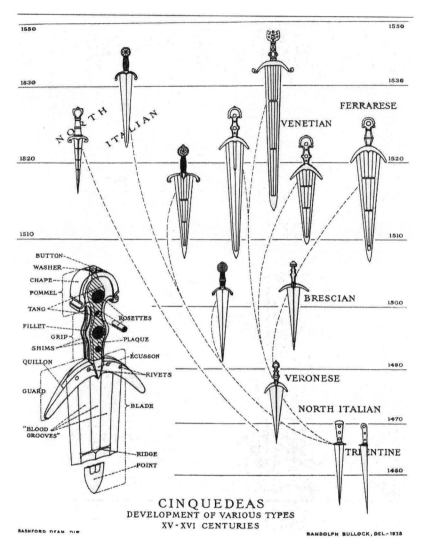

Compare with the "cinquedeas" branch in figure 5.12. Note the designation of critical characters in the lower left and that both anagenetic and cladogenetic modes are shown. (Not previously published.)

considered hybridization improbable. Given that Dean was curator of fishes at the American Museum and presumably knew evolutionary theory as it was at the time, he likely did not even consider hybridization of artifacts. Virtually

Figure 5.14
**Bashford Dean's Detailed Model of Phylogenetic Evolution in Rapiers
and Court Swords**

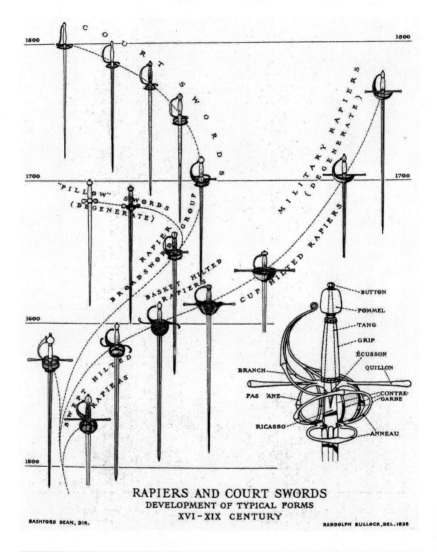

RAPIERS AND COURT SWORDS
DEVELOPMENT OF TYPICAL FORMS
XVI-XIX CENTURY

Compare with the "rapiers" and "court swords" branches in figure 5.12. Note the designation of critical characters in the lower right and that both anagenetic and cladogenetic modes are shown. (Not previously published.)

all phylogenetic trees drawn by biologists (e.g., Matthew 1926, 1930) were similar to those Dean constructed for weapons. This again underscores our take-home message: how we graph evolutionary history and the units we use to construct the graph will influence our interpretations of evolutionary mode among empirical phenomena. The next chapter in this volume builds on this recognition to provide a method for constructing graphs in a way that resembles Dean's.

Conclusion

The application of cladistics to artifacts is not without controversy, but the fact that seriation ultimately rests on the assumption of heritable continuity, just as cladistics does, in our view serves as a sufficient warrant for applying cladistics to artifacts (O'Brien and Lyman 2003a; O'Brien et al. 2001, 2002). One critical difference between seriation and cladistics is that the latter assumes that the evolutionary mode is always cladogenetic. Another difference is that in cladistics the temporal sequence of various taxa in different clades may be obscured. This is not a damning observation; cladistics is designed to demonstrate patterns of branching, whereas seriation is meant strictly to order phenomena lineally.

Phyletic seriation focuses on changes in character states that make up the definitions of artifact classes. As practiced by Petrie over a century ago and by Ford over a half-century ago, phyletic seriation can be used to graph any and all of the three modes of evolution. Frequency seriation, as typically implemented in a centered-bar graph, obscures evolutionary mode in favor of sequence. To make the mode clear, one must consider the definitions of the graphed classes rather than their frequencies of representation over time. We suggest that cladistics adds an important dimension to efforts to monitor phylogenetic history because of its analytical rigor and the fact that it requires explicit definitions of characters and character states. Further, it highlights the fact that the evolution of artifact lineages may well be cladogenetic.

The past decade or so has seen increasing efforts on the part of anthropologists and archaeologists to study the evolutionary history of various cultural lineages. We have shown here that both the scale of unit used to monitor phylogenetic evolution as well as the means used to graph it influence our inferences regarding evolutionary mode. This must be kept in mind when using any of the various methods and techniques discussed here. So should two other seemingly obvious points. First, although we focus on material items when we perform a seriation or cladistic analysis, it is not the materials per se that evolved but the ways people made them. Second, phylogenetic methods are only the first of a long series of steps that need to be taken in an evolutionary study. Enrico Coen (2002: 50) summed up both points beautifully in his discussion of Bashford Dean's diagram of helmet evolution: "[the diagram] tells a story about changes in how people fashion helmets in response to changing circumstances, materials, and traditions." It is in figuring out those circumstances, materials, and traditions where evolutionary studies become exciting.

Acknowledgments

We thank Enrico Coen of the John Innes Centre, Norwich, United Kingdom, for bringing Bashford Dean's work to light and for his subsequent correspondence with us. We also thank Stuart Pyhrr and Donald LaRocca, both of the Metropolitan Museum of Art, New York, for providing copies of Dean's drawings of artifact phylogenies; and Mary French of the University of Missouri for her assistance in obtaining the drawings. Mark Collard and Stephen Shennan provided helpful comments on an earlier draft.

6

The Resolution of Cultural Phylogenies Using Graphs

Carl P. Lipo

Evolutionary archaeologists (e.g., Dunnell 1982; Hunt et al. 2001; O'Brien and Lyman 2000a) commonly repeat biologist Richard Lewontin's (1974: 8) comment that "we cannot go out and describe the world in any old way we please and then sit back and demand that an explanatory and predictive theory be built on that description." This is not a trivial adage: theoretically and empirically robust explanations require that phenomena be described using variables embedded within a coherent theoretical framework. In the case of explanations that invoke Darwinian evolution as a process, two kinds of descriptions are critical: measures of performance differences and measures of relatedness.

Relatedness is an everyday way of talking about similarity that results from shared inheritance. Inherited similarity is considered to be the result of two entities sharing characteristics as a result of sharing a common ancestor. However, having a common ancestor is not the only possible explanation for why two entities share a feature. They could have developed it independently, converging on a common solution to a common problem. Likewise, it is possible that two entities are similar because one is the ancestor of the other.

This is as true for objects in the archaeological record as it is for organisms: similarity can potentially be a product of both kinds of ancestry. This means that archaeological explanations require two kinds of descriptions. First, the things we study must be arranged chronologically. Second, we must evaluate the degree to which similarities among observations have independent origins or are related through inheritance. Determining historical relatedness specifies if and how entities descended from one another. Together these lines of evidence form the foundation of explanations that take the form "descent with modification," the defining concept in evolution (O'Hara 1988).

Archaeologists are adept at determining chronology and inheritance and have been doing this since the early twentieth century (e.g., Kroeber 1916a, 1916b; Phillips et al. 1951; Sayles 1937; Spier 1917). Archaeologists routinely place items of material culture into so-called "time-space" charts that depict spatial, chronological, and historical relationships among artifact classes (Lyman et al. 1997; O'Brien and Lyman 1998, 2000; Spaulding 1955; Willey 1953). These charts form the core of our empirical knowledge of the archaeological record.

Figure 6.1 is one such chart. It shows Dunnell's (pers. comm. 2003) unpublished reconstruction of the evolution of eastern North American projectile

Figure 6.1
**Hypothetical Evolutionary Relationships among Types of
Projectile Points from Eastern North America**

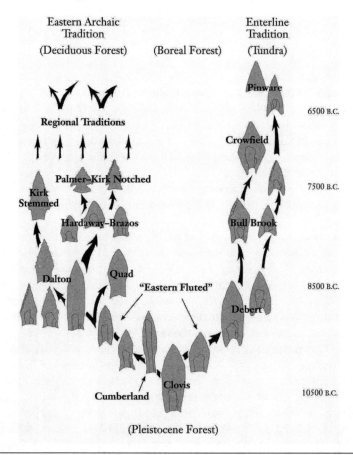

(R. C. Dunnell, pers. comm. 2003.)

points. It adds a spatial component to change through time that maps how projectile points diverge into two spatially and environmentally distinct traditions. What is clear from this and similar figures (e.g., those in chapters 1 and 5, this volume) is that we have the means of studying evolution within existing archaeological practices. In combining elements of time and relatedness to track the descent with modification of artifacts, these diagrams provide us with the products needed to generate evolutionary explanations.

It is tempting to think that the presence of these time-space charts preadapts archaeology to make use of evolutionary explanations in accounts of the past. However, despite the potential match between these products and the demands of evolutionary theory, archaeology continues to fall short of becoming an evolutionary science (Dunnell 1989). This failure is the result of a number of factors. First, the discipline has relied on common-sense-based descriptions of the archaeological record that are incompatible with measures of evolutionary relatedness (Dunnell 1982). For example, if we want to study historical relationships, it is necessary to build classifications that focus on the measurement of homologous similarity. Second, archaeology sorely lacks statistically defensible and quantifiable measures of relatedness. Although they form the basis of culture histories and take the form needed for evolutionary studies, time-space charts have relatively little statistical warrant. The creation of such charts is done primarily on the basis of intuition and arguments of authority rather than on repeatable measurements and quantitative evaluation (O'Brien and Lyman 2000a). This does not make the inheritance claims of culture historians wrong, just relatively limited in their usefulness.

Fortunately, these deficiencies can be overcome. By generating variables from theory, we can build descriptions of the archaeological record that are explicable within evolutionary frameworks (e.g., Lipo 2001). The potential of this approach has been powerfully demonstrated by Greenlee (2002) in an evolutionary account of prehistoric subsistence variability in eastern North America. Significant strides have also been made in adopting, developing, and modifying quantitative methods for studying patterns of cultural inheritance (e.g., Bettinger and Eerkens 1997, 1999; Lipo 2001; Lipo et al. 1997; Neiman 1995; O'Brien and Lyman 2003a; O'Brien et al. 2001, 2002; Shennan 2000; Shennan and Wilkinson 2001). Of these developments, two areas are of particular interest: seriation (e.g., Dunnell 1981; Graves and Cachola-Abad 1996; Lipo 2001; Lipo et al. 1997; O'Brien and Lyman 1998; Teltser 1995) and cladistics (e.g., Collard and Shennan 2000; Jordan and Shennan 2003; O'Brien and Lyman 2003a; O'Brien et al. 2001, 2002; Tehrani and Collard 2002).

Cladistics is a powerful means of building hypotheses about inheritance that is well established in biology and paleontology (Eldredge and Cracraft 1980; Felsenstein 2004; Hennig 1950, 1966; Nelson and Platnick 1981; Wiley

1981). Although initially created for the study of organisms, cladistics depends only on mapping the results of transmission of information among entities and is potentially applicable to any inheritance system (O'Brien and Lyman 2003a; O'Brien et al. 2001). Cladistic analyses of biological, genetic, and linguistic inheritance are conducted primarily by determining ancestral relationships among contemporaneous samples. Linguists, for example, reconstruct ancestry based on descriptions of languages taken at a specific point in time (e.g., Campbell 1999; Gray and Atkinson 2003; Gray and Jordan 2000; Jordan 1999; McMahon and McMahon 1995; Ringe et al. 2002). In the same way, geneticists make inferences based on samples of DNA taken from modern populations (e.g., Cavalli-Sforza 2000; Cavalli-Sforza and Feldman 2003; Underhill 2003). In many cladistic analyses, the ends of a phylogenetic tree—referred to as "terminal," or "sister," taxa—are contemporaneous samples, and nodes in the tree represent reconstructed ancestors that presumably existed in the past. Importantly, the nodes often are then shown as sister taxa, even though in a strict sense they may not be (see below).

Contemporaneity among taxa is rarely the case when we deal with objects in the archaeological record because characters (attributes) used to describe artifacts are chronologically variable. This means that it is highly unlikely that terminal taxa in an archaeological cladistic analysis are contemporaneous. The same is true in paleontology. It is important to point out that the presence of chronologically variable taxa does not violate assumptions of cladistics; the method still resolves relative degrees of relatedness. But we need to be aware of how cladistics may overestimate the amount of branching that may have taken place.

The problem gets more complicated with real data. Take for example, the tree produced by O'Brien et al. (2001) for early projectile points from the southeastern United States (figure 6.2). O'Brien and colleagues built this tree using seventeen taxa defined by the states of eight characters. Is distance in figure 6.2 a function of relatedness or simply of chronological position? Given that relatedness and chronology need not be linearly related, the order of branching between clades (an ancestor and all of its descendants) is problematic.

The problems that cladistics faces in handling non-contemporaneous taxa are widely recognized, but thus far there have been no easy solutions. Stratocladistics is one attempt by paleontologists to address this issue. Stratocladistic methods (e.g., Benton and Hitchin 1997; Benton et al. 1999; Fisher 1991, 1992, 1994; Forey 1992; Heyning et al. 1999) use stratigraphic data to evaluate hypotheses about phylogenetic trees. Despite its promise, however, the method is limited. Stratocladistics is a manual technique, and there is no agreement as to which solution should be given the stronger weight—stratigraphic order or cladistic analysis (Fisher et al. 2000; Fox et al. 1999; Heyning et al. 1999; Smith 2000). Is there an alternative?

Figure 6.2
The Cultural Phylogeny of Paleoindian-Period Projectile Points from the Southeastern United States

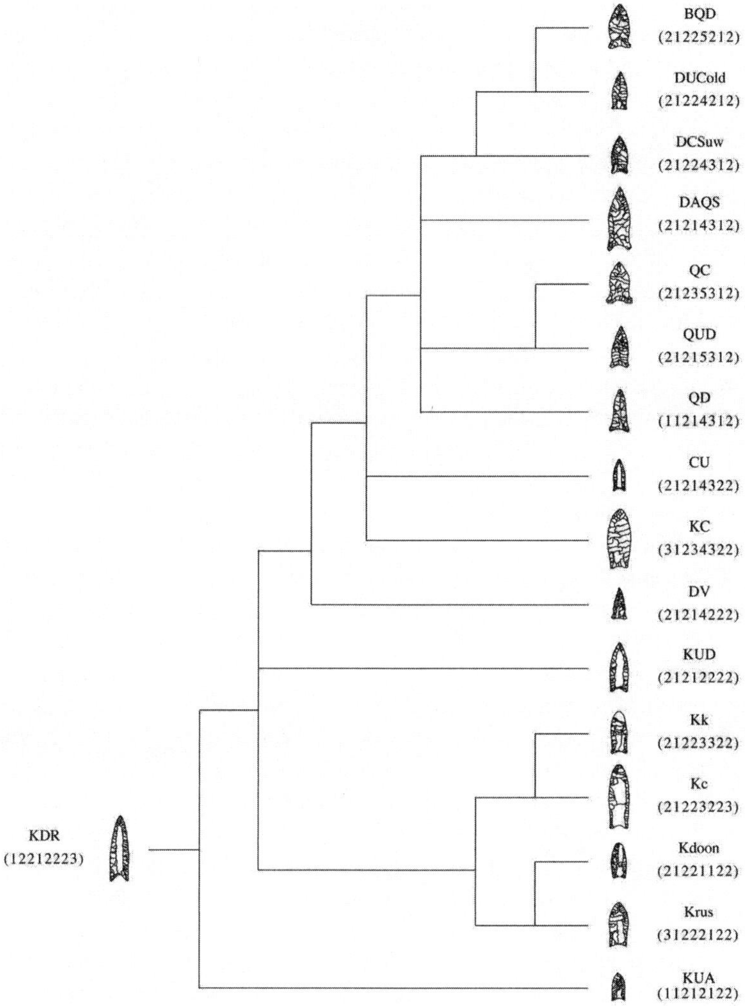

(From O'Brien et al. 2001.)

Mapping Cultural Phylogenies Using Graphs: A Complementary Method

In recognition of the limitations inherent in cladistics, a number of new approaches have been developed to model patterns of relatedness. These methods include the use of networks (e.g., Bryant and Moulton 2002; Huson 1998) and graphs (e.g., Baroni 2003, 2004) and are particularly robust when evolutionary processes such as recombination and hybridization may have been present in a dataset (Bryant and Moulton 2002). In the remainder of this chapter I describe one such method based on graph theory that can serve alongside cladistics. This method makes use of a simple set of assumptions for mapping transmission and is capable of detecting constraints, measurement problems, and processes that impact patterns of homologous similarity.

The key component of any method for studying relatedness is the careful construction of units for describing the empirical record. Here, I am interested in constructing descriptions in which the dimensions (characters) used to construct classes (taxa) are independent and measure neutral variation. Dimensional independence is critical; mechanically linked change between characters is likely a function of architectural and technological constraints and not of transmission. Thus, we need to exclude allometric effects (e.g., West et al. 1997), the "spandrels" of Gould and Lewontin (1979), and the design constraints of Conway Morris (2003). This requires developing general awareness of "evolutionary kinematics" (Fontana 2003; Stadler et al. 2001) when we build classifications and descriptions (see also chapter 2, this volume).

The use of stylistic descriptions—those that measure neutral variation only—is also a key component of the method. Stylistic descriptions make use of culturally transmitted, alternative traits that have no significant differences in fitness values and thus are said to be neutral with respect to selection (Dunnell 1978; Lipo and Madsen 2000; Neiman 1995). This feature of the descriptions helps ensure we are studying similarity derived from inheritance and not similarity resulting from convergence. If we measure variation using taxa built with these style-related criteria, cultural-transmission theory states that traits will change as a result of one of three distinct processes: social learning (transmission), individual innovation (mutation), and sampling error (chance).

Consider an artifact that is described by three characters (A, B, C), each of which has three character states (1, 2, 3). Taxon definitions take the form of a sequence of numbers where each digit represents a state of a separate character. In this example, taxa take the form of number strings such as 321 or 322. If we identify instances of taxa 321 and 322, for example, we can hypothesize that the difference in the third character was caused by innovation, cultural transmission, and/or chance. Using the principle of parsimony, we can order our descriptions using the smallest number of possible changes to form hypotheses about change (Felsenstein 2004).

The minimum number of character states that must change to convert one taxon to another is known as the "Hamming distance" (Hamming 1980). This method is akin to O'Brien et al.'s (2002) "occurrence method" for studying the distribution of character-state changes with a set of ordered taxa (see also chapter 5, this volume). The method works because we have specified that changes occur only because of transmission factors; the resulting order must be explicable in those terms. In this way, the patterns we generate can be inferred to reflect transmission in time and/or space. For example, if innovation and vertical transmission are the primary processes that structure patterns of character states, we can expect patterns of change to be linear. In this scenario, variation will reflect the passage of time. Additional factors will alter this simple pattern. As a result of the effects of innovation rate in a population that has limited horizontal transmission, we would expect that taxon definitions will diverge within the population.

Graph Representation

Patterns of stylistic descriptions ordered by the principle of parsimony can be represented visually in the form of an undirected graph. Graphs are a simple means of representing data structures when they are nonlinear and nonhierarchical (e.g., Flament 1963; Harary 1969; Wasserman and Faust 1994). Graphs are used frequently in computer science to solve problems such as finding the shortest airplane route between two cities. They are also used to begin to aid in the interpretation of trees (e.g., Morris, Asnake, and Yen 2003) and to visualize timelines of interaction (e.g., Morris et al. 2003). Visually, the graphs consist of a collection of nodes and edges, with the latter connecting the former.

We can create a graph representation of our data by connecting taxa that differ in only a single character. For example, Taxon 112 differs from Taxon 122 in only a single character. This allows us to map the order of changes between taxa and thus generate hypotheses about the processes responsible for change. In the case where innovation and vertical transmission are primary factors, a linear pattern is expected in which taxa are linked to only two neighbors (figure 6.3), each differing by character states in but a single character. The order generated is a hypothesized chronological order.

In fact, if we build taxa that allow only two states per character, absence/presence, the resulting graph (figure 6.4) takes the form of what we commonly recognize as an "occurrence seriation" (Lyman et al. 1998). This means that the construction of graphs using comparisons of taxa to generate connectedness is a general version of a method for mapping change that includes occurrence seriation as a special case when the character states are binary. In this respect, the graph method for arranging descriptions has the same constraints as occurrence seriation. For example, we need additional, external information in order to tell the top from the bottom. The theoretical rationale for linking the graph method with occurrence seriation comes from the inference that linear orders are primarily a result of mutation. Thus, orders are predominantly chronological. However, in its general form this can be true if we use traits that are binary or can take multiple states.

Figure 6.3
A Graph Linking Taxa (Nodes) Together into an Order

The taxa are defined by three characters (e.g., Taxon 111) and are linked by lines to other taxa that differ only in a single character.

Figure 6.4
Linear Graph of Taxa Ordered Using Binary Character States

This results in what is commonly recognized as "occurrence seriation."

The pattern we generate depends on the number of differences in dimensions that are used to determine nodes. Ordered taxa will differ in an increasingly large number of characters depending on the taxa that are compared. For example, Taxon 122 differs from Taxon 323 in two characters. Based on the assumptions of the model—that change in character states occurs only by mutation, cultural transmission, or chance—the method is most robust in explaining changes in only a single character. Concurrent multiple character changes mechanically create links to more than one taxon. With multiple character changes, no single order is possible, and without external information explanatory ambiguity can occur. The graph method allows one to identify the location in the taxon definition (the number string) that is causing multiple trees and thus where the results are ambiguous.

Explanations are simplest when descriptions that are being compared have a Hamming distance of one (e.g., 112 to 122). Of course, the minimum Hamming distance between pairs of descriptions will often differ by values greater than one. Larger Hamming distances (e.g., 113 to 122) can be potentially explained as (1) the distribution of taxa within the classification space; (2) a sampling problem that results in the absence of instances of intermediate forms available for measurement; or (3) an indication of linked characters. For example, taxa in figure 6.5a that differ in only one character are linked by thick lines. Taxa with differences in two characters are connected by thin lines. In this example Taxon 323 is equally different in two characters from taxa 222 and 122. This pattern potentially indicates that there might be missing intermediate taxa that could be placed between one of the two pairs of taxa (e.g., taxa 223 or 123 as shown in figures 6.5b and 6.5c). Locating instances of one of these would help us resolve whether 323 should be modeled as in figure 6.5b or as in figure 6.5c.

Graphs produced with nodes linked by minimum Hamming distances that are greater than one can produce useful results, but there will often be multiple solutions, given that the results are no longer deterministic. There also might be cases in which no intermediate ancestors exist, as traits have changed synchronously in multiple dimensions. This can indicate that characters are technologically linked. For example, in the case of projectile points, a character such as "basal stem angle" could be mechanically constrained by certain forms of notching. In this case, forms of notching may always result in changes in basal stem angle, and changes in the characters will be synchronous. Resolving this problem requires a reexamination of the classification and modification of the characters so that they are not technologically and/or functionally linked (chapter 7 and 12, this volume).

Unlike with occurrence seriation, linear patterns are not required. Indeed, this is one of the strengths of using the graph method for mapping relatedness: There are no constraints so long as the assumptions of the method are met. If, for example, we find an instance of Taxon 123 to help resolve the ambiguity in

Figure 6.5
Graphs of Taxa Defined by Three Characters, Showing the Potential Ambiguity that Arises When Taxa Simultaneously Show Differences in More than One Character

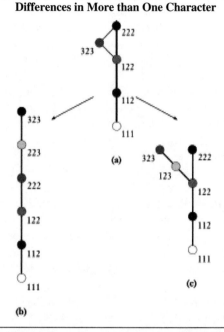

The thick lines indicate differences between taxa in only a single character, and the thin lines indicate two character differences between taxa. In (a) the placement of Taxon 323 is ambiguous, whereas in (b) and (c) intermediate taxa help resolve the placement.

Figure 6.6
Taxa Linked Together by Differences in Single Characters Showing a Divergent History

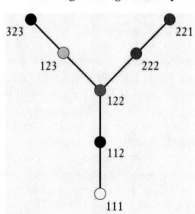

figure 6.5, we can definitively generate a graph that links each taxon with single character differences. In this case, Taxon 123 falls between taxa 122 and 323. When placed into the graph (figure 6.6), the resulting pattern is one of divergence.

Similarly, using the graph method we can also track convergence if it is present within a set of descriptions (figure 6.7), even in cases that also include divergence. From an inheritance perspective, patterns of convergence can be generated when traits are shared across lineages through horizontal transmission. In addition, we can map reticulate patterns that are present when there is a significant amount of horizontal transmission (figure 6.8). In cases where traits are exchanged in a way that is unconstrained, a dense network will appear, in which taxa are linked to many others in nonlinear patterns.

In figure 6.8, for example, taxa are shown linked by single differences in characters. If we had external information in order to orient the figure so that the bottom of the graph is early and the top is late, we could imagine that traits are being shared across a population in a way that is not strictly vertical. This kind of inheritance creates a bushy appearance that is characteristic of reticulate evolution and potentially a factor in cultural transmission (e.g., Kroeber 1948; Lyman 2001).

Given its flexibility, the use of graphs has significant potential for analyzing historical relatedness in phenomena that vary simultaneously in time, space, and inheritance. The strength of the method comes from the fact that graphs represent patterns of inheritance as determined by the assumptions of the method. Like determining the root of a cladogram or the orientation of an occurrence seriation, shape and orientation of the graph must be determined by external information. Using stratigraphic or absolute dates, for example, we can orient the graph chronologically. We can also evaluate hypotheses about spatial variation by assigning relative positions to nodes based on geographic locations. We can also add new data by moving and stretching the graph, and we can move nodes around by using ordinal- or ratio-scale data (e.g., dates and absolute positions).

Application to Archaeological Data: Projectile Points from the Southeastern United States

A reexamination of the data used by O'Brien et al. (2001, 2002) in their cladistic analysis of projectile points from the southeastern United States provides an example of how the graph method can analyze patterns of inheritance. The data in the original phylogenetic analysis consist of metric and morphological measurements made by combining eight characters, each consisting of two to six possible states (table 6.1). Using this classification system and measurements from eighty-three projectile points, O'Brien and colleagues identified seventeen unique taxa (table 6.2). For example, 21223223 is a pro-

Figure 6.7
Taxa Linked Together by Differences in Single Characters
Showing Convergent History

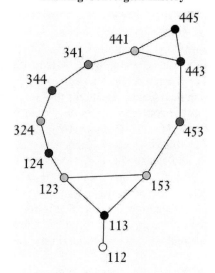

Figure 6.8
Taxa Linked Together by Differences in Single Characters Showing an
"Entangled Bank" that Can Be Produced by a Combination of
Divergence and Horizontal Transmission

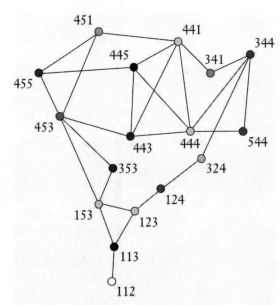

jectile-point taxon (abbreviated as Kc) that consists of a combination of states of eight characters and is commonly identified as "Clovis."

To build the graph, I first calculated the Hamming distance between each pair of taxa and placed them in a matrix. I then used NetDraw[1], a network-visualization program, to plot the taxa as nodes in a network and the edges as the distance between taxa. The key advantage of NetDraw is that it allows one to plot and visualize a network with different parameters of "connectedness," or in this case character-distance parameters. The algorithm used to generate the graphs places nodes in locations that are scaled by the number of differences in characters for each pair of descriptions.

Using this procedure, I generated a graph that consisted of the linkages between taxa with the fewest differences in characters. The results are shown in

Table 6.1
System Used by O'Brien et al. (2001) to Classify Projectile Points

Character *Character state*	Character *Character state*
I. Location of maximum blade width	V. Outer tang angle
1. Proximal quarter	1. 93°–115°
2. Secondmost proximal quarter	2. 88°–92°
3. Secondmost distal quarter	3. 81°–87°
4. Distal quarter	4. 66°–80°
	5. 51°–65°
	6. <50°
II. Base shape	VI. Tang-tip shape
1. Arc-shaped	1. Pointed
2. Normal curve	2. Round
3. Triangular	3. Blunt
4. Folsomoid	
III. Basal indentation ratio	VII. Fluting
1. No basal indentation	1. Absent
2. 0·90–0·99 (shallow)	2. Present
3. 0·80–0·89 (deep)	
IV. Constriction ratio	VIII. Length/width ratio
1. 1·00	1. 1·00–1·99
2. 0·90–0·99	2. 2·00–2·99
3. 0·80–0·89	3. 3·00–3·99
4. 0·70–0·79	4. 4·00–4·99
5. 0·60–0·69	5. 5·00–5·99
6. 0·50–0·59	6. 6·00

Table 6.2

Taxon Definitions, Abbreviations, and Common Type Names of Projectile-Point Taxa Used by O'Brien et al. (2001)

Taxon	Abbreviation	Common type names
21225212	BQD	Beaver Lake–Quad–Dalton
21214322	CU	Cumberland–Unidentified
21214312	DAQS	Dalton–Arkabutla–Quad–Simpson
21224312	DCSuw	Dalton–Cumberland–Suwanee
21224212	DUCold	Dalton–Unidentified–Coldwater
21214222	DV	Dalton–Vandale
21223223	Kc	Clovis
31234322	KC	Clovis–Cumberland
21221122	Kdoon	Clovis–Doon
12212223	KDR	Clovis–Dalton–Redstone
21223322	Kk	Clovis
31222122	Krus	Clovis–Russellville
11212122	KUA	Clovis–Unidentified–Arkabutla
21212222	KUD	Clovis–Unidentified–Dalton
21235312	QC	Quad–Cumberland
11214312	QD	Quad–Dalton
21215312	QUD	Quad–Unidentified–Dalton

figure 6.9. Not all of the taxa differ by only a single character. Six taxa differ from other taxa by two characters, and one taxon (12212223) differs by three characters. For the most part, the descriptions can be ordered into a branched pattern, where ten of the taxa can be linked with single steps. The remainder of the taxa are connected in a nearly linear pattern, with two exceptions. An ambiguity exists with Taxon 31222122, as it differs in two dimensions from four different taxa. It is possible that additional intermediate examples will resolve this problem. In addition, because Taxon 12212223 differs in three dimensions from two other taxa, its relationship is unclear.

It is necessary to determine the degree to which the graph results might have been determined by chance. It is possible to obtain patterns of connected nodes in random assignment of character states, especially when the size of the classification is small. The smaller the classification, the more likely chance will play a role in generating descriptions that differ by only a single character. The classification constructed by O'Brien and colleagues is reasonably large, consisting of 62,208 combinations of character states. With only seventeen taxa, the likelihood of the classification space constraining the descriptions is extremely small. This suggests that chance likely played a minor role in pro-

Figure 6.9
Graph Produced by Linking Taxa to Their Most Similar Neighbors

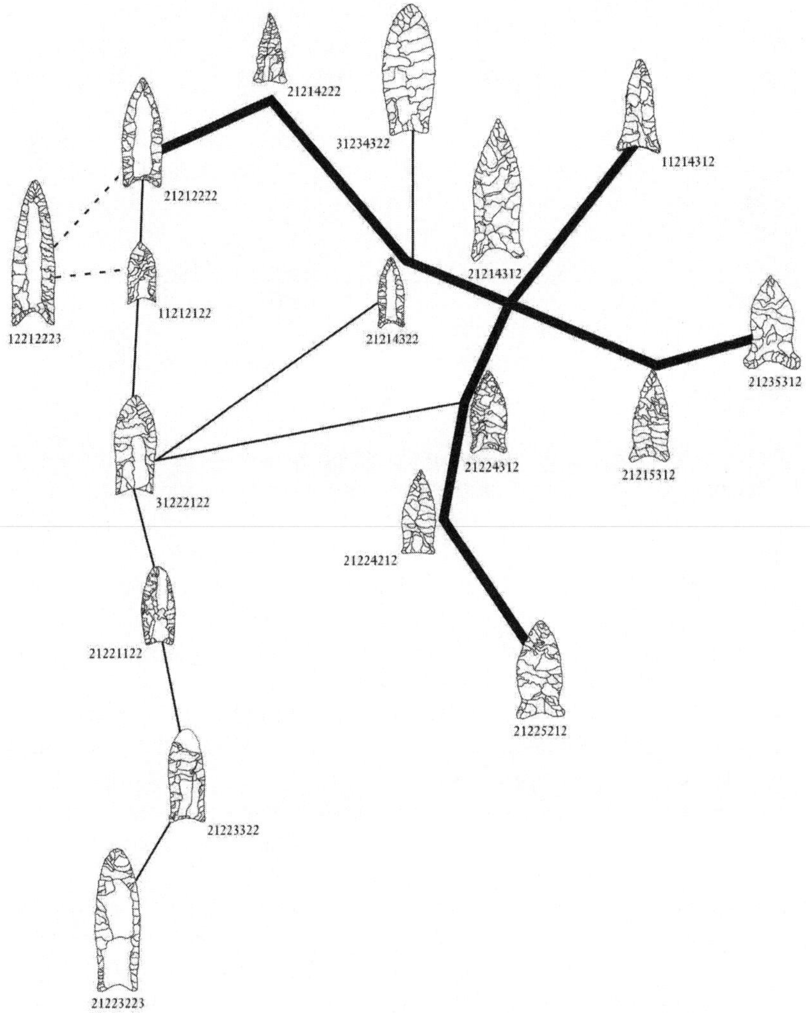

Bold lines represent differences in taxa of only a single character (single steps), and thin solid lines show differences in taxa of two characters. The dotted lines reflect differences of three characters. The multiple lines that connect Taxon 31222122 to other taxa reflect ambiguity caused by equivalent differences between multiple taxa. Additional information or intermediate specimens will potentially resolve which connection represents the evolutionary pathway. (Taxa from O'Brien et al. 2002.)

ducing the graph. However, we can determine a p-value for the results using a bootstrapping procedure (Efron and Tibshirani 1993). This is done by randomly bootstrapping the same number of taxa, calculating character distances for the bootstrapped set of taxa, and counting the instances in which the bootstrap set has at least the same number of single character differences as the actual data.

By repeating these steps a minimum of 10,000 times we can produce an estimate of the p-value for the graph. With respect to the projectile-point data, the likelihood that the observed pattern of single character differences was produced by chance alone is much less than one in a million. In other words, we can eliminate chance as a potential factor in producing the pattern of taxa. This leaves us with only cultural-transmission processes (social learning and innovation) as explanatory options.

Evaluation of Results

Although several ambiguities remain, the results of the graph suggest an overall linear pattern. Based on the assumptions of our model, we can infer that much of the similarity in the projectile-point data is structured by time and that the taxa form a chronological sequence. One portion of the graph around 21214312 (DAQS) is strongly branching, and the data suggest divergence or an increase in innovation relative to transmission and time. Although we can begin to generate hypotheses about portions of the graph on the basis of the methodological assumptions, we cannot assign absolute relationships without external data. We cannot determine, for example, which branch is the beginning and which branch is the latest without absolute dates. We need additional information to "root" the graph.

In addition to rooting the graph, adding temporal data provides a means of assessing our hypotheses for the processes that were responsible for producing patterns within the projectile-point taxa. Figure 6.10 shows the same graph as in figure 6.9, but it is coded with known temporal information for each taxon as determined by Anderson et al. (1996). Although there are deviations from the expected pattern, the overall expectations of our hypotheses are met: projectile-point taxa can be ordered into a chronological sequence until a point is reached where later taxa diverge from one another. This is a pattern that can be explained as the result of populations that are becoming isolated from one another as a result of geography or are experiencing increases in size and are subject to "isolation by density" (in the sense of Terrell 1986). Further archaeological and geographic analyses are necessary to assess these hypotheses.

At this point it is useful to draw attention to potential problems and to identify issues that demand further research. First, the robustness of the graph method for detecting patterns in cultural transmission strongly depends on the

Figure 6.10
Graph Analysis of Projectile-Point Taxa

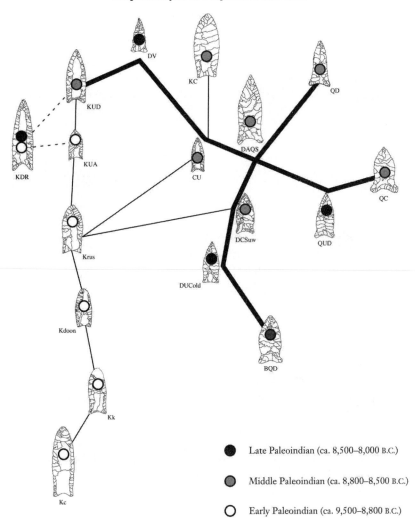

●	Late Paleoindian (ca. 8,500–8,000 B.C.)
◐	Middle Paleoindian (ca. 8,800–8,500 B.C.)
○	Early Paleoindian (ca. 9,500–8,800 B.C.)

Temporal information (from Anderson et al. 1996) is indicated by the shade of the circles.

quality of the classifications. If characters are not independent, for example, changes in taxa may reflect technological constraints and hence obscure patterns of transmission. Technological correlation, however, will not necessarily cause problems. In the case of the projectile-point classification, several characters are not completely independent of one another. There is, for example, a moderate to strong correlation (Pearson's $r = 0.72, p = 0.0011$) between characters VI and VII, outer tang angle and tang-tip shape (table 6.1). This suggests that the two characters are not fully independent or may be linked with another character such as base shape. Further research into the structure of the projectile-point classification is required to resolve the potential impact of this dependency.

Second, although chronology explains much of the structure of the graph, spatial variation may also play a role. The points described by the classification are located across eleven southeastern states. Although preliminary examinations (O'Brien and Lyman 2003a) do not indicate strong spatial patterning, it is reasonable to expect that at least some of the variation in taxa is a function of distance. Lack of spatial variation might be explained by the rate of cultural transmission relative to innovation and a suppression of regional variants, perhaps for functional or technological reasons, resulting in spatial autocorrelation.

Third, further work is required to refine the chronological assignments of the projectile-point taxa. Rather than typological cross dating, we need direct-dating information for as many representatives of each taxon as possible in order to build robust empirical estimates of the temporal distributions. Luminescence dating of catastrophically heated chert-tool manufacturing debris offers one promising avenue for generating direct chronological information on individual specimens (Wilhelmsen and Miles 2005).

Fourth, there are no empirical "packages" of information in cultural transmission, meaning that projectile points may not form a single unit of transmission. As Bettinger and Eerkens (1999) have pointed out, the set of instructions that produce what we know as projectile points may be the result of a variety of attributes and attribute sets, each with its own historical trajectory (see also chapter 11, this volume). Consequently, the patterns measured here can be considered to reflect only the history of one portion of the information required to produce projectile points—in specific, only the history of basal shape and fluting. Determining the scale of the transmission package is an empirical question that requires examining the history of multiple trait groups. Some trait groups may coincide, which implies either that the traits came as packages or that they came from consistent sources along consistent pathways, even if it happened over some period of time as opposed to all at once.

Conclusions

Developing methods for studying the archaeological record in a way that is founded in evolutionary theory is a critical task. As long as variation was measured in terms of discrete objects, culture historians had a reasonable but intuitive way for generating hypotheses about chronology, spatial pattern, and relatedness (Lyman 2001; Lyman et al. 1997). Although roughly capturing the broad features of culture history, time-space diagrams produced by culture historians had little theoretical foundation. More-recent attempts at producing tools for studying inheritance move us in the right direction, but the interpretation of results can be problematic in archaeological cases where observations vary simultaneously in terms of time, space, and relatedness.

The graph method described here provides a means of building and testing cultural phylogenies that is complementary to methods such as cladistics. The strength of the method is that it can be used to generate hypotheses about relatedness, spatial variation, and chronological relationships of artifacts based on homologous similarity. It is an excellent tool for examining evolutionary dynamics.

Note

1.   NetDraw is a shareware program available as part of the UCINET social network analysis package (Borgatti et al. 2002). This analysis used version NetDraw 1.0, which can be downloaded at http://www.analytictech.com.

Acknowledgments

I thank R. C. Dunnell, J. Eerkens, T. Hunt, D. Larson, R. L. Lyman, M. Madsen, H. Neff, D. Schechter and K. Wilhelmsen for their many discussions and inspiration while I was developing this chapter. M. J. O'Brien and M. Collard provided valuable comments and editorial assistance.

7

Measuring Relatedness

Robert C. Dunnell

Tracing patterns of historical relatedness, typically termed "phylogeny," is both central to historical science and a distinctive feature of it. Thus it is paradoxical that the means of discerning such relationships have been problematic from Darwin's day forward. The initial insight that led to the formation of historical science was that resemblance was a function of relatedness. With hindsight, it is apparent that the Linnaean taxonomic classification, developed in the second half of the eighteenth century and central to biology ever since, unconsciously embodied this notion. In the absence of any scientific explanation, the structure that it imparted to the living and fossil worlds was its warrant and remains so to this day.

Without a theoretical context, Linnaean classification was naïve (e.g., Hull 1965; Stafleu 1969). There were no specifications of how resemblance was to be measured. Indeed, it was not measured at all in the modern sense of the term. Thus the reasoning of the system was fundamentally circular. Organisms resembled one another because they belonged to the same species, genus, family, and the like according to their degree. What constituted an organism was even less overtly questioned.

The emergence of evolutionary theory in the mid-nineteenth century solved, or more properly seemed to solve, much of this conundrum by providing a mechanism that explained the structure of resemblance captured by the Linnaean hierarchy. The "apparent" hierarchy was taken to represent the results of descent, that is, more similar organisms shared a common ancestor more recently than less similar ones did. From that point on, evolution would be pursued by the twin strategies of paleontology (study of historical forms) and neontology (comparisons of contemporary forms). The virtue of the former is that it studies evolutionary linkages directly whereas the virtue of the latter is the ease of access to relevant phenomena (e.g., Harvey and Pagel 1991). Both depend, however, on the equation of resemblance with relatedness.

Importantly, it was quickly apparent from evolutionary analyses of everything from invertebrates to human social structure that relatedness is not the only cause of resemblance. In an evolutionary framework, resemblance can be caused by numerous distinct mechanisms, three of which I focus on here. First, resemblance can be a consequence of shared descent. This is the target in the biological notion of homology, as it is in my original formulation of the archaeological concept "style" (Dunnell 1978). Second, resemblance can also be a consequence of the action of external forces. This condition is embedded in the biological notion of analogous similarity. Those reared in an anthropological tradition will quickly recognize the debate between historicists and functionalists (Harris 1968; Kroeber 1935, 1945) in these two ideas and appreciate its latter-day expression in archaeology as the contest between culture historians (and particularist explanation) and the processualists (and generalist explanation) (Dunnell 1986). A similar story can be told in biology, where until the late 1950s it was heretical to suggest that the shape of biological evolution was attributable to any force but natural selection (Haldane 1956). These debates arose in each case because one set of mechanisms—historical or functional, homologous or analogous—was held to be dominant, either empirically or theoretically.

A third source of resemblance, chance, requires a greater sophistication in quantification than the first two and therefore was recognized somewhat later on. Simply put, similarity can occur without being indicative of any substantive mechanism. In an empirical and historical world of finite possibilities, occasional resemblances can arise in random variation, the frequency of which is inversely proportional to the complexity of the resemblances and proportional to population size.

Distinguishing among the three kinds of resemblance—relatedness, common function, and chance—is thus a crucial methodological component of historical science.[1] It is crucial because different mechanisms cause resemblance. Descriptions that mix kinds of resemblance will be constrained to indeterminate cause (Binford 1971; Dunnell 1971; Hull 1965; Jelinek 1976). This is why "style and function," at least in terms of how I defined the terms (Dunnell 1978), represent a fundamental dichotomy. Stylistic descriptions contain information only on transmission linkages. Otherwise they are random. Functional descriptions can be explained by selection.

Resemblance in an Archaeological Context

Three tacks have been taken in archaeology with respect to the question of why two things resemble one another. First, differences among the kinds of resemblance have been ignored, with only occasional criticism (e.g., Steward 1954). Standard practice has been to develop descriptive classes (artifact types) by trial and error (Lyman et al. 1997; O'Brien and Lyman 1999) and subject them to a test of historical significance, namely, time-space contiguity (e.g., Krieger 1944). This effectively singles out resemblances resulting from relatedness inasmuch as contiguous time-space distribution is a necessary condition for transmission (e.g., Lipo et al. 1997). Until recently (e.g., Lipo 2001; Lipo et al. 1997; Neiman 1995) this effort has been limited to the construction of chronology. Other equally legitimate and necessary concerns have been treated with ad hoc descriptive classes, and the results have been assumed to mark relatedness. This has led to such practices as treating the spread of "agriculture" as if it were a pottery style able to diffuse in the same manner (e.g., Griffin 1967) or inferring long-distance contact on the basis of chance resemblances (e.g., Meggers et al. 1965) in highly constrained media.

Such errors stimulated the development of, and provided intellectual cannon fodder for, the early processualists, who assumed that resemblance was the result of common function (adaptation), inasmuch as culture was viewed as an adaptive system. This is well illustrated by the debates between François Bordes and Lewis Binford (e.g., Binford 1973; Binford and Binford 1966; Bordes 1961; Bordes and de Sonneville-Bordes 1970) over the nature of differences between Mousterian variants. For Bordes, different variants meant different people and periods; for Binford they represented different functions and seasons. Significantly, neither party questioned the descriptions of the variants themselves, only how they were being interpreted. The underlying systematics were invisible to the combatants, who ended up confusing interpretation (stories) with meaning (significance).

The processualists were able to avoid developing a systematics to support their functionalist view because the ad hoc classes used by culture historians were drawn from Western culture, whose nouns are largely functional. The processualists simply borrowed them wholesale. This made the role of theory in the measurement of relatedness even more obscure and encouraged a systematic empiricism (Willer and Willer 1973).

This tack, the empiricist approach, is perhaps best illustrated by the rise and demise of "numerical taxonomy" (e.g., Sokal and Sneath 1963) in biology and in archaeology (e.g., Clarke 1968; Read 1974; Spaulding 1953; Whallon 1972; Whallon and Brown 1982). In biology, as in archaeology, the absence of any theory to guide description—that is, rules of description that could reliably partition variation into homologous and analogous similarity—led to a sense of ennui about classification. Taxonomists performed a kind of magic that on close inspection was circular. A character was chosen for use in distinguishing among species because it *did* distinguish among species (you had to have the species first). The same reasoning applied to archaeology with respect to the "phase" (see Dunnell 1971 on Willey and Phillips 1958). Numerical taxonomy arose in response to such circularity. It replaced the arbitrary judgments of the taxonomist with an algorithm for species construction. What this did, of course, was simply force the problem deeper, away from species to the characters used to define them. When pressed on this issue, numerical taxonomists claimed that they used all characters, later changing that to "all available characters," then finally to just "many characters." "Polythetic classification" became the rallying cry of the archaeological empiricists (e.g., Whallon and Brown 1982) just as it did of the biological empiricists (e.g., Sokal and Sneath 1963; Sokal et al. 1965).

Apart from the methodological untenability of such claims, they made sense for tracing phylogenies only if one assumed resemblance equaled relatedness or that resemblance was dominated by relatedness (O'Brien and Lyman 2003a). In effect, numerical taxonomists assumed that all, all available, or most characters were homologous when clearly this could not be sustained empirically (Hull 1988). In archaeology, cultural as well as genetic transmission plays a role in inheritance, and transmission is spread out, albeit unevenly, over a period of time instead of at the moment of conception. Consequently, the attractiveness of this empiricist position on description was limited. What currency it did enjoy was probably linked more closely to substituting methods for theoretical justification than to specific classificatory results.

A variant of the empiricist theme, stimulated by the work of Hennig (e.g., 1966), can be found in cladistics (O'Brien and Lyman 2003a; Robson Brown 1995, 1996). By providing algorithms for the construction of phylogenetic trees, biologists were attempting to circumvent the apparent judgmental element of classical taxonomy. But resemblances are not treated as unitary. Traits are identified as ancestral or derived, the latter being used as the basis for branching. But as any reading of the practical literature of cladistics shows, this approach has not escaped the circularity of traditional taxonomy, insofar as the ancestral or derived nature of a given trait is often deduced from the distributional information it is used to create. This is a simplification to be sure. For one thing, cladists have a defensible theoretical warrant in using branching, to the extent that branching (and extinction) characterizes evolution. Further as many of the authors in this volume demonstrate (e.g., chapters 1, 4, 10, 13, and 16), cladists exert considerable effort in iterative approaches in order to demonstrate that the particular circular solution is the most parsimonious one.

The third tack on the problem of partitioning resemblance into relatedness, function, and chance is theoretical. That is, evolutionary theory provides a set of methods for reliably distinguishing among kinds of resemblance. It is notable that evolutionary theory unites both historicism and functionalism into a single theoretical system, which is a necessary precondition for distinguishing among different kinds of variability. As a result, there are elements of both "isms" entailed in the theoretical tack; it is their integration that provides the synergy for a new approach.

Avoiding the Repetition of History

My initial exploration of some of these issues is represented by my paper, "Style and Function: A Fundamental Dichotomy" (Dunnell 1978), in which I attempted to link common usages of these words to evolutionary concepts to explain why, among other things, culture-historical attempts to construct chronologies using resemblance were for the most part successful. The most obvious connection with biology was in the concepts of analogous and homologous similarity, as others (e.g., Service 1964) had noted before me. But just because these notions are biological does not automatically insure that they are adequate from an analytical standpoint. Indeed, with regard to the issue of resemblance, they are decidedly inadequate (for both archaeology and biology) because they are not mutually exclusive.

This makes it clear why traditional biology has not resolved the partitioning issue. In the non-human context, biologists were content to assume that all traits of evolutionary significance were transmitted genetically and that all were under selection. All traits were thus both homologous and analogous. A trait could not be present if not by descent (save only mutations) nor could it be present if it were not functional (otherwise it would have been removed by selection). So long as these assumptions were made, it was impossible to describe resemblance in a way that partitioned it by causal mechanism. The construction of phylogenetic histories was constrained to be intuitive.

The solution—the neutral trait—is a classic case of the interplay between empirical results and theoretical advance in response. Defined as a character to which selection is blind—in the biological context a genotypic difference that does not result in a phenotypic difference—a neutral trait traces descent and descent alone. If one understood the cultural historical notion of "style" (not the English word style) as marking selective neutrality, the culture historical success in chronology construction was immediately explained. Thus, in "Style and Function" I defined style as neutral variation, as characters that are not under selection. Conversely, function became variation that is under selection. Any trait has to be one or the other at any given point in time.

The transmission component is now separated by recognizing that both stylistic and functional variability are initially stochastic, but in the case of function, variability is subsequently shaped by selection whereas style is shaped only by transmitter-population characteristics (Lipo and Madsen 2000; Neiman 1995; O'Brien and Leonard 2001). This implies a noncircular methodology for creating a language of observation that distinguishes between the two kinds of variability. Traits under selection have different spatial and temporal distributions than those that are not (O'Brien and Holland 1990; Wilhelmsen 1993). More accurately, there are necessary, but unfortunately not sufficient, differences in distributions (e.g., Kornbacher and Madsen 1999 [and other papers in the same volume]).

Traits not under selection will have unimodal distributions, the amplitude and duration of which are determined by the number of variants in the system (because of the closed-array measurements employed) and population characteristics; functional distributions have no such regular features because they are driven by, and thus correlate with, external conditions. But inasmuch that some applications (e.g., dating) entail using distributions, distinguishing between style and function requires a further analysis of their physical and chemical aspects in order to demonstrate the action of selection or the equivalence of cost between variants (avoiding circularity as well as overcoming distributional insufficiency).

It is not enough to note, for example, that a certain ceramic change increases hardness and claim fitness is thereby increased unless you can show that ceramic failure as a result of low abrasion resistance is actually a problem. In this manner, the problems posed by pleiotropy are likewise overcome. Traditionally, if intuitively, archaeologists have solved the problem posed by chance resemblance by focusing attention on "types"—sets of attributes—rather than on single attributes.

It is not difficult to imagine the kind of clarity that distinguishing among neutral, functional, and chance resemblance could produce in the analysis of projectile points, for example. Many, if not most, similarities among points may well be a result of chance once the broad functional characters (those related to stabbing, thrusting, throwing, and machine projection) are identified, thereby constraining the possible forms that can be produced by a particular technology. For example, haft smoothing (basal/lateral grinding) is an added, not alternative, cost, so it must be considered functional at the start of any analysis. A priori, this cost would be selected when the haft is subjected to considerable, sustained kinetic stress. Tools currently used as "knives" are such tools, having to bear up under hours of kinetic contact with a substrate. Projectile points used as "arrowheads" subject the haft only to a few microseconds of kinetic stress, all directed backward (when "properly" deployed; when not, breakage occurs).

Barbs, because they are an exposed part of the tool, must also be treated as functionally significant. They have no effect (separate from the distal angle) in penetration, but they have a considerable effect on the removal of the point. One might therefore suppose that the presence of barbs is a clear indicator of a technology in which the point is cast by hand or machine. The absence of barbs does not preclude casting but would be positively selected when it is important to be able to remove the point rapidly (e.g., when the user is on the end of a stick also attached to a big animal) or to facilitate recovery (e.g., when poison is used).

The weight of a projectile point is another obviously functional trait in any initial analysis, as the weight is a determinant of the amount of energy required to use a given point. Weight must interact with distal angle and edge sharpness in this regard. As a result, even intuitively, weight has been used to differentiate between arrows and spears. But the variability in weight, not just mean weight, requires consideration as well. Cast spears (javelins) and stabbing tools might well be of similar weights, but hand-held stabbing tools admit much greater variability in this parameter than cast tools. Different casting machines might similarly place different limits on variability as well as affect the mean weight. Variability in distal angle is likewise potentially informative as already noted; it interacts with the delivery energy. Some kinds of "projectile points" display a wide range of angles, from sharp to blunt, whereas others are much more limited. Axial symmetry is likewise a suspect for functional variability. Given that this is a major cost in manufacture, strong selection is indicated (once waste [Dunnell 1989] has been eliminated). Axial symmetry has a modest impact on resistance to breakage under axial stress but has a large impact on free-flight characteristics.

In short, virtually any attribute of the blade portion of a projectile point is suspect as functional. Likewise, anything that affects cost will be under selection unless the presence of waste can be demonstrated. Even haft elements, buried in the rest of the tool under use conditions, may be functional if the stresses placed on the haft are not constant and the performance of alternatives is not more or less equivalent in performance and cost. The point, no pun intended, is not to provide a detailed analysis here but simply to indicate the kinds of clarity that one would produce by looking at projectile points with a theoretically informed language of observation (see also chapter 12, this volume).

In the case of projectile points there appears to be at best only modest room for any stylistic attributes (some haft variability); the bulk of the variability is either functional or technological. "Clovis points" are not a distinctive early style of projectile point but probably a kind of long-handled Swiss Army knife. Even the fluting of the base, a hafting element to judge from its correlation with edge grinding, is not unique in formal terms. Many Danish and southern Scandinavian Neolithic points have a similar feature. Ultimately one is driven to suggest that only the manner in which this kind of basal thinning is accomplished has the potential of being stylistic. Even then, cost differences must be carefully considered. Thus there may not be a scrap of style in Clovis points, despite extensive manufacture. Yet projectile points are routinely used for drawing conclusions about age/ancestry in the preceramic era. This analysis does not mean that such conclusions are wrong, only that they are difficult to warrant. Chapter 12 in this volume provides a good example of the numerous steps required to profitably study relatedness in projectile points.

Similarly, it is easy to appreciate how the above speculations about function may be converted to hypotheses that can be tested using physics or chemistry. For example, "beveling" is frequently considered to be resharpening (e.g., Ballenger 2001; Goodyear 1974), though why this should be so is never clearly explained. Yet one suspects that as a blade feature it must be functional, that is, affect performance, and thereby be under selection. One hypothesis to account for beveling is that it is one variant that arose in early casting technologies before darts/javelins were fletched. The differential lift created by airflow over the trapezoidal section should rotate the tool in flight, improving accuracy much in the manner of fletching (Wilson 1898). Functional speculations about ad hoc variables lead nowhere. Theoretically informed variables are readily converted into testable hypotheses.

Understanding that most of the attributes of stone points are functional explains why points look much the same the world over when made by chipping even though the technologies are otherwise quite distinct. It also suggests that chronologies using point types should be regarded as suspect until proven otherwise. Even differences that have proved valuable as chronological markers over limited amounts of time and space (e.g., fluting or beveling) may turn out, on inspection, to be functional. That such markers "work" cannot be taken to suggest the distinction is unimportant. Function does change and during such periods will correlate with time. Such functional changes must be identified in the process of chronology/phylogeny construction, no matter how useful they may prove once the chronology or phylogeny is known, if we are to avoid mistaking ancestry with coping with similar problems in similar environments.

Conclusion

Archaeology's rich, dense record of rapid change, when coupled with the modern interest in physical/chemical analyses, offers an ideal context in which to undertake refinements of evolutionary theory, not just as applied to people but as a model for biology as a whole. We are in a better position to differentiate between neutral and functional traits, the crucial distinction underlying all of the methods used to construct phylogenetic trees. Were these methods generalized, archaeology could make a contribution to science as a whole. But nothing is guaranteed. After all, realizing that the phenomena called culture is, in an evolutionary framework, an additional system of trait transmission has not been a contribution of anthropology to the larger realm of science (e.g., Bonner 1980). One can only hope that we will not repeat history and let the attractiveness of new methods overcome the need for theoretical innovation.

Note

1. The number mechanics, both biological and archaeological, simply ignored this issue, presumably because to do otherwise would have done away with the rationale for their approach to unit construction (e.g., Cowgill, 1972; Spaulding 1960).

Part 3

Biology

8

Phylogenetic Techniques and Methodological Lessons from Bioarchaeology

Gordon F. M. Rakita

Phylogeny and phylogenetic methods may be new to archaeology, but an interest in quantitative examination of cultural relatedness is not new in anthropology. The early twentieth century witnessed considerable interest in quantifiable representations of cultural similarity and difference—for example, Driver and Kroeber's (1932) *Quantitative Expression of Cultural Relationships*—but the interest waned. The disenchantment with such studies no doubt was a result of a lack of integration within anthropology, itself perhaps an outgrowth of the increasing subfield specialization possible with the development of anthropological departments. Decreasing knowledge about developments in other subfields led to a decline in integrated research questions and research designs.

Over the past two decades, however, there has been increasing interest within anthropology in the development and application of explanatory models based on Darwinian evolutionary theory. This renewed attention has sparked a revitalized interest in quantitative assessments of cultural relatedness. As a result, phylogenetic studies have become more commonplace. My purpose here is to review phylogenetic approaches that have been used in physical anthropology. In particular, I highlight some of the insights that can be gleaned from many decades of phylogenetic analysis performed by bioarchaeologists—physical anthropologists who specialize in human skeletal remains from archaeological contexts. In this study, I focus on physical and morphological attributes; the following chapter (chapter 9) covers a discussion of genetic material derived from skeletal remains. I begin with a basic description of what biological-distance (biodistance) studies are and how they are conducted. I follow with a discussion of why such studies are relevant to cultural phylogenetics. I then provide a brief history of phylogenetic studies conducted on human skeletal materials from the American Southwest. This history provides examples of methodological hurdles that have been dealt with by bioarchaeologists. I end with a summary of some key technical issues that should be considered by anyone exploring phylogenetic methods of data analysis.

Biodistance Studies

Biodistance studies have been performed in one form or another for most of the twentieth century. The basic premise to biodistance analysis is the assumption that human physical similarity is an indication of shared ancestry. More specifically, bioarchaeologists assume that phenotypic similarity mirrors or is an indication of genotypic similarity. This similarity is assumed to be the result of gene flow between populations of interacting individuals. The sources of data for bioarchaeologists are the human skeletons excavated from archaeological sites. Buikstra et al. (1990: 1) describe biodistance studies as examining "variation in bone or tooth shape and form in order to define patterns that are thought to reflect genetic relatedness within or between past populations." More colloquially, a person's similarity to his or her parents and children is a direct reflection of the genetic material that they share.

Traditionally, two forms of data are used to quantify variation in bone and tooth morphology—data on metric traits and data on nonmetric traits (see Buikstra and Ubelaker 1994). Metric traits are commonly agreed upon, standardized linear measurements (or mathematical combinations thereof) of the distance from one point on the skeleton to another (e.g., Howells 1973). Examples of metric traits include the bizygomatic breadth—the distance between the most laterally situated points on the zygomatic arches—and the nasal index—the ratio of the width to height of the nasal aperture. Nonmetric traits, also referred to as discrete, epigenetic, or discontinuous traits, are variations in particular morphological features of the skeleton. Examples include the septal aperture—a small hole on the distal portion of the humerus—and the mylohyoid bridge—a bone ridge that develops over the mylohyoid canal of the mandible.

Analysis of metric and nonmetric data derived from skeletal samples involves the statistical examination and evaluation of levels of similarity in the variation exhibited in those samples. Samples that exhibit widely divergent metric or nonmetric characteristics are assumed to represent individuals or populations that are widely divergent in their genetic makeup. That is, such divergence in phenotypic traits is considered indicative of limited gene flow between the populations represented by the samples. One specimen (a skeleton) can be compared to another specimen, sets of specimens (a skeletal series) can be compared to other sets, and individual specimens can be compared to multiple sets. For biodistance studies, at least three samples or sets are needed so that the analyst can say that, for example, the biodistance between A and B is shorter than it is from either A or B to C. Biodistance is expressed either as a numerical estimate of similarity or dissimilarity and/or visually as spatial closeness on a phylogenetic tree or within two- or three-dimensional space.

As noted by Buikstra et al. (1990), biodistance studies can be conducted at a variety of analytical scales ranging from interracial, to interpopulation, to intraregional, to intrasite. Interracial studies attempt to assess the genetic distance between the "major races" of modern humans. Buikstra and colleagues found that such studies ceased to be published in the *American Journal of Physical Anthropology* after 1960. Interpopulational studies that examine biodistance among sets of skeletons representing national or state-level groups suffered a similar decline after 1960, although it was not as precipitous. Intraregional studies, on the other hand, increased dramatically after 1960 and represent a large proportion of biodistance studies published in the *American Journal of Physical Anthropology*. These studies concentrate on assessing microevolutionary processes using samples drawn from the same general geographic region. Intrasite studies, a growing but still minority approach in the 1970s and 1980s, represent analyses of the biological distance between specimens or sets of specimens excavated from a single archaeological site.

Several developments within the discipline impacted the nature of biodistance studies, perhaps the most pervasive of which was the establishment of new disciplinary goals for physical anthropology as a result of the influence of the evolutionary synthesis of the 1940s and 1950s. Washburn's (1951) seminal article called for the establishment of a "new" physical anthropology that focused its attention on processes of evolution that have affected both extant and extinct primates (both human and nonhuman). This contrasted distinctly with the "old" physical anthropology, which was "primarily a technique" and was characterized by an "emphasis on classification based on types" (Washburn 1951: 298).

To be sure, physical anthropologists prior to the 1950s were well aware of the variation exhibited in the specimens that made up their "types," but they did not see it as germane to their particular research questions. In terms of biodistance studies, the older period of research saw numerous descriptive studies of nonmetric traits, catalogs of summary statistics for metric variables for skeletal series, and a few examples of intraregional studies. Certainly intrasite studies were rare. Modern biodistance studies are far less concerned with classifying populations or specimens and more concerned with examining evolutionary processes affecting gene frequencies in samples. These processes include gene flow, genetic drift, population movements and migrations, and interpopulation interaction.

Related to the development of the new physical anthropology was the increasing distance anthropologists tried to establish between their research and racist explanations or interpretations of their data (Brace 1982; Caspari 2003). Although biodistance relationships can be illustrated using phyloge- netic trees, the use of such diagrams can suggest to the casual reader that speciation or a founding event has occurred. In many ways, the current lack of expressing biodistance relationships of modern *Homo sapiens sapiens* groups using such diagrams can be seen as a way of avoiding the appearance of typological thinking that harkens back to racist tendencies. Indeed, modern biodistance studies are often the target for recent claims that such research is inherently racist (Armelagos and Van Gerven 2003).

Finally, the development of novel multivariate statistical methods and the emergence of powerful personal computers hastened the advance of sophisti- cated quantitative applications. In his 1954 presentation of the coefficient of divergence, Spuhler (1954: 609) prefaced his discussion by stating that "it is not the statistical technique of preference. Discriminant analysis is the pre- ferred technique for classificatory problems. . . . Unfortunately, discriminant methods involve both difficult and extremely laborious computations. When more than a few populations and measurements are used, the amount of labor with the usual desk computational equipment is prohibitive." Things have changed to the point where most studies can benefit from powerful multivari- ate statistical procedures (e.g., Stojanowski 2003; Tomczak and Powell 2003), but there is a caveat: "Biological distance studies can become tedious me- chanical exercises unless they are meshed within the context of evolutionary theory and historical problem solving" (Buikstra et al. 1990: 5).

The Relevance of Biodistance Techniques

There are several reasons why bioarchaeological techniques and method- ological advances in biodistance approaches are relevant to cultural phylogenetics research. First, both bioarchaeologists and archaeologists are interested in asking similar questions of their data sets. Both are interested in the interactions and movements of populations in prehistory. Whereas archae- ologists have traditionally interpreted the magnitude of similarity in cultural traits as indicative of the magnitude of cultural interaction, bioarchaeologists have interpreted magnitude of phenotypic similarity as indicative of biologi- cal interaction. In effect, morphological similarity is assumed to represent genetic or cultural similarity. Thus one would assume that measures of similar- ity and the techniques of grouping similar samples or populations would be issues of mutual concern.

In some respects biodistance studies have outstripped the archaeological analysis of interactions among past human populations. As Konigsberg and Buikstra (1995: 203) note,

> much work has focused on the definition of archaeological boundaries from spatial distributions of artifact styles or the geographic organization of site types.... However,

boundaries can also be inferred through the study of past human skeletal features. In that the mechanisms for biological evolution are more readily understood than the processes defining culture change, human morphology can provide boundary definitions that are more easily interpreted than other classes of archaeological evidence.

Second, it has been suggested by those who reject evolutionary models for cultural phenomena that the reticulate nature of cultural transmission precludes a cladistic approach. Reticulations occur when the streams of cultural traditions merge. Kroeber in particular was concerned that reticulation made biological evolution a poor model for cultural phenomena. His perception of the differences between organic evolution and cultural evolution are illustrated in figure 8.1. However, reticulation also occurs in biological phenomena, as when genetic traits are passed between contemporaneous populations. Indeed, the possibility of genetic reticulation between *Homo sapiens sapiens* and *Homo sapiens neandertalensis* populations in Paleolithic Europe is still being debated (Klein 1999; O'Rourke 2003; O'Rourke et al. 2000; Wolpoff 1999). Bioarchaeologists are aware of these reticulations, and it is precisely these sorts of transmission processes that provide the basis for biodistance models.

Finally, both archaeologists and bioarchaeologists acknowledge that cultural transmission is often accompanied by or occurs together with genetic transmission. Thus the results of both cultural-distance and biodistance studies should be broadly comparable. Indeed, disjunctions between cultural and

Figure 8.1
A.L. Kroeber's Representation of Organic and Cultural Evolution

(a)   (b)

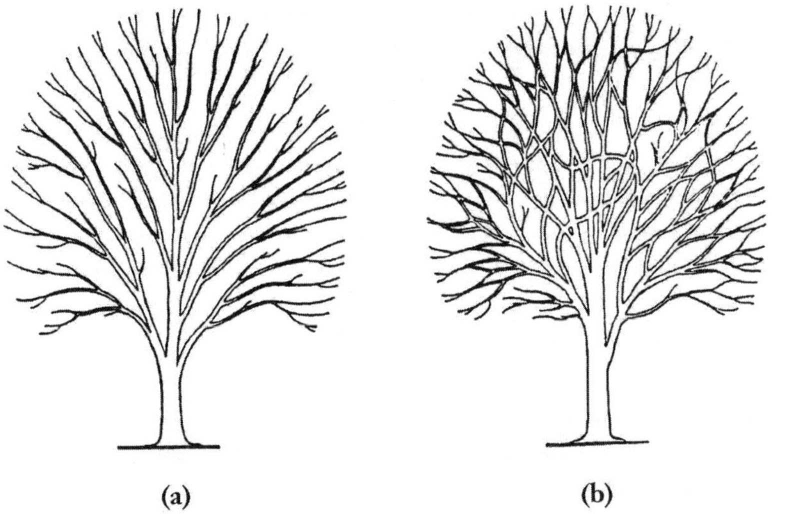

(After Kroeber 1948.)

genetic data should be illustrative of unique and potentially interesting situations. O'Brien and Lyman (2002: 27) have recently remarked that "the independence of biological and cultural evolution must be treated as a null hypothesis." Further, "it has long been observed that cultural transmission is independent of biological transmission, but this does not mean that cultural transmission will never be correlated with the degree of genetic relatedness between a transmitter and a receiver" (O'Brien and Lyman 2002: 27).

For these reasons, I would argue that an examination of bioarchaeological techniques and models for biological distance studies are extremely valuable to archaeologists interested in phylogenetic studies. Indeed, close cooperation between both sets of researchers promises to bear considerable fruit as each side learns from the other. In the meantime, what lessons have bioarchaeologists already learned that can usefully inform archaeological models of cultural phylogeny?

Biodistance Studies in the American Southwest

Beginning in the 1930s, bioarchaeological research in the Southwest, as well as in the rest of the country, began to undergo significant shifts in research agendas. Famous physical anthropologists such as Earnest Hooton, W. W. Howells, Aleš Hrdlička, Charles Seltzer, T. Dale Stewart, and James Spuhler tried their hands at quantitatively measuring the relatedness of various skeletal samples from the region. These researchers attempted to assess the relative genetic similarity of populations through examinations of observable metric features of the human skeleton, especially the cranium. Some of the crania from the ancestral Zuni site of Hawikku (referred to as "Old Zuñi"), along with others from the Southwest, constituted the primary data sets for a series of craniometric studies published in the 1930s and 1940s (Brues 1946; Hrdlička 1931; Seltzer 1944; Stewart 1940; see also Hooton 1930). Several of these investigations were aimed at answering questions about the ancestry of the modern Zunis (a question originally raised by Frank Cushing). However, most also attempted to reconstruct biological affinities of the prehistoric and contemporary inhabitants of the greater Southwest.

Hrdlička (1931) made the first biodistance study in the Southwest, using cranial measurements from numerous locations, including southern Utah Basketmaker sites, Puyé in the Jemez mountains of New Mexico, "Old Zuñi," Chaco Canyon, and Hopi Mesa. Using comparisons of various metric attributes of the crania, especially the cephalic index, Hrdlička arrived at several conclusions, including that the collections displayed two distinct morphological groups, one brachycephalic ("round-headed") and the other dolichocephalic ("long-headed"). Among the former fell the Utah Basketmaker specimens, and among the latter the Puyé and Hopi specimens. Additionally, Hrdlička noted that the geographic distribution of the two groups was unsystematic, which probably represented "considerable interpenetration."

Several years later, Carl Seltzer (1944) reanalyzed the collections, iteratively comparing the mean and standard deviation of over twenty metric traits and eleven indices of the skull for each pairing of the Hawikku collection against each other sample. He agreed with Hrdlička's conclusion that the Zuni crania were morphologically similar to the Utah Basketmaker samples (Corruccini 1972). He further argued that the Zuni collection resembled those from Chaco Canyon. However, he also argued that

> The supposedly sudden appearance of large numbers of deformed crania in the pre-Pueblo and the very earliest of Pueblo phases has caused the majority of archaeologists to believe that these deformed specimens marked the arrival of what they termed "a new race," "a round-headed invasion." The writer [however]. . . . is prone to believe that the deformed crania are more the expression of a change in fashion or ideals of beauty rather than in physical type. (Seltzer 1944: 25)

Stewart's (1940) analysis of skeletons excavated by Frank H. H. Roberts (1939, 1940) in the Zuni region lent support to this conclusion. Moreover, this interpretation of the skeletal remains challenged the traditional viewpoint of many archaeologists, including A. V. Kidder (1924), who suggested that the Basketmaker–Pueblo transition was marked by the arrival into the Southwest of a genetically dissimilar people.

Importantly, although Hrdlička and Seltzer (as well as Hooton and most other physical anthropologists of the day) referred to portions of their collections as belonging to this or that morphological "type," this was not an exercise in mindless, essentialist classification. Nor should it be seen as a glimpse into suspected racist attitudes on the part of early twentieth-century physical anthropologists. No doubt such attitudes existed (Brace 1982), but Seltzer, for example, was quick to point out that terms such as "dolichoid" were descriptions of overall sample sets and often did not necessarily characterize the significant variation within groups: "The impression conveyed by these statements is that all Basket Maker crania are dolichocephalic, that is, have indices below 75, and that all the Pueblo crania are brachycephalic with indices over 80. *This is not true*" (Seltzer 1944: 26, emphasis added). Physical anthropologists on the whole were cognizant of the variation exhibited in their collections. It was simply that their research interests did not lead them to explanations of that variation.

One drawback to these early biodistance studies was the cumbersome and statistically invalid assessment of similarity in metric attributes. Seltzer's iterative comparison of each of over thirty metric traits or indices from the Hawikku sample against over a half dozen other samples is illustrative of the mass of calculations necessary. Interpretation of the various results of such comparisons, together with concerns over the increasing experimental error rate, made individual researcher's interpretations of results both subjective and suspect. In an attempt to alleviate these issues, and in response to growing statistical sophistication, various multivariate measures of morphological similarity were developed. The most common early statistic used was the coefficient of racial likeness.

Although that coefficient was a computational improvement over previous methods, and although a few individuals continued to pursue craniometric biodistance studies into the 1950s, many of the techniques and assumptions of these research agendas were decried by both physical anthropologists (Stewart 1954) and archaeologists (Kraus 1954) alike. Stewart dealt a deathblow to the use of the coefficient of racial likeness and other similar measures in his critique of an analysis conducted by Spuhler (1954). Stewart (1954: 619) asked,

> Is the coefficient of divergence (CD), the new statistical device which Sphuler uses, so much better than the CRL [coefficient of racial likeness]? By his own admission, it has about the same faults: Correlation of characters is ignored, characters are not weighted according to their importance, size of sample is not taken into account, etc. Why then does he proceed with this analysis, knowing as he surely does the nature of the criticisms which will be leveled at him? Part of the answer is, I believe, that he regards the means of analysis as secondary to the problem under investigation.

What was the result of such a critique? Did it drive the final nail into the coffin of biodistance studies? Actually, no. As Buikstra et al.'s (1990) study showed, biodistance studies remained a consistent, if low-frequency, topic from 1955 to 1985. Whereas after 1955 there was a decline in biodistance studies in comparison to studies of diet and disease, the later years of the study period showed an upswing. This renewed interest correlated with published studies regarding trait associations, sources of measurement error, the genetic basis of phenotypic traits, and discussions of distance statistics and models of gene flow related to migration and interaction (Buikstra 1980; Cheverud and Buikstra 1978, 1981a, 1981b, 1982; Cheverud et al. 1979; Konigsberg 1988, 1990; McGrath et al. 1984; Richtsmeier et al. 1984).

In the Southwest, later studies also examined the phenotypic similarity of a skeletal collection from one site with those from multiple other locations throughout the region—what Buikstra et al. (1990) termed intraregional studies. These included studies by Benfer (1968) and Butler (1971) of the Casas Grandes (Paquimé) material of northwestern Chihuahua; by Bennett (1973) of the Point of Pines burials; by El-Najjar (1974) on remains from Canyon de Chelly; by McWilliams (1974) on the Gran Quivira sample; by Heglar (1974) on Cochiti; and by Birkby (1973), Corruccini (1972), and Lumpkin (1976) on various samples. Such studies tailed off in the 1980s and 1990s, perhaps in response to growing political pressure surrounding the passage and implementation of the Native American Graves Protection and Repatriation Act. However, a new generation of bioarchaeologists is once again asking questions about the interaction (both culturally and biologically) and movement of prehistoric populations in the Southwest, and their reports are more frequently showing up in research publications (e.g., Corruccini 1998; Howell and Kintigh 1996, 1998; Schillaci and Stojanowski 2000, 2002).

Methodological Lessons

Like most researchers studying phylogenetics, bioarchaeologists are careful to assess the selective pressures acting on possible traits used in biodistance studies. Traits whose frequency is heavily influenced by selection are more likely to yield information on biological adaptation rather then on population interaction. Biodistance studies, like analogous cultural-distance studies, require traits that are both heritable and influenced only by nonselective evolutionary forces such as drift. In this respect, the focus on neutral traits in archaeological analysis (Dunnell 1978; Hurt and Rakita 2001) may not be as misplaced as some believe. Stylistic traits, that is, those traits whose distribution in time and space is regulated by nonselective processes, are precisely the sorts of traits that would be most useful in cultural-distance models.

Of course, separating stylistic (neutral) from functional (adaptive) traits is not as simple as many of us would hope. As has been recently noted (Hurt and Rakita 2001; Hurt, Rakita, and Leonard 2001; Hurt et al. 2001), stylistic traits can become associated with functional traits such that they do not behave in a manner we would expect of traits not under selection. These sorted traits can have considerable impact on cultural-distance studies. For over thirty years, bioarchaeologists have noted the difficulties inherent in including traits that are correlated with each other. Indeed, it is standard in biodistance studies (e.g., Buikstra 1980; Konigsberg 2000; Pietrusewsky 2000) to check for intertrait correlations and to eliminate those traits that are found to be strongly associated with others.

Alternatively, proper selection of distance measures can eliminate or ameliorate the effects of trait correlations. Bioarchaeologists have turned to measures such as the Mahalanobis D^2 generalized-distance statistic in their examinations of the biological distance between populations. Generally speaking, Mahalanobis distance is the squared distance between two samples, taking into account any number of variables or characteristic states. One advantage of the Mahalanobis D^2 statistic is that it controls for intertrait correlations and mechanically satisfies the assumptions of a normal distribution of variables and an equivalence of covariance matrices. Mahalanobis distance has the added advantage of providing a single quantitative value that represents the dissimilarity between two groups, thus making it a useful first step in multivariate clustering techniques.

In a similar way, bioarchaeologists are careful to examine the level of correlation between traits used in their phylogenetic studies and other characteristics of their samples that may not be used in calculating biological distance. For example, traits highly correlated with the sex or age of individuals within their samples are eliminated. Again, the assumption is that such traits reflect developmental or sex-based etiology and not the genetic ancestry of an individual.

Bioarchaeologists are also quite wary about the possibilities of inter- and intraobserver error (Aftandilian 1995; Buikstra and Ubelaker 1994). These sorts of errors are introduced when two or more researchers collect information differently from each other or when one researcher collects information differently in different phases of the research. These sources of error have been largely neglected throughout archaeology's history (but see Boyd 1987; Fish 1978; Whittaker et al. 1998).

The translation of genotypic information into phenotypic expression is also of concern to bioarchaeologists. For example, many nonmetric traits exhibit what is referred to as "quasi-continuous" expression, or traits that have a "threshold model" of expression (Konigsberg 2000; Saunders 1989). Such traits are controlled by continuously distributed genotypic attributes, but phenotypic expression does not occur until that genotypic attribute exceeds a threshold. Thus what in reality is a continuously distributed genotypic trait is phenotypically expressed dichotomously. As Konigsberg (2000) points out, it is the underlying genotype that is of interest to researchers, not necessarily the phenotypic expression. Yet it is the phenotypic expression that is available for study. In like fashion, archaeologists attempting phylogenetic reconstruction of prehistoric cultures should consider how cultural ideas are translated into cultural materials. Schiffer and others (e.g., Schiffer 1999; Schiffer and Skibo 1997; Schiffer et al. 2001) have been building the literature on such issues, which should be consulted.

Numerous other methodological issues can also impact archaeological phylogenetics. For example, most phylogenetic case studies involve the use of intricate multivariate techniques, yet rarely are the assumptions of such statistics discussed. Grouping methods abound, but what are the advantages and disadvantages of each? Why is one chosen over another? And what do we do about differences in sample sizes? Randomization techniques, which have become common in bioarchaeological circles, may be helpful with this issue and may also provide useful methods for dealing with missing data. Discussions of these issues are found in archaeology, for example in Neff's (2002) discussion of quantitative techniques for analyzing ceramic compositional data. Bioarchaeologists have also struggled with these and other issues and have their own insights to add.

Conclusion

I would not argue in a similar vein as Stewart (1954) that archaeologists conducting phylogenetic studies regard phylogenetics as secondary to the problem under investigation. Quite to the contrary, phylogenetic methods are becoming more commonplace in archaeology. As archaeologists begin to use cladistics and other methods (e.g., O'Brien and Lyman 2003a), they can draw important lessons from others who share their interest in the cultural and biological history of human populations. Bioarchaeologists have been grappling with how to reconstruct the interactions and movements of prehistoric populations for over a century. Archaeologists might do well to heed the methodological mistakes, hurdles, improvements, and developments within the biodistance studies of bioarchaeology.

Equally important, however, archaeologists should not lose sight of the research questions they are asking. Stewart's concern was that bioarchaeologists in the 1950s were placing undo emphasis on the questions they were asking and not focusing enough upon the methods they were using. Conversely, I recommend that researchers using phylogenetic methods and techniques continually reassess their research goals in order to ensure that they are using the correct methods. Archaeologists should work to ensure that phylogenetic techniques are indeed answering the questions they wish to ask and are not simply becoming, as Buikstra et al. (1990: 5) put it, a "tedious mechanical exercise" devoid of theory.

9

Phylogeography of Archaeological Populations: A Case Study from Rapa Nui (Easter Island)

John V. Dudgeon

Reconstructing the history and geography of human populations is a worthy goal. The empirical distribution of people and their artifacts provides the basic data to generate historical explanations about not only population-level phenomena but also the individual behaviors of which they are composed. Evolutionary models that specify the underlying processes that create and sort variation structure the way we collect historical information. From these models, testable predictions are generated that measure the fit of the model to our observations. These have the potential of identifying significant large-scale historical events such as colonization, migration, interaction, and competition.

Evolutionary models that explain the empirical distribution of genetic structure over geographic space are well suited to bridge general evolutionary models with anthropological theory. This is largely a result of well-developed theory and attendant methods that explain empirical molecular variation developed by population genetics and evolutionary systematics over the past fifty years (Felsenstein 2004). These methods have been greatly enhanced by focused attention on the problem of explaining variation over nonlinear, heterogeneous geographic space (Avise 2000; Epperson 2003).

Understanding the distribution of genetic variation over geographic space, however, is not sufficient to explain the creation and maintenance of that variation. The latter requires models that specify the empirical outcomes of evolutionary change across ecologically and demographically heterogeneous landscapes. The goal of this class of models is to separate genetic patterning based on ancestry from that relating to subsequent interpopulation gene flow

(Templeton 1998). Teasing apart these components of molecular variation represents a major challenge for population genetics and evolutionary systematics.

In cases where the current geographic distribution is a small, discontinuous subset of a population's former range, analysis of modern genetic variability tends to fail to characterize historical population dynamics adequately (Pääbo 2000). Reconstruction of the evolutionary history of extinct or prehistoric populations using archaeological samples allows us to directly measure the effect of ecological and environmental variability on the molecular composition of a group of organisms under a variety of demographic scenarios. Well-studied archaeological populations offer the opportunity to test the utility of molecular approaches to reconstructing population structure and history.

The exploration of the social structure and spatial organization of the prehistoric inhabitants of Rapa Nui (Easter Island) (figure 9.1) is an example of how molecular studies can be integrated with detailed archaeological approaches and fine-scale geographic mapping. It is a story of changing social structure, influenced by dramatic long-term isolation and ecological deterio-

Figure 9.1
Map of Rapa Nui (Easter Island), with 50-Meter Contour Intervals Displayed

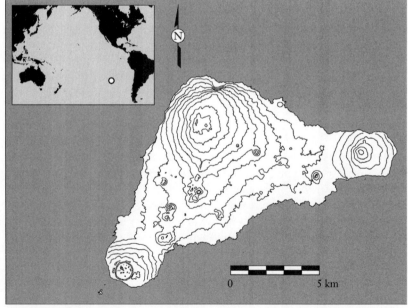

Over 3,700 kilometers west of Chile, of which it is a province, Rapa Nui is 2,250 kilometers southeast of the nearest inhabitable island, Pitcairn. For this reason, Rapa Nui is generally considered the most isolated continuously inhabited island on Earth (Bahn and Flenley 1992). (Figure courtesy B. L. Shepardson.)

ration. The historical processes responsible for the development of Rapa Nui populations are examples of extremes. After A.D. 400, a small colonizing population, perhaps as few as 100 individuals, made landfall on arguably the most isolated place on Earth. For over 1,300 years, these Polynesian voyagers evolved an elaborate, isolated local culture on only 172 square kilometers of land, with a population that may have reached as high as 10,000 individuals.

The population developed a tradition of monumental architecture and social competition of phenomenal proportions. These activities, so apparently successful for most of the culture's history, ended abruptly soon after European contact in A.D. 1722, when the island population collapsed through the combined effects of European slavery, land annexation, and introduced disease (McCall 1994). By 1877, population declined to around 100 individuals, all of whom were virtually imprisoned in the island's only urban center in the late nineteenth century. The processes responsible for the history of Rapa Nui were extreme. With such dramatic changes to the population, it is clear that an ahistorical description of human variation over geographic space can never explain or fully capture the details of the "esoteric efflorescence" (Sahlins 1955) of human culture on Rapa Nui.

The history of the island demands close attention to model construction. The conceptual framework with the greatest power to resolve the evolutionary history of situations such as Rapa Nui requires the integration of fine-scale geographic history with phylogenetic reconstructions of human lineages and a model that incorporates neutral genetic drift. Archaeological information about population growth and demographic structure allows us to generate hypotheses about the geographic structure of populations. Analyses of these sources of data can provide independent tests of hypotheses generated from phylogenetic models that predict spatial structure, but the burden of the method rests on the analysis of genetic variation.

It is only through studies of gene flow that the history of biological populations can be revealed. Granted, the number of variables involved in genetic models of population history (e.g., rates of gene flow, effective population size and demographic trajectory, geographic subdivision, coalescence times, and gene genealogies) is large and may be difficult to estimate in ancient populations. To complicate matters further, the situation on Rapa Nui adds necessary constraints to the development of the model, given that Polynesian populations flourished on the island for a relatively short period and were likely initially very small. Thus, the study of Rapa Nui requires a carefully constructed model that is tuned for the special case that the island's history represents. Specifically, we require a model that (1) is robust for small sample sizes from populations of shallow generational depth, with unknown but presumably high gene flow, and (2) is capable of estimating phylogeny and structure where drift, rather than mutation, is the primary mechanism for geographical subdivision and phylogenesis (Nielsen et al. 1998).

In this chapter, I discuss the scope of molecular-history studies that are focused on explaining cases such as Rapa Nui. Using these studies as a guideline, I frame several testable hypotheses that concentrate on the analysis of skeletal data that was generated by previous research. My goal is to make the results of these independent analyses comparable. The project advocated here uses previously studied skeletal populations. In addition, I make use of recent comparative data assembled from spatial analysis of archaeological features of habitation and monumental constructions. These archaeological remains are believed to represent population segmentation and temporally variable social organization—and by extension, genetic relatedness.

Rapa Nui Prehistory

The standard interpretation of the archaeological record of Rapa Nui holds that prehistoric populations consisted of a series of geographically distinct social groups (McCall 1979; McCoy 1976; Routledge 1919; Stevenson 1984, 2002). The artifactual record of Rapa Nui has generally been held up as a clearcut case of population differentiation and social competition in a restricted environment (Bahn and Flenley 1992; Flenley and Bahn 2002; Stevenson 2002). Three main sources of information have traditionally been marshaled to explain the apparently high degree of social competition, monumental construction, and overall "esoteric efflorescence" (Sahlins 1955) on Rapa Nui. These are ethnographic evidence, biological studies, and archaeological remains.

Ethnographic Evidence

Ethnographic accounts of indigenous Rapa Nui culture have been used to reconstruct the prehistoric and protohistoric social hierarchical and kinship system. The accounts are based on interviews with individuals from remnant populations and date to the late nineteenth and early twentieth centuries, several hundred years after the events being recorded (Lavachery 1936; Métraux 1940; Routledge 1919; Thompson 1889).

The accounts indicate that Rapa Nui was divided among various lineages. Called kainga, these geographically localized areas were held by descent groups (mata) that were defined as affiliations of extended and nuclear families. The mata and kainga were roughly equivalent spatially. The term mata denotes a type of relatedness usually expressed by the anthropological term "clan," and kainga are the geographic and possibly administrative areas occupied by clan-related individuals. Each kainga was anchored to a broad coastal territory, extending inland in pie-slice configuration. The kainga arrangement provided each mata a range of island environments for marine exploitation, inland and upland agriculture, and related subsistence activities (e.g., Stevenson et al. 2002). This coastal-inland arrangement of descent-based geography has been reported elsewhere in Polynesia (Handy and Pukui 1972) and has been employed in some general models of the evolution of agricultural systems and political hierarchy (e.g., Ladefoged and Graves 2000; Ladefoged et al. 1996). As I show below, the ethnographic accounts and various land-division schemes proposed for Rapa Nui, while not appropriate as explanations of social differentiation in themselves, can be used to generate some basic molecular spatial hypotheses.

Biological Evidence

Gill (1986, 1990; Chapman and Gill 1997; Gill et al. 1997) used a variety of methods to examine Rapa Nui skeletal variation. Stefan (1999, 2000), Zimple and Gill (1986), Chapman (1993, 1997), and others have used skeletal remains to examine intraisland population structure based on models of ethnohistoric social divisions. Stefan (1999, 2000), in his studies of minimum genetic distance and its contribution to phenotypic variability (Williams-Blangero and Blangero 1989), found evidence of greater between-group homogeneity within the male skeletal sample. This pattern appears to indicate higher islandwide mobility of males compared to females. However, his studies reveal no large-scale regional or lineage-based pattern of inbreeding. Stefan (1999: 416) concluded that, contrary to the story provided by ethnographic accounts, "differentiation of those tribes did not occur through the actions of cultural and genetic isolation."

Other studies do not agree with this conclusion. Some genetic isolation caused by group structure has been suggested based on studies of multiple individual burials in coastal caves (Shaw 2000). These studies suggest that there is evidence of small pockets of relative genetic isolation within segments of some subpopulations (Zimple and Gill 1986). The argument is based on the occurrence of three rare discrete traits of the postcranial skeleton. These are traits that achieve higher than expected frequency in discrete geographical locations (Gill and Owsley 1993; Shaw 2000; Stefan 1999). Other reports (e.g., Zimple and Gill 1986) have offered similar evidence for variable gene-flow schemes. These are based primarily on the appearance and frequency of rare discrete traits as well as on other heritable phenotypic markers.

Archaeological Evidence

Previous research into the development of lineages has focused on spatially patterned monumental architecture and the occurrence of discrete residences and subsistence features hypothesized to be associated with them (McCoy 1976; Stevenson 1984, 1986, 2002). In an extension of the ethnographic accounts and observations of historic settlement patterns for Rapa Nui (Lavachery 1936; Métraux 1940; Routledge 1919; Thompson 1889), several authors (McCall 1979; McCoy 1976; Stevenson 1984; Stevenson et al. 2002) have proposed a settlement-subsistence model in which habitations were clustered in a narrow margin along the coast, allowing access to both marine resources and inland farming areas. Habitation-site density decreases markedly beyond 1,000–1,500 meters inland from the coast, implying that in the absence of controlling topographic or hydrographic variability, settlement pattern is influenced by access to marine resources and in relation to the large ceremonial platforms (ahu). Temporally, the model suggests that the record was initially patterned by dispersed residences that were representative of local lineage autonomy and that coalesced in the middle period into increasingly nucleated, more densely clustered habitations. This accretion of small, widely distributed settlements is argued to represent the incorporation of autonomous local lineages into multiple lineage clusters.

In his analysis of obsidian-hydration dates for areas previously surveyed by McCoy (1976), Stevenson (1984) concluded that by the sixteenth century all previously independent lineages on the southern coast of Rapa Nui were incorporated into four politically autonomous multilineage descent groups, which persisted until the eighteenth century. The latter part of prehistory on Rapa Nui is roughly correlated with evidence of environmental deterioration and the beginnings of population-level resource and subsistence stress. The commonsense explanation for the development of multilineage political associations is that resource stress caused by high populations and the demands of monumental-statue construction and movement resulted in the need for greater cooperation among previously autonomous lineages. This arrangement lasted until the early eighteenth century, when multiple lineage centers were abandoned and the southern-coast populations reverted to the autonomous lineage-based configuration of two centuries earlier (Stevenson 1984). Coincident with the increase in settlement density and lineage fission-fusion was human-induced ecological deterioration and resource stress.

The central theme of these descriptions of late Rapa Nui prehistory is a common archaeological story, and its main tenets have been invoked to explain the Maya "collapse" (Santley et al. 1986) and the Anasazi "abandonment" of the American Southwest (Fish et al. 1994). After A.D. 1400, rapidly growing Rapa Nui populations were nucleating into high-density coastal centers characterized by elite residences and elaborate ceremonial architecture (Stevenson 2002). By around A.D. 1500, the coastal centers consisted of many intermixed, previously autonomous lineages. As population pressure and resource exploitation began to affect these large regional centers after A.D. 1550–1600, factionalism and warfare increased, and the politically unified regional centers dissociated along lineage lines, re-aggregating as dispersed, more evenly distributed low-density coastal and inland communities. By the time of European contact in A.D. 1722, Rapa Nui was still a viable island society, albeit at far lower population than its high in the sixteenth century. However, the construction of monumental statues and large ceremonial buildings—the central focus of outside interest in Rapa Nui for almost 300 years—had ceased (Kirch 1984).

Analytical Methods

A geographic model of population divergence and phylogenetic related-ness employing a molecular analysis of Rapa Nui skeletal material can pro-vide basic means for testing hypotheses of spatial segmentation of social groups through time. The model should include factors for small initial popu-lations, rapid population growth, and selective pressures of ecological dete-rioration. Molecular approaches are an excellent means for building these kinds of models. Molecular data are sensitive to small, isolated populations with limited mobility because social or competitive barriers to migration and interaction can be measured with fidelity that archaeological and biological approaches are unable to replicate.

Depending on the approach used, empirical variation can be viewed as (1) the result of demographic and biological processes leading to broad patterns of geographic differentiation within and between populations or (2) the result of a genealogical process, whereby discrete allelic states define probable an-cestor-descendant relationships. The former model employs pairwise mea-sures of frequency distributions of alleles across space to estimate the amount of gene flow or interaction occurring within and between subpopulations (Wright's [1931, 1943] F-statistics). Pairwise measures generate a coefficient of similarity between any two individuals or groups. The coefficient of simi-larity combines information about the evolutionary history between groups plus ongoing gene flow via migration. Teasing apart the relative contributions of each process becomes a difficult proposition but one that is informed by spatial arrangement or other historical information.

The latter model uses an explicitly phylogenetic, or coalescent, approach that postdicts the pattern of the merging of sampled lineages backward in time (Jobling et al. 2004). Moving backward, each generation subsumes individu-als possessing shared derived traits, such as novel genetic mutations, until all the individuals in the sample are joined to a common ancestor. The pattern of ancestral-state coalescence is the evolutionary description of the sampled population. Ongoing gene flow complicates the construction of gene gene-alogies under the coalescent method, but the genealogical history across dif-ferent genes can give clues to the amount of ongoing gene flow (Barton and Wilson 1995). Ultimately, coalescent models are more robust to sampling effects than F-statistics, given that the resulting coalescent tree describes the genealogical relationship of only those individuals sampled in that genera-tion. In contrast, measures of allelic diversity based on F-statistics are useful indicators of population structure and estimators of gene flow (Neigel 2002), especially when migration and drift, rather than mutation, are the primary forces for population differentiation.

To construct a model of genetic divergence and hierarchical population segmentation over time, we need to create expectations for detectable differences in molecular heterozygosity (i.e., patterns of different alleles at a given locus in regard to a given character) between subpopulations as a result of nonrandom migration and genetic drift. If many populations are compared in a matrix of pairwise genetic distance, and if mutation and selection pressure are low, this statistic reflects the amount of subpopulation differentiation resulting from restricted gene flow, provided that genetic drift is constant for all populations (Hutchison and Templeton 1999).

Population size in prehistoric and protohistoric Rapa Nui has been notoriously difficult to quantify for three reasons. First, the superposition of temporally unrelated archaeological features makes ground-based estimates of total population problematic (but see Stevenson 1984). Second, the loss of nearly the entire population from slave raids in the 1860s, as well as from introduced European diseases, creates a temporal, spatial, and cultural discontinuity. Third, a lack of good chronological dating of stone-lined chamber and cave bundle burials seriously limits paleodemographic reconstruction to estimate population sizes and demographic pressure across any temporal interval.

Population genetics tells us that the single most important parameter necessary when calculating loss of genetic diversity in small, isolated populations is the "effective population size," which is the sample of the population at large that typically participates in the founding of the next generation. Even within large, randomly mating populations, rarely is the effective population size the same as the total number of individuals. Reductions in absolute mating efficiency occur because of demographic differences in fertility between mating pairs or the unequal distribution of males and females.

A demographic model of population growth is needed to estimate the effective population size in Rapa Nui from initial colonization through the nineteenth century. In circumscribed geographic ranges, models that incorporate growth-rate reductions from resource stress are better predictors of population size through time. Density-dependent demographic models predict that populations that approach the environmental carrying capacity of the landscape they exploit will suffer population growth-rate declines from reduced fertility in stressful environments (Alstad 2001; MacIntyre 1999).

A density-dependent model of prehistoric population growth (figure 9.2) provides estimates of both intrinsic growth rate and total population through time and better approximates living systems in finite environments. Density-dependent growth models assume overall population size will affect the per-capita growth rate of the population as a negative linear effect that increases as the population approaches the carrying capacity of the environment (Alstad 2001). At colonization, small initial populations are significantly below carrying capacity, and the intrinsic population growth rate is near maximum. As the population nears carrying capacity, the negative effect on the growth rate results in reduction of intrinsic growth rate toward zero and eventually a stable equilibrium where the population size equals carrying capacity.

Numerous authors have speculated on both the time and size of initial colonization of Rapa Nui (Finney 1993; Irwin 1992; Kirch 1984). Some estimates favor a small founding population (40–150 individuals) and a settlement date as early as A.D. 400 (Heyerdahl and Ferdon 1961; but see Martinsson-Wallin and Crockford [2001] and Spriggs and Anderson [1993] for recent reassessments of the Rapa Nui radiocarbon chronology). The size of the prehistoric maximum population on Rapa Nui is an equally contentious issue. Most authors agree with the paleoenvironmental evidence that forest decline and population stress occurred by A.D. 1550 and that after that date the population leveled off and then began a slow decline toward a census

Figure 9.2
Density-Dependent Population-Growth Curves for Rapa Nui

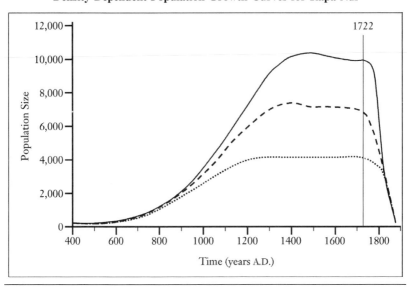

In this simulation, the intrinsic growth rate is set to 0.006, corresponding to roughly 12 percent population growth per generation (20 years). This growth rate, while generally in agreement with other estimates, is not crucial to total-population estimates, other than as a device for building population at a specific level at a certain time. Although low by comparison to modern developing nations, which often serve as analogues to prehistoric colonizing populations, this growth rate fits the expectation of a population maximum in the sixteenth century. Included in this graph is the hypothetical rapid population decline after about 1750A.D., which corresponds roughly to 10–15 percent population loss per generation. This decline reflects the combined effects of environmental deterioration, social instability, and introduced disease (syphilis, smallpox, and tuberculosis) subsequent to European contact in 1722 up to the census figure of 3000 in 1862. By 1880, only 111 native Rapa Nui remained.

population of 3,000 individuals in 1862. This is the year before the arrival of Peruvian slave traders, who exploited the local population for off-island mining concerns, reducing the total population to 111 people by 1877.

Estimates of population reached during the hypothesized prehistoric high in the sixteenth century range between 4,000 and 10,000 individuals, with most estimates between 6,000 and 8,000 (Bahn and Flenley 1992). Simulating population growth from a colonizing population size of 100 at an early date of A.D. 400 (Irwin 1992), and setting the intrinsic growth rate so that maximum population is reached by A.D. 1550, creates the population estimates shown in figure 9.2.

I expect the effective population size for the estimates of diversity loss to be some small fraction of the total potential breeding population (ca. 10,000 high census population) over the time period of interest. If we presume that the skeletal population represents a late-period population (A.D. 1500–1750), the effective population size over the 67.5 generations between A.D. 400 and A.D. 1750 is only 699 individuals. If the founding population that landed on Rapa Nui ca. A.D. 400 consisted of perfectly heterozygous ($H_0 = 0.5$) individuals, the expected heterozygosity is 0.476, meaning that less than a 0.03 reduction in genetic diversity is predicted over the 67.5 generations of continuous occupation.

If, however, we divide the island-wide effective population equally among the eleven ethnographically reported prehistoric tribal divisions shortly after contact, the expected tribe-level heterozygosity drops to 0.293. Table 9.1 demonstrates the expected reductions in heterozygosity under different levels

Table 9.1
Expected Heterozygosity Reduction Based on Estimates of Effective Population Size for Rapa Nui

Island effective population size (N_e) [a]	Heterozygosity reduction (H_{exp}) [b]		Hypothesized social division[c]
699	0.48	(0.02)	None (island-wide interaction)
350	0.45	(0.05)	Moiety (subdivided population)
64	0.29	(0.21)	Tribal/Corporate (eleven separate political entities)
32	0.17	(0.33)	Lineage-Based (two lineages/factions per tribe)

a Based on density-dependent growth rate and maximum census population of 10,000 individuals.
b Calculated reduction from initial heterozygosity of 0.5.
c Reported by Routledge (1919).

of population subdivision. Based on the assumptions of the model of random genetic drift, we might expect slightly greater losses in heterozygosity in our Rapa Nui population if nonrandom mating and fluctuating size within subpopulations occurred.

I hypothesize that the hierarchical population structure took the form of individual spatially defined lineages at the lowest level of inclusiveness and encompassed the entire island at its highest level. In between, the corporate descent unit described by Stevenson (1984, 2002) groups individual lineages, which are in turn nested into the ethnohistoric tribal boundaries (Routledge 1919) and moieties described by various authors (McCall 1984; Métraux 1940; Routledge 1919). Framing testable hypotheses for geographic genetic structure inevitably relies on ethnographic and archaeological social divisions. There exist few if any geographic barriers to gene flow by migration, and the island's small size precludes genetic models of isolation by distance (e.g., Malécot 1950; Wright 1943), unless mobility can be shown to be strongly and negatively correlated with population density. Nonetheless, geographically patterned population structure may emerge under several anthropological scenarios, including lineage-based marriage restrictions and social competition between descent groups (Métraux 1940).

Figure 9.3 provides a simple example of the effect of migration rate on the expected allelic frequencies in a hypothetical example of a developing population. Each simulation represents a subpopulation composed of ten demes, or subpopulations, each containing 100 individuals. Each deme interacts with the others, based on a migration rate of 0.15 per generation, averaged over all other demes. This migration rate corresponds to the exchange of fifteen individuals from each deme of 100 individuals in each generation. A migration rate of 0.15 per generation is considered relatively endogamous in human tribal populations (Birdsell 1973) and produces an average decrease in subpopulation heterozygosity from 0.5 to 0.479, reaching a semistable equilibrium after ten generations. If this simplistic model proves a robust approximation of the demographic history on Rapa Nui, random migration will mitigate genetic differentiation between subpopulations, and it might be difficult to discern subpopulation structure. We might also suppose that on Rapa Nui migration by mate exchange might have been significantly higher than modeled here. Routledge (1919: 221) noted that "in remembered times there were no group restrictions on marriage, which took place indiscriminately between members of the same or different clans."

Nonrandom Gene Flow

The notion that the population structure for Rapa Nui prior to the nineteenth century was hierarchically organized by lineage, and by extension, the family, offers hope that we can model these processes of genetic divergence within an anthropological framework integrated with genetic theory for small,

Figure 9.3
Allelic-Frequency Changes over Time as a Response to Random Genetic Drift and Gene Flow

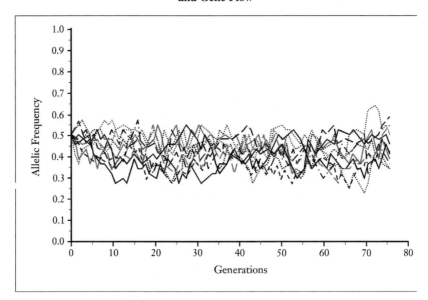

Simulation shows the rate and trajectory of heterozygosity change for a sample of 10 demes of 100 individuals, exchanging migrants at a rate of 0.15, or 15 individuals per generation. Initial frequency of alleles is 0.5 for all demes. This corresponds to a homogeneous colonizing population.

interacting populations. The simple model presented here assumes there are no spatial barriers to migration and that all migrant exchange per generation is random with respect to the target deme and the allelic frequency of each migrant. But humans, as with other social mammals, tend to migrate nonrandomly across space in related groups (Fix 1978), which might bias the sex ratio of migrants based on rules of kinship and resource partitioning (Flinn and Low 1986). Also, competition may generate barriers to migration along the boundaries or within existing subpopulations (Read and LeBlanc 2003), either through patch depletion or social competition from mating control (Flinn and Low 1986). To understand the specific lineage histories and evolution of genetic divergence in Rapa Nui, tests of population structure must be sensitive to nonrandom gene flow in any form predicted from prior anthropological or archaeological observations.

Models of kin-structured migration posit that the migration of related individuals has a positive effect on the maintenance of heterozygosity, especially measures of between-group to within-group variance, and may partially offset the homogenizing effect of random migration (Rogers 1987). Migration is

Figure 9.4
Example of Demographic Structuring and Its Effect on Lineage Evolution

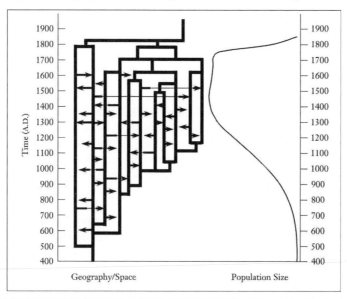

As Rapa Nui population growth accelerated after about A.D. 800, new lineages emerged, with subpopulations expanding into and colonizing new coastal areas (fission). After A.D. 1500, environmental deterioration coupled with social instability resulted in the fusion of previously independent lineages. The phylogeographic-branching pattern shown here represents averages of multiple lineages in regional descent groups.

expected to maintain heterozygosity in randomly interacting populations, reducing the visibility of population substructure. Kin-structured migration can generate the opposite effect, maintaining population substructure and creating visible effects over time and distance (Fix 1999). Included within this general class of nonrandom migration is the anthropological notion that on Rapa Nui, some groups or demes practiced marriage-exchange alliances (*tumus*), which structured mate exchange between specific tribes (Métraux 1940).

Also of interest for Rapa Nui is nonrandom gene flow through what Neel (1967) called the "lineal effect," which is the result of kin-based fission of local co-resident populations that produces new, kin-structured population migrations. Stevenson (1984, 1986) suggests that this kind of process explains late prehistoric populations based on his study of southern-coast settlement patterns after A.D. 1400. Neel and Salzano (1967) demonstrated that such fission and fusion processes could generate significant amounts of localized heterogeneity, a kind of kin-structured founder effect (Fix 1999).

Sex-biased gene flow, in the form of spatially structured male-female craniometric variation (Stefan 1999), may also have conferred localized heterogeneity. Analysis of sex-biased migration, especially for reconstruction of historical process in contrast to population structure (Templeton 1998; Templeton et al. 1995), will rely on sex-specific alleles (mtDNA, Y chromosome) and their relationship to dual-inheritance genetic variation (nuclear polymorphism). For Rapa Nui, the low mtDNA variation in eastern Polynesia (Murray-McIntosh et al. 1998) and the hypothesized small colonizing population may preclude resolving sex-biased migration as a historical process in the archaeological population.

Viewed in this way, analysis of subpopulation differentiation in Rapa Nui under nonrandom migration holds promise for testing previous observations of spatially clustered phenotypic traits. Gene flow via nonrandom migration may tend to maintain heterozygosity differentially with respect to random migration under various ideal models (Kimura and Weiss 1964; Malécot 1950; Wright 1943, 1951). If migration is viewed as a stochastic process under the ideal models, then nonrandom migration can be viewed as an augmentation (Fix 1999).

If prehistoric Rapa Nui is characterized by lineal fission and establishment of new coastal settlements during the period of rapid population growth (figure 9.4), then the effects of kin-structured migration will generate a spatial pattern of discrete pockets of low genetic variation and the appearance of greater isolation between geographically proximate subpopulations. Skeletal material in the caves on Rapa Nui's southern coast, although probably later than the period of rapid population expansion, suggests that long-term habitation by localized and isolated populations was occurring (Shaw 1996, 2000).

Conclusion

Analysis of prehistoric molecular variation over geographic space creates independent historical explanations that can be compared to archaeological or other spatial-temporal data. Critical to these explanations is the ability to discern spatial variation at scales pertinent to the demographic structure of the target population. Different classes of DNA polymorphism are capable of resolving population structure at multiple scales, depending on the evolutionary history of the organism. In order to generate meaningful explanations for hierarchical structure, defined subpopulations must show a reduction in the average proportion of population heterozygosity relative to the expected proportion of heterozygous genotypes in a randomly mating population (Hartl and Clark 1997).

Partial barriers to gene flow, in the form of geographic or social boundaries to migration or isolation by distance in a continuous population, can generate measurable discontinuous as well as clinal distributions of heterozygosity reduction, given sufficient time and effective population size. Whereas the reduction of heterozygosity through genetic drift within and between small populations is more rapid relative to larger populations, similarly small amounts of random gene flow from migration are required to obliterate the observation of hierarchical structure and subpopulation divergence (Crow and Kimura 1970).

Although it probably is true that estimating phylogenetic structure, especially in small, interacting populations, is better approximated by models that specify an explicit model of evolution (Nielsen et al. 1998; Templeton 1998), estimators of differentiation based on Wright's F-statistics will continue to serve a valuable role (Neigel 2002). The relationship between F-statistics and anthropologically important parameters such as population size and rate of migration between demes overcomes some of the loss of relevant data imposed by averaging allelic frequencies into genetic distances.

The question being asked here is not focused on genetic drift or heterozygosity reduction but on the amount of gene flow and heterozygosity maintenance that can be predicted from patterned variation in the interaction of genetic drift and gene flow. Genetic drift is a stochastic process, ratcheting variability out of populations in unpredictable ways. Modifications to the process of genetic drift, such as mutation, migration, and selection, provide data to generate explanations for the differential persistence of variation in a study population. Rapa Nui is an excellent laboratory in which to test our ability to resolve differences in human association through time and to identify and explain these differences under variable life-history strategies.

Here the goal is almost the opposite of standard phylogenetic analysis. Rather than elucidating structure through the identification of ancestral states and then explaining the differences according to bifurcating nodes, studies such as the one discussed here attempt to identify historically significant amounts of gene flow that enhance relatedness among otherwise geographically separate, bifurcating populations. Mitigation of genetic drift through population interaction, especially if the interaction is not purely negatively correlated with geographic distance (Wright 1943), has important implications that must be understood.

Part 4

Culture

10

Tracking Culture-Historical Lineages: Can "Descent with Modification" be Linked to "Association by Descent"?

Peter Jordan and Thomas Mace

Two key questions face anthropologists and archaeologists: (1) how are cultural attributes transmitted between generations and horizontally over space, and (2) do different elements of culture have separate descent histories or are they passed on as coherent cultural cores? On-going debates tend either to emphasize the potential for branching processes of descent akin to biological speciation or to stress that interaction and exchange lead to cultural blending. In this chapter, we develop an approach for tracking both branching and blending and thereby addressing whether culture is transmitted as cores or as independent packages. As Boyd et al. (1997: 386) argue, "identifying the upper limit for culturally coherent scales is a vital question"; perhaps large-scale anthropological survey such as we propose here might begin to answer that question. We make two contributions to the current debates, the first methodological, the second a case study of cultural transmission on the Northwest Coast of North America. We look both at processes of transmission and at the effects these have on the upper scale limit of coherent units of culture.

Cultural Transmission: Current Debates

Investigations of cultural transmission have focused on two debates. First, different accounts of human history and cultural diversification have stressed either blending or branching processes of cultural transmission (Boyd et al. 1997; Durham 1992; Moore 1994b; Terrell et al. 1997). Branching is thought to come about in a manner similar to speciation: as members of a population interact less, they split, carrying their traditions and cultural values with them (e.g., Rushforth and Chisholm 1991). In short, a new cultural assemblage will arise through the descent with modification of an ancestral assemblage (clado-genesis). Others have argued that the tendency for humans to interact means that this is unlikely and that human cultural history has always been character-ized by the predominance of horizontal blending between adjacent popula-tions (e.g., Terrell et al. 1997). Blending destroys or at least lessens our chances of reconstructing cultural phylogenies.

The term "ethnogenesis" is usually used to describe the process by which a new assemblage arises through the blending of elements from two or more contemporaneous assemblages. The precise contribution of these processes is hotly disputed, though there is growing consensus that biological methods that focus on the quantitative identification of descent, diffusion, and adapta-tional processes have much to contribute to modeling the operation of these cultural processes (Gray and Jordan 2000). Regrettably, this potentially fruit-ful area of research is being hindered by a frustrating lack of systematic cul-tural-survey data that record assemblages in sufficient variety and detail for these questions to be addressed in any rigorous quantitative manner. Conse-quently, without further empirical research these key debates remain in the domain of speculation.

The second set of debates is related directly to this "branching versus blend-ing" debate and involves issues of the size and time scale of coherent units of culture (Boyd et al. 1997). Poorly understood is the potential for different parts of culture to have quite different transmission histories, as work to date has tended to focus on the transmission of one set of traditions rather than on the broader body of cultural attributes carried by populations (Jordan and Shennan 2003; Tehrani and Collard 2002). Is a range of diverse cultural at-tributes transmitted as a coherent "core" combining language, craft traditions, ritual beliefs, and the like? Conversely, does each facet, or "package," of culture have a different descent history?

Scales of Cultural Coherence: Current Models

In their detailed analysis of the key similarities and differences between biological evolution and processes of cultural transmission, Boyd et al. (1997) identify a useful range of theoretical models, or hypotheses, that attach differ-ent degrees of importance to both the branching and blending processes of cultural transmission and to the relative scales of coherent units of culture:

- *Culture as species* – coherent units of cultural tradition generated entirely by branching descent with modification, essentially immune to outside influence;
- *Cultures with hierarchically integrated systems* – cultures comprise core traditions transmitted via cladogenesis and peripheral elements that are more fluid and susceptible to exchange and blending;

- *Cultures as assemblages of many coherent units* – no central culture core but rather an intermeshing of different traditions drawn from diverse sources and with different descent histories; and
- *Cultures as collections of ephemeral entities* – no overall coherence in cultural traditions.

Here we stress the need to investigate several areas of culture to evaluate each of these four models properly. It is clear that methods drawn from evolutionary biology have direct applicability to these research questions. In adapting and applying these methods to cultural problems we stress, however, that we have no prior subscription to either biological or cultural explanations of human cultures, or to branching or blending models of culture change. Instead, we believe that employing biological methods to similar problems (the identification of descent, diffusion, and adaptation relative to patterns of diversity) will enable us to generate concrete accounts of factors operating in particular cases.

For example, the methods enable us to quantify high levels of blending as predicted by the ethnogenesis hypothesis (Moore 1994b), and we are also able to detect cultural lineages, or traditions (Tehrani and Collard 2002). Our goal is to identify whether different "packages" of culture are all being transmitted in the same way. For example, if all these elements are being transmitted by the same set of factors that encourage branching transmission, then it might well be possible that unified cores are formed, as each different package of culture is being passed on in tandem.

How Do We Detect Cultural Cores?

Cladistics has seen increasingly widespread application in the analysis of cultural transmission, in particular the identification of the relative contribution of branching and blending processes. In this chapter, we employ the null model that new cultural assemblages arise entirely through the bifurcation of ancestral ones. Thus, the cladistic method attempts to account for the emergence of new cultural assemblages in the form of a branching-tree diagram that shows lines of cultural descent. Biologists developed the method to identify how ancestral species bifurcated through time into new but historically related forms. The key principle involves determining which similarities are a result of shared ancestry ("homologies") and which are a result of other processes, including borrowing ("homoplasies"). If the data fit the tree model well, we can assume that branching transmission has predominated. If the fit is poor, then other processes have affected patterns of historical descent.

How do we analyze the scale of coherent units of cultural tradition? At one scale, if a cultural assemblage does not fit a tree model well, then perhaps we can posit that innovation or blending, or both, has obscured phylogenetic history. This means we can use cladistics to attempt to identify the upper size limit affecting the transmission of coherent assemblages of culture—

traditions of weaponry manufacture, basketry weaving, clothing styles, and so on.

However, the upper size limit for coherent units of culture may extend beyond individual weaponry, clothing, or basketry lineages. Indeed, all these traditions may have been transmitted in tandem, perhaps also with language, thereby forming a unified cultural core. Indeed, this would equate with romantic and primordialist models of ethnic groups, which are argued to have uniform cultural "essences" combining a uniform material and social culture and distinct world view, all of which are transmitted through history en masse. Clearly, any community will have a wide range of traditions relating to different aspects of its life. These may be affected differently by innovation, by branching and blending processes of transmission, and by various kinds of selection and decision-making forces. Subsequent postlearning social interaction will also guide how cultural traditions are reproduced and the subsequent forms and patterns they take. The key point is that if these different traditions have been affected by similar sets of influences, they are likely to have similar transmission histories. If they do, then they will track each other with various degrees of fidelity through time, thereby forming cultural cores.

How do we test for the existence of cultural cores? First, we need to demonstrate that cladogenesis has affected the descent of different cultural packages. Second, we need to track the association of these separate lineages. If culture has been transmitted as a core, then separate lineages (for different packages of culture) will cluster together, via common descent histories, in unified bundles of cultural and linguistic tradition. Identification of cultural cores then becomes an empirical problem, one that evolutionary biologists have already approached, albeit through reference to biological rather than cultural datasets. We explore how these biological methods can be adapted to investigate the presence of cultural cores, where different cultural lineages have been transmitted in tandem.

There are two dimensions to this biological work. The first is the debate over the unified versus concerted response of different species to climate change, and the second is the host-parasite literature (Page 2003). This second area of research is perhaps a better analogy with cultural-transmission research as it not only addresses descent with modification but quantifies the degree of association by descent. Thus, the theme has seen extensive theoretical, methodological, and analytical attention, summarized recently by Page (2003). In simple terms, this research into association by descent identifies the degree of "co-speciation"—the joint speciation of two or more biological lineages that are ecologically associated, the paradigm being that of host and parasite (Page 2003).

Importantly, the relationship between the species need not be parasitic, and many other factors may lead to co-speciation. Central to the process are factors that lead to speciation. Generally, these are related to some degree of isolation, which means as the host speciates, associated factors make if difficult for the parasite to switch or disperse to other hosts. In short, parasite lineages are "forced" onto host phylogenies. The archetypal case study is the association between pocket gophers and lice, which form a textbook example of co-phylogenetic congruence. The reasons for this are found in interaction patterns between both host and parasite. The gophers live much of their life cycles alone in tunnels, from which they exclude other individuals. They have very low dispersal rates and distances and tend not to travel far from their natal homes, where they form patchy rather than continuous populations. This combination of factors blocks opportunities for lice dispersal among potential host species, which promotes congruence between host and parasite phylogenies (Clayton et al. 2003).

Biological processes might have parallels in cultural-transmission histories. Clearly, many forces—for example, diffusion and rapid innovation—can intervene to jeopardize a clear-cut parallel, but if Boyd et al.'s (1997) model of culture as either "species" or "hierarchically integrated units" is appropriate for the origins of cultural diversity, then at least some core traditions must have similar descent histories. That is, some cultural lineages must have tracked one another with various degrees of fidelity. Thus the most basic test for biological, as well as cultural, co-speciation is whether the topology of the host and parasite phylogenies (or two or more cultural lineages) is significantly more similar than would be expected as a result of chance alone. In other words, "if co-speciation were the only process occurring the host and parasite phylogenies would be mirror copies of one another" (Page 2003: 1).

Research Questions and Methods

To summarize, we are interested in testing the following hypotheses using data from the Northwest Coast:

Have individual cultural assemblages been passed on by branching or blending processes?

Are individual assemblages associated by descent, thereby forming cultural cores?

Is language history linked to cultural history?

Which of Boyd et al.'s (1997) models for cultural transmission provides the most convincing account for the origin of cultural diversity on the Northwest Coast?

What are the effects of geographic location on cultural transmission?

We use the methods in box 10.1 to explore these issues. Our data set is derived from Philip Drucker's (1950) extensive culture-element list, which resulted from systematic survey undertaken on the Northwest Coast in 1936

Box 10.1
Summary of Methods Used to Investigate Research Questions

General Question	Specific Issue	Test	Result
Branching or Blending?	Tree-to-data fit?	Consistency index	100% is perfect cladogenesis
	Strength of support for branches?	Bootstrapping	Shows percentage support for each branch
Fit among Trees?	Is there any difference among trees?	Kishino-Hasegawa	Determines if trees differ significantly
	Is association among trees random?	Triplets	Measures degree of nonrandom association

Box 10.2
Names and Linguistic Affiliations of the Northwest Coast Indigenous Communities Investigated

Code	Tribe/Division	Language	Branch	Family
NH	Hupachisat	Nootka	Nootkan	Wakashan
NT	Tsishaat	Nootka	Nootkan	Wakashan
NC	Clayoquot	Nootka	Nootkan	Wakashan
KK	Koskimo	Kwakiutl	Kwakiutlan	Wakashan
KR	Kwexa	Kwakiutl	Kwakiutlan	Wakashan
KW	Wikeno	Heiltsuk-Oowekyala	Kwakiutlan	Wakashan
BC	Bella Coola	Bella Coola	Bella Coola	Salishan
KO	Bella Bella (Oyalit division)	Heiltsuk-Oowekyala	Kwakiutlan	Wakashan
KC	Xaihais	Heiltsuk-Oowekyala	Kwakiutlan	Wakashan
KX	Xaisla (Kitamat)	Xaisla	Kwakiutlan	Wakashan
TH	Southern Tsimshian (Kitqata division)	Coast Tsimshian	Tsimshian	Tsimshian
TG	Tsimshian Proper (Gilutsa division)	Coast Tsimshian	Tsimshian	Tsimshian
GK	Gitksan (Kispiyox division)	Nass-Gitksan	Tsimshian	Tsimshian
HM	Massett or northern Haida	Haida	Haida	Haida
HS	Skidegate or southern Haida	Haida	Haida	Haida
LS	Sanyakwan	Tlingit	Tlingit	Tlingit
LC	Chilkat	Tlingit	Tlingit	Tlingit

and 1937. We extracted data relative to seventeen village groups located on the western side of Vancouver Island and along the length of the coast of British Columbia (figure 10.1). The names and linguistic affiliations (Thompson and Kinkade 1990) of the groups are shown in box 10.2.

Linguistically, the Northwest Coast is highly fragmented, being the second most (after California) linguistically diverse region of native North America (Thompson and Kinkade 1990). Despite their linguistic diversity, the many groups of the region are collectively distinctive (Suttles 1990). Their cultural repertoire largely represents adaptation to the region's mild climate, its temperate rainforest, and its rich marine life (Drucker 1955, 1965). The economy was highly dependent on fishing, especially for salmon, and the hunting of sea mammals. Woodworking technology was highly developed.

The culture area is fairly well bounded on the inland side by mountains (Suttles 1990), and given the difficulties posed by inland travel, travel by

Figure 10.1
Locations of Northwest Coast Indigenous Communities

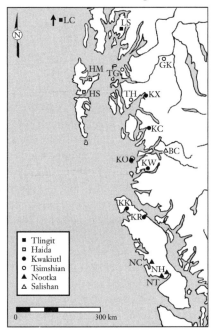

(See Box 10.2 for names and linguistic affiliation.)

canoe was the most viable means of linking one village to another (Kirk 1986). The head of a local kin group held important economic and ritual position, but there is no evidence that in prehistoric times there existed an overriding political authority linking the many autonomous villages. Social ranking based on a combination of birth and wealth was validated through formal gift-giving ceremonies known as *potlatches*. Although the level of craft specialization is not well known, trade was an important part of life. The household was the main economic unit, and it was this localized kin group that controlled access to resources and all forms of property (Ames and Maschner 1999). The concept of exclusive property rights in land and places of economic importance was highly developed, and marriage partners were often preferentially selected from within the tribe or extended family in order to retain these and other hereditary privileges (Drucker 1955).

Branching versus Blending

Cladistic methods were employed to investigate the relative contributions of branching and blending processes among the seventeen tribelets. The branch-

ing origin of contemporary cultures was reconstructed on the principle that
like begets like. As an isolated outlier of Salishan stock, the Bella Coola (BC)
was each time selected as the outgroup to root the tree. The "best fit" tree for
the data was selected using parsimony methods. Tests were performed using
PAUP* (Swofford 1998).

After we generated best-fit trees for twenty-two traits, it was readily apparent that both branching and blending processes had affected transmission and
cultural diversity. In short, degree of fit between tree model and data varied
considerably. The full scope of processes affecting these assemblages is detailed elsewhere (Mace 2003; Mace and Jordan n.d.). Our interest here is in
outlining a method for identifying the upper scale for coherent units of culture. Within Boyd et al.'s (1997) range of cultural models, this poor fit of tree
to data suggests that blending is eroding cultural lineages, making the formation of cultural cores impossible. We stress that both blending and branching
processes are important factors in cultural evolution, although we are interested here in detecting and accounting for the conditions that might favor the
transmission of cores.

We then selected the six cultural subsets that had the closest fit to the
branching-tree model: structures, dress and adornment, musical instruments,
potlatch, marriage, and female rituals. These were grouped in terms of material
and social-cultural attributes as in box 10.3. Phylogenetic trees are shown in
figures 10.2–10.7.

The main branching of the cultural trees frequently isolates a culturally
distinct northern subarea. The Tlingit, Haida, and Tsimshian speaking groups,
together with the most northerly Wakashan speakers, are closely related in
terms of variation in their structures, dress and adornment, musical instruments, marriage customs, and female rituals. Progressive bifurcation is less
typical of these more northerly tribes, which share many cultural attributes.
The bushlike origin of various cultural assemblages is probably indicative of
the intensity of social interaction among the groups, including the exchange
of goods, concepts, and even people.

Box 10.3
Summary Details of Social and Material-Culture Assemblages Investigated

Material Culture	Social Culture
Structures: materials, form, and internal features of dwelling houses, storehouses, and sweathouses	*Potlatches:* practice and occasions marked by potlatches as well as by concepts of wealth and display
Dress and Adornment: materials used for clothing, how the hair is worn, body ornaments, mutilation, and personal care	*Marriage:* ceremony, rules of residence, and types of marriage
Musical Instruments: variation in drums, rattles, and wind instruments	*Female Rituals:* puberty observances and menstrual customs

Clan alignment observed among the Tsimshian, Tlingit, and Haida for the purposes of intermarriage (Drucker 1955, 1965; Suttles 1990) and the concomitant shifts in population units back and forth across linguistic boundaries are likely mechanisms of cultural blending. The intensity of interaction among these groups has resulted in a distinctly northern community of culture; farther to the south the various groups behave more like cultural isolates. Hostilities between more distant tribes potentially posed a barrier to the more widespread diffusion of certain cultural attributes, and warfare and slave raiding, sometimes conducted over distances of over 600 kilometers, was endemic to the Northwest Coast by the time Europeans arrived (Kirk 1986).

The Nootka are distinct in terms of their potlatches, female rituals, and dress and adornment, suggesting their relative cultural isolation. Bifurcating lineages characterize the evolution of structures and marriage, especially among the groups of Vancouver Island, and the branching pattern among these traits for the southern Kwakiutl and Nootka is almost identical, suggesting that together these cultural assemblages constitute a larger cultural package.

Figure 10.2
Phylogenetic Tree for Structures

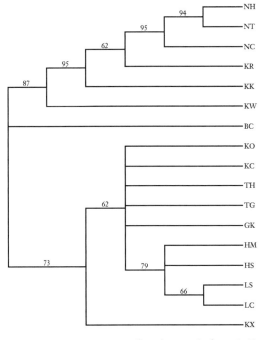

Consistency Index = 0.43

Analysis of Structures

There is a definite north-south regional pattern to structural styles (Drucker 1955, 1965). The Wikeno (KW), together with those groups located on Vancouver Island, form a distinct clade characterized by progressive bifurcation (figure 10.2). The branching pattern of these southernmost groups is strongly influenced by geographic proximity. Farther to the north, origins of descent are more bushlike, suggesting that processes of cultural blending have been significant. The bootstrap figures are consistently high, especially for the evolution of the southernmost groups.

Analysis of Dress and Adornment

The Bella Bella (KO), together with the more northerly groups, form a distinct clade (figure 10.3). The Haida, Tlingit, Tsimshian, and Xaisla (KX) are culturally closely related and are also closely related to the Haihais (KC) and Bella Bella (KO). The Nootka and Southern Kwakiutl form distinct cultural lineages in terms of their dress and adornment. In historic times, facets of dress and adornment signaled wider group affiliation and corresponded to regional networks of intermarriage. Marriageable women among groups farther to the

Figure 10.3
Phylogenetic Tree for Dress and Adornment

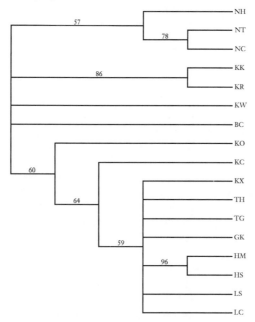

Consistency Index = 0.34

Figure 10.4
Phylogenetic Tree for Musical Instruments

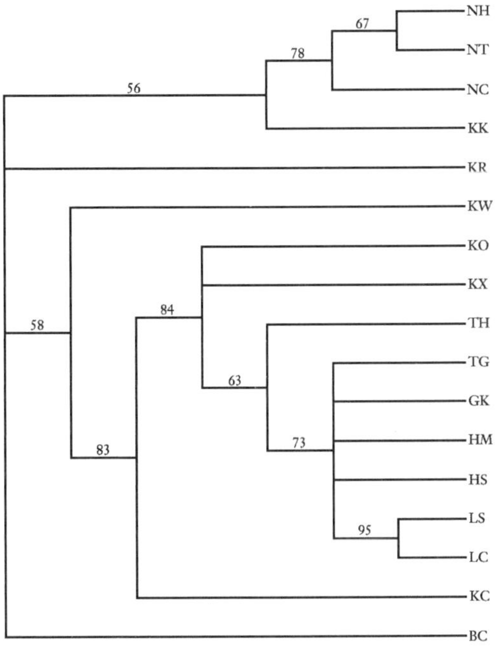

Consistency Index = 0.57

north had pierced lips for wearing labrets (lip plugs), whereas various styles of head deformation were practiced farther to the south (Suttles 1990).

Analysis of Musical Instruments

The consistency index for this tree (figure 10.4) is relatively high (0.57), which suggests that the data are consistent with the branching-tree model. Musical instruments were part and parcel of the system of kin-based privileges (Kirk 1986). Intermarriage would diffuse these privileges more widely, and on the tree this would be represented by multiple branches from a single node, as is the case among the northernmost groups, which are often related within the space of a couple of generations. The Nootka, together with the Koskimo (KK), form a separate clade, suggesting their relative cultural isolation.

Analysis of Potlatches

The Nootka, the centrally located Kwakiutl, the more southerly Kwakiutl speakers, and the more northerly groups comprise four distinct clades with respect to the potlatch (figure 10.5).

Figure 10.5
Phylogenetic Tree for Potlatches

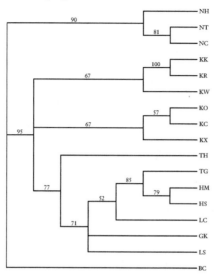

Consistency Index = 0.53

Figure 10.6
Phylogenetic Tree for Marriage

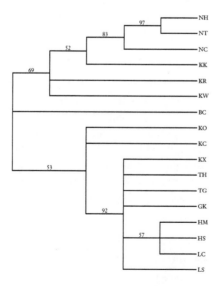

Consistency Index = 0.41

Analysis of Marriage

With respect to marriage, groups from the Wikeno (KW) south form a distinct clade characterized by progressive bifurcation, whereas the branching origin of more northerly cultures is more bushlike (figure 10.6). The branching pattern for the southernmost groups is almost identical to that seen with respect to structures.

Analysis of Female Rituals

Nootka speakers (the Hupachisat, the Tsishaat, and the Clayoquot) are distinct in terms of their female rituals and form a distinct clade with a high degree of probability (figure 10.7). Similarities arising through processes of cultural blending are relatively commonplace farther to the north, and the Tsimshian, Haida, and Tlingit are related within a couple of generations.

Degree of Association among Cultural Lineages, Geographic Distance, and Language

Were any of the cultural assemblages passed on in close association with language? How did distance constrain transmission? The search for a best-fit

Figure 10.7
Phylogenetic Tree for Female Observances

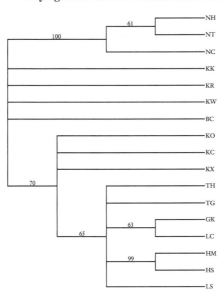

Consistency Index = 0.42

tree can be constrained by the hypothesis that transmission occurred in tandem with language, or in close association with distance. The Kishino-Hasegawa test (Kishino and Hasegawa 1989) adapted for PAUP* 4.0 (Swofford 1998) uses tree length (parsimony) as an optimality criteria for testing whether best-fit and constrained trees are significantly different. If they are, then the null hypothesis—here, for example, that linguistic affinity accounts for all the variation in structures—can be rejected. Note that this method tests only for perfect correlations between constraint and data trees. Looser associations— historical lineages tracking each other with significant but less than perfect fidelity—will not be identified.

Constraint trees for language and geographic distance were constructed manually in MacClade 4.05 (Maddison and Maddison 2000). The language classification of Thompson and Kinkade (1990) formed the basis of the language tree. For distance, measures of "as the crow flies" between groups were converted into a distance matrix, which was then converted into an average-linkage dendrogram. These two trees were then exported to PAUP* to create the constraint trees. This meant that the search for a best-fit cultural tree had to proceed within the structure defined by the new trees.

Test results are shown in table 10.1. None of the cultural trees is identical to the language tree of Northwest Coast groups. Partial correlation Mantel tests confirm that language is only a relatively weak influence on cultural variation (Mace and Jordan n.d.). Moreover, none of the trees fits well with distance, suggesting that proximity did not influence transmission. These results indicate that there are no close correlations among distance, culture, and language.

Are any of the cultural trees identical to one another, indicating association by descent? The search for a best-fit tree is constrained to fit within the structure of another, in this case cultural, tree. Degrees of fit between best-fit tree and constrained best-fit trees can then be measured statistically to test whether, for example, clothing was passed along with musical instruments. Repeated searches for a best-fit tree for structures were constrained by the best-fit trees for the other variables. When these trees were compared, all were significantly different to the best-fit tree for structures. This indicates that the branching model for structures is significantly different.

The procedure was repeated systematically for the other cultural assemblages. The search for a best-fit tree for dress was constrained by four other cultural trees (music, potlatch, marriage, and female rituals); music was constrained by three other trees (potlatch, marriage, and female rituals); potlatch was constrained by two trees (marriage and female rituals); and marriage was constrained by a single tree (female rituals). Taken together, these test results indicate that all the trees in all the tests were significantly different. In other words, none of the cultural trees had tracked another with perfect fidelity. We can therefore reject the hypothesis that association by de-

Table 10.1
Results of the Kishino-Hasegawa Test on Trees Constrained by Language and Geographic Distance

	Tree number	Length	CI [a]	RI [b]	Difference	K-H test [c]
Structures	2	183	0.46	0.64	0	Same
Constrained by language	1	215	0.40	0.52	32	Different
Constrained by distance	2	225	0.38	0.48	42	Different
Dress/adornment	2	292	0.39	0.51	0	Same
Constrained by language	1	326	0.34	0.42	34	Different
Constrained by distance	1	321	0.36	0.44	29	Different
Musical instruments	2	65	0.60	0.74	0	Same
Constrained by language	3	83	0.46	0.56	18	Different
Constrained by distance	6	86	0.45	0.53	21	Different
Potlatches	2	98	0.55	0.77	0	Same
Constrained by language	2	122	0.44	0.64	24	Different
Constrained by distance	2	131	0.41	0.60	33	Different
Marriage	1	143	0.45	0.65	0	Same
Constrained by language	1	170	0.38	0.62	27	Different
Constrained by distance	2	163	0.40	0.56	20	Different
Female rituals	4	239	0.47	0.56	0	Same
Constrained by language	1	259	0.39	0.50	20	Different
Constrained by distance	6	265	0.43	0.48	26	Different

Note: Constructed by stepwise addition, swapping on best only; $p < 0.05$; Bella Coola as outgroup; constraint tree for distance was a single-linkage dendrogram calculated in SPSS; language tree from Thompson and Kinkade (1990).

a CI = consistency index.
b RI = retention index.
c K-H test = Kishino-Hasegawa test.

scent has proceeded in its strictest sense—that different cultural assemblages have, in some way, been bound together so that branching of one assemblage automatically equates to the branching of all the associated assemblages. However, the fact that all these tree topologies are not identical does not mean that associations between them are no stronger than one would expect by chance. If topologies are similar, but not necessarily identical, then there might still be some mileage in the case for the existence of more loosely associated cultural cores.

Is Association among Trees Random?

There are several means of testing for overall tree similarity rather than the kinds of strict tree difference that the Kishino-Hasegawa test measures. Here we employ COMPONENT 2.0, written by Page (1993). Unlike PAUP*, the software does not infer trees from data but rather requires that pre-existing trees be entered into the program, after which comparison methods can be applied. Comparison of trees may employ a measure of similarity between two trees; the technique we employed represents the two trees as sets of simpler structures and then uses a measure of similarity between sets. We used the triplet, as this is the smallest possible informative subtree on a rooted tree, for which we again used the Bella Coola (BC) as the outgroup. A triplet is the rooted analogue of a quartet. COMPONENT uses an algorithm based on Douchette's (1985, cited in Page 1993) algorithm for quartets.

COMPONENT also generates random trees for use in, and as the basis for, statistical tests. The program uses a uniform random-number generator based on Schrage's (1979) FORTRAN implementation of the linear-congruence method. Measures of similarity between trees can then be compared with similarities between a set of random trees. If the similarity between two data trees—for example, structures and language—is closer than between random trees, then we can assume that their similarity is greater than one would expect as a result of chance alone (the higher the figure, the more different the trees). The results (table 10.2) show two distinct trends: random associations among culture, language, and distance; and significant associations by descent.

The first trend is based on the fact that the association between the topologies of many trees is no closer than one would expect by chance (triplets figures are within the range of values from 1,000 random trees (174 to 465 [table 10.2]). For example, comparing the dress and adornment and potlatch trees shows that 190 triplets are resolved differently in one tree or the other but not in both. This is within the range of triplets numbers measuring differences among the 1,000 randomly generated trees. Similarly, the value of the tree for dress and language is over 174, suggesting a random association. Most cultural assemblages have only random association with language, although there are some weak similarities between the trees for language and potlatch. The fact that Haida speakers and speakers of Kwakiutl dialects are sometimes shown

Table 10.2
Results of Triplets Tests for Tree Similarity

	Dress/ adornment	Female rituals	Marriage	Musical instruments	Potlatches	Structures	Language
Distance	223	213	225	248	272	252	245
Language	202	258	204	240	148	202	—
Structures	40	153	57	130	208	—	—
Potlatches	190	207	217	159	—	—	—
Musical instruments	110	79	131	—	—	—	—
Marriage	31	134	—	—	—	—	—
Female rituals	123	—	—	—	—	—	—

Note: 1000 similarities among random trees (mean = 372.25; SD = 34.12; minimum = 174; maximum = 465).

to be cultural sisters means that similarity in terms of potlatch is slightly more compatible with the language tree than are other cultural assemblages, but many major discrepancies remain.

Overall, there is little congruence between the historical descent relationships that can be established between languages and cultural assemblages. In fact, the level of cultural homogeneity of the study area is far higher than one might at first suppose, given the high linguistic diversity of the region, especially in the north. Indeed, the high linguistic diversity of the northernmost groups probably accounts for why there is only random association between language and geographic distance.

Interestingly, there is only random association between all cultural assemblages and geographic distance. Certainly cultural variation along the Northwest Coast is not geographically continuous. For cultural assemblages the main branching is often between the north and south. Nevertheless, one might assume that distance was a significant factor affecting the distribution of cultural lineages. Regional-interaction systems are a known feature of the culture area, and there is near agreement in the anthropological literature as to the composition and extent of a northern subarea (Suttles 1990). It appears that (1) the clustering of cultural elements causing the cultural dendrograms to be bushlike, especially among the more northerly tribes, and (2) the strong north-south culture divide reduce the fidelity with which the distance tree tracks the evolution of cultural assemblages, obscuring the relationship between culture and distance.

The second set of results is more interesting: several trees suggest that lineages to a certain degree have tracked one another through time. For example, the triplets score for marriage and dress and adornment is only 31—the lowest score on the table. This strongly indicates association by descent and suggests that similar factors have affected the transmission of the two lineages. Covariation between marriage rituals and dress and adornment fits well with what is known from the ethnography of the region. Variation in dress and adornment among women, for example, signaled their actual or potential participation in networks of intermarriage (Suttles 1990). By using these triplets measures it is possible to suggest that the topologies of trees for structure, dress, and marriage are most similar, with values between pairs being 31, 40, and 57 respectively. The branching pattern of structures and marriage among southernmost groups is almost identical. A second strong relationship links music and female rituals, with a score of 79. Other relationships between trees are less than by chance but less strong.

These results suggest the presence of both a loosely defined cultural core of assemblages associated by historical descent and a series of more independent cultural packages, each with an independent branching-descent history. However, the lack of complete congruence between the various cultural-assemblage trees suggests that there were no sharp cultural boundaries between each of the communities investigated.

Conclusions

We have attempted to identify the upper limit for coherent units of culture among seventeen communities of different linguistic affinity on the Northwest Coast. Employing methods drawn from evolutionary biology, including tests for co-speciation, we found that whereas there was no perfect association by descent among any of the cultural lineages, several lineages were associated quite closely, suggesting that similar sets of influences had affected their social transmission. Overall, then, we can state that there is a loosely defined cultural core, with certain characters being passed on in tandem.

Other assemblages have also been affected by branching patterns of descent, although theirs is an independent history unlinked to other lineages. Around these lineages we can detect the presence of cultural blending and innovation (the range of other cultural assemblages from Drucker [1950] that did not fit the tree model well and are not investigated here [but see Mace and Jordan n.d.]). Taken together, these factors point to the best model for cultural diversity on the Northwest Coast as being "culture as a hierarchically integrated system" (Boyd et al. 1997), so long as the closer association noted between several of the cultural lineages can be taken to represent a loosely defined cultural core.

However, despite our attempts to reconstruct the kinds of contexts that led to these observed patterns of cultural and linguistic diversity, we are always working backwards by reconstructing presumed historical associations, and then, by default, assuming that certain kinds of behavior were responsible for these patterns. The models we currently employ focus on broad-scale processes and the origins of regional-scale cultural diversity. Whereas human agency, innovation, individual interaction, and decision-making processes form central, albeit implied, mechanisms in these models, their operation is merely suggested through (cladistic) historical reconstructions of this kind.

As we look to the future of research on cultural transmission, it appears that the discipline is developing a coherent method, drawn primarily from evolutionary biology, for differentiating branching and blending contributions to transmission and for identifying the upper-scale limit for coherent units of culture. However, we believe that the new frontier of research lies in increasing our understanding of the social processes affecting the mode(s) of cultural transmission. Much recent work on transmission has an implicit emphasis on social learning, which has clear similarities with genetic transmission, rather than an emphasis on strategic contexts of social interactions that are the focus of anthropological inquiry.

In other words, we need to move beyond the initially inspiring deployment of the genetic analogy with culture. What people actually make in terms of pottery or the clothing they wear might depend less on what they learn/inherit and more on the kinds of actions they perform relative to a wider context characterized by socially sanctioned forms of interaction, innovation, and consumption. This means that at both the general and specific levels we need to know more about the range of living ethnographic contexts in which values and tastes are upheld, decisions are made, and certain kinds of transmission mechanisms and processes are encouraged.

New research is required in ethnographic contexts to connect, for example, the range of documented behaviors with outcomes that favor the formation of certain lineages or that blend and blur traditions across linguistic frontiers. This will require a greater empirical interest in the details of microscale processes as well as a consideration of the potential long-term outcomes of some of the day-to-day patterns of interactions observed in fieldwork. If we can develop a more coherent theory and method for linking specific behaviors to broader-scale outcomes, we might well be able to unite different and traditionally divergent spheres of anthropological research into a more holistic, ambitious, and socially grounded approach to cultural transmission.

Acknowledgments

This chapter develops and expands the insights of an unpublished M.A. thesis by Tom Mace carried out at the Institute of Archaeology and Prehistory, University College London. We thank Stephen Shennan for his insightful comments on this earlier work. We are grateful to Russell Gray for his suggestion to use the triplets measure to compare trees. In addition, Alex Bentley, Mark Collard, Clare Holden, Fiona Jordan, Stephen Shennan, and other members of the AHRB-funded Centre for the Evolutionary Analysis of Cultural Behaviour have all contributed to an exciting and dynamic research environment in which to pursue novel ideas and share ideas and discussions. During the period that this chapter was prepared, Peter Jordan was funded by a Leverhulme Trust Special Research Fellowship at University College London.

11

Cultural Transmission, Phylogenetics, and the Archaeological Record

Jelmer W. Eerkens, Robert L. Bettinger, and Richard McElreath

Phylogenetic studies of material culture (e.g., Jordan and Shennan 2003; Lyman and O'Brien 2000; O'Brien et al. 2001; O'Brien and Lyman 2002a, 2003a; Tehrani and Collard 2002) are gaining popularity in the anthropological sciences and are giving us new insights into the transmission of human culture in the past and present. But in their focus on phylogeny such studies tend to bypass extended discussion of the processes of transmission and modification that produce variability in the items of material culture. Yet as numerous anthropologists and others have discussed (e.g., Boyd and Richerson 1985; Cavalli-Sforza and Feldman 1981; Henrich 2001), cultural information can be passed on and modified in a multitude of ways. Surely, these different modes of transmission affect our ability to reconstruct and interpret phylogenetic trees.

Here we attempt to fill this vacuum in applications of phylogenetics to material culture by examining how well such analyses are able to reconstruct the descent of traits inherited through different cultural-transmission systems. In particular, we are interested in transmission systems of the kind discussed and defined by Boyd and Richerson (1985). We use computer simulation to assess the effects of different forms of cultural transmission on cultural phylogenies and evaluate these concepts to a dataset comprising projectile points from the Great Basin of North America.

Transmission Processes

Before describing our simulations, we briefly define the transmission systems modeled here. "Guided variation" entails transmission of information from a social model to a recipient, who then experiments with that information in search of a better or an optimal character state. Traits are acquired and modified individually in piecemeal fashion. For example, an individual might initially learn how to make a projectile point from his father, but later improve techniques of manufacture or selection of raw materials based on his own experience. "Conformist transmission" involves cases in which individuals survey the social-model pool and find the most common attribute or attribute state and adopt it. Again, this is done piecemeal for different attributes. In this form of transmission, an individual making an arrow point would seek to identify the most common raw material, the most common flaking tool, the most common point length, and so on. All of these traits would be combined during process of point construction. "Indirectly biased transmission" involves cases in which individuals survey the social-model pool and select a single social model on the basis of an indicator trait and then copy the entire cultural repertoire of this model. Here traits are not adopted one at a time but together as a package. For example, success in some communities might be judged by the number of surviving children. An individual might preferentially imitate the beliefs and behaviors of members of the community with the most children over the age of, say, five.

There are good reasons to suspect that all these potential transmission mechanisms exist in the real world. First, theoretical analyses suggest that no general cultural-learning strategy is optimal in all circumstances. Instead, social and ecological contexts strongly influence the efficacy of particular models and the payoffs that result from integrating their behaviors and beliefs into one's cultural repertoire (Boyd and Richerson 1985; Henrich and Boyd 1998). While social learning may have a low cost, it sometimes pays to ignore the behavior of others and rely on individual learning, or guided variation, to acquire behavior (Boyd and Richerson 1985; Rogers 1988). Second, evidence from psychology and other social sciences suggests that people employ a diversity of learning strategies, including the three outlined above. Bandura (1973, 1977), for example, found that people select models based on cues such as observed payoffs, prestige, and specific similarity between themselves and the model.

Psychologists (e.g., Asch 1952, 1955; Milgram 1974; Moscovici 1985; Rock 1990; Wilder 1977) have also observed a tendency for individuals to conform to the beliefs or behaviors of a majority. In addition, psychologists and economists working on individual choice and judgment have studied how people apply experience to modify existing beliefs and preferences, providing evidence for a mechanism that will lead to guided variation in natural circumstances. Lastly, evidence from the literature on the diffusion of innovations, such as hybrid corn or computers, suggests that people employ different imitation and learning strategies (Henrich 2001; Henrich and Boyd 2001; Rogers 1988), including conformity, indirect biases, and guided variation.

Simulation

We used a Microsoft Excel spreadsheet to model these transmission systems. Our simulations deliberately minimize the number of rules and initial conditions that govern transmission to expose the general patterns that emerge when a few simple traits are transmitted by simple rules in a relatively small population over a small number of generations. Our assumptions are highly unrealistic; they are certainly not intended to capture any specific real-world situation. However, the simulations define a simple transmission system with enough detail to directly observe how the mechanisms of transmission affect phylogenetic reconstruction. We think that more-complicated simulations would likely arrive at the same conclusions, but with much less clarity.

Each of our simulations models a population of individuals. The first generation of each population consists of a single individual, whom we refer to as the "founding father." This founding father creates two offspring (the second generation), each of whom creates two offspring of his own (the third generation), and so on until we reach the sixth generation, in which there are thirty-two individuals. In its basic form this simulation is akin to asexual reproduction. Each individual is characterized by four traits, so in each simulation there are 124 trait transmissions: $1 + 2 + 4 + 8 + 16 = 31$ parent-to-offspring transfers down the tree, each entailing four traits ($4 \times 31 = 124$).

Each of the four traits can take one of ten different states, coded in our simulations with numbers between 0 and 9. One way to envision this is as people who wear four articles of clothing (e.g., shirt, shoes, trousers, socks), each of which comes in ten possible colors. We follow that analogy in the discussions below. Two different types of models, directed and undirected, are presented. In the undirected models, each of the ten color states is equal in value, and there is no inherent ordering to the character states (i.e., the states are nominal variables). In the directed models, the ten states are ordered from 0 to 9, with 0 being the lowest and least desirable color and 9 the highest and most desirable state (i.e., the traits are ordered, integer-scale variables).

During transmission, one of three things will happen. First, with a pre-defined frequency, referred to as the "error rate," individuals miscopy the character state of their parents and randomly generate a new character state. This introduces heritable variation that is tracked during sequences of transmission events through the simulation run. For consistency, the copy-error rate was set at 5 percent for all runs. The introduction of error was necessary to track the transmission of heritable variation. Second, individuals employ an inheritance system to acquire character states from other individuals in the population. Inheritance between individuals occurs at a set frequency that is defined as the "cultural transmission rate." Third, if there is neither copy error nor cultural transmission, individuals simply inherit and keep the character state of their parent. Only one inheritance system was simulated at a time. That is, within a simulation run, individuals use one and only one mode of transmission—they cannot use guided variation for one trait and conformist transmission for another. In reality, individuals probably employ many mechanisms at once, even for the same traits, but our aim here is to illustrate the consequences of the transmission mechanism on phylogenetic reconstruction, so we keep the simulations simple.

In each simulation we know exactly how traits are transmitted and how populations are related to one another. In this study, our interest is in determining how well phylogenetic analyses are able to reconstruct an inheritance tree when traits are transmitted under the three systems of inheritance. To make this determination we used trait data from the sixth generation of each simulation run in a common cladistics package, PAUP* 4.0 (Swofford 1998). All thirty-two individuals in this generation were treated as independent terminal taxa even if they exhibited the same set of traits. We examined general trends by slowly increasing the amount of transmission that was allowed to take place under a particular inheritance system—guided variation, conformist transmission, and indirect bias—from 0 percent to 100 percent, recording the resulting inheritance tree (i.e., the tree directly created from the simulation data from every generation) and reconstructed tree (i.e., the tree produced using only data from the final generation).

Guided variation—inheritance followed by experimentation and learning—was simulated as follows. For each of the four traits, a random number between 0 and 99 was generated. If this random number fell within the range of the error rate (5 percent), a color between 0 and 9 was randomly assigned to that trait. If the random number fell within the range of cultural transmission, the trait was transmitted by undirected or directed guided variation. In the undirected model, where no trait value was recognizably better than any other, this was simulated by generating a random number between 0 and 9 corresponding to trait color. In the directed model, the parent trait value was raised by 1 with 90 percent chance and raised by 2 with 10 percent chance, up to the maximum value of 9. Thus, the undirected model simulates the outcome of experiments where all outcomes (trait values) are equally valuable or desirable by randomly generating a new trait value, whereas the directed model simulates experiments that lead to trait improvement by slowly pushing trait states toward the maximum value of 9. Finally, if the random number fell outside the combined ranges of error and cultural transmission, the value of the parent was adopted without change (neither copy error nor guided variation occurred). Figure 11.1 presents a flowchart depicting the simulation.

The simulation of conformist transmission operates in the same way. Again, for each trait a random number between 0 and 99 was generated. If this number fell within the range of copy error, a new color was randomly generated. If it fell within the range of conformist transmission, individuals surveyed the previous generation (the generation of their parent) and adopted the modal

Figure 11.1
Flowchart for Guided-Variation Model

For each of 4 characters (traits):

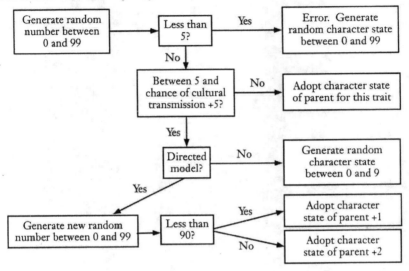

color displayed by individuals in that generation. If neither random copy error nor conformist transmission occurred, the color of the parent was adopted. Because conformist transmission is directed by definition toward modal behaviors, we did not model an undirected version. Figure 11.2 presents a flowchart for our simulation of conformist transmission.

Indirectly biased transmission was modeled slightly differently. In addition to the four character states, each individual also possessed an indicator trait (varying between 1 and 4) that informed the individual which locus (trait) to inspect when selecting a social model. In the undirected model, each individual also possessed a preference trait (varying between 0 and 9) that informed him of the value of the indicator trait that was to be sought in a social model. The indicator and preference traits were transmitted vertically from parent to offspring with a 5 percent copy error. Transmission copy error was modeled by generating a random number between 1 and 4 for a miscopied indicator trait and between 0 and 9 for a miscopied preference trait.

A random number was generated for each individual to determine whether all four traits would be obtained as a package by indirect bias. If so, in the undirected model individuals consulted their indicator trait, surveyed the previous generation for that specific trait, and if any individual in that generation displayed a value within 1 of their own preference trait, they copied all

Figure 11.2
Flowchart for Conformist-Transmission Model

For each of 4 characters (traits):

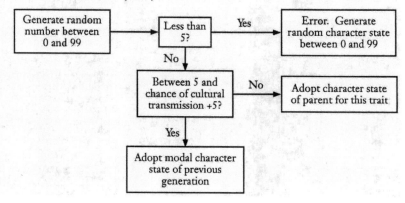

four traits of that individual perfectly, that is, copied their entire color scheme. If no individual in the preferred range was present, individuals simply adopted the full set of parental values. In the directed model, on the other hand, individuals consulted their indicator trait, surveyed the previous generation for that trait, selected an individual with the maximum value of that trait (at random, when two or more individuals displayed the maximum value), and copied all four traits of that individual perfectly. Figure 11.3 presents a flowchart for how we simulated indirectly biased transmission.

Results

We were interested in what happens to the pattern of inheritance when the amounts of guided variation, conformist transmission, and indirectly biased transmission are increased. More specifically, we wanted to know how much phylogenetic information would be retained in the terminal taxa as this occurred. Note that the data structure was constant across all simulations: thirty-two individuals (terminal taxa), each displaying four traits that can take any one of ten different states. The similarity in data structure allows us to compare results from the three transmission systems. The stochasticity built into all our simulations by the use of random numbers in decision making will generate variability. This obviously obscures patterns of central tendency but is highly informative about the process of transmission and the feasibility of constructing phylogenetic trees under the simulated conditions. Accordingly, in the discussion below we focus on both central tendency and variation. We report and compare two statistics reported by PAUP* across the different simula-

Figure 11.3
Flowchart for Indirectly Biased-Transmission Model

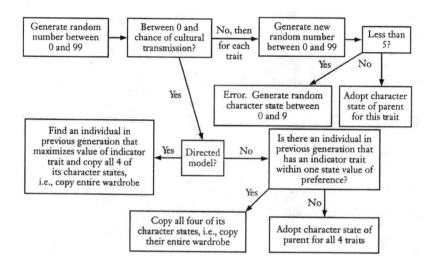

tions—tree length (TL) and consistency index (CI)—which are strongly and inversely correlated. Smaller TLs correspond to higher CIs. Both statistics help describe the amount or strength of the phylogenetic signal within a particular simulation run.

Guided Variation

The amount of guided variation (t) was increased from 0 percent (y = 0) to 95 percent (y = 0.95) in small increments (recall that the remaining 5 percent corresponds to copying error). Figure 11.4 shows the CI for the simulations for the undirected model. As the figure shows, when individuals never use guided variation (t = 0) they produce very consistent and simple trees with strong phylogenetic signals. Only random errors contribute heritable variability to the tree. At the other extreme, when individuals always use guided variation (t = 0.95), which means they always experiment with new colors (or make copy errors, which amounts to the same thing), they produce completely random trait sets with no phylogenetic signal. At this extreme (t = 0.95), CI values hover near 0.30, and TL approaches 120, indicating very long trees. However, experimentation removes phylogenetic signal long before guided variation becomes this common. As shown in Figure 11.4, this happens when guided variation accounts for 40% of all transmission events.

This result was expected. As people experiment more and more without direction (randomly), they produce more and more variation, which becomes

Figure 11.4
Consistency-Index Values with Increasing Strength of Undirected
Guided Variation

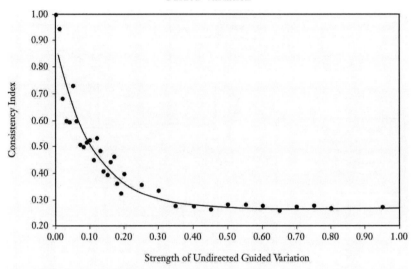

harder and harder to capture in a short, simple tree. This means that as undirected guided variation becomes more important, cladistic analysis becomes
less and less useful in reconstructing inheritance systems, simply because less
and less information is being transmitted across generations. The inheritance
"signal" is quickly lost due to variability from experimentation.

A different result obtains when we make individual experimentation directional. Figure 11.5 shows that as in the undirected version, when the strength
of directed guided variation is low, CI values are initially high, and as the
strength of guided variation (and experimentation) increases, CI values fall,
indicating weakening of the phylogenetic signal. However, at the point where
the undirected CI values hit their minimum (roughly at 35 percent guided
variation), the directed CI values begin to rise again. Although more and more
people are experimenting, they increasingly arrive at the same conclusion,
thereby decreasing overall variation. In other words, all individuals begin to
adopt the same character traits, much as they did when there was little experimentation and mostly vertical transmission.

Using cladistics, we would interpret this as a better phylogenetic signal
because of the higher CI and lower TL. Note, however, that this "better" signal
is not really the result of vertical transmission of heritable information. It is
really individuals separately arriving at the same optimal trait combination
through experimentation—the convergent evolution of analogous traits as a
result of the environment. In a variable environment in which different traits
are optimal in different places, strong guided variation will destroy phyloge-

Figure 11.5
Consistency-Index Values with Increasing Strength of Directed
Guided Variation

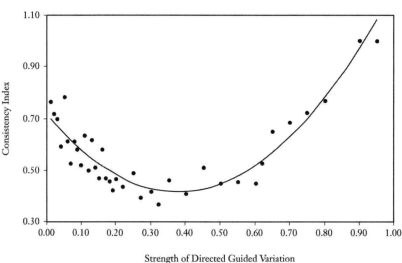

Strength of Directed Guided Variation

netic signals, just as strong natural selection destroys phylogenetic signals in genetic data. When a strong attractor erases variation, phylogenetic information is destroyed in any system. This observation points out the weakness of using CI (and TL) to estimate the "strength" of the phylogenetic signal in a data set. Other statistics are much better in this regard (see McElreath 1997), which we aim to employ in future work.

Conformist Transmission

We obtain still a different result when individuals acquire traits by conformist transmission. In contrast to guided variation, where CI values decrease (at least initially) as the force of transmission increases, with conformist transmission CI values increase as the force of transmission increases. CI values also vary much more around this basic trajectory. When conformist transmission is low, CI values are intermediate, between 0.65 and 0.75. When conformist transmission exceeds 50 percent, CI values consistently exceed 0.85. These trends are shown in figure 11.6.

This result was not unexpected, in that conformist transmission tends to decrease variation, at least within communities (Boyd and Richerson 1985; Henrich and Boyd 1998). As more and more individuals use conformist transmission to obtain traits, these individuals look more and more alike, which greatly increases the overall phylogenetic signal displayed by a population. The increased variability around this mean tendency is the result of the poten-

Figure 11.6
Consistency-Index Values with Increasing Strength
of Conformist Transmission

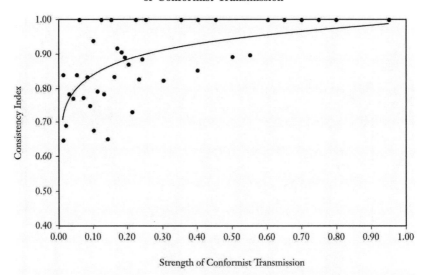

tial for novel recombination of traits when some are inherited vertically and others are acquired by conformist transmission, which results in the creation of new taxa (or color schemes in our simulations). As the strength of conformist transmission increases, the potential for novel recombination decreases, and the variability around the regression line decreases (right side of figure 11.6). Overall, in comparison to guided variation, conformist transmission tends to preserve a phylogenetic signal within terminal taxa. It follows, then, that traits acquired by conformist transmission are more suited to cladistic analysis than traits acquired through guided variation.

Indirect Bias

The undirected and directed simulations of indirectly biased transmission behave much like those of conformist transmission, but there is more variation around central tendencies. In both models as the strength of indirectly biased transmission increases, CI values increase, from around 0.7, when there is no indirect bias, to 1.0 as the frequency of indirect bias approaches 95 percent. This result is shown in figures 11.7 and 11.8. As with conformist transmission, CI values increase directly with the amount of indirect bias because indirect bias is in general a variation-reducing process. Because indirect bias does not generate any novel trait-value combinations, unless copy error is built into the system, TL will decrease, and CI values will increase monotonically as indirect bias increases.

Figure 11.7
Consistency-Index Values with Increasing Strength of Undirected Indirect Bias

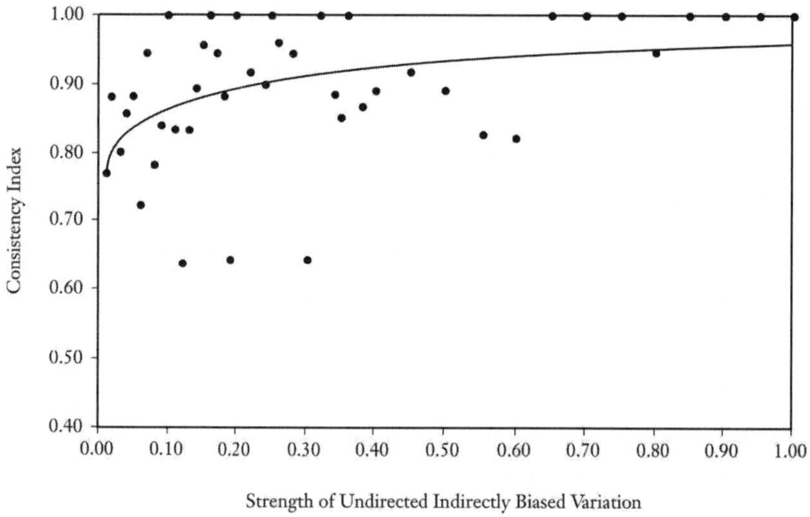

Strength of Undirected Indirectly Biased Variation

The relatively high variation around the regression lines in figures 11.7 and 11.8 is a result of these indicator- and preference-trait copy errors. The errors generate subsets of individuals whose color schemes are identical but whose indicator and preference traits are different because some were copied incorrectly. These random copy errors in the indicator and preference traits force sets of individuals who should have chosen the same social models to copy different social models. Whenever random copy errors generate significant within-generation variation in the indicator and preference traits, phylogenetic trees will become longer and more complicated. On the other hand, if we remove the 5 percent error rate built into the transmission of the indicator and preference traits, so that all individuals have the same value for these traits, indirectly biased transmission forces everyone to choose the same social model. If we use PAUP* to generate trees using data from these simulations, the amount of variation around the regression line is much lower, as expected. Overall, our studies suggest that indirectly biased transmission tends to preserve a phylogenetic signal as well or better than conformist transmission and better than guided variation.

Summary of Results

These analyses lead us to several observations about the possibilities for cladistic analysis in archaeology. First and most importantly, some transmission systems preserve phylogenetic signatures better than others. Phylogenetic signals are most likely to be retained in collections of archaeological traits that were culturally transmitted in packages by indirect bias, for example. Conversely, phylogenetic signatures are the least likely to be retained in trait complexes whose individual components were acquired one at a time (not as packages) by guided variation, particularly in instances characterized by experimentation over many generations. The phylogenetic signal will be stronger, and retained longer, if the individually transmitted components of such complexes are acquired by conformist transmission, but the signal will be weaker and shorter-lived when trait packages are obtained by indirectly biased transmission. Apart from this, the utility of cladistic analysis will decrease for traits that are subject to external (noncultural) evolutionary forces that lead to convergence, especially where guided variation is strong and to a lesser degree where indirectly biased transmission is strong. In the following section, we compare these generalizations against the results of phylogenetic analyses of projectile points from two areas—Owens Valley and Monitor Valley—in the western Great Basin of North America.

Application to Great Basin Projectile Points

Approximately half of the described projectile points in Owens Valley and Monitor Valley belong to either the Rosegate or Elko series. Rosegate represents the introduction and first phase of bow and arrow use, from roughly A.D. 600 to A.D. 1300. Rosegate replaced dart points belonging to the Elko series, which are similar in shape but larger and older than Rosegate; in Owens and Monitor Valleys Elko-series points date from roughly 1500 B.C. to A.D. 600.

Previous analyses (Bettinger and Eerkens 1997, 1999) of these two kinds of points led us to argue that Owens Valley Rosegate points were the product of a transmission system that depended heavily on experimentation—guided variation or something similar—that governed the introduction of bow-and-arrow technology in that area. Conversely, we argued that Monitor Valley Rosegate points were part of a transmission system characterized by conformist or indirectly biased transmission. Our simulations imply that if these things are true, Monitor Valley points should display a stronger phylogenetic signal than Owens Valley points.

To facilitate comparison, we quantified the point assemblages in much the same way as our simulated data. We sampled thirty-two points more or less at random from each area, giving preference to specimens that were independently dated by obsidian hydration in Owens Valley (where obsidian is common) and by stratigraphy in Monitor Valley (where obsidian is rare). For each point, we recorded four attributes that previous research suggested were governed by more or less neutral selective forces: length/width ratio, basal width, proximal shoulder angle, and thickness. Each attribute was rescaled into ten states (0 to 9) by subtracting the minimum value across the entire sample for each attribute from its observed value, dividing by the range for that type in that region, multiplying by 9, and dropping the values to the right of the decimal point. This mathematical manipulation transformed each projectile-point measurement from a continuous number (in centimeters or degrees) to an integer that varies between 0 for the lowest observed value and 9 for the largest.

The PAUP* results are presented in table 11.1 (rows 1 and 2). The results of our simulations of completely random and perfectly transmitted data are listed for comparison (rows 3 and 4). As can be seen, in both regions CI values are only slightly higher, and TL values only slightly lower, than the results obtained from random data, suggesting a negligibly small phylogenetic signal. Because our previous work suggested that guided variation dominated the transmission of projectile-point technology in Owens Valley, we expected this type of result for the Owens Valley points. That work, however, suggested that point transmission in Monitor Valley was dominated by conformist or indirectly biased transmission, which should have produced a stronger phylogenetic signal, but did not.

Further, although there was strict consensus of trees in all cases, these reconstructed trees do not predict point chronology. Hydration readings (Owens Valley) and stratigraphic positions (Monitor Valley) do not segregate by tree branch. Within these two regions at least, point morphology does not appear to vary over time in a way that it should under cultural transmission. The lack of tree-time correspondence is not an artifact of our continuous-scale to ordinal-scale (between 0 and 9) data transformation. For example, rescaling the data in units of standard deviation (so that each character state expresses the number of standard deviations between an individual observation and its mean) produces a narrower range of character states, between 0 and 5 in most cases. This results in a predictable increase in the CI (table 11.1, rows 5 and 6) as well as in the production of nearly identical trees. In short, changing the way data are quantified does not change how PAUP* reconstructs trees for these data sets.

Table 11.1
PAUP* Results on Rosegate Points from Owens and Monitor Valleys, California

	Data Set	CI	TL
1	Owens Valley Rosegate	0.33	109
2	Monitor Valley Rosegate	0.35	104
3	**Random Data**	**0.27**	**132**
4	**Perfect Transmission**	**1.00**	**1**
5	Owens Valley Rosegate – (rescaled)	0.59	34
6	Monitor Valley Rosegate – (rescaled)	0.63	35
7	Owens Valley Elko and Rosegate	0.36	99
8	Monitor Valley Elko	0.38	97

Attempts to detect a phylogenetic signal in Elko points were similarly unproductive (see table 11.1, rows 7 and 8). For the Owens Valley analysis, we were able to assemble only twenty-two points that were sufficiently complete for phylogenetic analyses. To obtain the requisite thirty-two terminal taxa, we augmented the sample with ten Owens Valley Rosegate points. With one exception, PAUP* did place the Elko and Rosegate points on different branches, but the PAUP* subgroupings of Elko points again failed to predict hydration readings, which were inconsistently distributed across the subgroups. This suggests that PAUP* is not detecting a temporal component in these data.

For Monitor Valley, Elko points from Gatecliff Shelter were also subjected to phylogenetic analysis in PAUP*. Low CI and high TL suggest a low phylogenetic signal here as well. PAUP* does divide these points into two major branches, however, which visual inspection suggests is primarily a function of thickness, (thinner vs. thicker points). Once again, this split fails to predict the stratigraphic position of Elko points within the Gatecliff deposit. Overall, points from different levels are indiscriminately mixed among all branches and subbranches, including the major thin-thick division.

Does this mean that information about projectile points was not transmitted and/or subject to evolutionary forces in prehistory in these two areas? No. One obvious possibility is that Rosegate and Elko points assumed their optimal forms almost immediately following their appearance and then drifted very tightly and nondirectionally around these optimal forms for the balance of the time they remained in use. In such cases PAUP* will probably not highlight changes that are related to time.

Conclusions

Our simulations demonstrate that all transmission systems do not act on variation in ways that are amenable to analysis using cladistic methods. Some systems, such as indirectly biased transmission, are variance reducing and lead to detectable signal preservation over time; others, such as guided variation, increase variation and cause loss of a detectable signal relatively quickly. The system in place prehistorically dramatically affects our ability to tease apart cultural inheritance with phylogenetic methods.

We did not detect phylogenetic signals in our projectile-point data, despite previous work suggesting we should have been able to (Bettinger and Eerkens 1997, 1999). Our lack of success may be a result of the scale of analysis. Most previous studies of projectile-point phylogeny have dealt with point types (Lyman and O'Brien 2000; O'Brien et al. 2001; O'Brien and Lyman 2002a), with distinct types being treated as terminal taxa that are assembled into a phylogenetic tree. In our analyses individual projectile points, not the types, are the terminal taxa, and it may be that the amount of inter-individual variability at any given time overwhelms what is being transmitted during the time a particular point style is in use. Thus, in practice, cladistic methods may be unable to highlight and segregate heritable variation at this more fine-scale level. This is unfortunate because on a theoretical level the technique is well suited to track the evolution of small heritable changes at such a scale.

This is not a failing of cladistic analysis per se. PAUP* detected heritable variability in our simulations, which was at the scale of the individual, though unrealistically simplified. The devil may be in the details of the real-life example. It may simply be that the majority of archaeological data at the individual level are too subject to idiosyncratic variation to be suitable for cladistic analysis. In other words, cladistic analyses in archaeology might be better suited to broad-scale changes rather than microscale ones. Unfortunately, while the modes of transmission at the individual level are relatively straightforward and the subject of substantial theoretical and empirical work (e.g., Boyd and Richerson 1985; Cavalli-Sforza and Feldman 1981; Henrich 2001; Henrich and Boyd 2001; McElreath 1997), an understanding of the processes that produce broad-scale changes are still a mystery. It seems to us, then, that there is still a substantial gap in our ability to link the trees produced by cladistic analyses of such broad-scale data (types) to prehistoric behavior.

Part of the problem may relate to the assumption of parsimony—that the best trees are those that minimize the number of evolutionary changes. In the biological sciences parsimony-based methods work well because heritable genetic changes are rare. However, as previously discussed by one of us (McElreath 1997), there is no good reason to assume this is true in the case of the transmission of human material culture. Indeed, the rate of change witnessed in the archaeological record over the last 10,000 years suggests that human material culture is characterized by an extremely high rate of change. The penchant for human learning suggests that sudden convergence may be much more common than in biological evolution. Perhaps part of our failing to find a phylogenetic signal in our projectile-point sample stems from the fact that specimens were subject to a high rate of evolutionary change, which included instances of convergence. Thus, the phylogenetic methods we employed may have failed because they naively assumed evolution to be rare.

12

Using Cladistics to Construct Lineages of Projectile Points from Northeastern Missouri

John Darwent and Michael J. O'Brien

The evolution of projectile points in the late Paleoindian and Early Archaic periods (ca. 8950–6000 B.C. uncalibrated radiocarbon years) in what is now northeastern Missouri (United States) was marked by a series of changes that first saw a radiation in diversity followed by a narrowing of variation (figure 12.1). The sequence began around 9250 B.C. with lanceolate Clovis points, which likely gave rise to Dalton points around 8850 B.C. (Bradley 1997; O'Brien et al. 2001; O'Brien and Wood 1998). Sometime thereafter, certainly by 7900 B.C., the radiation in point form began. Starting with the appearance of stems, every form of haft known from prehistoric Missouri, including side, corner, and basal notches, developed by 7500 B.C. Lanceolate points apparently were still being manufactured alongside these new forms (O'Brien and Wood 1998). This mosaic of point forms continued until 7000 B.C., when most hafting technologies began to disappear. With the exception of some stemmed forms, most projectile points made over the next 4,000 years were side notched. To understand why side-notched points came to ascendancy, we need to determine the sequence of changes that led to their development and that of other point forms of the period.

Here we present one portion of a much larger study in the use of cladistics to reconstruct the phylogeny of early projectile points in northeastern Missouri. We use cladistics because of its unique ability not only to create testable lineages of points but also to lay out sequences of character-state changes (O'Brien and Lyman 2002a, 2003a, 2003b; O'Brien et al. 2001, 2002). Thus, we can track the historical developments that eventually led to the appearance of side-notched points. The ultimate goal of this procedure is to explain why side notching was preferred over other hafting techniques.

185

Figure 12.1
Temporal Ranges of Specific Projectile-Point Types Found
in Northeastern Missouri

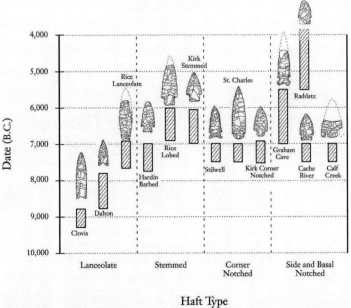

All ranges were assigned based on O'Brien and Wood's (1998) review of Paleoindian and Early Archaic–period projectile points in Missouri, with the exception of those for Kirk Corner Notched and Kirk Stemmed, which were drawn from Justice (1987).

Cladistics and the Archaeological Record

Cladistics is a method that "in its purest form, seeks to group taxa into sets and subsets based on the most parsimonious distribution of characters" (Forey 1990: 430). The underlying requirements for using cladistics to infer phylogenetic relationships for a set of phenomena are that the phenomena must evolve through decent with modification and be hierarchically related (Davis and Nixon 1992). Obviously, biological organisms fall within these parameters, but it has also been demonstrated that cladistics is applicable to the study of manuscripts and language (e.g., Platnick and Cameron 1977; Ross 1997) as well as other cultural and biocultural phenomena (e.g., Holden and Mace 1997, 1999; Mace and Pagel 1994; Sellen and Mace 1997), including those occurring in the archaeological record (Collard and Shennan 2000; Foley 1987; Jordan and Shennan 2003; O'Brien and Lyman 2000a, 2002, 2003a, 2003b; O'Brien et al. 2001, 2002; Tehrani and Collard 2002; chapter 13, this volume). We do not review this work, taking it for granted that there are no insurmountable theoretical or methodological obstacles to using cladistics to create artifact phylogenies (chapter 1, this volume). We also take for granted that the reader is familiar with the basics of cladistics.

Cladistic hypotheses are created without using temporal or spatial information, which makes them independent hypotheses concerning form alone. Consequently, they can be tested against time—the fossil/archaeological record—because there is an ordinal-scale sequence to the taxa on a phylogenetic tree that can be compared to the order in which the taxa arose in the fossil record—assuming that the history of life is reflected in the sequence of fossils (Benton 1995). When working with cultural phenomena, we assume that the history of cultural change is reflected in the sequence of artifacts in the archaeological record (chapter 6, this volume).

In order to examine trees in terms of the fossil record, they must be converted into trees where time is added. This is done by placing the terminal nodes of a tree at the point of earliest occurrence of fossil taxa (figure 12.2). In situations where there is complete congruence between the tree and the fossil record, a tree can be placed on the existing known temporal ranges of the taxa (figure 12.2a). However, in situations where a node of the tree must be lowered beyond the temporal range indicated in the known chronological sequence, the open space between the node and the taxa range is filled in with an extended, or "ghost," range in order to maintain a logical order based on derived characteristics (figure 12.2b).

Likewise, when the tree indicates a character developed before the divergence of two taxa, which results in it not being on a terminal branch of the tree, a "ghost taxon" is used to connect the nodes (Norell 1992, 1993) (figure 12.3). Just as with any other taxon, a ghost taxon has all the formal properties of a regular taxon; however, its range is determined by the sequence of the tree.

In simplest terms, the phylogenetic tree that needs the fewest ghost-range extensions in order to keep logical consistency is the best phylogenetic reconstruction. One way to assess this for a group of trees is to compare the number of range extensions that are needed to fit each tree to the fossil record. The tree requiring the fewest extensions is the best representation of the phylogeny, assuming that the fossil record is accurate (Benton 1995). In the example illustrated in figure 12.3, tree (a) fits better with the fossil record than tree (b) does because tree (a) requires only one range extension as opposed to the three needed by tree (b). Similarly, if we add the number of temporal intervals required for range extensions, tree (a) is again superior, as it requires two as opposed to thirteen intervals of range extension.

After a phylogenetic tree is calibrated to the fossil/archaeological record, it is possible to explore the temporal nature of each character change. At any time around a speciation event, there potentially could be taxa that have some, none, or different characters than the taxon that eventually arose. How-

Figure 12.2
Two Different Scenarios for Converting a Cladogram into a Calibrated
Phylogenetic Tree

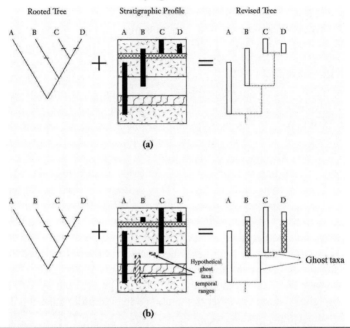

On the rooted cladograms, the positions of character changes are noted by horizontal lines on branches. The temporal range of each taxon is indicated in the stratigraphic profile by solid bars and on the phylogenetic tree by open bars. In (a), the nodes of the cladogram are simply mapped onto the existing stratigraphic ranges for the taxa because there is complete congruence between the position of the taxa on the cladogram and their occurrence in the stratigraphic profile. In (b), the ranges of taxa B and D need to be extended in order to keep the logical order of the cladogram intact, which are indicated by cross-hatched bars. Taxon B must come before Taxon C in temporal range because it comes before Taxon C on the cladogram. Taxa C and D are sister taxa because they depart from the same node; therefore, Taxon D's range must be extended back to the same time that Taxon C originated. Also depicted in this example are two ghost taxa and their predicted ranges in the stratigraphic profile, which are set by their position on the phylogenetic tree (Norell 1992, 1993).

ever, with the temporal information it is possible to begin to assess the rates of change within each character. On an individual level, it is possible to see which characters are relatively stable over time versus those that change rapidly or to see if some go through bursts of activity or are under constant change. On a group level, it is possible to discern periods when there is rapid change occurring in a number of characters versus times of relative stability.

It also is feasible to begin to formulate models concerning the nature of the origin of each character. For derived characters the simplest explanation is that

Figure 12.3
Comparison of Two Alternate, though Equivalent in Terms of Tree Length, Phylogenetic Hypotheses for the Same Character Matrix Using the Fossil Record

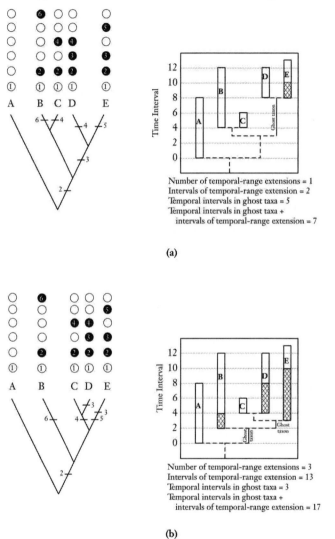

Number of temporal-range extensions = 1
Intervals of temporal-range extension = 2
Temporal intervals in ghost taxa = 5
Temporal intervals in ghost taxa + intervals of temporal-range extension = 7

(a)

Number of temporal-range extensions = 3
Intervals of temporal-range extension = 13
Temporal intervals in ghost taxa = 3
Temporal intervals in ghost taxa + intervals of temporal-range extension = 17

(b)

On the left are two rooted cladograms with the data matrix specified in the overhead circles (derived characters in filled circles) and the position of each change indicated on the branches. On the right are two phylogenetic trees, with the open bars indicating taxa ranges and the cross-hatched bars depicting temporal range extensions. Tree (a) is a superior hypothesis of the phylogeny because it requires less temporal range extensions and total number of increments of range extension than tree (b) does.

they are part of a line of heritable continuity. However, characters that are the result of homoplasy in archaeological phenomena can be the result of independent invention in a line of heritable continuity or of horizontal transmission (Mace and Pagel 1994). With a phylogenetic tree it is possible to speculate as to which form of transmission was related to the character change. Similar character changes that occur temporally (and spatially) closer to each other are more likely to be the result of horizontal transmission than those that are not. For example, if certain identical character changes appear simultaneously across several lineages, it might signify that the traits are the result of horizontal transmission. However, if such traits appear in staggered order through time, each change is more likely to have been the result of independent invention. Unfortunately, there is no method to prove whether a similar character change in two lineages at roughly the same time is the product of horizontal transmission. Even with the addition of spatial evidence into such speculations, all such conclusions are circumstantial because past cultural transmission cannot be observed.

Methods and Materials

A paradigmatic classification based on thirteen characters was used to classify projectile points, with most of the characters relating to the hafting area (see figure 12.4 for measurement locations and table 12.1 for characters and states). We believe the haft is the most likely area to exhibit the effects of transmission (Beck 1995, 1998) and thus is likely to carry a strong phylogenetic signal (O'Brien et al. 2001). We used fairly small-scale characters and character states. For example, instead of having one character that broadly categorizes a haft as being side, corner, or basal notched, or as contracting, straight, or expanding stemmed, we have four characters that together monitor the lower shoulder angle/upper notch angle, the notch shape, the notch depth, and the lower notch angle. By taking this approach, we attempted to make our characters as independent as possible.

We selected twenty-one classes of points that included five corner-notched, four lanceolate, four side-notched, and seven stemmed specimens, as well as one basal-notched point (figure 12.5; table 12.2). When choosing these classes, we tried to include as many specimens as possible from Zone III of the Pigeon Roost Creek site—the most thoroughly studied stratified archaeological site in northeastern Missouri (O'Brien and Warren 1983). Most of the projectile points recovered from this zone fell into established point types associated with either the late Paleoindian period or the Early Archaic period (table 12.2) and were below Middle Archaic–period points and radiocarbon dates (O'Brien and Wood 1998).

We selected a Clovis point from the Kimmswick site in Jefferson County, Missouri, to serve as the outgroup (table 12.2). This choice was made because Clovis points likely preceded all others in the region, and there is technological evidence that suggests that Dalton points evolved out of Clovis points

Table 12.1
Definitions of Characters and States for Projectile-Point Classification

Character	Definition	State
I	Length-to-width ratio	1. < 1.4
		2. 1.5–2.9
		3. > 3.0
II	Blade shape	1. Straight
		2. Excurvate
		3. Incurvate
		4. Ovate
		5. Incurvate/excurvate
III	Outer shoulder angle	0. No shoulder present
		1. 1–30º
		2. 31–60º
		3. 61–90º
		4. 91–120º
		5. 121–150º
		6. 151–180º
IV	Inner shoulder angle	0. No shoulder present
		1. 1–45º
		2. 46–90º
		3. 91–135º
		4. 136–180º
V	Lower notch angle	0. No notch present
		1. 136–180º
		2. 90–135º
		3. 46–89º
		4. 1–45º
VI	Basal tang-tip shape	1. Pointed or rounded
		2. Blunted
		3. Squared
VII	Neck-constriction–height ratio (neck height/length)	1. < 0.1
		2. 0.1–0.19
		3. > 0.19
VIII	Basal-concavity ratio	1. < 0.8
		2. 0.8–0.99
		3. 1.0
		4. > 1.0
IX	Blade-to-base ratio (blade width/base width)	1. < 0.9
		2. 1.0
		3. 1.1–1.9
		4. 2.0–4.0
		5. > 4.0
X	Notch-depth ratio (notch depth/notch width)	0. No notches
		2. 0.01–0.5
		3. 0.51–1.0
		4. > 1.0
XI	Outside tang angle	0. No outer tang/tang shape pointed or rounded
		1. 0º
		2. 1–45º
		3. 46–89º
		4. 90–135º
		5. 136–179º
XII	Notch shape	0. No notches present (lanceolate)
		1. Squared interior; lower margin length < 2x upper margin length (notch)
		2. Rounded interior; lower margin length < 2x upper margin length (notch)
		3. Rounded interior; lower margin length > 2x upper margin length (stem)
		4. Angled interior; lower margin length > 2x upper margin length (stem)
		5. Ground crescent-shaped notches
XIII	Neck-width-to-blade constriction ratio (neck width/blade width)	1. 1.0–0.80
		2. 0.79–0.60
		3. < 0.60

Figure 12.4

Illustration of the Measurements Taken on Projectile Points, along with Morphological Features of Projectile Points Used in the Text

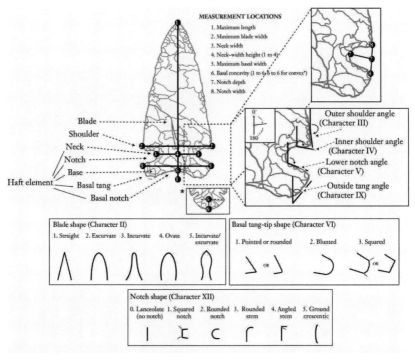

These measurements are used to calculate the character states listed in table 12.1. The two cut-away boxes on the right illustrate measurements and angles for notches and other features. All angle measurements were made between 0 degrees and 180 degrees, with 0 degrees always directed toward the tip, parallel to the long axis of the point. The lower three boxes illustrate various shapes of blades, basal tang tips, and notches.

(Bradley 1997; O'Brien et al. 2001; O'Brien and Wood 1998). Although these criteria are not hard and fast requirements for outgroup selection (Nixon and Carpenter 1993), using a point class that appears to have a direct ancestral relationship with the twenty-one ingroup taxa can be expected to enhance the phylogenetic reconstruction.

Results

Using the branch-and-bound algorithm of the phylogenetics program PAUP* (Swofford 2002), four equally most parsimonious trees were generated for the twenty-two taxa, each having seventy-two steps, a consistency index of 0.49, and a retention index of 0.66 (figures 12.6 and 12.7). Note that the two trees shown in each figure are identical except for the placement of two taxa—

Figure 12.5
**Illustration of Specimens in Each of the 22 Classes Included
in the Cladistic Analysis**

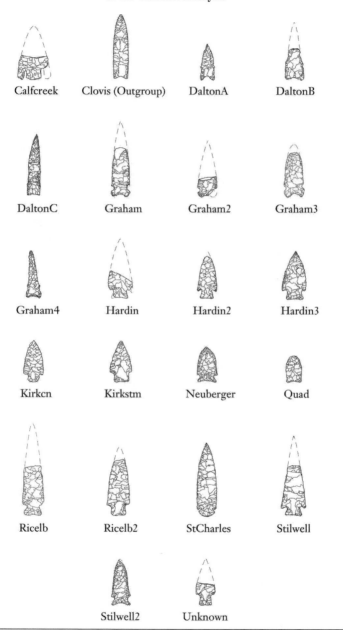

Each specimen is at 22.5 percent of original size.

Table 12.2

Classes with Assigned Point Types, Temporal Ranges, and Provenience

Class name	Code	Point type assigned	Temporal range	Provenience [a]
Calfcreek	226411244023	Calf Creek	7,500–7,000 B.C.	Pigeon Roost Creek, Zone III (300–310 cm B.S.)
Clovis (outgroup)	340001123001	Clovis	9,250–8,950 B.C.	Kimmswick, Jefferson County, Missouri
DaltonA	234112321351	Dalton	8,500–7,900 B.C.	Pigeon Roost Creek, Zone III (310–320 cm B.S.)
DaltonB	236002321030l	Dalton	8,500–7,900 B.C.	Pigeon Roost Creek, Zone III (320–330 cm B.S.)
DaltonC	336111123205l	Dalton	8,500–7,900 B.C.	Hendricks
Graham	3562232213212	Graham Cave	7,000–5,500 B.C.	Collins
Graham2	2262232121211	Graham Cave	7,000–5,500 B.C.	Pigeon Roost Creek, Zone III (320–330 cm B.S.)
Graham3	2262233212221	Graham Cave	7,000–5,500 B.C.	Cooper
Graham4	3351232212521	Graham Cave	7,000–5,500 B.C.	Pigeon Roost Creek, Zone III (300–310 cm B.S.)
Hardin	2413122233333	Hardin Barbed	7,800–7,000 B.C.	Pigeon Roost Creek, Zone III (320–330 cm B.S.)
Hardin2	241311223043	Hardin Barbed	7,800–7,000 B.C.	Cooper
Hardin3	2213112232033	Hardin Barbed	7,800–7,000 B.C.	Collins
Kirkcn	2413132433223	Kirk Corner Notched	7,500–6,900 B.C.	Pigeon Roost Creek, Zone III (320–330 cm B.S.)
Kirkstm	2262122232232	Kirk Stemmed	6,900–6000 B.C.	Pigeon Roost Creek, Zone III (290–300 cm B.S.)
Neuberger	2563122233212	Neuberger	~7,500–7,000 B.C.	Collins
Quad	2400023230501	Quad (-like)	Late Paleoindian Period	Hendricks
Ricelb	3162122233233	Rice Lobed	6,900–6,000 B.C.	Collins
Ricelb2	3562132232233	Rice Lobed	6,900–6,000 B.C.	23MN802
StCharles	3413212434023	St. Charles	7,500–7,000 B.C.	23MN898
Stilwell	2563232233312	Stilwell	7,500–7,000 B.C.	Ross
Stilwell2	2554122233213	Stilwell	7,500–7,000 B.C.	Collins
Unknown	2262113432033	Unknown	Early Archaic Period	Pigeon Roost Creek, Zone III (290–300 cm B.S.)

a All provenience information from O'Brien (1985) except for Kimmswick (Graham et al. 1981); B.S. = below surface.

Figure 12.6
Two of Four Equally Parsimonious Rooted Cladograms for the 22 Taxa Included in the Analysis

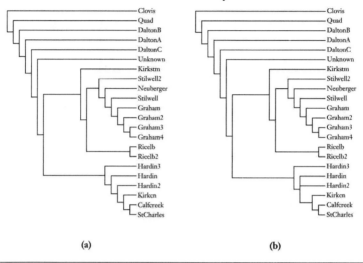

(a)   (b)

Each has 72 steps, a consistency index of 0.49, and a retention index of 0.66. Differences between the two are restricted to the order of the Hardin and Hardin2 classes.

Figure 12.7
The Remaining Two of Four Equally Parsimonious Rooted Cladograms for the 22 Taxa Included in the Analysis

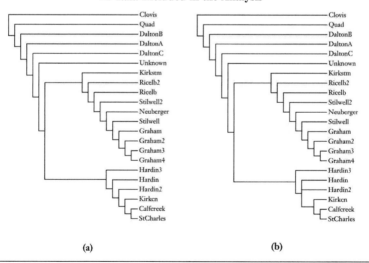

(a)   (b)

Again, differences between the two are restricted to the order of the Hardin and Hardin2 classes.

Figure 12.8
Strict Consensus Tree for the Four Most-Parsimonious Cladograms

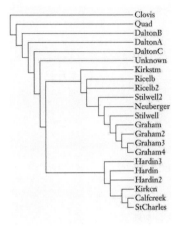

Because of the similarities among the four most-parsimonious cladograms, the majority-rules consensus tree is identical to the strict consensus tree.

Hardin and Hardin2. Through a rare set of circumstances, related to the position of Ricelb and Ricelb2, the majority-rules consensus tree and the strict consensus tree are identical. The tree is shown in figure 12.8.

In order to choose the best representation of the phylogeny, we compared the trees to the archaeological record by evaluating the congruence between the order of the classes in the trees and their known temporal ranges. Pictured in figures 12.9 and 12.10 are the four trees calibrated to the archaeological record, with the open bars representing the known temporal ranges of the points (see table 12.2 for assigned ranges) and the cross-hatched bars representing instances where we had to extend the taxa ranges in order to keep the logical consistency of the tree. Notice again that the only difference between the two trees shown in each figure is the placement of the Hardin and Hardin2 classes.

In instances where several classes have specimens from one established point type (e.g., Stilwell and Stilwell2), the first class with the type in the temporal ordering of taxa is given the full range of the point type, and subsequent classes with the type are given a more restricted range (e.g., the Stilwell2 class is given a range of 7500–7000 B.C., whereas the more derived Stilwell class is given a range of 7450–7000 B.C.). There are no "penalties" assigned to the trees in terms of correspondence to the archaeological record because classes with reduced ranges have specimens that are more derived and therefore would naturally come later in time.

Figure 12.9
Two of Four Phylogenetic Trees Calibrated with the Archaeological Record
Created for the Four Most-Parsimonious Cladograms

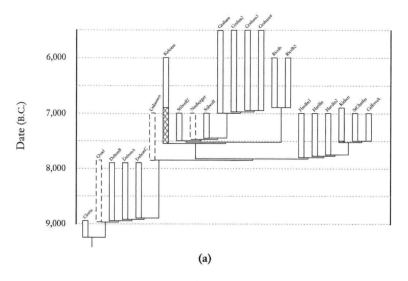

(a)

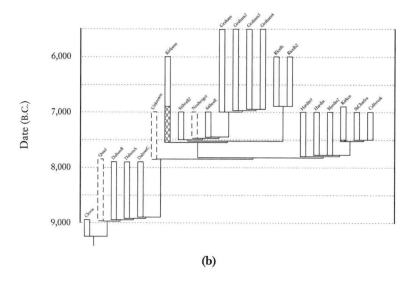

(b)

The trees differ in terms of the splitting events connected with the Hardin taxa. Open bars represent known class ranges, cross-hatched bars depict temporal range extensions, and dashed-lined bars indicate estimated ranges for classes without clear temporal information. The minimal time interval between speciation events is 25 years.

Figure 12.10
The Remaining Two of Four Phylogenetic Trees Calibrated with the
Archaeological Record Created for the Four Most-Parsimonious Cladograms

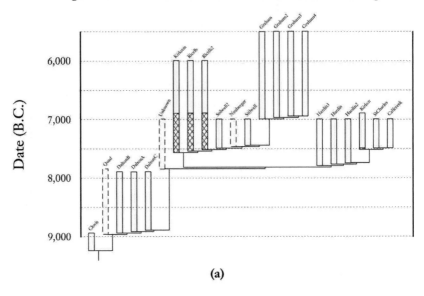

(a)

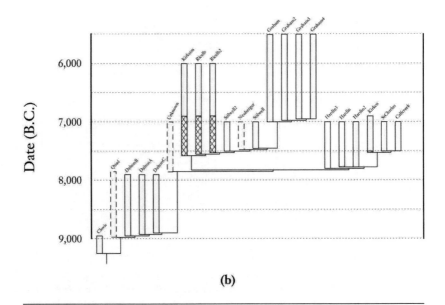

(b)

See the figure 12.9 caption for symbols.

We use bars with dashed lines to indicate classes that had specimens from unknown point types or from types with poorly defined temporal ranges, and we set their ranges based on what is known about the type and the position of the class on the tree. Although each taxon-origination event is depicted as being minimally twenty-five years apart, the gap could be considerably smaller. In theory there could be a speciation event over the course of one knapping session, which is virtually instantaneous in terms of archaeological time. However, if one or several speciation events occur in such a limited period of time, then other speciation events will have be proportionately longer. Therefore, we use twenty-five years only for the sake of convention.

Evaluating the trees in terms of congruence with the archaeological record, the trees in figure 12.10 are less acceptable because they require range extensions for three of the classes as opposed to one for the trees in figure 12.9. In

Figure 12.11
Phylogenetic Tree of the Most-Preferred Tree with Class Illustrations

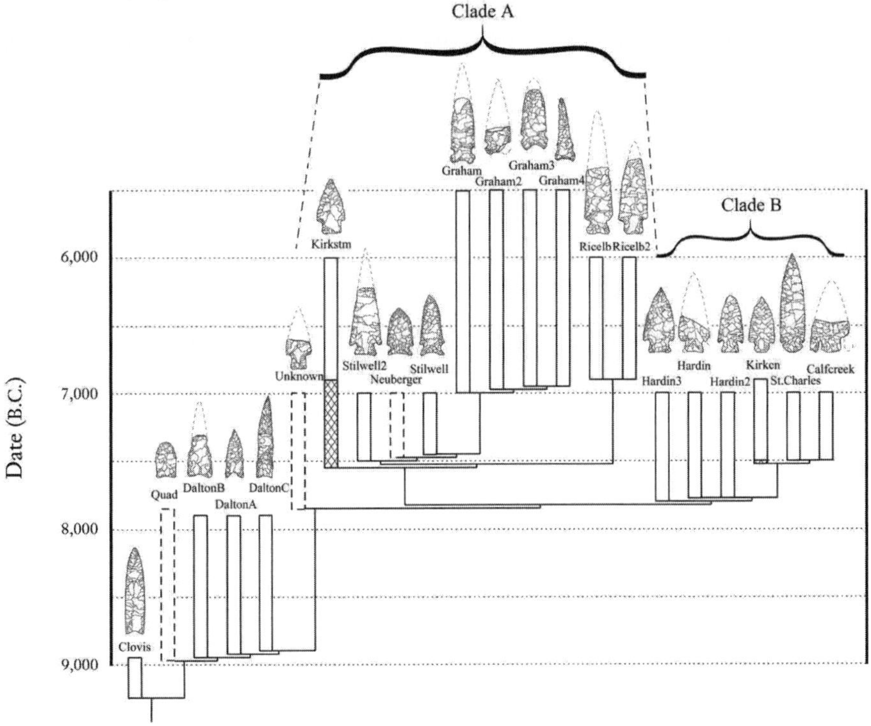

Clade A comprises Kirkstm + Ricelb + Ricelb2 + Stilwell2 + Neuberger + Stilwell + Graham + Graham2 + Graham3 + Graham4, and Clade B comprises Hardin3 + Hardin + Hardin2 + Kirkcn + StCharles + Calfcreek. Open bars represent known class ranges, cross-hatched bars depict temporal range extensions, and dashed-lined bars indicate estimated ranges for classes without clear temporal information.

figure 12.10 Ricelb and Ricelb2 must be extended below 7500 B.C. in order logically to appear before the Stilwell2 class. If we add the number of years of extensions needed for each tree, those in figure 12.10 require 1975 years of additional range, whereas those in figure 12.9 require only 675 years.

The two trees in figure 12.9 are equivalent in terms of the archaeological record because they require the same number of extensions and have the same number of range extensions and ghost taxa. Thus, to decide between these two, we compared the arrangement of taxa to the consensus tree, under the premise that if a particular tree matches the consensus tree, then it has the most support in terms of character-state distribution. The tree shown in figure 12.9b, reproduced in more detail in figure 12.11, has more support in terms of characters and thus is the best hypothesis of projectile-point development.

Implications in Terms of Character Evolution

Viewing the tree in terms of hafting allows us to generate an overall picture of point evolution, but it does not allow us to formulate explanations as to why certain clades developed in the manner they did. However, one of the powerful aspects of using cladistics for examining technological change is that we can move down from the taxic level to examine historical change in individual characters. In theory almost every character change could represent a functional change in the performance of a projectile point, any of which could benefit or hinder its success as a weapon (Beck 1998). Characters such as weight, blade shape, width, and haft all affect how deeply a projectile penetrates its target, how much bleeding it causes, how accurately it can be propelled to the target, how far it can be effectively shot, how well the projectile will withstand impact, and even ease of manufacture (Christenson 1986; Hughes 1998; Musil 1988). The design of every projectile point represents a series of compromises among these factors and reflects the needs its manufacturer perceives as necessary for successful use.

Unfortunately, the results of cladistics cannot determine whether a character change represents a functional change in projectile-point design, nor do we have informants who can tell us why they changed a particular feature. However, the engineering properties of different characters can give us some insight (O'Brien and Holland 1990; O'Brien et al. 1994).

We selected six characters to monitor—IV (inner shoulder angle), V (lower notch angle), VI (tang-tip shape), IX (blade-to-base ratio), XII (notch shape), and XIII (neck-width/blade-width ratio (table 12.1). Characters VI, IX, and XIII were chosen because they are connected with the ability of a projectile point to withstand damage during use. Characters IV, V, and XII were selected because they are tied to certain aspects of the performance of a projectile point.

For character XIII, the strength of a point should increase with a lower neck-width/blade-width ratio because the neck is larger in proportion to the blade. This should reduce the effects of side slap or bending force during impact with either the target or the ground (Van Buren 1974). Although two dimensions that were not included in the analysis—thickness and cross section—also play a role (Cotterell and Kamminga 1992; Hughes 1998), a smaller blade will have less area to exert pressure on the neck than will a larger blade. However, the tradeoff for a smaller blade in proportion to the neck is that the penetration of the point could be affected because the blade will have less ability to create an opening through which the bindings can pass (Musil 1988).

The size of the base in proportion to the blade (character IX) should also be a measure of the durability of a projectile point. On the one hand, a proportionally larger base should be able to withstand more shock than a smaller base and be able to better distribute force across the shaft or foreshaft of the projectile, thereby lessening the likelihood of damage. In addition, bindings can be wrapped more effectively around the bottom of a larger base, which helps lessen the force of impact on a shaft. On the other hand, with an enlarged base there is a reduction in size or effect of shoulder barbs. This could reduce the ability of a point to cause bleeding (Christenson 1986).

Another component that possibly influences the strength of the base of a point is tang-tip shape (character VI). Although we have three states for this character—pointed, blunted, and squared—the main division in terms of strength is between pointed versus blunted and squared shapes. Blunted and squared tangs tend to create more robust bases than do pointed tangs. They might also allow for more secure hafting.

The lower notch angle (character V) also plays a role in how securely a projectile point can be fastened to a shaft or foreshaft. The closer the lower notch angle comes to 90 degrees, the more perpendicular it becomes in relation to the shaft, which should increase the ability of the bindings to keep the point attached to the shaft when it is withdrawn from an animal. Although this might be an advantageous characteristic in terms of reuse of projectiles, in some instances the desired effect might be to have the point remain behind in the target to cause additional tissue damage and bleeding.

The presence or absence of shoulder barbs on a projectile point is a factor of the inner shoulder angle (character IV) because any projectile point that has an inner shoulder angle greater than 90 degrees effectively has barbs. Functionally, barbs increase the ability of a projectile point to cause bleeding by holding the point in the target, which could cause more damage by further cutting brought about by backward pressure produced by the shaft. As Christenson (1986: 117) put it, "a wide, barbed point will rankle and cause more bleeding than a narrow, unbarbed one."

Despite the effectiveness of barbs in causing bleeding, there are tradeoffs that come with them in terms of durability and reuse because barbs themselves are relatively fragile (for examples, see Flenniken and Raymond 1986), and they are often associated with smaller bases and neck widths. The effectiveness of a barb is partially controlled by its angle, but the proportional size of the blade to the base also has an effect because the greater the width of the base in proportion to the blade, the less ability the barbs will have to hold.

Although there are six divisions for the shape of the notch (character XII), the importance of the character for this discussion relates the presence of a notch to the upper length of the notch margin versus the lower length of the notch margin. This character is obviously related to how a projectile point is hafted to a shaft or foreshaft but also to issues concerning reuse and material usage. According to Musil (1988: 376), lanceolate hafts are not very efficient because "a large amount of lithic material is discarded when [they are] broken, there is less opportunity for remanufacture, and [there is a greater possibility for] increased damage to the shaft upon impact." Similarly, Musil reasons that stemmed points are more efficient than lanceolate points because they allow for more rejuvenation of the blade before the point is exhausted or broken. Notched points are even more efficient because they can easily be renotched if the base is snapped off.

Figure 12.12 shows the preferred phylogenetic tree (from figure 12.11) with each of the changes for the six characters illustrated. Although the first change for the six characters occurs at node 42, where character VI changes from state 1 (pointed or rounded basal tangs) to state 2 (blunted basal tangs), the first important set of changes in the characters occurs at node 40. Here Dalton points presumably were initially ground on the lateral margins to the degree that lower section of the point came to resemble a broad crescent-shaped notch, and a slight shoulder was formed (denoted by character XII changing from 0 to 5). With this change the inner shoulder angle and lower notch angle originated, as character IV moved from 0 (no notch present) to 1 (1–45 degrees) and character V moved from 0 (no notch present) to 1 (136–180 degrees). Although these changes are depicted as occurring as early as 8850 B.C., it is impossible to determine from the current temporal data associated with the Dalton type whether this was the case. The creation of this new structure probably led to points becoming more securely hafted than straight-sided lanceolate points.

The next major change in the characters occurs after node 38. Character V remains the same, but character IV moves from 1–45 degrees (state 1) to 46–90 degrees (state 2), and character XII changes from a ground, crescent-shaped notch (state 5) to an asymmetrical notch, meaning the lower margin of the notch is twice as long as the upper margin, with a rounded interior (state 3). This new configuration created a stem in terms of large-scale hafting technology.

If we follow Musil's (1988) scenario, the change from lanceolate to stemmed hafts might have occurred because of the greater efficiency in terms of material use that stemmed points provided. In addition to this supposition, we propose that the decreased blade-width-to-neck-width ratio would have allowed the blade to create a larger opening in a target through which the bindings of the

Figure 12.12

Phylogenetic Tree of the Most-Preferred Tree with the Temporal Position of Characters IV, V, VI, IX, XII, and XIII Plotted along with Illustration of Each Character Change

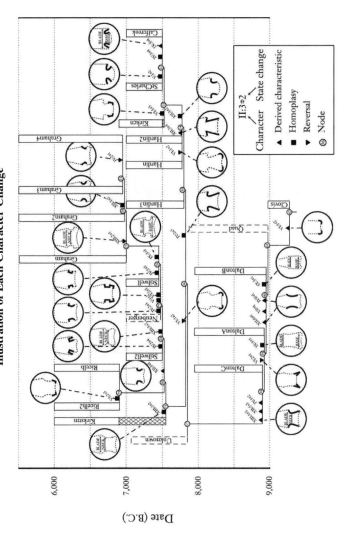

The locations of character changes in the illustrations (circles) are designated by solid lines or text in combination with arrows specifying the direction of change. Dashed lines in the illustrations (circles) represent the nonchanging characters. All illustrations are proportional, with angles set to the midpoints of their ranges (e.g., a character with a range of 90–135 degrees would be drawn at 112 degrees) and blade, neck, and base widths drawn relative to one another. The type of character change is denoted by a symbol listed in the legend, and each node is labeled with a number for reference.

haft could pass. This change, in effect, could have increased the penetration of a projectile into an animal. However, the reduced neck-width-to-blade-width ratio might have also made the new stemmed points fundamentally weaker than the previous lanceolate points. Therefore, it can be questioned whether the new haft was more efficient in terms of reuse unless it provided increased protection for the shaft. Unfortunately, there is little in the way of experimental data that could determine this, one way or the other.

A division creating two major clades of Early Archaic–period projectile points (noted in figure 12.11) occurs after node 36, with one of the changes being character IV moving from state 2 (46–90 degrees) to state 3 (91–135 degrees). This new state is one of the defining derived characteristics for Clade B, despite its occurrence in classes in Clade A, and it does not change again on the clade with the exception of the Calfcreek class, where the angle becomes even more pronounced. In terms of morphology, this character change effectively makes the taxa in Clade B barbed. Based on the temporal range of the Hardin3 class on the following node, the change in character IV happened prior to 7800 B.C., but how much earlier is not resolvable.

The rest of the changes in characters IV, V, and XII for Clade B occur after nodes 34 and 32. One change of note in character XII occurs after node 34, where there is a reduction in the size of lower margin of the notch (state 3 to state 2). This modification created some points that traditionally would be considered corner notched depending on the width of the notch. Based on the position of the node, this change occurred approximately between 7750 and 7525 B.C.

After node 32, characters IV and V move in opposite directions. On the one hand, character IV moves from state 3 (91–135 degrees) to 4 (136–180 degrees) to roughly parallel the angle of character V, which creates a basal-notched configuration found in the Calfcreek class. On the other hand, character V moves from state 1 (136–180 degrees) to state 2 (90–135 degrees) to form the distinct corner notches present on the specimen of the StCharles class. Both of these character changes became fixed around 7500 B.C. and represent some of the last innovations in this clade along with one last change of note. Character IX changes on the Calfcreek class after node 32, when the blade becomes larger in proportion to the base, moving from state 3 (1.1–1.9) to state 4 (2.0–4.0).

The development of blunted basal tangs after node 36 is one of the defining features of Clade A, despite similar changes in the taxa of Clade B and its status as a reversal. After node 36, character IV changes from state 1 (pointed or rounded basal tangs) to state 2, which begins the development of more robust bases in Clade A. Subsequently, character IV changes from blunted (state 2) to squared (state 3) basal tangs on the main lineage after node 27 and independently after node 29 for the Ricelb2 class. Never does the character revert to pointed or rounded tangs. Because of the position of node 29 in relation to the Hardin3 class, this change had to have occurred before 7800 B.C.

The sequence of change in characters IV, V, and XII for Clade A represents an interesting case where the hypothetical ancestor has a different configuration than the taxa branching off the nodes. Following the departure of the Ricelb and Ricelb2 classes from node 30, the next three classes to arise all have hafts that would be considered as corner notched based on the angles of their notches. However, the ghost taxa from which these points branched appear to have been side notched. The incongruity begins after node 30, where character XII changed from 3 to 1 prior to 7500 B.C. This transformation involved a shortening of the lower margin accompanied by a "squaring" of the interior of the notch instead of a rounded arch. Although some points with this new configuration might be considered corner notched, it is likely that many would be classified as side-notched points, depending on factors such as the width of the notch and the shape of the base. The subsequent shift of character V after node 27 from state 1 (136–180 degrees) to state 2 (90–135 degrees) would have created points that undoubtedly would be classified as side notched. Thus it is likely, based on the character changes on the hypothetical ancestor, that side-notched points were present in the region around 7500 B.C.

The three taxa that branched off from the hypothetical ancestor after node 30 all had variations in character IV. After node 28 the Stilwell2 class branched off with a change from state 2 (46–90 degrees) to state 4 (136–180 degrees), which in this case made the inner shoulder angle roughly parallel to the lower notch angle. After nodes 27 and 28, both the Neuberger and Stilwell classes independently changed from state 2 (46–90 degrees) to state 3 (91–135 degrees). Each of these three character changes is a homoplasy. The shift to state 4 in character IV also occurs in the Calfcreek class, and the shift from 2 to 3, while obviously shared between the Neuberger and Stilwell classes, also occurs after node 36. All of these changes arise relatively close to each other in time, around 7500 B.C. Because of this temporal proximity, we suspect that the similarities are the result of horizontal transmission, although additional spatial information is needed to enhance this argument. Regardless, if the changes in character IV in the three taxa were the result of independent invention, they represent experimental offshoots from a lineage that retains an ancestral characteristic.

The alterations in characters IV, V, and XII were accompanied by changes in characters IX and XIII. After node 28, the neck-width-to-blade-width constriction ratio (character XIII) changed from < 0.60 (state 4) to 0.79–0.60 (state 3). This change likely occurred around 7500 B.C. on the hypothetical ancestor but also occurred independently after node 31 for the Kirkstm class before 7500 B.C. Further expansion of the neck in relation to the blade continued, and after node 25 the ratio changes from 0.79–0.60 (state 2) to 0.80–0.99 (state 1). However, based on the position of this character state in relation to the Graham class, this change likely occurred around 7000 B.C. and thus was not a rapid one. One change occurred for character IX, where the base became wider than the blade as the blade-to-base ratio shifted from 1.1–1.9 (state 3) to < 0.9 (state 1). This change occurred between 7000–7500 B.C., but further resolution is impossible.

Stepping back to compare Clade A and Clade B, both are similar in that notching arose out of stemmed technology twice. The initial steps toward notching are relatively similar if we compare the hypothetical ancestors from node 30 on Clade A and node 34 on Clade B, as both have similar inner shoulder angles and lower margin angles. Although the changes after node 34 are depicted as being earlier than those after node 30, in actuality node 34 could be as late as 7525 B.C. and node 30 as early as 7800 B.C., and thus they could have been coeval. If we subscribe to Musil's (1988) hypothesis concerning the efficiency of notched points over stemmed points in terms of material use, the move to notching in both clades is not surprising and provides an explanation as to why these clades parallel each other in this regard. However, in addition appears that development of the clades represents two different approaches to maximizing projectile-point efficiency.

It appears that the innovations of Clade A were directed largely towards increasing the strength and, consequently, the reusability of projectile points. Although taxa in the clade obviously remained pointed, there is a lack of development of features that could have enhanced killing power. Conversely, many of the developments in Clade B reflect efforts to improve the killing power of projectile points, which likely came at the expense of projectile-point strength. Our reasoning for these conclusions is based on trends in the patterns of character development in each clade.

There are two lines of evidence for projectile-point durability increasing in Clade A. First, changes in characters VI and IX indicate that bases became more robust. This trend first started with the division between Clade A and Clade B, when basal tangs became blunted and eventually the base became wider than the blade. As discussed, larger bases likely made points more resistant to impact shocks as well as dampened the load on the shaft of the projectile. Second, the size of the neck in relation to the blade (character XIII) increased over time. This new adaptation also would have increased the strength of specimens, although probably at some expense to penetration power because bindings would have been closer to the margins of the blade.

In addition to the possible increases in durability, another series of changes that might have increased point reusability is the decrease in lower notch angle (character V). As it moved closer to 90 degrees, this shift increased the perpendicularity of notches in relation to the shaft of a projectile, which likely increased how securely the bindings could attach the point to a shaft or foreshaft. Consequently, these points would more likely stay with the shaft of the projectile when being withdrawn or knocked loose. This effect was likely enhanced by the retention of the ancestral inner shoulder state (character IV, state 2), which precluded the development of barbs that would have made extraction more difficult. Although there was experimentation with barbs on the branches of the Stilwell, Neuberger, and Stilwell2 classes, this character did not change on the hypothetical ancestor. The lack of barbs also eliminated the potential of breakage of these weaker structures.

In a different trajectory, the development of points in Clade B seems to have been more focused on increasing their killing power. This conclusion is based on the development of shoulder barbs and the overall lack of character changes that might impede their function. The appearance of barbs is one of the defining characters of Clade B after node 36, which reaches ultimate expression in the Calfcreek class at the crown of the clade. Barbs would have not only caused more bleeding but also created larger openings for haft bindings to slip through unimpeded. There are no changes in the blade-width-to-neck-width (character XIII) and blade-width-to-base-width ratios (character IX), nor changes in the lower notch angle (with the exception of the StCharles class) that would have hampered these functions. In the Calfcreek class the blade-width-to-base-width ratio actually became smaller, which would have increased the effectiveness of its barbs.

The downside of the development of barbs and the retention of the ancestral states of characters V, IX, and X (as well as the derived state of characters IX in the Calfcreek class) was that point durability was never enhanced and possibly was reduced. This might be best represented by specimens in the Calfcreek class. Although points in this class were highly efficient killing implements, they are usually found with broken ears (O'Brien and Wood 1998; Powell 1995). Therefore, the strategy in using these points, and other points of Clade B, was that the potential for causing more damage upon a successful hit outweighed the risk of point breakage and loss.

Conclusion

We have outlined how cladistics can be used to derive explanations for technological change in the archaeological record. In terms of interpreting the results, there is a need for better understanding of the performance standards (Schiffer and Skibo 1987) of different characters. This information can be obtained through experimenting with the properties of different characters and examining breakage patterns in archaeological specimens.

From our analysis it appears that the rise of side-notched points to dominance in northeastern Missouri in the Early Archaic period came through a series of character changes that enhanced projectile-point durability. Although another, competing tradition arose that appears to have emphasized increasing the killing power of projectile points, the benefits that this tradition conferred did not outweigh its costs to its manufacturers.

Acknowledgments

We thank Dan Glover for producing the figures; Lee Lyman for many helpful conversations; and Mark Collard and Stephen Shennan for advice on strengthening the chapter.

13

Reconstructing the Flow of Information across Time and Space: A Phylogenetic Analysis of Ceramic Traditions from Prehispanic Western and Northern Mexico and the American Southwest

Marcel J. Harmon, Todd L. VanPool, Robert D. Leonard, Christine S. VanPool, and Laura A. Salter

Phylogenetic analysis was originally developed and used by biologists to classify organisms and to reconstruct genealogical relationships, or historical lineages (Brooks and McLennan 1991; Felsenstein 2004; Kitching et al. 1998). A "lineage," or clade is a group of related entities, all of which have descended from a common ancestor. Figure 13.1 shows such a lineage composed of members of a multigenerational family. The children (generation 2) and the grandchildren (generation 3) all form part of this lineage, descending from the progenitor (generation 1), shown here as a male. Groups of organisms may form lineages as well.

Learning lineages (intellectual traditions), composed of information transmitted between individuals and their larger groups, also form clades. Figure 13.2 shows an intellectual clade for the Chinese martial-arts style known as Pa Kua Chang. All the individuals listed are "related" in the sense that they are receivers and/or transmitters (students and/or teachers) of the information contained within the fighting system of Pa Kua, and all are intellectually "descended" from the common "ancestor," Tung Hai-Ch'uan.

The clade in the Pa Kua example is composed of individual humans, but intellectual clades can also include the things people manufacture and use, such as Ford pickups, buildings, stone tools, and ceramic vessels. The infor-

Figure 13.1
A Lineage Composed of Individual Members of a Single Family, All Descending from the Progenitor in Generation 1

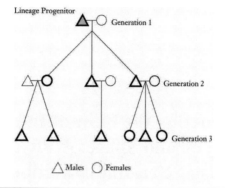

The progenitor is represented by a bold, shaded triangle. The lineage is composed of the progenitor, the children of generation 2, and the grandchildren of generation 3, each represented by either a bolded circle or triangle.

Figure 13.2
One of Many Theorized Learning Lineages for the Chinese Martial-Arts Style Known as *Pa Kua Chang* (Eight Changes of the Palm)

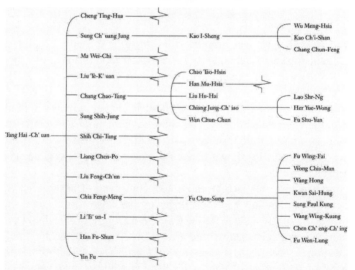

This diagram is a clade, consisting of four generations of *Pa Kua* practitioners starting with their common intellectual ancestor, Tung Hai-Ch'uan. Each successive generation is composed of the students of the teachers in the previous generation. The lines and brackets trace the specific information paths between teachers and students. Only a portion of the lineage is depicted here. (Figure adapted from Johnson and Crandall 1990.)

mation required to design, manufacture, and use these objects was taught, learned, and copied by both individuals and groups, who transmitted it across time and space. In this chapter we use phylogenetic analysis to construct an intellectual clade of design iconography using the information embedded within the designs found on prehistoric pottery from western and northern Mexico and the American Southwest.

Phylogenetics Reconstructs Information Transmission

At its very core, phylogenetics is a method for hierarchically organizing a group of objects, organisms, species, and the like (generally referred to as "taxa") based on the distributions of character states among the taxa. "Characters" are definable features, such as feathers, a genetic marker, or a particular design element on a ceramic vessel (for example, the images of twins). "Character states" refer to the series of alternate forms that particular characters may take. In the case of feathers, different character states might include those related to color, length, width, and shaft-wall thickness. For DNA sequences, the character states are the four bases: adenine, cytosine, guanine, and thymine. And for the case of images of twins, the character states might include the type of image, whether of a human, a bird, or a serpent. For some characters, the states might be presence or absence.

The analysis produces a hierarchical organization, termed a "phylogenetic tree." Figure 13.3 shows the hierarchical, or nested, relationships among four dinosaur taxa. These relationships are based in part on the distribution of four morphological characters. Each node represents a hypothetical ancestor, and each theoretical ancestor and its respective descendants form a clade.

The trees produced by phylogenetics are essentially hypotheses about the transmission of information. In the case of biological reproduction, genetic information is passed along from parent(s) to child. In DNA sequences the information is encoded using the aforementioned four bases. For humans, this encoded information is what gives us two hands, five fingers, blue or brown eyes, a bulbous nose, and so on. In the case of the dinosaur tree (figure 13.3), the information in a stegosaurus's genes produced a skull without a shelf at the back, whereas the genes of a triceratops did produce such a shelf. However, all dinosaur genes produced a hole in the pelvis into which the femur fits (the acetabulum). By looking at how the morphological expression of the information encoded in the genes of these four different dinosaur taxa is distributed among the taxa, it is possible to build a tree, or hypothesis, of how that information has been transmitted over time. In this case, it is hypothesized that the dinosaur groups pachycephalosaurus and triceratops were more closely related to each other than they were to parasaurolophus or stegosaurus.

In contrast to genetics, the processes of cultural replication are not well understood. We do not have a clear understanding of how information is physically manifest inside the minds of individuals. Nor do we completely under-

Figure 13.3
A Phylogenetic Tree Depicting the Hierarchical, or Nested, Relationships among
Four Dinosaur Taxa

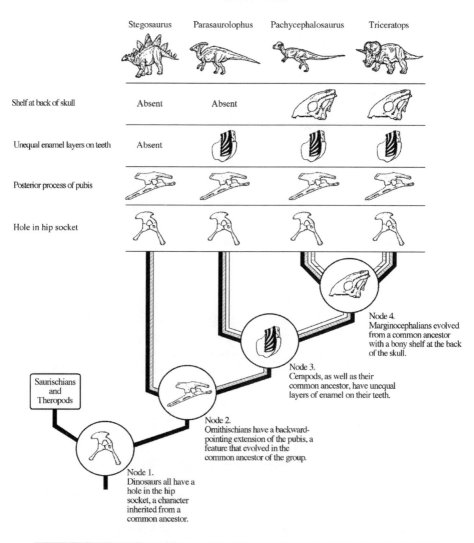

These relationships are based in part on the distribution of the following four characters: (1) shelf at the back of the skull, (2) unequal enamel layers on teeth, (3) the posterior process of pubis, and (4) a hole in the hip socket. Each node represents a theoretical ancestor, and each theoretical ancestor and its respective descendants form a clade. Therefore node 4 + Pachycephalosaurus + Triceratops form a clade; node 3 + node 4 + Parasaurolophus+ Pachycephalosaurus + Triceratops form a clade; and so on (after Gaffney et al. 1995).

stand the brain's activities during information transmission or how the brain converts information into behavior, such as the manufacture of tools (Hull 2000). Despite this, phylogenetic analysis can still be used to reconstruct the historical developments of cultural lineages. There are two main reasons for this.

First, phylogenetics cares only that information is passed between individuals and groups and that this information is subsequently used to "build" things—things that may be biological or cultural in nature. Examples include building a biological organism, the decorations on a ceramic vessel, or a suspension bridge. These "things" have particular characters and character states as a result of the specific bits of information that have been transmitted between individuals and groups. In a phylogenetic analysis, the physical manifestation of these packages of information becomes the character states used to reconstruct the nested relationships of the groups under study. The interpretation of the results as lines of heritable transmission is based on an understanding that the distributions of character states represent the transfer of information, whether that information is biological or cultural (e.g., O'Brien and Lyman 2003a). The specific information content, its manifestation, and its associated transmission processes only affect *how*, not *if*, phylogenetics can be used.

Second, phylogenetics constructs lineages by distinguishing between homologous and homoplastic similarities. "Homoplasy" is the product of similar responses to similar conditions, or convergence, whereas "homology" is the product of heritable transmission, be it cultural or biological. Within a lineage, the similarities that descendant phenomena have with ancestral phenomena are the result of some type of information transmission between the two. Thus they are homologous similarities. In contrast, homoplastic similarities (such as the independent development of hatching on pottery or bat versus bird wings) do not indicate the transfer of information and therefore do not reflect heritable relationships. Conflating the two will potentially lead to inaccurate conclusions concerning both biological and cultural transmission.

A complete discussion of phylogenetics in general (Brooks and McLennan 1991; Felsenstein 2004; Kitching et al. 1998; Sober 1988; Swofford et al. 1996), and with regard to cultural data in particular (Harmon 2000; Harmon et al. 2000; Leonard et al. 2002; Mace and Pagel 1994; O'Brien and Lyman 2003a; O'Brien et al. 2001; Sellen and Mace 1997; Tehrani and Collard 2002; VanPool et al. 2000), is beyond the scope of this chapter, but the reader is referred to the aforementioned references.

Typically, a phylogenetic software package is used to construct a tree by analyzing the distribution of the characters and character states within a group of taxa. In many cases an optimality criterion is defined to evaluate a given tree, and then an algorithm is used to construct a tree that has the best value given that optimality criterion (Swofford et al. 1996). For our analysis, we have made use of two such criteria—maximum parsimony (MP) and maximum likelihood (ML).

Maximum Parsimony and Maximum Likelihood

When used to evaluate scientific hypotheses, the principle of parsimony states that we select the explanation or hypothesis that requires the fewest assumptions and supporting conditions (Kitching et al. 1998; Sober 1988). MP operates within the general framework of parsimony by searching for the "simplest solution." It constructs a tree in such a way that changes from one character state to another, and independent developments of character states, are minimized across a tree. Figure 13.4 shows an example with two states, *a* and *b*, of a single character. Taxa 1 and 3 and the outgroup possess state *b* (the ancestral state), whereas taxa 2 and 4 possess state *a* (the derived state). In general, the outgroup is a taxon that ideally is the most closely related to the primary taxa under study (the ingroup); it is a taxon that shares a common ancestor (node 1) with the primary taxa.

Because the outgroup possesses state *b*, it is hypothesized that the theoretical ancestor at the root, or node 1, also possesses state *b*. These two trees depict two hypothetical ways in which the states could have arisen in each of the four

Figure 13.4
These Two Trees Demonstrate How Maximum Parsimony Searches for the "Simplest Solution" by Constructing a Tree in Such a Way that Changes from One Character State to Another Are Minimized across a Tree

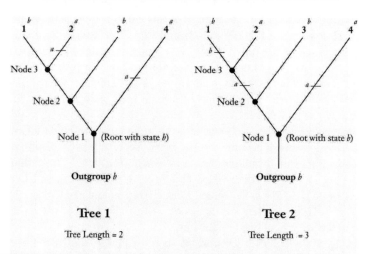

In tree 1, state *a* is introduced twice; the tree length is two. In tree 2 state *a* is introduced twice, and state *b* reintroduced once; the tree length is three. Therefore, tree 1, which has the shorter length, is the more parsimonious tree. However, the *most* parsimonious solution would actually be a tree of length 1 that groups taxa 1 and 3, and taxa 2 and 4.

"ingroup" taxa. In tree 1, it is hypothesized that state *a* was introduced on two separate occasions, once in the branch leading to Taxon 4 and once in the branch leading to Taxon 2. In this case, tree 1 has a tree length of 2. In tree 2 it is hypothesized that state *a* was introduced twice (in the branch leading to Taxon 4 and in the branch leading to node 3), and that state *b* was reintroduced in the branch leading to Taxon 1. Tree 2 therefore has a tree length of 3. State *a* was introduced twice in both trees, but state *b* was reintroduced only once in tree 2. Therefore, tree 1, which has the shorter tree length, is the more parsimonious tree. The most parsimonious solution would actually be a tree of length 1 that groups taxa 1 and 3, and taxa 2 and 4.

ML distinguishes itself from MP by being a model-based optimality criterion (Lewis 2001) with many explicit evolutionary assumptions. This implies that MP is a "model-free" criterion, but as Swofford et al. (1996) point out, minimizing the changes in character states across a tree as MP does makes a key assumption (even if implicit) about how information has been transmitted, or "evolved." Nevertheless, ML provides an alternative to MP by being able to evaluate many more models or explicit assumptions about information transmission. ML approaches are formulated on stochastic models of evolutionary change (Huelsenbeck and Bollback 2001; Swofford et al. 1996), or in this case a model of cultural transmission operating under the constraints of various evolutionary mechanisms such as natural selection and drift.

Figure 13.5
**Maximum Likelihood Is a Model-Based Optimality Criterion that Makes Use of
Stochastic Models of Evolutionary Change**

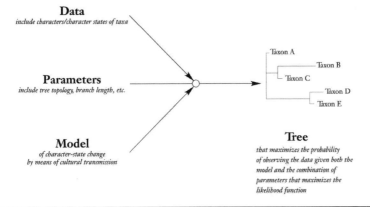

It uses this model to construct a tree that maximizes the probability of observing the characters fed into the analysis. In addition to the model, the probability of observing the data depends on several unknown parameters such as tree topology and tree branch lengths. These parameters are either estimated as part of the process or known ahead of time.

Essentially ML uses this model to construct the tree that maximizes the probability of observing the characters fed into the analysis (Swofford et al. 1996) (figure 13.5). In other words, using a specific model of change in conjunction with the observed data (taxa and the characters), ML identifies the most likely sets of relationships among the taxa. The model is a statement about the probability of specific types of changes within a phylogenetic context. The model does this by giving the "probability of a change from one [character] state to another over a specified evolutionary distance" (Huelsenbeck and Bollback 2001: 419). This probability of change is based on various characteristics of the data set. For example, some changes (such as minor changes in a previously existing motif) may be considered more likely, whereas others (such as the introduction of a new motif) are less likely. And some changes may be directional, such that a character is less likely to revert to an ancestral state once a change has occurred.

In addition to the model, the probability of observing the data depends on several unknown parameters that include tree topology, the tree branch lengths (something that MP does not take into account), and potential variation in the rate of character-state change from branch to branch. These parameters are either assumed a priori or estimated by "finding that combination of parameter values that maximizes the likelihood function" (Huelsenbeck and Bollback 2001: 426). ML therefore must solve two problems—"finding the maximum likelihood combination of parameters for distinct trees and finding the tree that has the greatest likelihood" (Huelsenbeck and Bollback 2001: 426). The success of ML methods for reconstructing phylogenies depends on the appropriateness of the model of character evolution that is specified.

Are MP and ML Appropriate for Analyses of Cultural Transmission?

MP assumes that it is less likely for a complex trait, such as a horned-serpent icon, to develop independently twice instead of developing once and then being transmitted. Although it is in fact possible for a character to develop independently more than once, the chance of this decreases as character complexity increases, such as simple triangle decorations versus more complex horned-serpent icons. Everything else being equal, this means that independent, analogous similarities are less likely to occur than transmitted, homologous similarities—a point consistent with MP.

We therefore argue that MP is applicable to analyses of cultural-information transmission because (1) evolution tends to be conservative over the long term (Jones 2000; Sober 1984); (2) the presence of the same complex characters are more likely to be the result of transmission rather than independent development; (3) the specifics of cultural replication and transmission are not well understood; and (4) the specific behavioral and cultural details of humanity's past are historically contingent and therefore difficult to access (O'Brien and Lyman 2000a). Points one and two are consistent with MP's goal of minimizing change in the character states across a tree, and points three and four suggest that adding explicit assumptions (regarding how information transmission occurred), in addition to those that MP makes, will be difficult and perhaps invalid. However, evolution is not always conservative, and analogous occurrences do happen. At what point a character is too complex to realistically be a product of independent development may not always be clear. Assuming homology when homoplasy is actually the case will result in erroneous tree reconstructions by MP. In these cases, ML offers an alternative means for assessing the phylogeny.

Whether or not ML is appropriate for the analysis of cultural transmission depends largely on the specific model used. Ours is based on a model proposed by Lewis (2001), which we believe is appropriate for the following reasons. First, no character state is designated ancestral or descendant a priori, and this is certainly appropriate in analyses of any type of transmission where this is unknown to begin with, as in our data set. This is also the assumption that our MP analysis makes. Second, a character along any branch can change state at any instant in time. The probability of such a change is equal for every time interval of equal length along a branch, and each time interval is independent with respect to this probability. This appears to be a valid assumption for any type of transmission where the specific day-to-day, and even minute-to-minute, historical contingencies of the process remain unknown.

Third, the probability of change between character states is considered symmetrical (the instantaneous probability of change from state a to state b is the same as from state b to state a). Our MP analysis makes the same assumption. Again, while such an assumption for specific characters may be unlikely for certain historical contingencies, the examination of broad cultural traditions over a large span of time (as in this case) makes such an assumption a reasonable place to begin because the historical contingencies for specific characters remain unknown.

Lastly, the model does not emphasize either graduated or punctuated change over the other (Lewis 2001: 917). Since the equations use the average amount of change, it does not matter whether the change along any particular branch occurred gradually or at specific moment(s) in time. A potential problem with the model is the assumption that the instantaneous rate of change is the same for all characters when in fact it may not be. Such an incorrect assumption could result in poor likelihood scores. There are ways to account for rate heterogeneity (Lewis 2001), and our future analyses will make use of such methods for comparison purposes.

Regions of Analysis and Data Set

The analysis under discussion here is a broad comparison based on the presence of complex associations of designs within five geographically and temporally defined ceramic traditions—the Comala Phase of western Mexico,

Figure 13.6
The Approximate Spatial and Temporal Distributions of the Five Ceramic Traditions Examined in This Analysis

1) Comala	100 B.C.–A.D. 375
2) Classic Mimbres	A.D. 1000–1150
3) Viejo	A.D. 700–1200
4) Medio	A.D. 1200–1450
5) Salado	A.D. 1300–1425

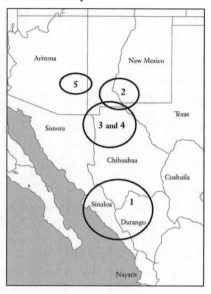

Viejo- and Medio-period occupations of the Casas Grandes region of northern Mexico, the Classic Mimbres occupation of the Mimbres Mogollon region of New Mexico, and the Salado occupation of southern New Mexico and Arizona (figure 13.6). Although we clearly recognize the difference between periods and what commonly are referred to as "cultures," we do not distinguish between them here. Rather, we view the above five nominal categories as cultural units. In terms of the phylogenetic analysis, they represent the taxa.

The presence and nature of designs in smoker effigies, fish effigies, dual/twin images, horned serpents, horned men, datura (Jimson weed) effigies, anthropomorphs, and two-headed serpents form the basis of the characters used in the analysis. Characters recorded for the horned-serpent motifs and icons are horn number, horn direction, and the color of the serpent. The character recorded for macaw motifs and icons is the type of design—effigy, isolated macaw head, or opposing macaw heads. The character recorded for twin images is the type of animal, and in the case of two-headed serpents, the type of serpent head. The presence and position of smoking individuals was also considered. Finally, the presence of horned men (anthropomorphic individuals with horns protruding from their foreheads), datura effigies, fish effigies, and anthropomorphic "fish people" and "macaw people" were also included.

The characters are coded in four different ways (tables 13.1–13.4) because of the various pros and cons of different character-coding schemes (see details

Table 13.1
Summary of Characters and Character States in Matrix 1: Two-State with Larger General Category

1.	Smokers	(0) Absent	(1) Present
2.	Kneeling Smoker	(0) Absent	(1) Present
3.	Crouching Smoker	(0) Absent	(1) Present
4.	Macaws	(0) Absent	(1) Present
5.	Red Macaw Effigies	(0) Absent	(1) Present
6.	Polychrome Macaw Effigies	(0) Absent	(1) Present
7.	Isolated Macaw Heads	(0) Absent	(1) Present
8.	Opposing Macaws	(0) Absent	(1) Present
9.	Fish	(0) Absent	(1) Present
10.	Twin Images	(0) Absent	(1) Present
11.	Human Twin Images	(0) Absent	(1) Present
12.	Bird Twin Images	(0) Absent	(1) Present
13.	Mountain Sheep Twin Images	(0) Absent	(1) Present
14.	Opposing Horned Serpents Twin Images	(0) Absent	(1) Present
15.	Horned Serpents	(0) Absent	(1) Present
16.	Horned Serpent Forward Horn Direction	(0) Absent	(1) Present
17.	Horned Serpent Reverse Horn Direction	(0) Absent	(1) Present
18.	Horned Serpent Horns in Two Directions	(0) Absent	(1) Present
19.	Red Horned Serpent	(0) Absent	(1) Present
20.	Black Horned Serpent	(0) Absent	(1) Present
21.	White Horned Serpent	(0) Absent	(1) Present
22.	Polychrome Horned Serpent	(0) Absent	(1) Present
23.	Horned Men	(0) Absent	(1) Present
24.	Datura	(0) Absent	(1) Present
25.	Anthropomorphs	(0) Absent	(1) Present
26.	Fish Men Anthropomorphs	(0) Absent	(1) Present
27.	Macaw Men Anthropomorphs	(0) Absent	(1) Present
28.	Two Headed Macaws and/or Serpents	(0) Absent	(1) Present
29.	Two Serpent Heads	(0) Absent	(1) Present
30.	Macaw and Serpent Heads	(0) Absent	(1) Present
31.	Two Macaw Heads	(0) Absent	(1) Present

in Kitching et al. 1998; O'Brien and Lyman 2003a; Swofford et al. 1996; Wiley et al. 1991). Matrix 1 consists of two-state characters (presence/absence) and a larger general category. For example, because kneeling smokers and crouching smokers were present, a general category of smoker was added. Matrix 2 consists of two-state characters but without the larger general category. Because of our present understanding of these traditions, we proposed that the addition of these larger general categories would more clearly resolve the hierarchical relationships among the taxa. However, it is possible that this

Table 13.2
Summary of Characters and Character States in Matrix 2: Two-State with No Larger General Category

1.	Kneeling Smoker	(0) Absent	(1) Present
2.	Crouching Smoker	(0) Absent	(1) Present
3.	Red Macaw Effigies	(0) Absent	(1) Present
4.	Polychrome Macaw Effigies	(0) Absent	(1) Present
5.	Isolated Macaw Heads	(0) Absent	(1) Present
6.	Opposing Macaws	(0) Absent	(1) Present
7.	Fish	(0) Absent	(1) Present
8.	Human Twin Images	(0) Absent	(1) Present
9.	Bird Twin Images	(0) Absent	(1) Present
10.	Mountain Sheep Twin Images	(0) Absent	(1) Present
11.	Opposing Horned Serpents Twin Images	(0) Absent	(1) Present
12.	Horned Serpent Forward Horn Direction	(0) Absent	(1) Present
13.	Horned Serpent Reverse Horn Direction	(0) Absent	(1) Present
14.	Horned Serpent Horns in Two Directions	(0) Absent	(1) Present
15.	Red Horned Serpent	(0) Absent	(1) Present
16.	Black Horned Serpent	(0) Absent	(1) Present
17.	White Horned Serpent	(0) Absent	(1) Present
18.	Polychrome Horned Serpent	(0) Absent	(1) Present
19.	Horned Men	(0) Absent	(1) Present
20.	Datura	(0) Absent	(1) Present
21.	Fish Men Anthropomorphs	(0) Absent	(1) Present
22.	Macaw Men Anthropomorphs	(0) Absent	(1) Present
23.	Two Serpent Heads	(0) Absent	(1) Present
24.	Macaw and Serpent Heads	(0) Absent	(1) Present
25.	Two Macaw Heads	(0) Absent	(1) Present

is imposing a degree of hierarchy not present in the data set, and we therefore chose to include the matrix 2 coding scheme as well.

As an alternative to matrices 1 and 2, matrix 3 consists of multistate characters without an absent state, thereby minimizing the effect of ordering the taxa by absences of character states as opposed to their presence (except of course for the few presence/absence characters that were unavoidably part of the multistate matrices). For the purposes of comparison we also created matrix 4, which adds an absent state to the multistate characters. The primary disadvantage of multistate coding schemes, which led us to also include two-state presence/absence schemes, is that the algorithms used to construct the trees may have more difficulties resolving the hierarchical structure (depending on the data set), resulting in more than simply dichotomous splits at tree nodes. For example, referring to figure 13.4, the branch leading to taxon 2 may instead extend from node 2 as opposed to node 3, creating what is known as a

Table 13.3
Summary of Characters and Character States in Matrix 3:
Multistate with No Absent States

Character	Character state
1. Smokers	(0) Kneeling Smoker
	(1) Crouching Smoker
2. Macaws	(0) Red Macaw Effigies
	(1) Polychrome Macaw Effigies
	(2) Isolated Macaw Heads
	(3) Opposing Macaws
3. Fish	(0) Absent
	(1) Present
4. Twin Images	(0) Humans
	(1) Birds
	(2) Mountain Sheep
	(3) Opposing Horned Serpents
5. Horned Serpent Horn Direction	(0) Forward
	(1) Back
	(2) Two
6. Horned Serpent Color	(0) Red
	(1) Black
	(2) White
	(3) Polychrome
7. Horned Men	(0) Absent
	(1) Present
8. Datura	(0) Absent
	(1) Present
9. Anthropomorphs	(0) Fish Men
	(1) Macaw Men
10. Two Headed Macaws and/or Serpents	(0) Two Serpent Heads
	(1) Macaw and Serpent Head
	(2) Two Macaw Heads

"polytomy," or a group of three or more taxa where the relationships among the members are unknown.

For each character, a character state was recorded if it was known to be applicable to at least one vessel within each respective ceramic tradition. If it was known that none of the character states for a particular character was present on any vessels within a particular ceramic tradition, then it was listed as inapplicable for that ceramic tradition. If it was unknown one way or the

Table 13.4
Summary of Characters and Character States in Matrix 4: Multistate with Absent States

	Character	Character state
1.	Smokers	(0) Absent
		(1) Kneeling Smoker
		(2) Crouching Smoker
2.	Macaws	(0) Absent
		(1) Red Macaw Effigies
		(2) Polychrome Macaw Effigies
		(3) Isolated Macaw Heads
		(4) Opposing Macaws
3.	Fish	(0) Absent
		(1) Present
4.	Twin Images	(0) Absent
		(1) Humans
		(2) Birds
		(3) Mountain Sheep
		(4) Opposing Horned Serpents
5.	Horned Serpent Horn Direction	(0) Absent
		(1) Forward
		(2) Back
		(3) Two
6.	Horned Serpent Color	(0) Absent
		(1) Red
		(2) Black
		(3) White
		(4) Polychrome
7.	Horned Men	(0) Absent
		(1) Present
8.	Datura	(0) Absent
		(1) Present
9.	Anthropomorphs	(0) Absent
		(1) Fish Men
		(2) Macaw Men
10.	Two Headed Macaws and/or Serpents	(0) Absent
		(1) Two Serpent Heads
		(2) Macaw and Serpent Head
		(3) Two Macaw Heads

other, then it was recorded as unknown for that region. The Comala-phase ceramic tradition of western Mexico, because of its distance in time and space from the other four traditions, was used as the outgroup.

The data matrices were constructed using the NEXUS Data Editor version 0.5.0 (Page 2001a) and then imported into PAUP* version 4.0b10 (Swofford 1998) for the phylogenetic analysis. The MP analyses were run using the AllTrees command to perform an exhaustive search of all possible tree topologies (of which there are only fifteen as a result of having only five taxa). The ML analyses were run using the HSearch command with the addition sequence set to random, the number of addition sequence replications set to 1000, the base frequencies set to equal, and the branch-swapping algorithm set to tree bisection-reconnection. All output was exported to TreeView version 1.6.6 (Page 2001b) for graphic manipulation and presentation.

ML historically has been set up to analyze molecular data, paying little attention to morphology, and PAUP* reflects this. However, the program provides two general methods for organizing molecular data—the data either contain all four bases (ACGT for DNA; ACTU for RNA) or are divided into purines (represented by A) and pyrimidines (represented by C). In that the latter choice gives two-state characters, an ML analysis can actually be performed on morphological data if the data are coded as present/absent. We therefore were able to run ML analyses only on data matrices 1 and 2.

In addition, there are two important problems/limitations to performing an ML analysis on cultural or biological morphological data in PAUP* as it is currently configured. First, unknowns and inapplicable codings are treated as being the same. These have distinctly different meanings with regard to our cultural data and will have to be differentiated in the future. Second, PAUP* currently does not have the capability to compute a conditional likelihood (conditional on the fact that only variable characters are present in the data [see Lewis 2001]). We are currently working on a program that will incorporate these items, and for the time being these ML results must be seen as tentative.[1]

Results

Figure 13.7 shows the resulting two tree topologies (out of the possible fifteen fully resolved tree topologies) that have the combined best support from both the MP and ML analyses. Using both optimality criteria, these were the only two topologies that occurred in all four matrices as either one of the most parsimonious trees or one of the trees with the best likelihood score. However, two statistical tests that were run suggest caution. The first is the bootstrap statistic, in which the original data set is resampled with replacement multiple times to produce several "fictional" samples of the same size. A separate tree is estimated for each fictional sample, and the confidence in individual groups (clades) is then assessed by computing the percentage of the samples in which that group is present (Felsenstein 2004). For both the MP

Figure 13.7
Out of the Possible 15 Fully Resolved Tree Topologies that Occur with Five Taxa, These Two Have the Combined Best Support from Both the MP Analysis of All Four Matrices and the ML Analysis of the Two Presence/Absence Matrices

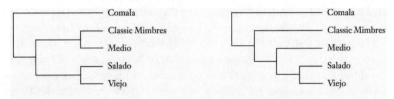

Tree Topology 1

MP: Appears in all four character matrices as
    one of the most parsimonious trees.
    For matrices 1 and 2, this topology is
    the sole most parsimonious tree if the Two
    Headed Macaw character is weighted as
    2.0 or if the Horned Serpent Twin
    Image character is excluded.

ML: Appears in both matrices 1 and 2 as
    one of the trees with the best ML score.

Tree Topology 2

MP: Appears in all four character matrices as
    one of the most parsimonious trees.
    For matrices 1 and 2, this topology is
    the sole most parsimonious tree if the
    Horned Serpent Twin Image character is
    weighted as 2.0 or if the Two Headed
    Macaw character is excluded.

ML: Appears in both matrices 1 and 2 as
    one of the trees with the best ML score.

They were the only two topologies that occurred in all four matrices as either one of the most parsimonious trees or one of the trees with the best likelihood score.

and ML analyses, the Salado and Viejo-period group was the only consistent grouping to appear more than 50 percent of the time, suggesting that this data set is having difficulty resolving the relationships among the Comala-phase, Medio-period, and Classic Mimbres traditions.

The second test run was the Shimodaira-Hasegawa test (Shimodaira and Hasegawa 1999), which was performed on the ML trees to determine if there were any statistically significant differences between their ML scores. Unfortunately, this test did not find any statistically significant differences between the best likelihood scores and the scores of 20^2 other trees that were within 2.21944 log-likelihood units of these two best topologies. However, this test tends to be conservative, perhaps overly so in some cases (Goldman et al. 2000; Shimodaira and Hasegawa 1999). Future analysis will include exploring other options for testing differences among likelihood-tree topologies.

While caution is warranted from these two statistical tests, the g1 statistic (Hillis 1991) did indicate a fair amount of underlying phylogenetic signal (hierarchical, branching structure) was present relative to how the characters have been coded (matrix 1: -1.098209; matrix 2: -0.618957; matrices 3 and 4: -1.500000). This discrepancy with the previous two statistics as well as the inability to choose between the two topologies shown in figure 13.7 may be the result primarily of two factors. First, a few of the Comala-phase characters were assigned an unknown state (data matrix 1, with thirty-one characters total [six characters unknown]; data matrix 2, with twenty-five characters total [six characters unknown]; data matrices 3 and 4, each with ten characters total [two characters unknown]). These unknowns contribute to the multiple most parsimonious solutions and the multiple statistically indistinguishable log-likelihood values that show different relationships among the Comala-phase, Medio-period, and Classic Mimbres traditions.

Second, for matrices 1 and 2, the two topologies (figure 13.7) appear to be tied to different single characters. Topology 1 appears to be linked to the "Two Macaw Heads" character (character 31 for matrix 1; character 25 for matrix 2). Topology 2 appears to be linked to the "Opposing Horned Serpents Twin Images" character (character 14 for matrix 1; character 11 for matrix 2). For both matrices, Topology 1 becomes the sole most parsimonious tree if either the "Two Macaw Heads" character is weighted[3] as 2.0 or if the "Opposing Horned Serpents Twin Images" character is excluded. Doing the opposite to these characters results in Topology 2 as the sole most parsimonious tree. No similar relationship was noted for matrices 3 and 4, but in these cases the two separate signals may be weakened because these two individual characters are integrated into larger multistate characters in matrices 3 and 4.

These relationships were not as visible in the likelihood analysis. For matrix 1, Topology 2 resulted as the tree with the sole best likelihood score if character 14 (Opposing Horned Serpents Twin Images) was weighted as 4.0. For matrix 2, Topology 1 resulted if character 25 (Two Macaw Heads) was weighted as 5.0. However, the other character weighting and exclusionary relationships just noted for the parsimony analysis did not occur. While somewhat less apparent from the ML analysis, this still indicates that there are perhaps two somewhat different intellectual "trajectories" embedded within these data sets, perhaps focused around these two characters. And neither weighting nor excluding any of the other characters resulted in a single tree for any of the matrices using either MP or ML. If this is the case, it would help explain why the bootstrap and SH test results were poor, despite the apparent hierarchical structure of the data set.

Discussion

We can say with some degree of caution that one of the two topologies in figure 13.7 is the best choice to represent the unknown correct tree. A choice between the two cannot be made based on these analyses alone, but filling in the character-state unknowns for the Comala-phase tradition may help clarify this. This uncertainty may also be the result of the two potential intellectual "trajectories" detected, represented by each of the topologies.

Although our analyses did not conclusively result in one single tree, we can say the following: (1) there appears to be an intellectual break between the Viejo-period and subsequent Medio-period traditions; (2) there does not appear to be a strong intellectual connection between the contemporary Medio-period and Salado traditions; and (3) the Medio period appears to have some type of intellectual-descendant relationship with both the Classic Mimbres and the Comala phase of western Mexico. The relationship between the Medio-period tradition and the Classic Mimbres is probably stronger than between the Medio period and Comala phase because of the latter's greater disjunction in time and space; and (4) there is a possibility that this data set is actually tracing two intellectual subtraditions following slightly different trajectories. One is represented by Topology 1 and focused to some degree around the Two Headed Macaw character, and the other is represented by Topology 2, focused to some degree around the Horned Serpent Twin Image character.

We can also formulate two specific hypotheses (supported by both phylogenetic analyses), which can be tested through other means. The hypotheses are as follows. First, there is a direct historic and heritable connection between the intellectual traditions underlying the symbolic systems of the Classic Mimbres and Medio-period Casas Grandes symbolic systems, which share a more ancestral relationship with western Mexico. Second, the Medio-period

Figure 13.8
Two Images Depicting Similarities between Comala-Phase and Casas Grandes Medio-Period Smoker Effigy Vessels

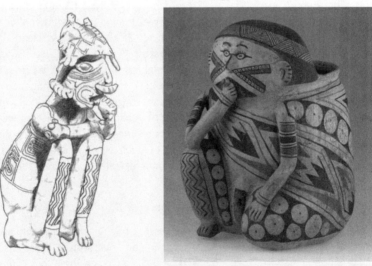

Comala Smoker Effigy Vessel

Casas Grandes Medio Smoker Effigy Vessel

Image 1 (Comala phase) redrawn from Furst (1998:figure 1); image 2 (Casas Grandes Medio period) courtesy Natural History Museum of Los Angeles County (photograph by C. Coleman).

Figure 13.9
**Two Images Depicting Similarities between Classic Mimbres and Casas Grandes
Medio-Period Horned/Plumed-Serpent-Headdress Figures**

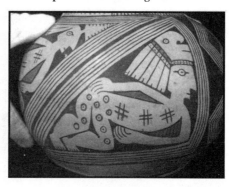

<table>
<tr><td>Classic Mimbres Figure with
Horned Serpent Headdress</td><td>Casas Grandes Medio Figure with
Horned Serpent Headdress</td></tr>
</table>

Image 1 (Classic Mimbres) redrawn from Davis (1995:180); image 2 (Casas Grandes
Medio period) courtesy Centennial Museum, University of Texas at El Paso (catalog no.
36.85.18).

Figure 13.10
**Two Images Depicting Similarities between Comala-Phase and Casas Grandes
Medio-Period Horned-Men Figures**

Comala Horned Man Effigy Vessel   Casas Grandes Medio Horned Man Image

Image 1 (Comala phase) from Graham (1998:figure 2); image 2 (Casas Grandes Medio
period) redrawn from Di Peso et al. (1974[6]:272).

Figure 13.11
Two Images Depicting Similarities between Comala-Phase and Casas Grandes
Medio-Period Macaw Effigy Vessels

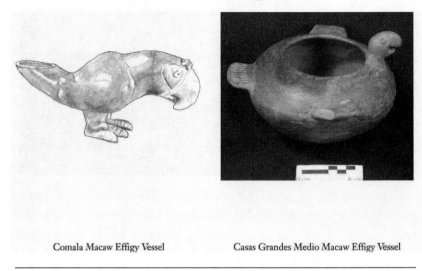

Comala Macaw Effigy Vessel   Casas Grandes Medio Macaw Effigy Vessel

Image 1 (Comala phase) redrawn from Schöndube (1998:figure 17); image 2 (Casas Grandes Medio period) courtesy Centennial Museum, University of Texas at El Paso (catalog no. A. 36.1.64).

symbolic tradition is less heavily influenced by the intellectual traditions of the preceding Viejo-period tradition and the contemporaneous Salado tradition. Similarities among the Comala-phase, Classic Mimbres, and Medio-period intellectual traditions are shown in figures 13.8–13.11. In addition, the reader is referred to Furst (1998: figure 29) and Brody (1983: plate 40) for a comparison between Comala-phase and Classic Mimbres "Fish Eating Man" effigy vessels.

There are numerous other lines of evidence that support the results of the phylogenetic analyses and the resulting two hypotheses presented above. Space does not allow a full discussion, but two examples follow. First, a phylogenetic analysis by VanPool et al. (2000) of horned/plumed-serpent imagery from the American Southwest found that Mimbres, Jornada Mogollon, Casas Grandes, and Pottery Mound serpent imagery demonstrated a historical relationship. Imagery from those cultural units was more distantly related to Salado and Pueblo III horned/plumed-serpent imagery. Second, a biodistance study by Turner (1999) suggests Medio-period occupants of Paquimé, a Casas Grandes site in northern Mexico, shared a close genetic relationship with the preceding Mimbres populations and the pre-Hispanic occupants of the Sinaloa region in western Mexico, and a much weaker genetic similarity with other groups such as the Salado.

Conclusions

Phylogenetic analysis is a method for tracing the transmission of information in order to reconstruct both biological and cultural clades, or lineages. Both MP and ML are appropriate optimality criteria to apply to cultural data, and both can be used to check the results of the other. We illustrated this by applying both optimality criteria to a phylogenetic analysis of five ceramic traditions from prehispanic northern Mexico, western Mexico, and the American Southwest, and found a strong probability for the following two statements. First, there was a direct historical, heritable connection between the intellectual traditions underlying the symbolic systems of the Classic Mimbres and Medio-period Casas Grandes symbolic systems, which share a more ancestral relationship with western Mexico. Second, the Medio-period symbolic tradition was less heavily influenced by the intellectual traditions of the preceding Viejo period and the contemporaneous Salado tradition.

Although our MP and ML analyses need further work, these two statements are supported by (1) the congruence between analyses using different optimality criteria (MP and ML) as well as different character-coding schemes, and (2) the multiple lines of supporting evidence that include such things as other cultural phylogenetic analyses and biodistance studies. Perhaps even more important than the specific results of these analyses is the enforcement of the notion that additional strength is added to phylogenetic analyses by using multiple optimality criteria. Those of us interested in cultural systemtics should continue to explore the combined implementation of ML and MP in our work.

Notes

1.   Shortly before this book appeared, one of the authors—Laura Salter—finished the program, SSAMK. The program is now available at http://www.stat.unm.edu/~salter/software
2.   This number includes trees with both fully resolved and unresolved topologies (trees with polytomies).
3.   Weighting involves the process of making the change from one character state to another more costly (Felsenstein 2004; Wiley et al. 1991) or more conservative (it is less likely to change). In this case, weighting a character as 2.0 means that the other characters, which are weighted as 1.0, are twice as likely to change states as this character. Or one could say that this character has twice the cost to change states compared to the characters with a weight of 1.0.

Acknowledgments

We thank the editors for putting together this important and timely volume on the use of phylogenetic methods in anthropology and for inviting us to contribute to it.

14

Archaeological-Materials Characterization as Phylogenetic Method: The Case of Copador Pottery from Southeastern Mesoamerica

Hector Neff

In an earlier paper on the interface between evolutionary theory and technological analysis of ceramics, I suggested that "historical continuity and transmission can be approached from the perspective of continuity of shared resource-procurement patterns defined through compositional analysis" (Neff 1993: 32). The basic argument is an extension of the use of materials characterization to distinguish local from nonlocal products—an application that has a long and venerable history in American archaeology (e.g., Shepard 1936, 1948).

The linkage between ceramic-materials characterization and lines of cultural descent depends on two interrelated assumptions. First, it must be assumed that relationships of descent among ceramics can be traced *by some means*. To many (e.g., Dunnell 1980, 1989; Lipo 2001; Lipo et al. 1997; Neff 1992, 1993; Neiman 1995; Shennan 2002; Tschauner 1994), this assumption is an obvious and basic implication of recognizing that culture constitutes an inheritance system. The assumption is also a virtual *sine qua non* of culture history and the taxonomic frameworks that were developed under the culture-historical paradigm (Lyman et al. 1997; Neff 1993). Although many would consider such an assumption nonproblematic, J. O. Brew's (1946: 53) comment that relationships of descent "do not exist between inanimate objects" still echoes in some quarters. For example, an anonymous reviewer of a paper by Neff et al. (1999) objected that "pottery is not alive" in reference to inferences made about ceramic traditions in the Guatemalan highlands. However, pottery does not have to be alive for relationships of descent to be traceable; the fact that potters must learn their craft through some kind of apprenticeship means that relationships of descent do, in fact, link potters (and therefore their pots) into historically continuous lineages, or "ceramic traditions." Identifying pots that pertain to specific lineages and describing the topology of linkages among those pots are central methodological problems in evolutionary archaeology.

The other part of the argument connecting materials characterization to cultural descent is the assumption that because ceramic-resource choice and paste-preparation practices (like other aspects of ceramic production) are inherited culturally, compositional uniformity will tend to be greater in a group of ceramics that represent a single tradition than in a heterogeneous mix of ceramics produced by potters working in several traditions. Potters working within a ceramic tradition will tend to live near one another and thus have access to the same ceramic environment. Further, by definition they share traditional knowledge, so they will know about the same local clay and temper sources, and they will share recipes for mixing those raw materials. Potters who combine materials from the same sources in similar ways may be expected to create compositionally similar ceramic end products.

Ethnographic studies (e.g., Arnold et al. 1991, 1999, 2000; Thieme and Neff 1993) document that the products of a single community of potters tend to be compositionally uniform and distinct from products of other communities. One remarkable instance of long-term continuity of resource use and paste preparation is the Gray-ware tradition of San Bartolo Coyotepec, in the Valley of Oaxaca, Mexico. Modern sherds and prepared raw materials from Coyotepec fall within the range of elemental variation of the main group (Gris-1) of Formative-period Gray ware from Monte Albán and other Oaxacan sites, and the modern and ancient gray wares are easily discriminated from other Oaxacan elemental profiles (figure 14.1). This compositional evidence is consistent with the hypothesis that a single, historically continuous line of inheritance links the gray bowls of Monte Albán II times with the shiny gray effigies and miniatures produced for tourists in Coyotepec today.

Of course, compositional uniformity cannot by itself prove historical continuity. Patterns of ceramic compositional diversity reflect not just resource choices and preparation practices of potters but also the structure of the local ceramic raw-material environment. In the Coyotepec case, for example, modern potters might produce ceramics that are chemically similar to Formative-period ceramics simply because they live in the same region and just by chance exploit clay beds that are chemically similar to clay beds used by unrelated potters at an earlier time period. But given that Oaxaca is geologically diverse and ceramics from the region show multiple distinct compositional profiles (figure 14.1), the fact that gray pottery from several different time periods is chemically uniform favors the hypothesis that the resource

Figure 14.1
**Sodium and Ytterbium Concentrations in Gris (Gray), Crema (Cream), and
Café (Brown) Ceramics from Monte Albán and Other Sites in Oaxaca, Mexico**

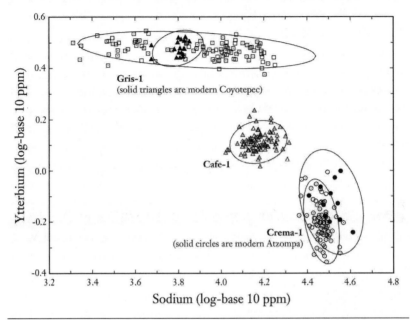

Solid symbols are ethnographic pottery and raw materials that exceed 1 percent probability of membership in the Gris-1 (solid triangles) or Crema-1 (solid circles) groups (probabilities are based on Mahalanobis distances from the group centroids, calculated using 31 elemental concentrations determined by INAA). All ethnographic samples that fall within the range of variation of the Gris-1 group are from Coyotepec; all ethnographic samples that fall within the range of variation of the Crema-1 group are from Atzompa; one raw clay from an archaeological context at Monte Albán is included in the Crema-1 group as well.

choices and pyrotechnology used to produce gray ware form a single, continuous lineage.

Another qualification to bear in mind is that the signal of continuity in resource use and paste-preparation practices can be attenuated by changes in resources. For example, if all or part of a lineage of potters migrates, the émigrés will be forced to adopt new resources in their new home. Alternatively, conditions in the local environment may select for resource shifts. An ethnographic example of such a case is Ticul, Yucatán, Mexico, where Arnold et al. (1999, 2000) document the dramatic compositional changes in Ticul ceramics following the exhaustion of a traditional clay source and the switch in 1992 to a new source located in Campeche, approximately eighty kilometers from Ticul. It is worth pointing out in this case, however, that whereas pre-1992 products are distinct from post-1992 products, the post-1992 products are nonetheless

chemically distinct from contemporary ceramics made in other pottery-pro-
ducing communities near Ticul. Post-1992 Ticul still has a distinctive local
signature, but it is different from the pre-1992 signature.

In sum, although one cannot argue that compositional uniformity invari-
ably identifies connections of common descent among ceramics, nor that common descent guarantees compositional uniformity, uniformity nonetheless
constitutes an important piece of evidence bearing on the issue of historical
continuity. Curiously, however, despite fairly widespread use of materials characterization in "provenance research," few studies have explicitly addressed
descent and taxonomy. Here I present an example in which elemental characterization discriminates between two competing hypotheses about lines of
cultural inheritance among serving vessels in the southeastern Maya area.
This is not a contrived example but rather one that shows how materials characterization can help resolve real questions about artifact phylogeny that
standard typological analysis cannot settle.

Copador and Other Serving Vessels of the Southeastern Maya Periphery

The example concerns the genealogy of a well-known Late Classic Maya
ceramic known as Copador (figure 14.2). Copador vessels are polychrome
cylinders or bowls that are distinguished by painted anthropomorphic figures
and repetitive glyph-like designs. The name "Copador" was coined by A. V.
Kidder in recognition of the Copán, Honduras, and Salvadoran associations of
this distinctive polychrome ceramic (Willey et al. 1994). A survey by Beaudry

Figure 14.2
Copador Polychrome Vessel from Copán, Honduras

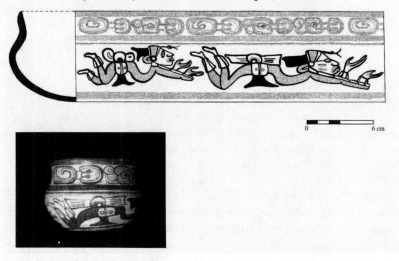

(After Willey et al. 1994).

Figure 14.3
Map of the Maya Area Showing Locations Mentioned in the Text

(1984) indicates that Copador is common across western El Salvador and adjacent southeastern Guatemala and at Copán and nearby sites in western Honduras (figure 14.3).

John Longyear (1952) provided the first detailed description of Copador in a monograph on the ceramics of Copán. Based on abundance in excavated assemblages, he considered Copán and Tazumal, El Salvador, equally likely "homes" of the Copador tradition. To resolve the provenance issue, he relied on features of the polychrome decorative style, particularly the glyphic elements and the postures of human and anthropomorphic figures. He considered these features to be distinctly Maya in character, and on this basis argued that Copador was a product of the Copán Maya:

> Copador certainly seems to have been strongly influenced by the hierarchic cult of the Maya.... I have tried to show how many of its glyph motifs stemmed from actual hieroglyphs, and have suggested that the positions assumed by its human figures find their counterparts in the attitudes of gods and personages depicted in the codices. If this is the case, Copador pottery should have originated in a center occupied by devotees and participants of the Maya hierarchy. (Longyear 1952: 63)

Longyear actually presented a more comprehensive model of Maya polychrome phyletic relationships (figure 14.4). He followed Sylvanus Morley in seeing Maya elite culture as developing in the Petén region of northern Guatemala, where basal-flange bowls and cylindrical tripods were the preferred polychrome serving vessels of the Early Classic period. According to this view, the elite groups that expanded out of the Petén, such as the founders of

Figure 14.4
Graphical Depiction of Longyear's (1952) Model of Diversification of Maya Polychromes from the Early Classic through Late Classic Periods

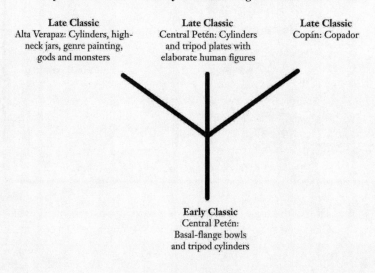

Late Classic
Alta Verapaz: Cylinders, high-neck jars, genre painting, gods and monsters

Late Classic
Central Petén: Cylinders and tripod plates with elaborate human figures

Late Classic
Copán: Copador

Early Classic
Central Petén:
Basal-flange bowls
and tripod cylinders

the Copán dynasty, initially either imported or made local copies of Petén vessels. Eventually, however, the Petén-derived polychrome tradition diversi-fied into several daughter lineages, such as the figure-painted plates and cyl-inders of the Petén, the "genre paintings of gods and monsters" of the Alta Verapaz, and the Copador tradition of Copán.

Additional phyletic assumptions are embedded in Longyear's summary chart of the Copán ceramic sequence (figure 14.5). Copador is shown continu-ing out of the Early Classic Maya basal-flange bowl/cylindrical-tripod tradi-tion, as just indicated. This polychrome lineage also includes "polychrome simple bowls," but it excludes both red-on-orange and burnished orange, both of which turn out to be relevant to the question of Copador ancestry (see below).

Based on his analysis of the ceramic collection from Chalchuapa, in west-ern El Salvador, Robert Sharer (1978) suggested that Copador was produced in several places. Like Longyear, Sharer suggested a close relationship between Copador and "polychrome simple bowls," to which he gave the name "Gualpopa polychrome." In his summary of the Chalchuapa pottery traditions (figure 14.6), Sharer depicted Gualpopa and Copador polychrome as being derived from an earlier cream-slipped monochrome called Huiscoyol.

Another line of descent for Gualpopa and Copador is implied by Willey et al. (1994: 34; see also Beaudry [1984] and Demarest [1986]), who suggest that the application of red paint to Usulutan vessels constituted "the starting point for the evolution of the polychrome tradition." "Usulutan" is the name given to wavy-line resist-decorated vessels that attained peak popularity in south-eastern Mesoamerica during the Late Formative period, when they occurred across a wide area of El Salvador, Guatemala, and Honduras. Although Sharer originally divided Usulutan vessels from Chalchuapa into cream- and orange-slipped variants (figure 14.6), he and Arthur Demarest (Demarest and Sharer 1982; Demarest 1986) later argued that both variants developed out of a long tradition of resist decoration that can be traced through the Early and Middle Formative periods of western El Salvador (figure 14.7). The time depth of the Usulutan tradition in western El Salvador implies that it is indigenous to that region. The addition of red paint in the Early Classic created a type designated "Chilanga" by Sharer (1978); this is what Longyear (1952: figure 5) earlier called "red-on-orange" at Copán. Both plain and red-painted Usulutan vessels are also known from Kaminaljuyú (Wetherington 1978) and Bilbao (Parsons 1967), in southern Guatemala.

Typological studies of ceramics from the southeastern Maya area thus have embraced one hypothesis about the genealogy of Copador polychrome, while also supplying the rudiments of an alternative hypothesis. Although Longyear's (1952) proposal that the figure painting and pseudo-glyphs indicate a connec-tion with the Classic Maya of Copán still holds sway among Maya ceramicists (e.g., Willey et al. 1994), those same ceramicists have also begun to link

Figure 14.5
Longyear's (1952) Summary of the Ceramic Sequence at Copán, Honduras, Showing Typical Vessel Forms and Kinds of Decoration

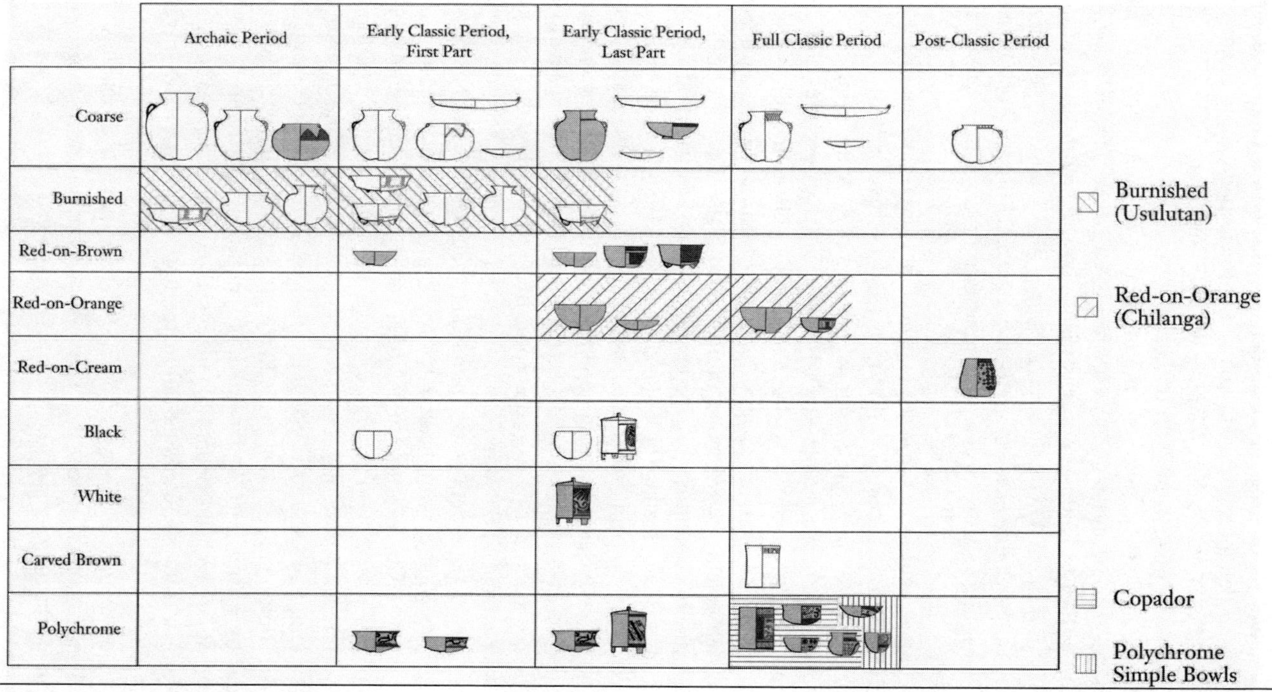

Copador is shown as continuing the "Polychrome" tradition, earlier manifestations of which are the basal-flange bowls and tripods of the Early Classic period. "Full Classic" polychromes also include "polychrome simple bowls," which would now be called "Gualpopa." "Red-on-Cream" vessels of the Early and Full Classic periods would now be called "Chilanga" Usulutan. Other Usulutan varieties are subsumed under the "Burnished" category.

Figure 14.6

Sharer's (1978) Summary of the Pottery Traditions at Chalchuapa, El Salvador

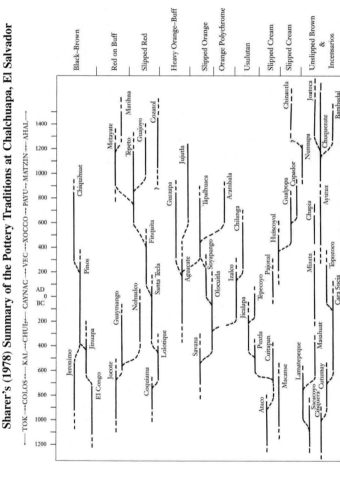

Note that Jicalapa (cream slipped) Usulutan, Chilanga (red painted) Usulutan, and Gualpopa/Copador (polychromes) are shown on three separate lineages.

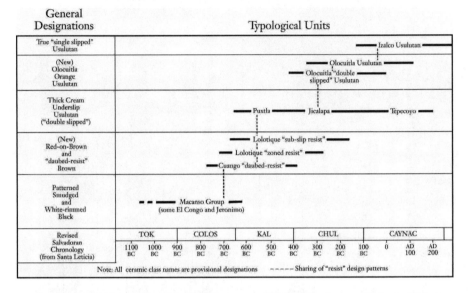

Figure 14.7
Demarest and Sharer's (1982; also Demarest 1986)
Reconstruction of Relationships among the Formative-Period Resist-
and Usulutan-Decorated Ceramics of Western El Salvador

Copador and Gualpopa with Usulutan, a tradition with deep roots in the Formative period of western El Salvador.

Characterization Studies of Copador and Related Ceramics

Longyear (1952: 64) and Sharer (1978: 55) both suggested that materials
analysis would be necessary to resolve the question of where Copador originated, and such an investigation was eventually undertaken by Ron Bishop
and Marilyn Beaudry (e.g., Beaudry 1984; Bishop and Beaudry 1994; Bishop
et al. 1986). The project involved instrumental neutron-activation analysis
(INAA) of Copador and other serving vessels from El Salvador, Guatemala,
and Honduras. Most Copador was found to fall into a single compositional
group that also included a majority of Gualpopa polychrome. The initial INAA
results thus confirmed earlier suggestions (e.g., Longyear 1952; Sharer 1978)
that Copador and Gualpopa pertain to a single. Late Classic polychrome ceramic tradition. Moreover, the fact that most Copador and Gualpopa
polychromes fall into a single compositional group contradicts Sharer's hypothesis of multi-locus production, indicating instead that production was
confined to a single raw-material procurement zone in which potters shared a
tradition of raw-material procurement and paste preparation.

Bishop and Beaudry's INAA study also bolstered the emerging realization,
mentioned above, that Copador and Gualpopa are related to red-painted

Usulutan (Beaudry 1984; Demarest 1986; Willey et al. 1994). The large compositional group that included Copador and Gualpopa also contained a sizable representation of Early Classic Chilanga red-painted Usulutan from Copán, Chalchuapa, and elsewhere (Bishop and Beaudry 1994). Copador and Gualpopa thus are the products of ceramic evolution within a single tradition of resource exploitation that extends back at least into Early Classic times, when potters began to apply red paint to Usulutan vessels.

Was the cream-paste tradition that eventually produced Copador polychrome associated with the Copán Maya, as argued originally by Longyear, or a Salvadoran product derived from the Usulutan tradition, as the INAA study might suggest? Despite the compositional link between Copador and the Usulutan tradition and the resulting implication that Copador might be a Salvadoran product, Bishop and Beaudry (Beaudry 1984; Bishop and Beaudry 1994; Bishop et al. 1986) argued that this cream-paste tradition was indigenous to the Copán Valley. More specifically, Beaudry (1984) suggested that Chilanga, Gualpopa, and Copador were all produced by part-time specialist potters who resided in several locations around the Copán center. The Maya-like elements of Copador, moreover, were introduced so that the vessels could be "marketed as visible symbols of participation in the Maya tradition" (Beaudry 1984: 256).

The case for a Copán Valley source for Copador was far from clear, however (Neff et al. 1999). The INAA project actually showed that local Copán domestic wares are chemically distinct from Copador, and no raw material analyses were reported (Bishop and Beaudry 1994). Instead, it was argued (1) that the high frequency of Copador at Copán favors a Copán attribution and (2) that the geology of the Copán Valley is diverse enough that "the geological possibility of Copador clay sources in the valley is realistic" (Bishop and Beaudry 1994: 426). Of course, neither of these arguments applies exclusively to Copán: Copador is also a frequent occurrence at Chalchuapa, El Salvador, and western El Salvador would qualify as a potential source under the "geological possibility" criterion. Longyear's conviction that Copador sprang from Maya roots cast a long shadow, however, and the weaknesses in the arguments for a Copán Valley provenance went unrecognized, even by investigators who perceived that Copador and Gualpopa polychrome might descend from the Usulutan tradition (Willey et al. 1994).

Almost accidentally, more evidence bearing on the origins of Chilanga, Gualpopa, and Copador arose in the course of a compositional study of Formative-period cream-paste pottery from southern Guatemala (Neff et al. 1999). Initially the study was designed to explore the potential of supplementing bulk elemental characterization by INAA with microprobe analysis using X-ray spectrometers on a scanning electron microscope. It led, however, to a discovery that Chilanga, Gualpopa, and Copador are made from the same clay and temper sources as earlier cream-paste Usulutan pottery and to an inference that those sources lie in western El Salvador.

The cream-paste study focused primarily on Sacatepequez White Paste White ware (SAWH) and Ivory ware. Earlier INAA results (Neff et al. 1990, 1994) had shown that Late Formative SAWH, which is confined to the central Guatemalan Highlands and adjacent Pacific coast (see figure 14.3), is chemically uniform. Ivory ware and Ivory Usulutan also comprise a homogeneous chemical group and are found at many of the same sites as SAWH (e.g., Monte Alto and Kaminaljuyú; see figure 14.3) and in similar shapes and sizes. Moreover, the chemical differences between SAWH and Ivory can be argued to result from subtle paste-preparation differences, perhaps among potters exploiting the same ceramic resource base (Neff et al. 1990, 1994). Because SAWH is securely attributed to production centers in the central Guatemalan Highlands, the distributional, typological, and chemical similarities between SAWH and Ivory seemed to favor a highland Guatemalan origin for Ivory as well (Neff et al. 1994). The microprobe study was designed to test this hypothesis by determining whether the bulk chemical differences between SAWH and Ivory are created by use of different clay sources, different volcanic-ash temper sources, or both.

The hypothesis of a common source for SAWH and Ivory was falsified by the microprobe study, which showed that both clay matrix and volcanic-ash inclusions are chemically distinct (Neff et al. 1999, 2003). This evidence demonstrates that, rather than being created by a subtle paste-recipe difference, the chemical differences between SAWH and Ivory result from the producers of the two wares exploiting completely different ceramic environments.

Additional INAA of Usulutan-decorated pottery undertaken in association with the microprobe study cast further doubt on the hypothesis that Ivory ware vessels are Highland Guatemalan products. Cream-slipped (Jicalapa) Usulutan samples from Nueve Cerros, Chalchuapa, and Santa Leticia (figure 14.3) were found to pertain to the same range of chemical variation as Ivory and Ivory Usulutan from Kaminaljuyú, Monte Alto, and other sites in south-central Guatemala. Vessels derived from the Ivory-ware source thus were consumed not only in south-central Guatemala but across an area that extends from Kaminaljuyú, across eastern Pacific coastal Guatemala, and into western El Salvador. Unfortunately, neither the microprobe study nor the INAA study of Formative-period Guatemalan pottery provided a clear indication of where within this broad region the Ivory-ware source might lie.

In seeking to develop alternative hypotheses about where Ivory-composition vessels originated, my colleagues and I (Neff et al. 1999) stumbled onto the fact that cream-paste vessels of the Chilanga-Gualpopa-Copador tradition pertain to the same range of chemical variation as Ivory, Ivory Usulutan, and Jicalapa Usulutan vessels of the Ivory compositional group. Searches of several southern Mesoamerican INAA data sets for specimens similar in composition to Ivory identified a cluster of close similarities in a data set of

Figure 14.8
Canonical Discriminant-Analysis Results Based on Ivory-, SAWH-, and
Tiquisate-Ware Compositional Groups

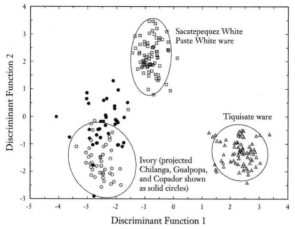

Tiquisate ware is used as an outgroup for comparison. Chilanga, Gualpopa, and Copador specimens are projected onto the two discriminant axes (solid circles), but they were not included in the Ivory Group used in calculating the axes. Ellipses represent the 90 percent confidence level for membership in each group.

Figure 14.9
Canonical Discriminant-Analysis Results Based on Ivory-, SAWH-, and
Tiquisate-Ware Compositional Groups

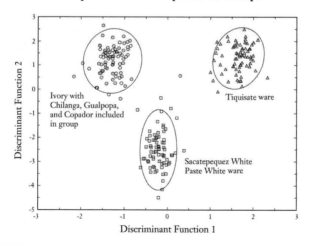

Tiquisate ware is used as an outgroup for comparison. In this case, Chilanga, Gualpopa, and Copador specimens are included in the Ivory Group used in calculating the axes. Ellipses represent the 90 percent confidence level for membership in each group.

ceramics from El Salvador analyzed at Brookhaven National Laboratory. "Similar" in this case was defined as falling closer than a Mahalanobis distance corresponding to 1 percent probability of membership in the Ivory reference group. All but two of thirty-eight matching specimens were either Chilanga, Gualpopa, or Copador, and twenty-five of the thirty-eight matches were members of Bishop and Beaudry's (1994) "Copán-focus Copador" reference group.

When projected onto axes obtained from discriminant analysis of three light-firing compositional groups (figure 14.8), the thirty-eight matching Chilanga, Gualpopa, and Copador specimens group with the Ivory-composition specimens. When the discriminant analysis is rerun with the matching Salvadoran specimens included in the Ivory group, the pattern is accentuated further (figure 14.9). Likewise, Mahalanobis distance-based probabilities for the Chilanga, Gualpopa, and Copador rise above 5 percent (average 48 percent, almost exactly the 50 percent expected average) after they are included in the reference group. These comparisons demonstrate unequivocally that the "Copán-focus Copador" group defined by Bishop and Beaudry (1994) coincides closely with the range of compositional variation subsumed by the Ivory compositional group in the sample of Formative-period cream-paste pottery from Guatemala.

The only region where all representatives of the Ivory/Copán-focus Copador compositional profile occur together is western El Salvador. Copador and Gualpopa are all but absent in south-central Guatemala, and none of the various Formative types known to make up the Ivory compositional group (Ivory, Ivory Usulutan, and Jicalapa Usulutan) has yet been identified in the Copán Valley. These and other considerations (Neff et al. 1999) clearly favor the inference that vessels in both the Formative Ivory compositional group and the Classic "Copán-focus Copador" compositional group originated in western El Salvador. Sampling and analysis of ceramic raw materials in western El Salvador are needed to test this provenance hypothesis more definitively.

Discussion

Based on the INAA results, the Classic-period ceramic tradition that produced Copador, which Longyear (1952) thought was derived ultimately from Petén Maya elite culture, can now be extended back into the Late Formative period, long before the founders of the Copán Maya dynasty took over in western Honduras. The earliest known representatives of this tradition are Jicalapa Usulutan from western El Salvador and Ivory and Ivory Usulutan from Guatemala. (The differences in nomenclature are simply a reflection of typological inconsistencies.) By the Early Classic period, red paint was added to the cream-slipped Usulutan surface to produce Chilanga. Later, black and orange paints were added to the red to produce Gualpopa polychrome, and specular hematite red, together with black and orange, were used to produce the glyphic- and figure-painted Copador vessels.

Not only did the cream-paste tradition precede the Copán Maya dynasty, but as discussed above, there seems little possibility that it was even indigenous to the Copán Valley. If Copán were the source for cream-paste-tradition vessels, then all representatives of that tradition, starting with the earliest (Ivory, Ivory Usulutan, or Jicalapa Usulutan) should be represented there. This is not the case. Although some Usulutan pottery appears at Copán during the Late Formative period, the only reported variety is Izalco, which is orange slipped rather than cream slipped, like the Jicalapa included in the Ivory compositional group. Based on Demarest and Sharer's (1982) study, cream-slipped Usulutan, which eventually yielded Jicalapa, was being produced by the Middle Formative period in western El Salvador, long before the orange-slipped subtradition that led to Izalco (figure 14.7). In short, the weight of evidence now indicates that the history of the cream-paste tradition that eventually produced Copador is rooted in western El Salvador, not in the Copán Valley.

As a Salvadoran product, Copador was made by potters outside the immediate orbit of the Copán Maya elite dynasty. Yet Copador has elements that are sufficiently Maya-like that Longyear's (1952) hypothesis of Classic Maya ancestry for the vessels has remained plausible until very recently. Perhaps the fact that the glyphs are really just decorative and have no meaning in the Maya script should have tipped off earlier investigators to Copador's non-Maya pedigree. Still, the glyphic elements as well as the anthropomorphic representations were clearly designed in emulation of things Maya.

Why would the cream-paste potters of western El Salvador have shifted to production of several varieties of polychrome, one of which (Copador) is clearly designed to mimic Maya decorative conventions? One conspicuous possibility is that shifting interaction networks favored the decorative innovations. During the Formative period, western El Salvador was incorporated into a southern Mesoamerican interaction network that has been called the "Miraflores sphere" (Demarest 1986; Demarest and Sharer 1986). Although the Miraflores sphere was originally thought to have arisen mainly through wide sharing of ceramic decorative conventions, recent provenance determinations (Kosakowsky et al. 1999; Neff et al. 1999) make it clear that actual movement of ceramics played a major role in creating the observed similarities among Late and Terminal Formative assemblages.

Establishment of the Copán dynasty in the fifth century A.D. brought a dramatic rearrangement in the Formative-period interaction pattern, and western El Salvadoran products flowed almost exclusively toward the north and east, with Copán receiving the lion's share of exports. This reorientation toward a new market in turn favored decorative innovations that made Salvadoran cream-paste pottery more attractive to a Maya audience (Neff et al. 1999). Thus, establishing the provenance and pedigree of Copador also tells us something about the selective pressures that may have shaped its evolutionary history.

Conclusion

Archaeological-materials characterization is not usually considered to be a phylogenetic method, but the case of Copador pottery discussed above demonstrates that identifying groups of compositionally similar specimens and linking those groups to raw-material source zones can provide crucial evidence about how lines of cultural descent are manifest in the ceramic contents of the archaeological record.

Hypotheses about descent relationships can come from many sources. Longyear, Sharer, and others used intuition about the ceramic collections they were studying in order to develop the hypotheses examined here, and most codified ceramic-sorting procedures, such as the type-variety system (Wheat et al. 1958), are in fact based on intuition (sometimes referred to as "ceramic feel"). Numerical taxonomy (e.g., Doran and Hodson 1975) or cladistic analysis (e.g., O'Brien et al. 2001) can be used to the same end (Neff 1993). The mistake would be to take the hypotheses suggested by intuition, cladistics, or any other technique as the end of the story. Ideally, intuitive or systematic pattern recognition should yield multiple competing phylogenetic hypotheses with contrasting test implications. In the case of Copador, the contrasting test implications concern the patterns expected in ceramic compositional data, and the results clearly falsify the hypothesis that Copador is a Classic Maya ceramic tradition.

Acknowledgments

I thank Carl Lipo for the invitation to participate in the symposium where material for this chapter was first presented. Also thanks to my collaborators on various phases of the cream-paste study, including Dean Arnold, Barbara Arroyo, Ron Bishop, Fred Bove, Jim Cogswell, Francisco Estrada Belli, Laura Kosakowsky, Lou Ross, and Genie Robinson. Perhaps the most important contribution to acknowledge is that of Marilyn Beaudry and Ron Bishop, who undertook the original INAA study of Copador and provided important feedback on aspects of my study. Analytical data on which this chapter is based were generated with funding from the National Science Foundation, under grants no. BNS89-11580, BNS88-01707, SBR91-02016, SBR95-03035, and SBR96-00334. Analyses at Brookhaven National Laboratory were undertaken under the auspices of the U.S. Department of Energy.

Part 5

Language

15

The Spread of Bantu Languages, Farming, and Pastoralism in Sub-Equatorial Africa

Clare J. Holden

Phylogenetic methods developed in evolutionary biology have recently begun to be applied in linguistics and anthropology, both to infer language trees (e.g., Gray and Atkinson 2003; Gray and Jordan 2000; Holden 2002; Rexová et al. 2003) and to investigate the evolution of other biocultural traits (e.g., Holden and Mace 1997, 1999, 2002, 2003). These methods enable us to use linguistic and ethnographic data from modern populations to make inferences about prehistory, providing new insights into the evolution of biocultural diversity in modern humans. A phylogenetic approach can provide insights into the biological or cultural evolution of traits that are rarely preserved in the archaeological record. These include aspects of culture such as language, kinship, and wealth inheritance, all of which are far more richly documented in the ethnographic record than they are for archaeological populations. Phylogenetic methods let us make better use of linguistic and ethnographic data to make inferences about prehistory, both in broad outline and often in surprising detail.

In this chapter I review recent research on linguistic and cultural evolution in Bantu-speaking populations using phylogenetic methods. Bantu is a language family of around 450 languages that are spoken across sub-equatorial Africa (figure 15.1). Bantu belongs to the Niger-Kordofanian phylum (a maximal group of related languages), which includes some 1,500 languages spoken in West Africa as well as in the southern half of the continent (Williamson and Blench 2000). For the purposes of comparative analysis, Bantu-speaking populations provide a large cross-cultural sample for which both linguistic and ethnographic data have been published (Bastin et al. 1999; Murdock 1967). Additionally, focusing on related cultures from a single region makes it

Figure 15.1
Map of 75 Bantu and Bantoid Languages in the Dataset

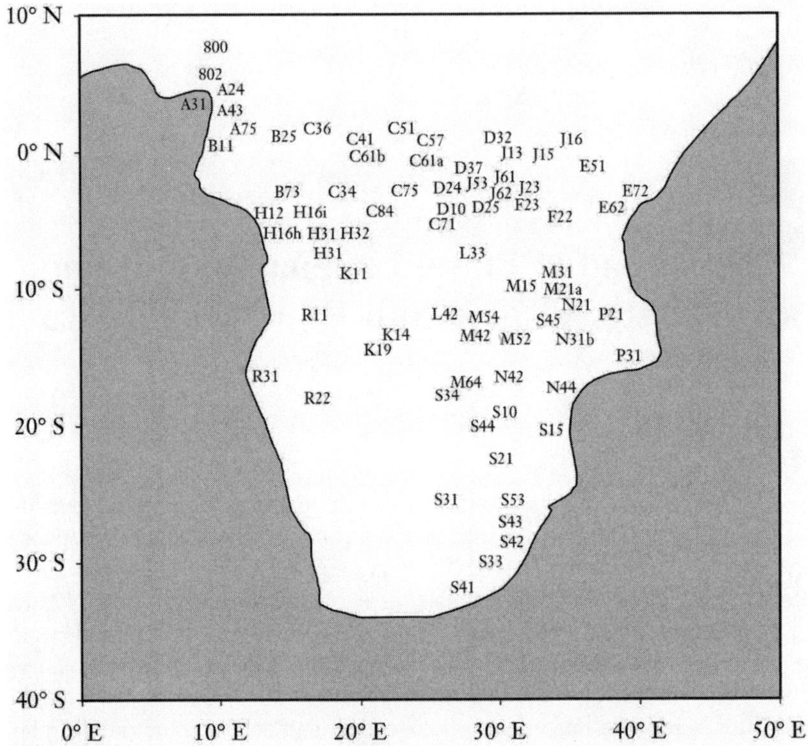

Languages are labeled by a code originally assigned by Guthrie (1967–1971), taken from Bastin et al. (1999). The language that appears to be in the ocean, A31, is Bubi, spoken on Bioko Island.

more likely that cultural traits are comparable across the sample (Eggan 1954; Goodenough 1957).

In the first part of the chapter, I describe the construction of a phylogenetic tree of Bantu languages. It is thought that Bantu languages were spread in tandem with the advance of farming between ca. 3000 B.C. and A.D. 200 (Clist 1989; Ehret 1998; Holden 2002; Huffman 1989; Phillipson 1993; Vansina 1990). The Bantu language tree described here closely reflects archaeological evidence for the spread of farming across sub-equatorial Africa, supporting the hypothesis that Bantu languages were spread by an agricultural dispersal. This suggests that the Bantu language tree reflects the broader cultural history of the region, specifically the spread of farming populations.

In the second part of the chapter, I describe how the Bantu language tree was used as a model of population history to test the hypothesis that the spread of cattle led to a change from matriliny to patriliny. A phylogenetic comparative method was used to test for co-evolution among cattle keeping and descent while controlling for the historical relatedness of Bantu-speaking populations. Results suggest that adopting cattle led to the loss of matrilineal descent in Bantu-speaking populations and its replacement by patrilineal or other descent rules. This may be because cattle confer greater fitness benefits on men than on women, so it is adaptive for parents (in terms of maximizing their number of grandchildren) to transfer cattle to sons rather than to daughters. In contrast, matrilineal Bantu-speaking societies provide women with greater rights to land, the main productive resource, land. In matrilineal parts of Malawi and the surrounding region, land inheritance from mother to daughter is the norm (Davison 1997; Holden et al. 2003). The spread of cattle may thus have had profound effects on gender relationships and female status among Bantu-speaking populations. Although cattle are a form of wealth, one may speculate that they may often have had a negative effect on women's status.

Phylogenetic Methods, Languages, and Population History

Languages often reflect population history because languages diverge after speech communities divide, in a process similar to speciation among isolated biological populations. (A "speech community" is a group of individuals speaking a common language.) If part of a speech community migrates to a new area, then, over time, the languages spoken in the separated populations will diverge, as words gradually change or are replaced. This process of linguistic divergence gives rise first to separate dialects, which are distinct but mutually comprehensible, and later to mutually incomprehensible languages. The development of two new languages from a common ancestral language is thought to take about 500 years (Swadesh 1971). Over centuries, this process of continued splitting and divergence among languages gives rise to groups of hierarchically related languages.

Darwin (1871: 59) observed that the processes of linguistic diversification and biological speciation are "curiously the same." Because of the similarities between linguistic and biological evolution, we can use phylogenetic methods developed in evolutionary biology to infer language trees. Recently, phylogenetic methods have been applied to several language groups including Indo-European (Forster and Toth 2003; Gray and Atkinson 2003; Rexová et al. 2003), Austronesian (Gray and Jordan 2000), and Bantu (Holden 2002). Phylogenetic methods have a number of advantages over previous methods for constructing language trees, including lexicostatistics and the linguistic comparative method. (Unfortunately, both linguists and biologists use the term "comparative method" but with different meanings. In linguistics it is a method for inferring language trees, in evolutionary biology it refers to methods for testing whether two traits co-evolve.)

Lexicostatistical trees are constructed from distances between language pairs, measured by the percentage of shared cognates using a standard list of 100, 200, or 500 items of basic vocabulary. Cognates are meanings (words) whose form shares a common root in two or more languages. Basic vocabulary refers to meanings that are present in all languages, for example, "man," "woman," "one," "two," "tongue," and "ashes." The word forms of basic vocabulary are thought to change more slowly than other meanings and to be less subject to borrowing (diffusion of linguistic elements between neighboring languages). Basic vocabulary can retain evidence of common ancestry for thousands of years (McMahon and McMahon 2003; Swadesh 1971).

Lexicostatistical trees have been criticized because they are based on the overall similarity between languages, including retentions as well as innovations (in biological terms, both "primitive" and "derived" characters). This produces a misleading tree when the rate of evolution varies, as slowly evolving languages will tend to be grouped on the basis of shared primitive characters (Blust 2000; Nurse 1997; Sober 1988). In contrast to lexicostatistical methods, the linguistic comparative method uses only innovations (derived characters) to identify descent groups (Nichols 1997). However, linguists do not use an explicit optimality criterion to choose the best tree or trees, so the linguistic comparative method has been criticized for being subjective (Gray and Jordan 2000; McMahon and McMahon 2003).

Phylogenetic methods use only derived characters (innovations) to define subgroups and use an efficient computer-implemented algorithm to search for the best tree(s) according to an a priori optimality criterion. Phylogenetic methods that operate directly on discrete data avoid the loss of information inherent in distance-based (lexicostatistical) methods. To date, the most widely used phylogenetic method is maximum parsimony, an optimality criterion that minimizes the number of character changes on the tree (tree length). Maximum-parsimony language trees have been constructed for Indo-European, Austronesian and Bantu, using both basic vocabulary lists (Holden 2002; Rexová et al. 2003) and a wider lexical set (Gray and Jordan 2000), depending on the available data.

The Bantu Language Tree

Guthrie (1967–1971) classified and coded Bantu languages[1] into fifteen zones (A to S) based on geography and linguistic criteria. A modified version of Guthrie's codes, from Bastin et al. (1999), is used here (figures 15.1 and 15.2). There are significant disagreements among previous studies about relationships among Bantu languages. Probable reasons for these disagreements are that different samples of languages, as well as different methods, were used in the different studies (Bastin et al. 1999; Nurse 1996). Guthrie's zones, often do not form coherent groups on trees.

Figure 15.2
Tree of 75 Bantu and Bantoid Languages

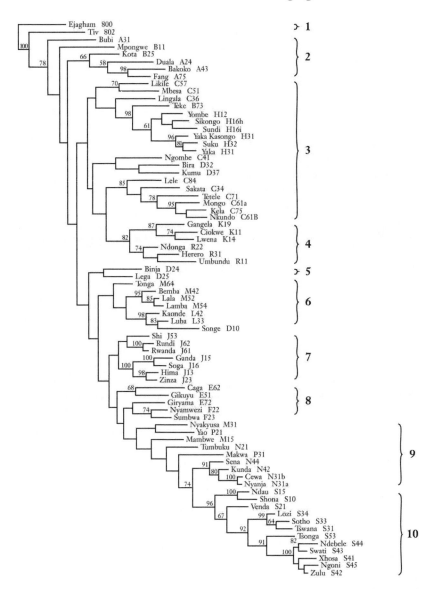

Languages are labeled by name and by their Guthrie code, taken from Bastin et al. (1999). Node labels are bootstrap values. Unlabeled nodes were recovered in fewer than 50 percent of bootstrap pseudoreplicates. Numbered bars on the right are subdivisions assigned for convenience to illustrate the possible spread of Bantu languages (see figure 15.3).

Most previous studies agree that the North West Bantu languages are the most divergent compared to other Bantu languages, suggesting that Bantu originated in the North West Bantu region. North West Bantu includes zones A, B and sometimes parts of C and D. Many linguists recognize two large groupings, West and East Bantu, among the non–North West Bantu languages. Other linguists dispute the composition of these groups (especially West Bantu). West Bantu usually includes languages spoken in the equatorial forest, Southwest Africa, and parts of Zambia. This includes zones H, J, K, L, and R plus parts of C, D, and M. Alternatively, L and M languages are sometimes grouped in a separate Central Bantu group or with East Bantu. East Bantu languages are spoken in east andsoutheast Africa and usually include zones E, F, J, N, P, and S. Most published Bantu language trees were constructed using lexicostatistical methods (Bastin et al. 1999; Heine 1973; Henrici 1973; Nurse 1996). Holden (2002) published a maximum-parsimony tree of seventy-five Bantoid and Bantu languages, described here (figure 15.2).

Data and Methods

The Bantu language tree I published elsewhere (Holden 2002) included seventy-three Bantu and two Bantoid languages—the seventy-five languages shown in figure 15.1. The sample included all Bantoid and Bantu languages for which both linguistic and ethnographic data (from the corresponding culture) were published. The linguistic data consisted of ninety-two items of basic vocabulary (meanings) that had previously been coded for cognates by Bastin et al. (1999). The ninety-two-item list was a subset of Swadesh's 100-word standard list of basic vocabulary. Eight meanings from the 100-word list were excluded by Bastin et al. (1999) as they were not present in Bantu (for example, "snow" [see Bastin 1983]). Languages with more than 5 percent missing data (data on fewer than eighty-eight cognates) were excluded from the analysis.

The two Bantoid languages Tiv and Ejagham were used as outgroups to root the tree. Linguistic, geographical, and archaeological data suggest that these are suitable outgroups for Bantu. Tiv is spoken in central Nigeria; the Ekoi in Cameroon speak Ejagham. It is likely that the ancestors of Bantu-speaking populations came from this general area.

The seventy-five languages in the dataset are spoken by culture groups in Murdock's (1967) *Ethnographic Atlas*, enabling the tree to be used to study other aspects of cultural evolution. Languages were matched to ethnographic populations by name and geographical location. Further ethnonyms and dialect names were found in Voeghlin and Voeghlin (1977) and Middleton and Rassam (1995). Where more than one vocabulary sample was available for a language, the sample that was geographically closest to the focus of ethnographic study was chosen.

The heuristic-search option in PAUP* 4.0 (Swofford 1998) was used to search for the most parsimonious tree or trees. Five hundred replications using tree bisection-reconnection (TBR) with random addition were performed, storing 2,000 trees in memory per search. Meanings with more than one character state (cognate form) in a particular language were treated as polymorphic. Character states were unordered. Characters were then reweighted using the rescaled consistency index (RC), according to their fit on the eighty-eight unweighted trees. Using weighted parsimony gives meanings that are less prone to homoplasy (from borrowing or convergence) greater weight in build-ing the tree. Another heuristic search for the shortest tree was run using TBR with random addition, with 1,000 replications, storing up to 2,000 trees in memory.

Bootstrap analysis was performed on the weighted characters to test the level of support in the data for individual clades on the tree. Five hundred bootstrap pseudoreplicates were sampled, using heuristic search with twenty TBR random-addition replicates. Clades recovered in the bootstrap analysis are probably supported by several linguistic innovations, and languages in a clade must have few or no conflicting relationships (for example, resulting from linguistic borrowing) with any language outside that clade.

Results and Discussion

Using unweighted parsimony, eighty-eight trees were found with a tree length of 2,533. The consistency index excluding uninformative characters (CI) was 0.65, the retention index (RI) was 0.59, and the rescaled consistency index (RC) was 0.38. Using RC weighted parsimony, three trees were found with a tree length of 841 (CI = 0.72, RI = 0.68 and RC = 0.49). Trivial variation among the three-weighted parsimony trees was found among branch lengths of languages of Bantu zone H.

One RC-weighted parsimony tree is shown in figure 15.2. Bootstrap values are shown on the nodes. Not all clades on the tree were recovered in the bootstrap analysis, especially clades toward the root of the tree (earlier splits). Nodes without a bootstrap value were found in fewer than 50 percent of boot-strap replicates.

The tree agrees with previously published Bantu language trees (e.g., Bastin et al. 1999; Ehret 1998; Heine 1973) in many respects. This is reassuring, given that phylogenetic methods are still relatively new in linguistics (McMahon and McMahon 2003). The first three splits on the tree are within the North West Bantu languages of zones A and B (labeled "2" on figure 15.2), agreeing with other studies that these are the most divergent Bantu languages.

East Bantu languages (spoken in East and Southeast Africa) form a clade, supporting the hypothesis that this is a true historical group. East Bantu lan-guages are labeled 7–10 on figure 15.2. This clade was not recovered in the bootstrap analysis. A clade comprising sixteen Bantu languages spoken in Southeast Africa was recovered in 74 percent of bootstrap pseudoreplicates, including all languages of Bantu zones S and N (except Tumbuka, N21). Bantu zones S and N remain distinct within this clade. This clade corresponds to the "Kusi" group of Ehret (1998).

West Bantu broadly defined (including languages of zones C, D, H, K, L, M, and R) is paraphyletic, meaning that these languages do not share a unique common ancestor. Languages spoken in and around modern Zambia (zone L and parts of M) form a clade that is referred to here as "Central Bantu" (6 on figure 15.2). Central Bantu is coordinate with East Bantu. The South West Bantu languages (zones K and R, labeled 4 in figure 15.2) form a clade, which was recovered in 82 percent of bootstrap pseudoreplicates. The place of this clade on the tree is unclear. On some unweighted parsimony trees this clade is an outlier attached to the clade containing Central and East Bantu. However, on most trees, including some unweighted parsimony trees and all weighted trees, these languages are most closely related to languages spoken in rainforest, mainly zones C and H (labeled 3 on figure 15.2).

Some authors have questioned whether trees can adequately model linguistic evolution. We know that there is some borrowing or diffusion of linguistic elements between neighboring speech communities, but trees show only branching and divergence, not borrowing between neighboring languages. If borrowing is widespread, then relationships among languages will be reticulate (netlike) rather than treelike (Bastin et al. 1999; Forster and Toth 2003; Hinnebusch 1999). How far linguistic relationships are treelike is part of a wider debate on the level of interconnectedness among human cultures. This debate focuses on whether branching or merging is the predominant process in intercultural relationships (e.g., Bellwood 1996a; Moore 1994b)—a point addressed by most authors in this volume.

We can assess how well a tree model explains the Bantu data by measuring how well the data fit on the tree, using the consistency and retention indices (Swofford 1991). Cases of borrowing will appear to be homoplastic—they will appear as the convergent evolution of the same character in different branches, decreasing the level of character fit. A high level of character fit is consistent with words being transmitted primarily by inheritance within speech communities.

Compared to biological trees with a similar number of taxa, the CI of the Bantu tree is high (Sanderson and Donoghue 1989). This suggests that Bantu languages evolved primarily by a branching process, with relatively little borrowing or convergence, at least for the basic vocabulary. Borrowing may have been more widespread for nonbasic items of vocabulary, such as words for technological innovations such as "iron" (Vansina 1990). A number of recent studies have found a surprisingly good fit between languages and tree models, especially for Indo-European (Gray and Atkinson 2003; Rexová et al.

2003), Bantu (Holden 2002), and Austronesian (Gray and Jordan 2000). All these language families are thought to have been spread as a result of agricultural dispersal, so they may reflect an underlying population history of expansion and divergence and thus fit a tree model well.

Bantu Languages and the Spread of Farming

The maximum-parsimony Bantu tree reflects archaeological evidence for the spread of farming across the whole region of modern Bantu-speaking Africa (Holden 2002; Huffman 1989; Phillipson 1993; Vansina 1990). Archaeological evidence shows that farming spread across the modern Bantu-speaking region between ca. 3000 B.C. and A.D. 200. Figure 15.3 shows a possible scenario for the spread of Bantu languages. The major subgroups of Bantu (from figure 15.2) were drawn onto a map, joining those subgroups as they are related on the tree. The tree broadly reflects archaeological evidence for the spread of farming both temporally and spatially. The relative order of splitting of the major subgroups on the tree is consistent with archaeological dates for the first farmers in each region—the deepest splits on the tree occur in the area of the oldest farming sites. The geographical areas where the major subgroups are found today (figure 15.1) also correlate with distinct archaeological traditions associated with the spread of farming. The correlation between the Bantu tree and the spread of farming is consistent with the hypothesis that the Bantu languages were spread by farmers, and it suggests that the Bantu tree reflects the population history of those farming populations.

The earliest Neolithic sites have been found in the same area as some of the most divergent North West Bantu languages (in group 2 on figures 15.2 and 15.3). The earliest archaeological dates have been obtained from sites in coastal Gabon (3000–1000 B.C.) and at Obobogo near Yaoundé in Cameroon (1000–600 B.C.) (Clist 1989).

During the first millennium B.C., farming spread to the interior and south of the forest, to the areas where West Bantu languages of zones B, C, and H are spoken today (including languages in groups 2 and 3 on figures 15.2 and 15.3). Neolithic (and probable Neolithic) traditions in this region are diverse. They include Tchissanga on the Congo coast (from 580 B.C.) (Denbow 1990); Okala near Libreville in Gabon (510–320 B.C.) (Clist 1987, 1989); Imbonga in Equateur, northern Zaire (440–90 B.C.) (Eggert 1993); Ngovo in Bas Zaire (200 B.C. to A.D. 100) (Clist 1989); and Batalimo in Centrafrique and the related Maluba tradition in northern Zaire (from 140 B.C.) (Clist 1989).

In contrast to the northwest and forest regions, the first farmers in East and Southern Africa belonged to the Early Iron Age (EIA). All Early Iron Age archaeological traditions in this region seem to be closely related, but three distinct traditions have been identified: the Urewe tradition around Lake Victoria, which is probably ancestral, and two "streams" by which Early Iron

Figure 15.3
Possible Spread of Bantu Languages Based on the Branching Order of Major Bantu Subgroups on the Tree

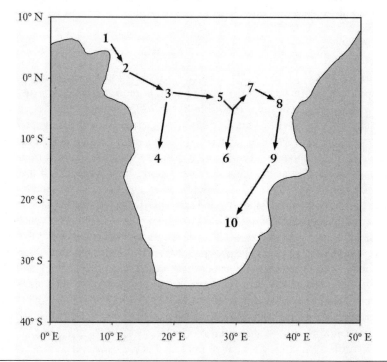

Numbers correspond to the subgroups shown in figure 15.2.

Age farming spread into Southern Africa—the Eastern Stream in Southeast Africa and the Western Stream in southwest Africa (Denbow 1990; Huffman 1989; Phillipson 1993).

The earliest EIA sites belong to the Urewe tradition around Lake Victoria, which probably dates to the last centuries B.C. (Schmidt 1975; Sutton 1972). In our sample, Zone J (Lakes Bantu) languages, plus Lega (D25) and Binja (D24), are spoken in this region today (labeled 7 and 5 respectively in figures 15.2 and 15.3). Other EIA archaeological traditions in East Africa include Lelesu in Tanzania and Kwale in Kenya, the latter dated to ca. A.D. 200 (Phillipson 1993; Shillington 1995; Soper 1971). Languages spoken in the Lelesu and Kwale areas today belong to Bantu zones E and F (labeled 8 in figures 15.2 and 15.3).

From the second century A.D., Early Iron Age peoples spread into southern Africa in at least two distinct traditions, the Eastern Stream in Southeast Africa and the Western Stream in Central andSouthwest Africa (Phillipson 1993).

The area of the Eastern Stream corresponds with the distribution of modern Bantu languages of zones N, P, S, and parts of M (labeled 9 and 10 on figures 15.2 and 15.3). The maximum-parsimony tree suggests that there was a single long spread of East Bantu languages from the Lake Victoria area, first to the rest of East Africa and then to Southeast Africa.

Western Stream archaeological sites are found in the area where Central and South Western Bantu languages are spoken today (groups 6 and 4 respectively in figure 15.3). The origins of the Western Stream in Southwest Africa remain unclear. Possibly it derives from farther north, perhaps from the Iron Age Madingo Kayes site on the Congo coast (Denbow 1990), or it may have originated at least partly in the Urewe tradition. Early Iron Age farming techniques and metallurgy were probably acquired from the east. Perhaps the reason why the South West Bantu languages are difficult to place on a tree is because they have borrowed elements from both East and West Bantu languages. The Western Stream later spread across Southwest Africa (Denbow 1990; Ehret 1998; Huffman 1989).

In summary, maximum-parsimony trees of Bantu languages reflect archaeological evidence for the spread of farming across the whole area of modern Bantu-speaking Africa. The correlation between archaeology and language groups suggests that the major subgroups of modern Bantu stem from the Neolithic and Early Iron Age, with relatively minor subsequent movements by speech communities.

Using Language Trees in Phylogenetic Comparative Analysis

In so far as the Bantu language tree reflects past relationships among Bantu-speaking populations, it can be used as a model of population history when investigating other aspects of cultural evolution. The remainder of this chapter will illustrate how a language tree may be used to test whether two cultural traits co-evolve, using a phylogenetic comparative method. Knowledge of population history is essential for this type of analysis because it enables one to distinguish between correlations that result from shared ancestry and those that result from convergent cultural evolution; only the latter are evidence for a functional relationship between two variables.

Related cultures (like related languages) share many similarities because cultural traits are transmitted from older to younger generations within populations (Cavalli-Sforza and Feldman 1981; Guglielmino et al. 1995; Hewlett and Cavalli-Sforza 1986; Hewlett et al. 2002; Holden and Mace 1999, 2002). This means that cultures cannot be treated as independent units in a statistical analysis. This is known as "Galton's problem." As a consequence, if two cultural traits are correlated across cultures, this does not necessarily imply that those traits are functionally related, because such correlations often arise from the shared history of cultures in the sample. For example, Bantu languages are characterized by a complex noun-class system (Williamson and Blench 2000), and most Bantu-speaking societies have lineal descent systems (Murdock 1967). However, noun classes and lineal descent are not functionally related; they arose separately in prehistory and were inherited by modern Bantu-speaking populations. To test whether two correlated cultural traits are functionally related, we need to know how many times they have independently co-evolved.

Mace and Pagel (1994, 1997) suggest that phylogenetic comparative methods from evolutionary biology could be used for cross-cultural comparison. In phylogenetic comparative methods, biological taxa or cultures are placed on a tree, which is used as a model of the past relationships among populations in the sample. Internal nodes on the tree represent hypothetical ancestral populations. Past character states are inferred from the distribution of characters in contemporary populations (at the tips of the tree). Rather than testing for a correlation between two or more variables in the sample (in modern populations), phylogenetic methods test for correlated evolution along the branches of the tree (Felsenstein 1985; Harvey and Pagel 1991).

The Co-Evolutionary Hypothesis

For over a hundred years, anthropologists have hypothesized that when matrilineal societies acquire domestic livestock they become patrilineal (Aberle 1961; Morgan 1877; Murdock 1949). Matriliny is a rare, although recurrent, type of social organization in which kin relationships through women are culturally more significant than relationships through men. In matrilineal societies, an individual belongs to his or her mother's descent group. Property inheritance and political succession are normally transferred from the mother's brother to his sister's son or from mother to daughter (Davison 1997; Flinn 1981; Murdock 1967; Schneider and Gough 1961). This contrasts with patrilineal societies, in which relationships through males are more important, and with other societies that have dual or ambilineal descent, or bilateral kinship, which give more equal significance to relationships through males and females. In the Standard Cross-Cultural Sample (Murdock and White 1969), a widely used worldwide dataset on 186 cultures, 17 percent of societies are matrilineal, 41 percent are patrilineal, and 42 percent have other forms of kinship and descent.

Matrilineal societies are usually horticultural—farmers who do not use the plow or keep large domestic livestock. Aberle (1961) tested the ecological correlates of matriliny in a worldwide cross-cultural sample of 565 cultures. He found that matriliny is highly significantly associated with horticulture and negatively associated with livestock. He concluded that "the cow is the enemy of matriliny, and the friend of patriliny" (Aberle 1961: 680). However, Aberle's analysis did not control for the fact that cultures are historically related, thus not statistically independent. Therefore, it remained uncertain whether the ecological correlates of matriliny were the result of cultural adaptation or history.

Holden and Mace (2003) tested the hypothesis that the spread of cattle led to the loss of matrilineal descent in Bantu-speaking populations, using the phylogenetic comparative method DISCRETE (Pagel 1994). They used Holden's (2002) Bantu language tree (figure 15.2) as a model of population history. The method DISCRETE provides a test for correlated evolution among traits. In addition, it allows one to test the direction of evolution—which of two co-evolving traits probably changed first. Testing which of two co-evolving traits changed first allows one to move beyond simply testing for a correlation among traits and to approach questions of causality. For instance, if it were found that cultures tend to switch from matriliny to patriliny before adopting cattle, this would be evidence that cattle were not the cause of the change in descent rules.

Data and Methods

Holden and Mace (2003) used the sample of seventy-five Bantoid and Bantu-speaking cultures that was used by Holden (2002) to build the language tree, except that seven cultures that lacked data on descent rules or cattle were excluded from the analysis. Their final sample included sixty-six Bantu-speaking and two Bantoid-speaking cultures. Data were taken from Murdock's (1967) *Ethnographic Atlas* (data on descent were taken from columns 20, 22, and 24; data on cattle were taken from column 39). Most Bantu-speaking populations have lineal descent, meaning that group membership is traced through one sex only, either matrilineally or patrilineally. (This contrasts with European populations, which mainly have bilateral kinship.) Of the sixty-eight cultures in the sample, twenty-four (35 percent) were matrilineal and thirty-seven (53 percent) were patrilineal. Cattle were present in thirty cultures (44 percent).

This range in cultural variation, especially in cattle keeping and in the relatively high proportion of matrilineal societies, made Bantu-speaking populations a good sample with which to test the hypothesis. Matrilineal descent is found mostly in a "matrilineal belt" across Central Africa. Cattle are found primarily in Eastern and Southern Africa (Figure 15.4). Cattle and descent rules are shown on the language tree in figure 15.5. Both traits show a clear tendency to cluster within linguistic groups, suggesting that using a phylogenetically controlled method is essential when testing for co-evolution among these traits. For the analysis, the presence or absence of cattle was coded as a binary variable. Matriliny and patriliny were coded as two separate binary variables (present or absent). Cultures with other descent rules, such as dual or ambilineal descent, were coded as neither patrilineal nor matrilineal.

The phylogenetic comparative method DISCRETE was used to test for co-evolution between cattle and matriliny and between cattle and patriliny. This method tests for correlated evolution between two binary characters on a tree

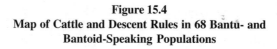

Figure 15.4
Map of Cattle and Descent Rules in 68 Bantu- and
Bantoid-Speaking Populations

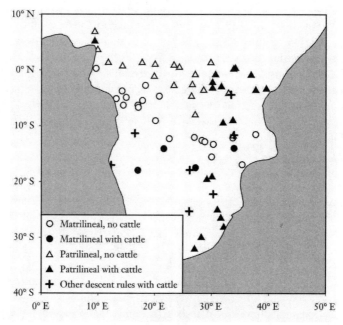

(Pagel 1994, n.d.). The relationships between matriliny and cattle and between patriliny and cattle were tested separately.

In this method the likelihood of the data—the character states observed at
the tips of the tree—is estimated, given the tree and the model of evolution.
Evolution in each character along the tree branches is modeled as a Markov
process, in which the probability of change in a trait is dependent on its
current state. Two models are fitted, an independent model in which evolution
in each trait is independent of the state of the other trait and a dependent
model in which the probability of change in one trait is dependent on the state
of the other trait. The likelihoods of the two models, LI and LD respectively,
are compared using a likelihood ratio (LR) test. If the dependent model fits the
data significantly better, this is evidence that the state of one trait affects the
probability of change in the other, indicating that the two traits co-evolve.
One hundred Monte Carlo simulations were run to generate a null distribution
of likelihood ratios in order to test the significance of the observed LR (Pagel
1994, n.d.).

DISCRETE can also be used to test the probable direction of evolution—
which of two traits changed first. Holden and Mace (2003) tested whether
adopting cattle preceded the loss of matrilineal descent and/or the adoption of

Figure 15.5
Cattle and Descent Rules in 68 Bantu- and Bantoid-Speaking Populations, Shown on the Language Tree

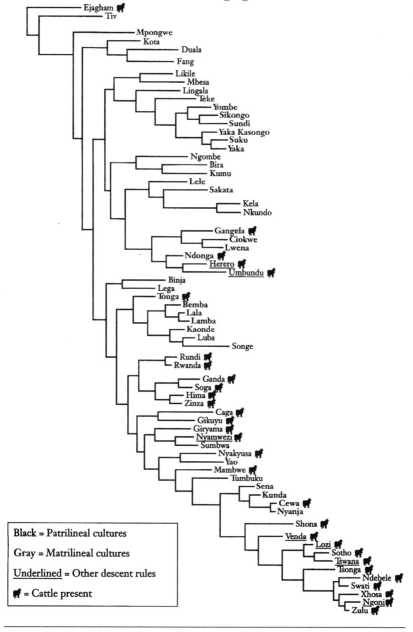

Black = Patrilineal cultures

Gray = Matrilineal cultures

Underlined = Other descent rules

🐂 = Cattle present

Other descent rules, includes dual and ambilineal descent and bilateral kinship.

patrilineal descent. They set each cultural change in turn to zero and tested whether this reduced the overall significance of the model. They then constructed a "minimum model" (Pagel 1994) showing which transitions could be set to zero without the overall significance of the model being affected (figure 15.6). The minimum model retains all individually significant transi-

Figure 15.6
Transitions between Cultural States for Matriliny and Cattle

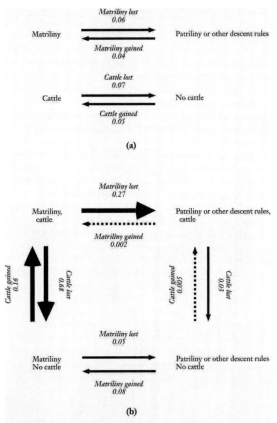

(a) independent model, in which the four possible transitions include the gain and loss of matriliny and cattle; (b) dependent model, in which the eight possible transitions include the gain and loss of matriliny and cattle, dependent on the state of the other variable. The likelihood of the dependent model is significantly higher than the independent model, indicating that cattle and matriliny co-evolve (LI = -62.52, LD = -56.80, LR = 5.72, p = 0.02). Transition rates for the unrestricted eight-parameter model are shown next to each arrow. Thick black arrows indicate rates of change 10 times higher than that shown by thin arrows, and dotted arrows indicate nonsignificant transitions whose rates do not differ from zero. The ancestral state for Bantu-speaking cultures was an absence of cattle, but the type of descent is unknown.

tions plus at least one transition to and from each state, choosing the transition with the higher rate. Holden and Mace (2003) also tested whether matriliny is more likely to be lost in cultures with cattle, by fixing the rate for the loss of matriliny to be equal in cattle-keeping and noncattle-keeping populations, and testing whether this reduced the significance of the model.

Results and Discussion

Results showed that in the prehistory of Bantu-speaking populations, adopting cattle led to the loss of matriliny and to its replacement by patriliny or mixed descent. There was no evidence that adopting cattle led to the adoption of exclusively patrilineal descent. Some cultures with cattle developed dual or ambilineal descent or bilateral kinship. These results support the first part of Aberle's (1961: 680) conclusion, that "the cow is the enemy of matriliny," but not the second part, that the cow is also "the friend of patriliny."

Comparing the independent and dependent models of evolution showed that when matriliny was contrasted with all other types of descent (including patriliny and mixed descent), cattle and matriliny were significantly negatively related (LI = -62.52, LD = -56.80, LR = 5.72, p = 0.02). However, when patriliny was contrasted with all other types of descent, there was no evidence that these two variables were related (LI = -69.88, LD = -68.40, LR = 1.49). The independent and dependent models of evolution are shown in figure 15.6.

Six parameters were retained in the minimum model (figure 15.6). The two nonsignificant transitions were as follows: (1) cultures with cattle and patrilineal or mixed descent do not become matrilineal, and (2) cultures without cattle with patrilineal or mixed descent do not gain cattle directly. Rather, they first become matrilineal, then acquire cattle, and then lose matrilineal descent. Being matrilineal with cattle appears to be a very unstable state. Such cultures are likely either to lose their cattle or to lose matrilineal descent, adopting patrilineal or mixed descent. In contrast, patrilineal or mixed descent with cattle appears to be a stable cultural state. Transition rates out of this state, either by losing cattle or in particular by becoming matrilineal, are low.

Setting the transition rates for losing matriliny to be equal in cattle-keeping and non-cattle-keeping cultures reduced the fit of the model. This indicates that matriliny is significantly more likely to be lost in cattle-keeping cultures compared to cultures without cattle.

These results provide insights into cultural evolution in Bantu-speaking populations, which add to evidence from archaeology and from the reconstruction of past vocabulary by historical linguists. (Reconstructing vocabulary is distinct from the construction of language trees described above.) Archaeology and reconstructed vocabulary suggest that cattle were absent in the earliest Bantu-speaking populations in West-Central Africa (Van Neer 2000; Vansina 1984). Cattle are still absent in this area, as they are not adapted to living in the forest. Both matrilineal and patrilineal populations are found in West-Central Africa today (figure 15.4). Factors other than cattle must be responsible for the variation in descent in this region.

The results shown in figure 15.6 suggest that non-cattle-keeping populations that were already patrilineal or had mixed descent did not acquire cattle. Instead, cattle were adopted by matrilineal populations, who then lost matriliny. This suggests that Bantu-speaking populations in Eastern and Southern Africa, who keep cattle and have patrilineal or mixed descent rules, may have formerly been matrilineal. This inference is also supported by evidence from historical linguistics. Ehret (1998) has reconstructed vocabulary items relating to kin institutions in the early Bantu-speaking communities of East and Southern Africa. He argues that these societies had both matrilineages and patrilineages (dual descent) but that matrilineages were originally more important in their social organization. He also states the Bantu-speaking societies in the Lakes region, which are mostly patrilineal today, were originally matrilineal, as shown in their feminine metaphors for "lineage," which include "belly" and "house," both items being associated with women.

Why Did the Spread of Cattle Lead to the Loss of Matrilineal Descent?

And finally, why did the spread of cattle lead to the loss of matrilineal descent and its replacement by other forms of descent, such as patriliny, dual descent, or bilateral kinship, all of which place more emphasis on kin relationships between males? Livestock probably promotes son-biased wealth inheritance because they confer greater fitness benefits on sons than on daughters. In many African societies livestock is used for bridewealth, a marriage payment from the groom or his family to the bride's family that enables men to marry, often polygynously. Herds also require defending against raiders, which may be more effectively done by sons than by daughters. It is therefore adaptive for parents (in terms of increasing their number of grandchildren) to transmit livestock to sons (Hartung 1982; Holden et al. 2003; Lancaster 1976; Mace 1996; Orians 1969). Even if daughters could use livestock to acquire husbands in the same way that men acquire wives, that is, if livestock was used as dowry and not as bridewealth, daughters could not increase their number of children proportionately by having several husbands, given the lower female reproductive rate.

Unlike cattle, horticultural land may confer equivalent fitness benefits on sons and daughters. Holden et al. (2003) found that men and women in a Chewa population in Malawi benefited equally from the size of their household's landholding. Subsistence in this population is based on horticulture and fishing, with no cattle. Among the Chewa and other matrilineal populations in the region, most land is passed on from mothers to daughters (Davison 1997). Land inheritance by daughters leads to matrilineal social organization based on co-residence of female kin (Morris 1998). Holden et al. published a model showing when it would be adaptive for parents to transmit wealth to either sons or daughters. The direction of parental sex bias in wealth inheritance depended on two factors: the additional benefits of wealth to sons (relative to daughters) and the level of paternity uncertainty. For parents, the risk of their wealth being transmitted to a nonrelative in the following generation, if their sons are cuckolded, makes daughter-biased inheritance adaptive if the benefits of wealth for sons and daughters are similar. However, if parents possess a form of wealth such as cattle, which provides additional fitness benefits to sons that outweigh the risk of nonpaternity among the sons' children, then it will be adaptive for parents to practice son-biased wealth inheritance.

This can be expressed as: if Bs/Bd > 1/P, where Bs is the benefit of wealth to sons, Bd is the benefit to daughters, and P is the probability of paternity, then it is adaptive to give wealth to sons. If Bs/Bd < 1/P, then daughter-biased wealth inheritance is adaptive. This could explain why most matrilineal societies are horticultural and also why matriliny tends to be replaced by son-biased wealth inheritance if cattle are introduced. These results suggest that among Bantu-speaking cultures the spread of cattle led to a change from social organization based on female inheritance of rights in land to social organization based on the inheritance of cattle by sons.

Conclusions

This chapter has described how phylogenetic methods can be used to construct language trees and to study the evolution of other biocultural traits on trees, illustrated by Bantu-speaking populations in Africa. The phylogenetic tree of Bantu languages appears to reflect the spread of farming in the region. This allows one to use the tree as a model of population history when investigating other aspects of cultural evolution in Bantu-speaking populations. The Bantu tree was used to test for co-evolution between cattle and descent rules, using a phylogenetic comparative method. Results showed that the spread of cattle led to the loss of matriliny in Bantu-speaking populations and to its replacement by patriliny or other forms of descent.

Note

1.   The term Bantu is used here in the sense of Ruhlen's (1991) "Narrow Bantu."

16

Are Accurate Dates an Intractable Problem for Historical Linguistics?

Quentin D. Atkinson and Russell D. Gray

Ancient population movements and cultural transformations have left us with a fascinating legacy of archaeological, genetic, and linguistic data. Synthesizing these historical archives allows us to reconstruct the past with more detail and greater certainty than would be possible on the basis of any discipline on its own. One important aspect of historical inference is the dating of ancient events. Unfortunately, date estimates based on historical linguistics are often viewed with skepticism, with some investigators preferring to rely solely on dating methods available in archaeology and genetics. However, as we have previously demonstrated (Gray and Atkinson 2003), the problems associated with traditional linguistic date-estimation techniques can be overcome by applying methods from evolutionary biology. Here we explain our rationale and methodology in more detail.

Limitations of the Comparative Method and Glottochronology

Traditionally, the most popular means of extracting diachronic information from linguistic data has been the "comparative method," which groups languages through knowledge of current and historically attested language syntax, word form, and phonology. By examining systematic sound correspondences among languages, linguists can reconstruct a likely series of phonological innovations. Exclusively shared innovations are used to infer historical relationships and construct a language-family tree. For example, the Germanic language family can be characterized by a sound change from an initial $*p$ in the ancestral Proto-Indo-European to "f" in Proto-Germanic (Campbell 1998). Hence *pater* in Greek and Latin has changed to *father* in English.

The comparative method provides two useful sources of historical information. First, the inferred family tree reveals major language groupings and the relative chronology of divergence events. Figure 16.1 shows the Indo-European language tree as constructed using the comparative method (Campbell 1998). We can see that the Celtic languages, for example, form a monophyletic group (i.e., a set of languages descended from a common ancestor) and that the initial Celtic split occurred between the Insular and Continental varieties. A second source of information lies in an approach known as "linguistic paleontology." Borrowed or inherited words can be used to draw inferences about the environment, culture, and daily life of a protolanguage's speakers. For instance, we can be reasonably confident that Proto-Mayan culture possessed agriculture because the vocabulary of Proto-Mayan, reconstructed from thirty-one of its descendant languages, exhibits a large number of agricultural terms, including those for "maize," "corncob," and "to harvest" (Campbell 1998).

Although language trees and linguistic paleontology are important lines of investigation, neither can produce objective estimates of absolute time depths. In the case of language-family trees, although linguists can infer relative chronology with some confidence, estimates of absolute time depth are at best intuitive guesses based on the perceived similarity between languages. There is no objective criterion for calculating time depth and no measure of the statistical error associated with an estimate. Conversely, date estimates based on linguistic paleontology can be obtained only by identifying a reconstructed protolanguage with a particular culture evident in the archaeological record.

An alternative approach that claims to provide an objective estimate of absolute time depth is Morris Swadesh's (1952) "glottochronology," which is a derivative of "lexicostatistics." Lexicostatistics uses the percentage of shared cognates between languages to make inferences about historical language relationships. Two words are judged to be cognates if they have a similar meaning and show recurrent sound correspondences thought to result from common ancestry. For instance, it can be shown that English *foot*, Greek *podos*, and Hittite *pata* are cognates because the words in each language can be traced back to a common ancestor in Proto-Indo-European. Usually, lexicostatistics is restricted to the Swadesh word list, a set of 100 or 200 basic vocabulary terms thought to be relatively universal and resistant to borrowing. The set includes numerals, kinship terms, terms for body parts, and basic verbs. Table 16.1 shows a sample of Swadesh word-list items across a selection of Germanic languages as well as Greek.

Glottochronology is used to estimate language divergence times under the assumption of a constant rate of lexical change through time, or "glottoclock." The more cognates shared between two languages, the more recently they are thought to have diverged, with the relationship conforming to an exponential decay curve. Thus, the time at which two languages began to diverge can be

Figure 16.1
Indo-European Language Tree Constructed Using the Comparative Method (after Campbell 1998)

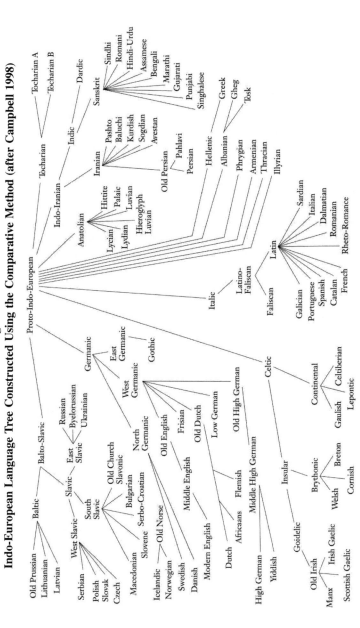

Although it is possible to infer the relative chronology of divergence events from this topology, absolute-date estimates are at best educated guesses.

Table 16.1

A Sample Dataset of Five Swadesh-List Terms across Six Germanic Languages (and Greek)

English	And [1]	Big [1]	Fire [1]	Meat [1]	Rub [1]	Water [1]
German	Und [1]	Gross [2]	Feuer [1]	Fleisch [2]	Reiben [1]	Wasser [1]
Dutch	En [1]	Groot [2]	Vuur [1]	Vleesch [2]	Wrijven [1]	Water [1]
Swedish	Och [2]	Stor [3]	Eld [2]	Kott [3]	Gnida [2]	Vatten [1]
Icelandic	Og [2]	Stor [3]	Eldr [2]	Hold [3]	Nua [3]	Vatn [1]
Danish	Og [2]	Stor [3]	Ild [2]	Kod [4]	Gnide [2]	Vand [1]
Greek	Ke [3]	Meghalos [4]	Fotia [3]	Kreas [5]	Trivo [4]	Nero [2]

Note: Superscripts refer to cognates within columns. For example, "and," "und," and "en" are cognates; similarly, "och" and "og" are cognates. Simplified orthography from Dyen et al. (1997).

calculated based on the inferred genetic distance between the languages using the equation:

$$t = \frac{\log C}{2 \log r}$$

where t is time depth in millennia, C is the percentage of cognates shared, and r is the "universal constant," or rate of retention (the expected proportion of cognates remaining after 1,000 years of separation [Swadesh 1955]). For the Swadesh 200-word list, a value of 81 percent is often used for r. If two languages share terms for 150 (75 percent) of the 200 words in the list, then according to the above equation we would infer that they separated about 680 years ago (figure 16.2).

Although glottochronology was initially received with enthusiasm, the method has since fallen out of favor as a result of problems identified with both glottochronology and distance-based methods of historical inference in general. These problems can be grouped into four main categories:

1. *Information loss* – The presence or absence of each cognate in each language usually represents a specific evolutionary event and constitutes evidence for grouping a particular subset of languages. By summarizing individual cognate data into percentage-similarity scores between languages, much of the information in the data is lost, greatly reducing the power of the method to reconstruct topology and branch lengths accurately (Steel et al. 1988).

2. *Inaccurate tree-building techniques* – Distance-based tree-building techniques, such as the "unweighted pair group method with arithmetic mean," can produce inaccurate trees under some conditions. Where rates of change are unequal, these methods tend to group languages that have evolved more slowly rather than languages that share a recent common ancestor (Blust 2000). Figure 16.3 illustrates an example of this sort of error. The correct relationship

among four languages is shown on the tree. If rates of retention are equal (e.g., 90 percent per millennium) across the tree, then distance methods reconstruct the correct relationships among the languages. Language A will be grouped most closely with language B, and language C will be grouped most closely with language D. However, if language D evolves more impiclly than languages A, B, or C after it has split from language C (e.g., retention rate of 80 percent per millennium), then distance methods will group language C with languages A and B rather than with language D, the correct placement.

3. *Borrowing* – Borrowing of words between languages can produce erroneous trees and confound divergence-time estimates. Where borrowing is common, the percentage of shared cognates may be a poor indication of relatedness, producing spurious relationships between languages. Borrowing may also confound divergence-time estimates, given that apparent lexical change depends on the degree of contact between languages as well as on the time since separation.

4. *Rate variation* – Glottochronology is based on the assumption of a constant rate of lexical change, but languages do not always evolve at constant rates. Rather, the rates vary as a result of sociolinguistic, cultural, and environmental factors. Rate variation can occur between languages, between individual meanings within a language, or through time (Pagel 2000). Bergsland and Vogt (1962) compared a number of contemporary languages with their archaic forms and found significant rate variation between languages. For example, Modern Icelandic and Norwegian were compared with their common ancestral language, Old Norse, spoken between 1,200 and 800

Figure 16.2
Curve Showing Exponential Decay of the Percentage of
Shared Cognates with Time

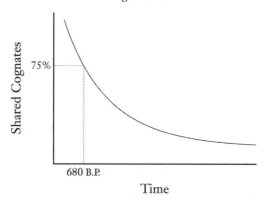

For example, if two languages share cognates for 75 percent of the terms in the Swadesh list, then glottochronology would predict a divergence time of 680 B.P.

years ago. The retention rate for Norwegian since the time of divergence from Old Norse was found to be 81 percent, consistent with a 1,000-year-old divergence event. However, Modern Icelandic produced a retention rate of 96 percent for the same interval, wrongly suggesting that it had diverged from Old Norse less than 200 years ago. Bergsland and Vogt's results demonstrated that under conditions of rate heterogeneity, glottochronology can produce erroneous age estimates.

These problems mean that most linguists are, at the very least, highly skeptical of the results of glottochronology. Indeed, the negative sentiment surrounding glottochronology is so strong that many have abandoned any attempt to date language divergence using linguistic data. As we discuss below, this

Figure 16.3
Illustration of the Effect of Rate Variation on Distance-Based
Tree-Building Methods (after Blust 2000)

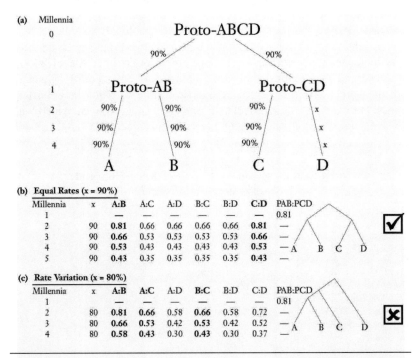

(a) shows the true topological relationship among four hypothetical languages A, B, C, and D. The vertical axis corresponds to time, and numbers along each branch are rates of retention per millennium (90 percent, or x percent in the case of the leaf leading to C); (b) shows the distance calculations for constant rates (x = 90 percent). Here the method retrieves the true tree; (c) shows the same calculation under conditions of rate heterogeneity (x = 80 percent). In this case the method will reconstruct the wrong ancestral relationships.

may be premature in the light of date-estimation techniques recently developed in evolutionary biology.

A Biological Solution to a Linguistic Problem

Since Darwin's time it has been recognized that the "formation of different languages and of distinct species, and the proofs that both have been developed through a gradual process, are curiously parallel. . . . We find in distinct languages striking homologies due to community of descent, and analogies due to a similar process of formation" (Darwin 1871: 59–60). Indeed, fundamental processes in biological evolution, such as cladogenesis, selection, drift, and mutation have linguistic analogues (Pagel 2000) (table 16.2). Just as species are subject to natural selection, so languages are subject to social selection. Processes of random drift and mutation operate on "linguemes" (Croft 2000) just as they do on genes. Most fundamentally, just as biological lineages split and diverge into family trees, so too do language lineages. These parallels mean that both evolutionary biology and historical linguistics seek answers to similar questions; both encounter similar difficulties; and often both use similar methods to arrive at a solution.

In Darwin's wake, Schleicher (1863) put forward what was essentially an evolutionary tree of the Indo-European family. Since then, methods have been borrowed from biology for use in linguistics and vice versa (see Atkinson and Gray [2005]). Table 16.3 shows some of the methodological parallels between biology and linguistics. Recent linguistic studies using phylogenetic meth-

Table 16.2
Conceptual Parallels between Biological and Linguistic Evolution

Biological evolution	Language evolution
Discrete heritable units (*e.g.*, genetic code, morphology, behavior)	Discrete heritable units (*e.g.*, lexicon, syntax, phonology)
Homology	Cognates
Mutation (*e.g.*, base-pair substitutions)	Innovation (*e.g.*, sound changes)
Drift	Drift
Natural selection	Social selection
Cladogenesis (*e.g.*, allopatric speciation [geographic separation] and sympatric speciation [ecological/reproductive separation])	Lineage splits (*e.g.*, geographical separation and social separation)
Anagenesis	Change without split
Horizontal gene transfer	Borrowing
Plant hybrids (*e.g.*, wheat, strawberry)	Language Creoles (*e.g.*, Surinamese)
Correlated genotypes/phenotypes (*e.g.*, allometry, pleiotropy)	Correlated cultural terms (*e.g.*, "five" and "hand")
Geographic clines	Dialects/dialect chains
Fossils	Ancient texts
Extinction	Language death

Table 16.3
Methodological Parallels between Biology and Linguistics

Biology	Linguistics
Species trees	Language trees
Synapomorphies vs. symplesiomorphies	Innovations vs. retentions
Monophyletic group	Minimal group
Infer ancestral states and origins	Infer ancestral states and origins
Divergence times—molecular clock	Time depth—glottoclock
Tracing character changes—genes, proteins, morphology, behavior	Tracing character changes— grammar, syntax, sound, lexicon
Sequence alignment	Sound change correspondences

ods include those by Gray and Jordan (2000), who examined the expansion of Austronesian languages across the Pacific; by Holden (2002), who conducted a similar study on Bantu languages in Africa; and by Gray and Atkinson (2003), who reexamined the spread of Indo-European languages across Europe.

Biologists, like linguists, are interested in the dates associated with nodes on evolutionary trees, and both encounter similar problems when estimating divergence times and time depth. Recently, however, biologists have developed techniques to overcome their equivalent of the four problems outlined above. These techniques allow the estimation of divergence times from genetic data without the assumption of a strict molecular clock. Linguists and those interested in using linguistic data archaeologically can benefit from what these techniques offer.

Overcoming Information Loss

Distance-based tree-building methods result in information loss in biology just as they do in linguistics. Discrete information about the presence or absence of genes, nucleotides, morphological features, or behavior is condensed into distance scores between species. Penny (1982) has shown that information is lost when sequence data are converted to distances because the resulting distance matrix does not allow the original sequence to be recovered. Thus biologists prefer to use character-based phylogenetic methods such as parsimony and maximum likelihood. Rather than using genetic distance as a proxy for evolutionary change, parsimony and maximum-likelihood methods retain individual character information and reconstruct the evolution of each character across a phylogeny.

Applied to linguistics, character-based methods ensure that information about the presence or absence of individual word forms or grammatical and phonological features (the characters) can be retained. *This means that unlike lexicostatistics we never count cognates or calculate ages based on pair-wise distances.* Table 16.4 shows a matrix of 1's and 0's that expresses the presence or absence of cognates across the seven languages listed in table 16.1. Each row represents a language and each column a character (in this case a cognate set). The sequence of 1's and 0's for each language can be viewed as analogous to the gene sequence of a species. Character-based methods use this information directly, without having to convert the data into distance scores.

Overcoming Inaccurate Tree-Building Methods

The most recently developed phylogenetic methods in biology employ maximum-likelihood models of evolution and Bayesian inference of phylogeny. These methods allow us to overcome the problems identified with the distance-based tree-building methods used in lexicostatistics.

By improving the accuracy of tree topology and branch-length estimation, maximum-likelihood methods generally outperform distance and parsimony approaches in situations where there are unequal rates of change (Kuhner and Felsenstein 1994). Maximum likelihood integrates three related components: the observed data, a model of character evolution, and an evolutionary tree or a set of trees. The method is based on the premise that we should favor an explanation that makes our observed data most likely. In biology the observed data are usually a set of gene sequences. For languages, the observed data can take the form of a binary matrix that codes cognate presence or absence, as in the example shown in table 16.4.

Maximum likelihood combines these data with an explicit statistical model of character evolution to reconstruct character-state changes across a tree. The evolutionary model is usually expressed as a rate matrix representing the relative probabilities of all possible character-state changes. More-complicated models can be implemented to account for phenomena such as site-

Table 16.4
Germanic (and Greek) Cognates from Table 16.1 Expressed in a Binary Matrix

	Meaning					
	and	big	fire	meat	rub	water
English	1 0 0	1 0 0 0	1 0 0	1 0 0 0 0	1 0 0 0	1 0
German	1 0 0	0 1 0 0	1 0 0	0 1 0 0 0	1 0 0 0	1 0
Dutch	1 0 0	0 1 0 0	1 0 0	0 1 0 0 0	1 0 0 0	1 0
Swedish	0 1 0	0 0 1 0	0 1 0	0 0 1 0 0	0 1 0 0	1 0
Icelandic	0 1 0	0 0 1 0	0 1 0	0 0 1 0 0	0 0 1 0	1 0
Danish	0 1 0	0 0 1 0	0 1 0	0 0 0 1 0	0 1 0 0	1 0
Greek	0 0 1	0 0 0 1	0 0 1	0 0 0 0 1	0 0 0 1	0 1

specific rate variation and unequal character-state frequencies. Table 16.5 shows the "general time-reversible" rate matrix used by biologists to model nucleotide substitution. Each cell corresponds to a probability of character-state change. A gamma shape parameter can also be added to allow for rate variation between sites. We can model lexical evolution by applying the same approach to linguistic data to allow rate variation between cognate sets (Pagel 2000). Because rate variation can be incorporated into the tree-building process, maximum-likelihood methods are not as susceptible to problems associated with rate heterogeneity.

Table 16.6 shows a rate matrix that might be used for modeling lexical evolution. Each cell represents the relative probability of gaining or losing a cognate. Again, a gamma shape parameter can be added to allow for rate variation between words. The gamma distribution provides a range of rate categories for the model to choose from when assigning rates to each cognate set. The distribution of these rates is determined by the gamma shape parameter. Figure 16.4 shows the gamma distribution for three possible values. For small values, (e.g., 0.5), most cognate sets evolve slowly, but a few can evolve at higher rates. As the value increases (e.g., 50), the distribution becomes more peaked

Table 16.5
The General Time-Reversible Rate Matrix Used to Model Nucleotide Evolution [a]

	A	C	G	T
A	$-u(a\pi_C+b\pi_G+c\pi_T)$	$ua\pi_C$	$ub\pi_G$	$uc\pi_T$
C	$ua\pi_A$	$-u(a\pi_A+d\pi_G+e\pi_T)$	$ud\pi_G$	$ue\pi_T$
G	$ub\pi_A$	$ud\pi_C$	$-u(b\pi_A+d\pi_C+f\pi_T)$	$uf\pi_T$
T	$uc\pi_A$	$ue\pi_C$	$uf\pi_G$	$-u(c\pi_A+e\pi_C+f\pi_G)$

a From Swofford et al. 1996. Model parameters are u (the mean substitution rate), a, b, c ... f (the relative rate parameters, which allow all of the possible transformations to occur at different rates), and A, C, G, and T, which represent the relative frequencies of the different bases A, C, G, and T.

Table 16.6
Simple Maximum-Likelihood Rate Matrix Adapted for Modeling Lexical Replacement in Language Evolution [a]

	1	0
1	$-u_0$	u_1
0	u_1	$-u_1$

a This is a time-reversible model that allows for unequal equilibrium frequencies of 1's and 0's (cognate presence and absence). The model parameters are u (the mean substitution rate) and 0 and 1, which represent the relative frequencies of 1's and 0's.

Figure 16.4
The Gamma Distribution Used to Model Rate Variation

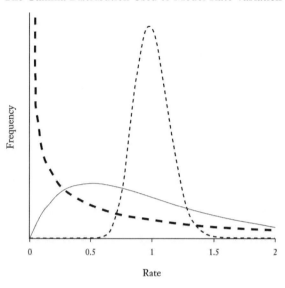

Three possible values are shown (0.5, 1, and 50). For small values (e.g., 0.5--), most cognate sets evolve slowly, but a few can evolve at higher rates. As the value increases (e.g., 50--), the distribution becomes more peaked and symmetrical around a rate of 1. In other words, rates become more equal.

and symmetrical around a rate of 1. In other words, rates become more equal (Swofford et al. 1996). Although the variables in the rate matrix and the gamma shape parameter can be assigned values prior to analysis, it also is possible to estimate model parameters from the data and to test the comparative ability of different model types to explain the data. This allows *a priori* assumptions about the process of evolution to be minimized and is thus a major advantage of the maximum-likelihood approach (Pagel 1997).

For a given model of evolution, trees are evaluated according to their likelihood scores, which represent the probability of a specific tree giving rise to the observed data under the model. The greater the likelihood of producing the observed data, the more favorable we find the tree. The basic procedure for calculating the likelihood score is outlined in figure 16.5 using the data from table 16.4. Two trees are evaluated so that their likelihood scores can be compared. First, presence/absence information for a particular cognate set is selected (figure 16.5a) and mapped onto each tree (figure 16.5b). Next, ancestral character states are hypothesized, and the likelihood of the resulting scenario is calculated (figure 16.5c). The likelihood is contingent on the substitution probabilities per unit time as defined in the model. This process is repeated for

Figure 16.5
Calculation and Comparison of Likelihood for Two Language Phylogenies

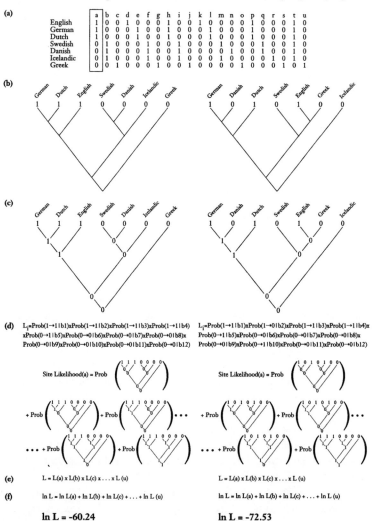

(a) presence/absence information for a particular cognate set is selected from the data in table 16.4; (b) this information is mapped onto each tree; (c) ancestral character states are hypothesized and the probability or likelihood of the resulting scenario is calculated; (d) the likelihood of each tree, for this single cognate set, is the sum of the probabilities of all possible ancestral-state combinations; (e) the overall log-likelihood score is calculated by summing the logs of the likelihood scores of all cognate sets. The tree with the least negative log-likelihood is the most favorable; (f) comparing the final log-likelihood scores of each tree we see that, consistent with what linguists already know of Germanic-language relationships, the tree on the left is more favorable.

all possible combinations of ancestral character states. The likelihood of each tree, for this single cognate set, is the sum of the probabilities of all the possible ancestral-state combinations (figure 16.5d).

The overall likelihood of each tree for all of the data in table 16.4 can be calculated by taking the product of all twenty-one individual cognate-set likelihoods. This value is often very small (especially for larger data sets), so the log of the likelihood is usually used instead. The less negative the log-likelihood is, the more likely the tree is. The overall log-likelihood score can thus be calculated by summing the logs of the likelihood scores of all cognate sets (figure 16.5e). In comparing the final log-likelihood scores of each tree, we see that, consistent with what linguists already know about Germanic-language relationships, the tree on the left is more favorable. It should be noted that this is a highly simplified example based on a very small data set. More information in the form of more characters allows for more powerful inferences; hence real linguistic and biological data sets typically include thousands of characters.

Although it is preferable to evaluate the likelihood of all possible trees, this is not usually computationally feasible. The number of possible tree topologies that must be evaluated increases exponentially with the number of taxa. For seven taxa there are 945 possible unrooted trees, for ten taxa there are over 2 million trees, and for twenty taxa there are over 2×10^{20} trees. Current processor speeds do not allow us to reconstruct character-state changes, estimate model parameters, and calculate likelihood scores across all possible trees for anything more than a few taxa. We are, however, able to employ heuristic methods that allow us to make inferences about the optimal tree topology and model parameters without having to evaluate all possible trees.

Bayesian inference of phylogeny evaluates trees according to their posterior probability distribution. Bayes's theorem relates the posterior probability of a tree (the probability of the tree given the data) to its likelihood score (the probability of the data given the tree) and its prior probability (a reflection of any prior knowledge about tree topology that is to be included in the analysis). Evaluating the posterior probability analytically is almost always impractical. However, we can use Markov Chain Monte Carlo (MCMC) algorithms (Metropolis et al. 1953) to generate a sample of trees in which the frequency distribution of the sample is an approximation of the posterior probability distribution of the trees (Huelsenbeck et al. 2001; Lutzoni et al. 2001). In other words, the more likely the tree, the more likely it is to appear in the sample distribution. The MCMC algorithm is usually started from a random phylogeny and from uninformative ("flat") model parameters known as "priors." The algorithm essentially works by proposing changes to the tree and model parameters and accepting these changes in proportion to their likelihood. After a "burn-in" period, the algorithm should sample trees in proportion to their posterior probability.

A consensus tree representing the most likely evolutionary scenario can be generated from the Bayesian sample distribution. Figure 16.6 shows a Bayesian consensus tree generated from the sample Germanic data set. As well as tree topology and branch length information, the consensus tree shows the degree of support for each clade within the phylogeny. Clade support is usually expressed in the form of the posterior probability of a clade—the percentage of time that the clade appears in the sample distribution. A value of 100, for example, indicates that the clade occurs in all sampled trees. Lower values indicate lower statistical confidence. Although clade-support values are low in figure 16.6 because of the very small size of the example data set, the topology is broadly consistent with what linguists know of Germanic history. The consensus tree includes the widely recognized North and West Germanic clades.

Another advantage of the Bayesian approach is that the sample distribution allows us to approximate uncertainty (in tree topology and branch lengths) and to incorporate this into subsequent analyses. This is impossible using either the comparative method or traditional glottochronology, and yet the effect of phylogenetic uncertainty is a crucial consideration if results are to be used to test historical hypotheses. For example, rather than restricting divergence-time analyses to a single optimal tree, such as in figure 16.6, we can analyze the entire Bayesian sample distribution and determine the error in

Figure 16.6
Bayesian Consensus Tree for the Germanic Sample Data Set

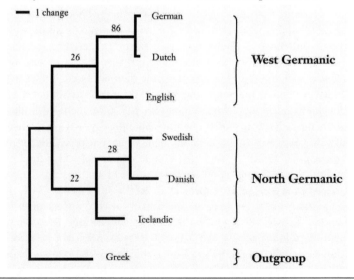

Branch lengths are proportional to the inferred amount of change. Posterior probability values for clades are shown above the branch immediately ancestral to each clade.

date estimates resulting from phylogenetic uncertainty (Huelsenbeck et al. 2001). This would include the 26 percent of trees with a West Germanic clade as well as the 74 percent without the West Germanic clade. The resulting distribution of divergence times would thus not be contingent on the existence of a West Germanic clade.

Alternatively, we may wish to incorporate prior knowledge into the analysis by imposing constraints on the tree topology. In the case of Germanic, we happen to know on the basis of other linguistic and historical evidence that the true tree must in fact include a West Germanic clade. If we wanted to include this information in our analysis, we could repeat the above process searching only within the subset of trees that include a West Germanic clade.

Overcoming Borrowing

Borrowing between languages is analogous to horizontal gene transfer in biology. Biologists use computational methods such as split decomposition (Huson 1998), which do not force the data to fit a tree model, to check for non-treelike signals in the data. This procedure has also been applied to historical linguistics (Bryant et al. 2005). In linguistics, the influence of borrowing can be minimized by restricting analyses to basic vocabulary such as the Swadesh word list. For example, although English is a Germanic language, it has borrowed around 60 percent of its total lexicon from French and Latin. However, only about 6 percent of English entries in the Swadesh 200-word list are clear Romance language borrowings (Pagel 2000). These known borrowings can be removed prior to analysis. Any remaining reticulation can be detected using methods that can identify conflicting signal, such as split decomposition and NeighbourNet (Bryant and Moulton 2002; see also chapter 6, this volume). In addition, because maximum-likelihood methods incorporate an explicit model of evolution, it is much easier to test assumptions about evolutionary processes such as borrowing. For example, it is possible to include borrowing between languages as part of the evolutionary model itself. We can then simulate data sets with varying degrees of borrowing and compare them to real data (see Nichols and Gray [2005] and Atkinson et al. [2005] for analyses using synthetic data).

Overcoming Rate Variation

Biologists base divergence-time estimates on the concept of a molecular clock, similar to the glottoclock in linguistics. Unfortunately, in biology, as in linguistics, rates of evolution vary between the characters of interest as well as between lineages. For example, Excoffier and Yang (1999) found evidence for rate variation between sites in mitochondrial human and chimp DNA, and Wu and Li (1985) have shown that rates of nucleotide substitution are higher in

rodents than in *Homo sapiens sapiens*. As described above, maximum likelihood allows us to account for rate variation between individual sites/words
using a gamma distribution. We can also account for rate variation between
lineages and through time by relaxing the assumption of a strict molecular-/
glotto-clock.

Biologists have recently developed rate-smoothing algorithms to model
rate variation across a phylogeny and thus estimate divergence times without
the assumption of a molecular clock. One such approach is the "penalized-
likelihood" method (Sanderson 2002a) of rate smoothing, which allows for
rate variation between lineages while incorporating a "roughness penalty"
that costs the model more if rates vary excessively from branch to branch.
Sanderson (2002b) has shown that the penalized-likelihood optimization procedure performs significantly better under conditions of rate heterogeneity
than procedures that assume a constant rate of evolution.

We can apply the same methods to linguistic data. Again, using the sample
Germanic dataset as an example, we begin by constructing an evolutionary
tree with branch lengths proportional to the inferred amount of change, such
as the consensus tree from the sample Germanic data. Known divergence times
based on historically attested dates are then used to calibrate rates of change
across the tree (figure 16.7). For example, we know from historical information
that the Anglo-Saxons began to settle in Britain in A.D. 449. This would

Figure 16.7
Estimating Divergence Times Using the Sample Germanic Data Set

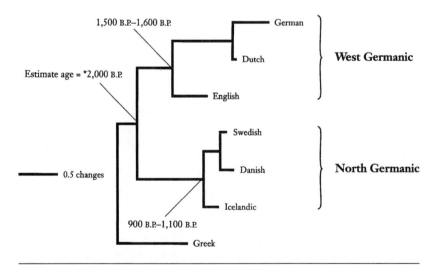

The age of the nodes corresponding to the North and West Germanic divergence is constrained
in accordance with historically attested dates. Rate smoothing is then used to estimate the
age of the split between the North and West Germanic lineages.

suggest that the English lineage split from the other West Germanic languages at some point during the fifth century A.D. We can constrain the age of this node on the tree accordingly. Similarly, we can date the break up of the North Germanic languages to around the end of the first millennium A.D. and constrain the age of this node on the tree. The penalized-likelihood model is then used to smooth rates of evolution across the tree and to calculate divergence times. We can thus reconstruct the age of the node of the tree in figure 16.7, representing the break-up of West Germanic and North Germanic. This procedure can then be repeated on all of the trees in the MCMC Bayesian sample distribution. The result is a distribution of divergence times rather than a single estimate. This distribution can be used to create a confidence interval for the age at any node. Figure 16.7 shows a meaningferred age for the North/West split of 2,300 B.P. Due to the very small example data set the potential error associated with this esstimate is large—the 95% confidence interval for the North/West split is between 1,600 and 10,000 B.P.

The Origin of Indo-European

In 1786, Sir William Jones noted similarities among Sanskrit, Greek, Celtic, Persian, Gothic, and Latin, which led him to conclude that these languages had "sprung from some common source" (Jones 1807: 34–35). The duly christened Indo-European language family today includes most of the indigenous languages of Europe and many from the Near East, all of which are considered to be descendants of an ancient ancestral tongue, Proto-Indo-European (PIE). Despite over 200 years of study, the question of where and when this common source arose remains controversial. Indeed, the origin of the Indo-European language family has recently been described as "the most intensively studied, yet still most recalcitrant, problem of historical linguistics" (Diamond and Bellwood 2003: 597).

There are currently two major competing theories of Indo-European origin. The more traditional view, championed by Gimbutas (1973a, 1973b), centers on possible archaeological evidence of an invasion by Kurgan horsemen from their homeland in southern Russia and Ukraine into an area of Europe and the Near East, which corresponds roughly to the attested Indo-European territory (Trask 1996). Archaeologists date the Kurgan "conquest" to some time after 6000 B.P. (Gimbutas 1973b). Linguistic paleontology provides evidence of an association between the Kurgan culture and PIE. Words reconstructed in PIE, including terms for "wheel" (*rotho-, *kwel-), "axle" (*hakhs-), "yoke" (*iak'om), "horse," (*ekhwo-) and "riding" (*mar-kho-), have been claimed to correspond with Kurgan cultural innovations in the archaeological record such as the domestic horse and the introduction of wheeled vehicles to Europe (Mallory 1989). This correspondence is taken as evidence that Indo-European is a child of the Kurgan expansion and hence no older than 6,000 years.

The opposing theory, put forward by Renfrew (1987, 2000a), holds that Indo-European languages expanded with the spread of agriculture from Anatolia between 8,000 and 10,000 years ago. This spread of agriculture into Europe is well documented in the archaeological record. Radiocarbon dates from the earliest Neolithic sites across Europe suggest that agriculture arrived in Greece at some time during the ninth millennium B.P. and had reached as far as Scotland by 5500 B.P. (Gkiasta et al. 2003). Renfrew contends that linguistic arguments for the Kurgan theory are based too heavily on a few enigmatic word forms. He points out that similar word forms across different languages might be the result of borrowing or semantic shift and hence do not imply that the technological innovations to which they supposedly refer were in existence prior to any divergence. Renfrew also challenges the idea that the Kurgans could have conquered such a vast area in a time when even small cities did not exist. Far more credible, he argues, is a scenario in which PIE spread passively across Europe with the spread of agriculture.

Other, more controversial theories of Indo-European origin have also been put forward. These proposals advocate homelands that include central Europe (Devoto 1962), the Balkans (Diakonov 1984), and even India (Kumar 1999), with hypothesized ages ranging from 4,000 to 23,000 years ago (Otte 1997).

As a result of slow rates of genetic change, admixture, differences in transmission mode, and the relatively recent time scales involved, genetic analyses have been unable to resolve debates about Indo-European cultural history (Rosser et al. 2000). Early genetic studies based on protein polymorphisms (e.g., Menozzi et al. 1978) supported a Neolithic population spread originating from the Near East. More recent studies using mtDNA and non-recombining Y-chromosome markers (e.g., Chikhi et al. 2002; Richards et al. 2000; Semino et al. 2000) also support a Near Eastern origin, although there is debate over the relative contribution of Neolithic farmers and Paleolithic hunter-gatherers to the European gene pool.

Languages change much faster than genes and so contain more historical information at shallower time depths. Thus there is an opportunity for a linguistic contribution to the question of Indo-European origin. Here we take advantage of the fact that the Kurgan hypothesis and the Anatolian-farming hypothesis both imply very different age ranges–6000 B.P. and 9000 B.P., respectively—and test the hypotheses by constructing a confidence interval for the age at the base of the Indo-European language tree.

Data and Coding

Linguistic data were derived primarily from Dyen et al.'s (1997) comparative Indo-European database, which records word forms and cognancy judgments in ninety-five languages across the 200 semantic categories of the Swadesh word list. Languages are grouped into cognate sets for each term on the list. Similar word forms known to be the result of borrowing are not coded as cognates. Some of the languages in the database are represented by multiple speech varieties, eleven of which were not included in the analyses because the languages to which they correspond were already in the database and had been identified by Dyen et al. (1992) as less desirable data sources. To assist the reconstruction of basal relationships in the tree, we added three extinct languages that are thought to have branched off relatively early from the main Indo-European stock (Hittite, Tocharian A, and Tocharian B). From the modified database we created a binary matrix representing the presence/absence of 2,449 cognate sets in eighty-seven languages. We found only limited evidence of reticulation in the data (Bryant et al. 2005). Examining subsets of languages using split decomposition revealed a strong treelike signal in the data, and a preliminary parsimony analysis produced a consistency index of 0.48 and a retention index of 0.76, well above what would be expected from biological datasets of a similar size (Sanderson and Donoghue 1989).

Tree Construction

Maximum-likelihood models of evolution and Bayesian inference of phylogeny were used to reconstruct Indo-European language relationships. We employed the "restriction site" model of binary-character evolution implemented in MrBayes (Huelsenbeck and Ronquist 2001). This allows for unequal character-state frequencies and gamma-distributed character-specific rate heterogeneity. Model parameters, including the rate matrix, branch lengths, and gamma-distribution shape parameter were estimated from the data. Ten million postburn-in trees were generated using the Bayesian-inference procedure. To ensure that consecutive samples were independent, only every 10,000th tree was sampled from this distribution, producing an effective sample size of 1,000. Trees were rooted with Hittite in accordance with linguistic evidence (Gamkrelidze and Ivanov 1995; Rexová et al. 2003).

The consensus tree from the resulting distribution of 1,000 trees is shown in figure 16.8. The topology of the tree is consistent with the traditional Indo-European language groups (Campbell 1998), correctly reconstructing the Celtic, Germanic (including North and West divisions), Romance (including Iberian-French division), Balto-Slavic (including Baltic and Slavic divisions), Indo-Iranian (including Indic and Iranian divisions), Albanian, Greek, Armenian, and Tocharic groups. All these groups are monophyletic and are supported by high posterior probability values. Recent parsimony and compatibility analyses have also supported these groupings as well as a Romano-Germano-Celtic supergroup, the early divergence of Greek and Armenian lineages (Rexová et al. 2003), and the basal position of Tocharian (Ringe et al. 2002).

Although the consensus tree summarizes much of the information in the Bayesian sample distribution, it should not be interpreted as the "true" tree.

Figure 16.8
Majority-Rule Consensus Tree Based on the MCMC Sample of 1,000 Trees

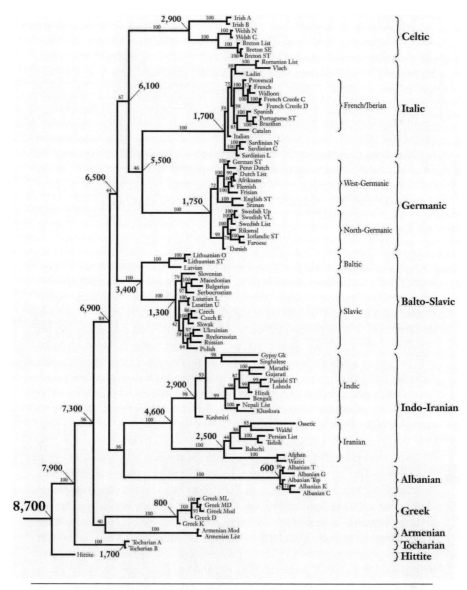

Branch lengths are proportional to the inferred maximum-likelihood estimates of evolutionary change per cognate. Values above each branch express the Bayesian posterior probabilities as a percentage. Values in bold beside selected nodes show the inferred ages of nodes in years B.P.

There is uncertainty in the branch-length estimates and topology of any reconstructed phylogeny. For instance, historical linguists have not resolved the position of the Albanian group, and this uncertainty is clearly reflected in the tree—the posterior probability of the Albanian/Indo-Iranian group is only 0.36. *One major advantage of the Bayesian approach is that results need not be contingent on a single phylogeny.* By estimating divergence times across the MCMC sample of trees we can account for variation in the age estimates that results from phylogenetic uncertainty.

Divergence-Time Estimation

We estimated divergence times by constraining the age of fourteen nodes on each tree in accordance with historically attested events (table 16.7). The age constraints employed do not represent the most precise dates available, but rather express a conservative feasible range on which to base the analysis. Relatively broad date ranges were chosen in order to avoid making disputable, a priori assumptions about Indo-European history. Another advantage of the Bayesian approach is that prior knowledge can be incorporated into the analyses. We were thus able to filter the sampling distribution of trees to include only those trees consistent with what linguists know of Indo-European history. For example, those trees that did not include the French/Iberian subgroup (2 percent) were excluded.

We used penalized-likelihood rate smoothing to calculate divergence times across the sample distribution without the assumption of rate constancy. Figure 16.8 shows reconstructed ages (in years B.P.) for selected nodes on the consensus tree (discussed in more detail below). The resulting divergence-time distribution for the age at the base of the Indo-European tree is shown in figure 16.9a. This distribution produced a 95 percent confidence interval of between 9800 and 7800 B.P.

Testing Robustness

An important part of any Bayesian analysis is an assessment of the robustness of the results. Most obviously, results must be robust to alterations in the starting values, or priors, used for the different model parameters (e.g., branch lengths and rates of change). To test the susceptibility of the results to alterations of the priors, we repeated the analysis using a range of prior values and found no appreciable effect. For example, repeating the analysis with an exponential branch-length prior produced a 95 percent confidence interval for the basal divergence time of between 9200 B.P. and 7100 B.P.

Cognancy judgments are another potential source of error. The Dyen et al. (1997) database contains information about the certainty of cognancy decisions, meaning cognates are coded as either probable or doubtful. In the initial analysis, both probable and doubtful cognancy decisions were coded as cog-

Table 16.7
Age Constraints Used to Calibrate Divergence-Time Calculations Based on Known Historical Information

Divergence	Age constraint	Historical information
Iberian-French	A.D. 450–800	Death of last writers knowing classical Latin and repetition of Latin liturgical formulas without comprehension in 6th to 8th centuries A.D. Strasburg Oaths, A.D. 842 [a, c]
Italic-Romanian	A.D. 150–300	Last Roman troops withdrawn to south of Danube, A.D. 270. Dacia conquered by Rome, A.D. 112 [a, b, c]
North/West Germanic	A.D. 50–250	Germanic tribes united against Rome, A.D. 1. Gothic migration to Eastern Europe, A.D. 180. Earliest attested North Germanic inscriptions date from 3rd century A.D. [a, b, c, f]
Welsh/Breton	A.D. 400–550	Migrants from Britain colonize Brittany in 5th century A.D. [a, e]
Irish/Welsh	before A.D. 300	Archaic Irish inscriptions date back to the 5th century A.D. Divergence must have occurred well before that time. [e, f]
Indic	before 200 B.C.	Singhalese records dating from as early as 2nd century B.C. indicate that Indic languages had begun to diverge by that time. [b, c]
Iranian	before 500 B.C.	By 500 B.C. Old Persian was distinct from the Eastern Iranian dialects. [b, c, f]
Indo-Iranian	before 1,000 B.C.	Rgveda, an identifiably Indic epic, is thought to date to 1450–1000 B.C. The Avesta, a similar Iranian epic, has been recorded in oral tradition since before 800 B.C. [b, c, f]
Slavic	beforeA.D. 700	Old Church Slavonic and East Slavic texts date to beginning of 9th century and indicate significant divergence by that time. The split must have occurred after the Balto-Slavic divergence. [b]
Balto-Slavic	1,400 B.C.– A.D. 100	Distinct Slavic culture and language known to pre-date A.D. 100 on the basis of Tacitus's "Germany." Archaeological evidence suggests the split may have occurred as early as 1,400 B.C. [b, c]
Greek split	before 1,500 B.C.	Earliest form of an ancient Greek dialect is Mycenaean, attested in Linear B texts dating from 15th century B.C. [b, d, f]
Tocharic	140 B.C.– A.D. 350	Tocharian languages are thought to have diverged shortly after the fall of Bactria (135 B.C.) and no later than 100 years before the first known inscriptions of Tocharian B. [b, c]
Tocharian A & B	A.D. 500–750	Earliest texts from later half of 1st millennium A.D. No texts after A.D. 750, by which time Tocharians are thought to have been assimilated with Turkish invaders. [b, c]
Hittite	1,800–1,300 B.C.	Oldest Hittite text of King Anittas from the 18th century B.C. Latest texts from the 14th–13th centuries B.C. [b, c]

a Embleton (1991).
b Gamkrelidze (1995).
c *Indo-European Chronology*, 2002.
d Champion et al. (1984).
e Ringe et al. (1998).
f Mallory(1989).

Figure 16.9
Distribution of Divergence-Time Estimates at the Root of the
Indo-European Phylogeny

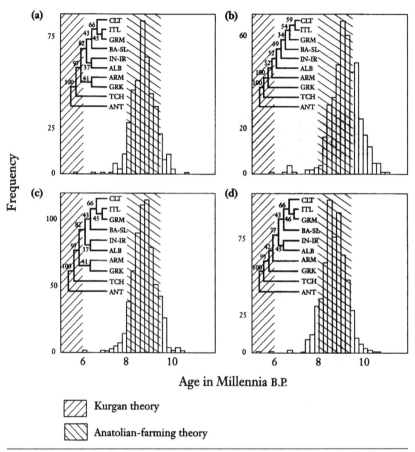

For (a) initial-assumption set using all cognate information and most stringent constraints [(Anatolian, Tocharian, (Greek, Armenian, Albanian, (Iranian, Indic), (Slavic, Baltic), ((North Germanic, West Germanic), Italic, Celtic)))]; (b) conservative cognate coding with doubtful cognates excluded; (c) all cognate sets with minimum topological constraints [(Anatolian, Tocharian, (Greek, Armenian, Albanian, (Iranian, Indic), (Slavic, Baltic), (North Germanic, West Germanic), Italic, Celtic))]; (d) missing-data coding with minimum topological constraints and all cognate sets. Shaded bars represent the implied age ranges under the two competing theories of Indo-European origin. The relationship between the major language groups in the consensus tree for each analysis is also shown, along with posterior probability values.

nate. Doubtful cognates, however, are more likely to be the result of chance borrowings and may produce spurious relationships on the tree. To test the effect of changing the stringency of cognancy judgments, we reran the analysis with only the probable cognancy decisions coded as cognate. This more conservative data set produced a similar topology and divergence time range to that of the initial analysis (figure 16.9b).

The constraint tree used to filter the sampling distribution also contained assumptions about the history of Indo-European that could have biased the results. We thus repeated the analysis using a more relaxed set of constraints. Again, this produced a similar divergence time distribution to the initial analysis (figure 16.9c).

Another source of error lay in the potential influence of uneven sampling across the languages. In the initial analysis, potentially missing cognate information was coded as an absence (0) in the data matrix. However, the extinct languages at the base of the tree may have more missing data as the result of the limited sources of information about these languages. This may have falsely inflated branch lengths at the base of the tree. We thus recoded the database to allow for the effect of missing data in these ancient languages. For each language, cognates were coded as either present (1), absent (0) or missing (?). Coding missing cognate information in this way means that the likelihood model can account for uncertainty in the data itself. The analysis of this modified data set also produced a similar consensus-tree topology and date range to the initial analysis (figure 16.9d).

Finally, although there is considerable support for Hittite as the most appropriate root for Indo-European (Gamkrelidze and Ivanov 1995; Rexová et al. 2003), rooting the tree with Hittite could be claimed to bias the analysis in favor of the Anatolian hypothesis. We thus reran the analysis using the consensus tree in figure 16.8 rooted with Balto-Slavic, Greek, Tocharian, and Indo-Iranian as outgroups. This increased the estimated divergence time from 8700 B.P. to 9600 B.P., 9400 B.P., 9900 B.P., and 10,100 B.P., respectively.

The consensus-tree topology and divergence-time distribution of all four analyses support the Anatolian theory of Indo-European origin. The pattern and timing of expansion suggested by the consensus tree is consistent with archaeological evidence documenting the spread of agriculture from Anatolia. Moreover, the resulting 95 percent confidence interval for the age of Indo-European is way outside the date range implied by the Kurgan hypothesis. Interestingly, the date range for the Kurgan expansion does roughly correspond to a rapid period of divergence on the consensus tree. According to the divergence-time estimates shown in figure 16.8, some of the major Indo-European subfamilies (Indo-Iranian, Balto-Slavic, Germanic, Italic, and Celtic) diverged between 5,000 and 7,000 years ago, close to the hypothesized time of the initial Kurgan expansion. Thus, as Cavalli-Sforza et al. (1994) observed, these hypotheses need not be mutually exclusive. It is possible that there were two distinct phases in the spread of Indo-European: an initial phase, involving the movement of Indo-European with agriculture, out of Anatolia into Greece and the Balkans some 8,500 years ago; and a second phase (perhaps the Kurgan expansion), which saw the subsequent spread of Indo-European languages across the rest of Europe and east into Persia and Central Asia.

The Potential Pitfalls of Linguistic Paleontology

A number of linguists have claimed that there is a compelling reason why the arguments we have presented must be wrong: wheels did not exist in Europe 9,000 years ago and yet Proto-Indo-Europeans are claimed to have had a word for "wheel." Trask (2003a) repeats this well-known argument in a commentary on our work that appeared on the World Wide Web:

> we can reconstruct for PIE a number of words pertaining to wheeled vehicles in general and horse-drawn chariots in particular. The last speakers of PIE must therefore have been familiar with these things. But the archaeologists tell us that these things were not invented before about 6000 B.P. So, how could a language that was last spoken around 10,000 years ago have words for things that were not invented until 4,000 years later?

This argument is nowhere near as compelling as Trask and other commentators have claimed. There are at least two alternative explanations for the distribution of terms associated with wheeled transport: independent semantic innovations from a common root and/or widespread borrowing of technological terms. To describe the case for the former, we can do no better than quote Trask (1996: 355–356) himself:

> There is a PIE word *ekwo-"horse," as well as *wegh-"convey, go in a vehicle," *kwekwlo-"wheel," *aks-"axle," and *nobh-"hub of a wheel." This has led some scholars to conclude that the PIE-speakers not only rode horses but had wagons and chariots as well. This is debateable, however, since everyone places PIE at least 6,000 years in the past, while hard evidence for wheeled vehicles is perhaps no earlier than 5,000 years ago. Watkins (1969) considers that these terms pertaining to wheeled vehicles were chiefly metaphorical extensions of older IE words with different senses (*nobh-, for example, meant "navel"). The word *kwekwlo-"wheel" itself is derived from the root *kwel-"turn, revolve." Nevertheless, the vision of fierce IE warriors, riding horses and driving chariots, sweeping down on their neighbours brandishing bloody swords, has proven to be an enduring one, and scholars have found it difficult to dislodge from the popular consciousness the idea of the PIE-speakers as warlike conquerors in chariots.

In other words, independent semantic innovations from a common root are a likely mechanism by which we can account for the supposed PIE reconstructions associated with wheeled transport. For example, upon the development of wheeled transport, words derived from the PIE term *kwel-, meaning "to turn, rotate," may have been independently co-opted to describe the wheel. On the basis of the reconstructed ages shown in our paper (Gray and Atkinson 2003), as few as three such semantic innovations around the sixth millennium B.P. could have accounted for the attested distribution of terms related to *kwekwlo- "wheel" (one shift just before the break up of the Italic-Celtic-Germanic-Balto-Slavic-Indo-Iranian lineage, one shift in the Greek-Armenian lineage, and one shift [or borrowing] in the Tocharian lineage). The pitfalls of linguistic paleontology are well known. Linguists can reconstruct word forms with much greater certainty than their meanings.

The second explanation, widespread borrowing, also seems a viable alternative for the distribution of terms pertaining to wheeled vehicles. Good ideas spread. Terms associated with a new technology are often borrowed along with the technology. The spread of wheeled transport across Europe and the Near East 5,000–6,000 years ago seems a likely candidate for borrowing of this sort. In a later posting on the Web, Trask (2003b) attempted to address this possibility: "There's a big difference between words which are inherited from a common ancestor and words which have merely diffused from one language to another. . . . [T]he regular changes in pronunciation in the daughter languages demonstrate that [*<kwekwlos> "wheel"] has been inherited from PIE, and not merely borrowed from language to language."

It is true that linguists are able to identify many borrowings (particularly more recent ones) on the basis of the presence or absence of certain systematic sound correspondences. However, borrowings cannot always be identified in this manner. For example, Geraghty (2004) points out that "it is possible to reconstruct the Proto-Micronesian word for 'motor-car,' with regular reflexes in all the relevant daughter languages (e.g., Pohnpei sidôsa, Woleai sitôosa), even though it is patently obvious that the word is a twentieth century loan from Japanese." So, if terms associated with wheeled transport were borrowed some 6,000 years ago, can we expect to identify them as borrowings? Our consensus tree indicates that all of the main lineages went through a long period of divergence post 5000-6000 B.P. before breaking up into their present-day daughter languages. If terms associated with wheeled transport were borrowed at the beginning of this period, as we would expect, then the terms in each of the major lineages will have undergone all the sound changes that characterize that lineage. This would make the words appear native to the lineage and thus inherited from PIE when in fact they could have been early borrowings.

Tasks for the Future

Numerous questions warrant further investigation. First, it should be evident from the consensus tree that the deeper relationships among language groups are generally not as clearly resolved as are the younger relationships. This undoubtedly is partly a result of increasing statistical noise in the data at greater time depths. As we attempt to infer deeper relationships, the phylogenetic signal present in the data is reduced, and the confounding effect of chance similarities and borrowing increases. If, for example, we assume a constant rate of word loss of 19 percent per 1,000 years (a figure suggested by Swadesh [1955]) and project this loss rate back 8,500 years to the base of the tree, we find that we would expect only about 17 percent of words from 8500 B.P. to be present in any language today.

This restricted data set, combined with the influence of chance similarities, means that we cannot expect the same degree of certainty in reconstructing the deeper language relationships. This was not a problem for testing between the Kurgan and Anatolian hypotheses because we were able to incorporate phylogenetic uncertainty into our analysis. However, the error associated with the basal relationships in the tree could be significantly reduced with the inclusion of more extinct languages reconstructed from ancient texts. As well as Hittite (3800 B.P.) and Tocharian (1300 B.P.), suitable examples include Old Norse (800 B.P.), Old Church Slavonic (1100 B.P.), Archaic Irish (1500 B.P.), Latin (2000 B.P.), Ancient Greek (2800 B.P.), and Sanskrit (3000 B.P.). Adding these extinct languages to the database and repeating the analyses could shed light on the deeper relationships within Indo-European as well as produce a narrower confidence interval for the age at the base of the tree (see Atkinson et al. 2005).

Second, nonlexical characters such as grammatical and phonological features of each language can also be used to reconstruct evolutionary language trees. When constructing species trees, biologists use genetic data from multiple loci as well as morphological and behavioral data. The results from any one data source can be validated against the other sources. Conversely, inconsistencies between sources may help to elucidate historical anomalies or problems with the model. For the same reasons, phonological and morphological language data could be incorporated into our analyses.

Conclusion

Computational phylogenetic methods are powerful tools with which to probe the mysteries of our past, including the evolution of language. They not only supplement traditional historical-linguistic methods in several important ways. First, the maximum-likelihood approach allows us to create explicit evolutionary models of language change, which can account for problems such as rate variation between words and lineages. Model parameters can be estimated from the data, reducing the need for restrictive, a priori assumptions about the evolutionary process. Where assumptions are made, we can evaluate the efficacy of the implied evolutionary models and test the robustness of our results. Second, we can measure phylogenetic uncertainty using Bayesian inference of phylogeny. Not only does this provide an estimate of the strength of any signal in the data, the uncertainty can be incorporated into future analyses. We can estimate the error associated with our results and hence test between alternative hypotheses in a scientifically rigorous way. Third, rate-smoothing algorithms allow us to estimate divergence times without making the flawed assumption of rate constancy across a tree.

Clackson (2000: 451) rather pessimistically claimed that linguists cannot answer the question of when PIE was spoken "in any really meaningful or helpful way." In light of the methods outlined above, this assertion seems a little premature. Maximum-likelihood models, Bayesian inference of phylogeny, and rate-smoothing algorithms are powerful investigative tools for research in historical linguistics, just as they are in evolutionary biology. Using these methods, we have been able to focus the age of Indo-European to within 1,200 years of 8700 B.P.–a meaningful range that certainly helps us answer the question of when PIE was spoken.

Acknowledgments

We thank S. Allan, B. Blust, L. Campbell, L. Chikhi, M. Corballis, S. Greenhill, J. Hamm, J. Huelsenbeck, G. Nichols, A. Rodrigo, F. Ronquist, M. Sanderson, and S. Shennan for useful advice and/or comments on the manuscript.

Part 6

Concluding Remarks

17

Afterword

Carl P. Lipo, Michael J. O'Brien, Mark Collard,
and Stephen J. Shennan

Efforts to build a science of human variation have a long history. Although a synthesis has yet to be reached, there is growing appreciation among social scientists that a Darwinian evolutionary perspective on variation can provide fruitful avenues of research. The key point of departure for incorporating Darwinian evolution within the social sciences is recognizing that evolution is a theory about history. Evolutionary explanations are historical because they concern themselves with how and why things change over time. Two points are worth making in this regard. First, evolutionary explanations explore "any net directional change or cumulative change in the characteristics of organisms and populations over many generations" (Endler 1986: 5). In this sense, the focus of evolutionary studies is on tracking change through time. Second, and related, evolutionary explanations rest on our ability to reconstruct genealogy. The key question here is: are two things similar because they are related phylogenetically, or are they similar as a result of other processes such as convergence and borrowing?

Interest in phylogeny has long been part of the research agenda for the social sciences. It is largely because of this interest that anthropologists have developed robust accounts of cultural, behavioral, biological, and linguistic histories for much of the world. These "culture histories" link modern, historical, and prehistoric populations through time and across space and are evolutionary accounts in the sense that they are narratives about relatedness. Indeed, the process of defining a culture-historical tradition consists of isolating a group of things that are linked in ancestor-descendent relations. Thus, evolutionary thinking fits comfortably with the kinds of analyses that anthropologists have routinely done for the better part of a century. The chapters in this book reflect the wide range of subject matter that can be studied phylogenetically, including projectile points, pottery designs, pottery composition, marriage patterns, puberty rituals, basketry, languages, and genes. These phenomena represent the broad spectrum of human variation and underscore the basic principle that phylogenetic methods are applicable to anything that is structured by a system of inheritance.

Several lessons stem from the study of this array of data classes. A key recognition is that the patterns derived through phylogenetic analyses often reflect unique histories of inheritance that depend at least in part on the characters of interest. Characters can be independently transmitted through a population and may not form coherent sets; each has its own history that may or may not be correlated with other characters in the population. In some cases, characters reveal strong branching patterns consistent with vertical transmission as the primary mode of inheritance. In these instances, variation among characters is produced by divergence caused by isolation of portions of a population from each other. In other examples, distributions of characters are consistent with blending, which occurs when inheritance is predominantly horizontal and patterns of relatedness are geographically structured so that similarity is correlated with spatial distance. Of course, horizontal inheritance can also produce tree structures, but they are orthogonal to the trees produced by vertical transmission—for example, a feature that spreads from one group to another, undergoes an innovation, and then spreads to another group. This means that each case needs to be evaluated independently.

In general, this observation of the nature of cultural transmission reflects our appreciation of the subtleties of phylogenetic approaches, and it underscores the fact that phylogenetics is clearly not the end point of analyses but rather an integrated and iterative part of the explanation of cultural phenomena. Methodological advances such as the ones represented in the chapters of this volume have resulted from improved and expanded models of transmission as well as from the development of statistical methods for evaluating the fit of data to the predictions of the models.

The chapters highlight a number of conceptual distinctions. One of the more substantial issues concerns the appropriate units of analyses: populations versus specific artifacts and/or characters. Some authors argue that groups of individuals can be analyzed as coherent units because groups share characters despite having somewhat permeable boundaries. Other contributors are critical of attempts to use cultures or societies as units, and suggest that populations cannot be treated simply as analogues for species. The resolution of this issue will depend on whether one can make a case for evaluating relatedness in sets of characters or populations of individuals exhibiting those characters. The latter situation is likely to characterize the study of ethnographic populations, whereas the former characterizes archaeological cases.

Another area in which authors' perspectives vary is the degree of confidence in identifying the factors that produce the variation we study. For some, it is not clear that our methods, whether adopted from biology or built from scratch, are fully in alignment with our theoretical understanding of cultural transmission and the processes by which humans inherit cultural, behavioral, and linguistic information. Indeed, several contributors express concern over whether the methods are racing ahead of the theory that we use to explain the results of phylogenetic analyses. On the one hand, we have good reason to be cautious. The allure of statistical techniques and their success in the natural sciences is all too often used as an excuse to adopt and implement new numerical methods within the social sciences. On the other hand, we should recognize the iterative nature of theory construction and method implementation. As we build an evolutionary approach to the study of human diversity, we can expect a degree of interplay between theory and empirical evaluation as we try different approaches and determine the degree to which they produce falsifiable hypotheses.

With respect to method, the chapters demonstrate that there is no single approach that necessarily addresses all phylogenetic issues. At least two kinds of approaches are represented. Many of the authors adopt the view that human diversity can be explored productively using methods originally devised to study biological evolution. This view centers on the notion that cladogenetic models can be applied to the study of human diversity. Deviations from this model are detectable using a variety of statistical means. Other authors suggest alternative avenues of inquiry that have their roots in the social sciences. Both approaches appear to be fruitful.

The diversity in approaches used in phylogenetic analyses has other implications. There is, for example, no single procedure for studying relatedness. The examples in the volume vary from the use of compositional analysis to map patterns of relatedness among artifacts to the use of biological phylogentic software such as PAUP* and MacClade. In addition, graphical representations of relatedness can take the form of relatively familiar treelike representations as well as network topologies.

To some degree, the differences reflected in phylogenetic approaches suggest the overall immaturity of our efforts, as social scientists explore the rich assortment of statistics and methods already existing within biology. These resources provide us with countless opportunities to experiment and investigate their application within anthropological, linguistic, and archaeological data sets. The adoption of methods from the biological sciences is unlikely to be abated; perusal of the phylogenetics literature suggests that ongoing innovations will fuel years of adaptations in the social sciences. Of particular interest to anthropologists will likely be new means of statistically inferring and evaluating trees under different types of assumptions (e.g., Felsenstein 2004), methods for studying biological phenomena such as reticulation among bacteria (e.g., Makarenkov 2001; Woese 2000), and new methods for dealing with temporal issues such as those found in the paleontological record (e.g., Huelsenbeck and Rannala 1997, 2000).

Where Should We Go Next?

Our first step is to recognize that phylogenetic theory is not as far along in anthropology as is our ability to evaluate variation statistically. In general, we need more information on how traits are transmitted within and between populations and a more sophisticated understanding of how population configurations influence patterns of relatedness. We need, for example, better means of estimating the effects of varying rates of interaction, methods for determining the impact of structured spatial distributions of individuals, and models for assessing the role of interpersonal rules for transmission. In addition to increasing our understanding of empirical processes, we also need a more refined grasp of measurement issues such as sampling effects and the construction of units for studying transmission. Simulations likely will be an important component of this kind of research as a means to assess the effects of our assumptions on the results of our analyses. We also need to determine how varying the properties of transmission and changing our measurement procedures influence the patterns we detect with cladistics and other phylogenetic techniques.

In summary, this volume is only a starting point, a place from which further theory, models, methods, and techniques can be constructed. The work reported here represents the frontier of phylogenetic applications within the social sciences and shows that by gaining an understanding of the abilities and limitations of existing phylogenetic methods, new statistics and models will emerge that more closely match the empirical nature of anthropological and archaeological phenomena. This is the kind of focused development that will be needed to move the phylogenetic study of cultural phenomena from the adaptation of biological techniques into a fully formed integrated field of research. We believe phylogenetic methods are ultimately a key development within the social sciences, as they offer a quantitative means of explaining human diversity. There is still much to accomplish, but it promises to be exciting work.

References

Aberle, D. F. 1961. Matrilineal Descent in Cross-Cultural Comparison. In *Matrilineal Kinship,* edited by D. Schneider and K. Gough, pp. 655–730. University of California Press, Berkeley.

Abouheif, E. 1999. A Method for Testing the Assumption of Phylogenetic Independence in Comparative Data. *Evolutionary Ecology Research* 1: 895–909.

Aftandilian, D. K. 1995. *Mass Graves or Family Plots? An Intra-Site Spatial Analysis of Burial Patterning in the Dickson Mounds Display Excavation.* M.A. thesis, Department of Anthropology, University of Chicago. Chicago.

Alstad, D. N. 2001. *Basic Populus Models of Ecology.* Prentice-Hall, Upper Saddle River, N.J.

Alvard, M. S. 2003. The Adaptive Nature of Culture. *Evolutionary Anthropology* 12: 136–149.

Ames, K. M., and H. D. G. Maschner. 1999. *Peoples of the Northwest Coast: Their Archaeology and Prehistory.* Thames and Hudson, London.

Ammerman, A. J., and L. L. Cavalli-Sforza. 1984. *The Neolithic Transition and the Genetics of Populations in Europe.* Princeton University Press, Princeton, N.J.

Andersen, E. S. 2003. The Evolving Tree of Industrial Life: An Approach to the Transformation of European Industry. Paper presented at the Second Workshop on the Economic Transformation of Europe, Torino, Italy.

Anderson, D. G., L. D. O'Steen, and K. E. Sassaman. 1996. Environmental and Chronological Considerations. In *The Paleoindian and Early Archaic Southeast,* edited by D. G. Anderson and K. E. Sassaman, pp. 1–15. University of Alabama Press, Tuscaloosa.

Archie, J. W. 1989. A Randomization Test for Phylogenetic Information in Systematic Data. *Systematic Zoology* 38: 219–252.

Armelagos, G. J., and D. P. Van Gerven. 2003. A Century of Skeletal Biology and Paleopathology: Contrasts, Contradictions, and Conflicts. *American Anthropologist* 105: 53–64.

Armstrong K. 1993. *A History of God.* Ballantine, New York.

Arnold, D. E., H. Neff, and R. L. Bishop. 1991. Compositional Analysis and "Sources" of Pottery: An Ethnoarchaeological Approach. *American Anthropologist* 93: 70–90.

Arnold, D. E., H. Neff, R. L. Bishop, and M. D. Glascock. 1999. Testing the Interpretive Assumptions of Neutron Activation Analysis: Contemporary Pottery in Yucatan, 1964–1994. In *Material Meanings: Critical Approaches to Interpreting Material Culture,* edited by E. S. Chilton, pp. 61–84. University of Utah Press, Salt Lake City.

Arnold, D. E., H. Neff, and M. D. Glascock. 2000. Testing Assumptions of Neutron Activation Analysis: Communities, Workshops and Paste Preparation in Yucatán, Mexico. *Archaeometry* 42: 301–316.

Arnold, M. L. 1997. *Natural Hybridization and Evolution.* Oxford University Press, New York.

Asch, S. E. 1952. *Social Psychology.* Prentice-Hall, New York.

Asch, S. E. 1955. Opinions and Social Pressures. *Scientific American* 193(5): 31–35.

Atkinson, Q. D., and R. D. Gray. 2005. Curious Parallels and Curious Connections— Phylogenetic Thinking in Biology and Historical Linguistics. *Systematic Biology* 54: 513–526.

Atkinson, Q. D., P. Nicholls, D. Welch, and R. D. Gray. 2005. From Words to Dates: Water into Wine, Mathemagic or Phylogenetic Influence. *Transactions of the Philological Society* 103: 193–219.

Atran, S. 2001. The Trouble with Memes. *Human Nature* 12: 351–381.

Aunger, R. 2000. *Darwinizing Culture: The Status of Memetics as a Science.* Oxford University Press, New York.

Avise, J. C. 2000. *Phylogeography: The History and Formation of Species.* Harvard University Press, Cambridge, Mass.

Bahn, P., and J. Flenley. 1992. *Easter Island, Earth Island.* Thames and Hudson, London.

Baker, R., and R. DeSalle. 1997. Multiple Sources of Character Information and the Phylogeny of Hawaiian Drosophilids. *Systematic Biology* 46: 654–673.

Ballenger, J. A. M. 2001. *Dalton Settlement in the Arkoma Basin of Eastern Oklahoma.* Sam Noble Oklahoma Museum of Natural History, R. E. Bell Monographs, no. 2. Norman.

Bandura, A. 1973. *Aggression: A Social Learning Analysis.* Prentice-Hall, New York.

Bandura, A. 1977. *Social Learning Theory.* Prentice-Hall, New York.

Barnosky, A. D. 1987. Punctuated Equilibrium and Phyletic Gradualism: Some Facts from the Quaternary Mammalian Record. *Current Mammalogy* 1: 109–147.

Baroni, M. 2003. Hybrid Phylogenies. Paper presented at the Workshop on New Trends in Phylogenetics and Genomics 2003. Zentrum für Bioinformatics, Tübingen, Germany.

Baroni, M. 2004. Using Directed Graphs to Represent Reticulate Evolution. Paper presented at the 2004 Annual New Zealand Phylogenetics Meetings, Mount Ruapehu, North Island, New Zealand.

Barth, F. 1966. *Models of Social Organization.* Royal Anthropological Institute, London.

Barth, F. 1987. *Cosmologies in the Making: A Generative Approach to Cultural Variation in Inner New Guinea.* Cambridge University Press, Cambridge.

Barton, N. H., and I. Wilson. 1995. Genealogies and Geography. *Royal Society London, Philosophical Transactions* B349: 49–59.

Bastin, Y. 1983. Classification Lexicostatistique des Langues Bantoues (214 Releves). *Bulletin des Séances, Académie Royale des Sciences d'Outre-Mer* 27: 173–199.

Bastin, Y., A. Coupez, and M. Mann. 1999. *Continuity and Divergence in the Bantu Languages: Perspectives from a Lexicostatistic Study.* Annales Sciences Humaines du Musée Royal de l'Afrique Centrale de Tervuren 162. Tervuren, Belgium.

Bateman, R., I. Goddard, R. O'Grady, V. A. Funk, R. Mooi, W. J. Kress, and P. Cannell 1990. Speaking with Forked Tongues: The Feasibility of Reconciling Human Phylogeny and the History of Language. *Current Anthropology* 31: 1–24.

Beaudry, M. P. 1984. *Ceramic Production and Distribution in the Southeastern Maya Periphery: Late Classic Painted Serving Vessels.* British Archaeological Reports, International Series 203. Oxford.

Beck, C. 1995. Functional Analysis and the Differential Persistence of Great Basin Dart Forms. *Journal of California and Great Basin Anthropology* 17: 222–243.

Beck, C. 1998. Projectile Points as Valid Chronological Units. In *Unit Issues in Archaeology: Measuring Time, Space, and Material,* edited by A. F. Ramenofsky and A. Steffen, pp. 21–40. University of Utah Press, Salt Lake City.

Bellwood, P. 1995. *Prehistory of the Indo-Malaysian Archipelago.* Academic Press, Sydney.

Bellwood, P. 1996a. Phylogeny vs. Reticulation in Prehistory. *Antiquity* 70: 881–890.

Bellwood, P. 1996b. The Origins and Spread of Agriculture in the Indo-Pacific Region: Gradualism and Diffusion or Revolution and Colonization? In *The Origins and Spread of Agriculture and Pastoralism in Eurasia,* edited by D. R. Harris, pp. 465–498. University College London Press, London.

Bellwood, P. 1998. The Archaeology of Papuan and Austronesian Prehistory in the Northern Moluccas, Eastern Indonesia. In *Archaeology and Language II: Correlating Archeological and Linguistic Hypotheses,* edited by R. Blench and M. Spriggs, pp. 128–140. Routledge, London.

Bellwood, P. 2001. Early Agriculturalist Diasporas? Farming, Languages, and Genes. *Annual Review of Anthropology* 30: 181–207.

Bellwood, P., and C. Renfrew (editors). 2003. *Examining the Farming/Language Dispersal Hypothesis.* McDonald Institute for Archaeological Research, Cambridge.

Benfer, R. A. 1968. *An Analysis of a Prehistoric Skeletal Population, Casas Grandes, Chihuahua, Mexico.* Ph.D. dissertation, Department of Anthropology, University of Texas. Austin.

Bennett, K. A. 1973. *The Indians of Point of Pines, Arizona.* University of Arizona, Anthropological Papers, no. 23. Tucson.

Bennyhoff, J. A. 1994. Central California Augustine: Implications for Northern Archaeology. In *Toward a New Taxonomic Framework for Central California Archaeology: Essays by James A. Bennyhoff and David A. Fredrickson,* edited by R. E. Hughes, pp. 65–74. University of California, Archaeological Research Facility, Contribution, no. 52. Berkeley.

Benton, M. J. 1995. Testing the Time Axis of Phylogenies. *Philosophical Transactions: Biological Sciences* 349: 5–10.

Benton, M. J., and R. Hitchin. 1997. Congruence between Phylogenetic and Stratigraphic Data on the History of Life. *Royal Society London, Proceedings* 264B: 885–890.

Benton, M. J., R. Hitchin, and M. A. Wills. 1999. Assessing Congruence between Cladistic and Stratigraphic Data. *Systematic Biology* 48: 581–596.

Bergsland, K., and H. Vogt. 1962. On the Validity of Glottochronology. *Current Anthropology* 3: 115–153.

Bettinger, R. L., R. Boyd, and P. J. Richerson. 1996. Style, Function, and Cultural Evolutionary Processes. In *Darwinian Archaeologies,* edited by H. D. G. Maschner, pp. 133–164. Plenum, New York.

Bettinger, R. L., and J. Eerkens. 1997. Evolutionary Implications of Metrical Variation in Great Basin Projectile Points. In *Rediscovering Darwin: Evolutionary Theory and Archeological Explanation,* edited by C. M. Barton and G. A. Clark, pp. 177–191. American Anthropological Association, Archeological Papers, no. 7. Washington, D.C.

Bettinger, R. L., and J. Eerkens. 1999. Point Typologies, Cultural Transmission, and the Spread of Bow and Arrow Technology in the Prehistoric Great Basin. *American Antiquity* 64: 231–242.

Binford, L. R. 1973. Interassemblage Variability–The Mousterian and the 'Functional' Argument. In *The Explanation of Culture Change: Models in Prehistory,* edited by C. Renfrew, pp. 227–254. Duckworth, London.

Binford, L. R., and S. R. Binford. 1966. A Preliminary Analysis of Functional Variability in the Mousterian of Levallois Facies. *American Anthropologist* 68: 238–295.

Binford, S. R. 1971. The Significance of Variability: A Minority Report. In *The Origin of Homo sapiens,* pp.199–210. Ecology and Conservation, Vol. 3. UNESCO, New York.

Bininda-Emonds, O. R. P., and A. P. Russell. 1996. A Morphological Perspective on the Phylogenetic Relationships of the Extant Phocid Seals (Mammalia: Carnivora: Phocidae). *Bonner Zoologische Monographien* 41: 1–256.

Birdsell, J. B. 1973. A Basic Demographic Unit. *Current Anthropology* 14: 337–356.

Birkby, W. H. 1973. *Discontinuous Morphological Traits of the Skull as Population Markers in the Prehistoric Southwest*. Ph.D. dissertation, Department of Anthropology, University of Arizona. Tucson.

Bishop, R. L., and M. P. Beaudry. 1994. Appendix B: Chemical Compositional Analysis of Southeastern Maya Ceramics. In *Ceramics and Artifacts from Excavations in the Copán Residential Zone*, by G. R. Willey, R. M. Leventhal, A. A. Demarest, and W. L. Fash, pp. 407–443. Peabody Museum of Archaeology and Ethnology, Papers 80. Cambridge, Mass.

Bishop, R. L., M. P. Beaudry, R. M. Leventhal, and R. J. Sharer. 1986. Compositional Analysis of Copador and Related Pottery in the Southeast Maya Area. In *The Southeast Maya Periphery*, edited by P. A. Urban and E. M. Schortman, pp. 143–175. University of Texas Press, Austin.

Blackmore, S. 1999. *The Meme Machine*. Oxford University Press, New York.

Blomberg, S. P., and T. Garland. 2002. Tempo and Mode in Evolution: Phylogenetic Inertia, Adaptation and Comparative Methods. *Journal of Evolutionary Biology* 15: 899–910.

Blomberg, S. P., T. Garland, and A. R. Ives. 2003. Testing for Phylogenetic Signal in Comparative Data: Behavioral Traits Are More Labile. *Evolution* 57: 717–745.

Blust, R. 2000. Why Lexicostatistics Doesn't Work: The 'Universal Constant' Hypothesis and the Austronesian Languages. In *Time Depth in Historical Linguistics,* edited by C. Renfrew, A. McMahon, and L. Trask, pp. 311–332. McDonald Institute for Archaeological Research, Cambridge.

Boas, F. 1904. The History of Anthropology. *Science* 20: 513–524.

Bonner, J. 1980. *The Evolution of Culture in Animals*. Princeton University Press, Princeton, N.J.

Boone J. L., and E. A. Smith. 1998. Is It Evolution Yet? A Critique of Evolutionary Archaeology. *Current Anthropology* 39:S141–S173.

Bordes, F. 1961. Mousterian Cultures in France. *Science* 134: 803–810.

Bordes, F., and D. de Sonneville-Bordes. 1970. The Significance of Variability in Paleolithic Assemblages. *World Archaeology* 2: 61–73.

Borgatti, S. P., M. G. Everett, and L. C. Freeman. 2002. *UCINET for Windows: Software for Social Network Analysis.* Analytic Technologies, Natick, Mass.

Borgerhoff Mulder, M. 1989. Reproductive Consequences of Sex-Biased Inheritance for the Kipsigis. In *Comparative Socioecology,* edited by V. Standen and R. A. Foley, pp. 405–427. Blackwell, Oxford.

Borgerhoff Mulder, M. 1995. Bridewealth and Its Correlates: Quantifying Changes over Time. *Current Anthropology* 36: 573–603.

Borgerhoff Mulder, M. 2001. Using Phylogenetically Based Comparative Methods in Anthropology: More Questions Than Answers. *Evolutionary Anthropology* 10: 99–111.

Borgerhoff Mulder, M., C. L. Nunn, and M. C. Towner. 2005. Macroevolutionary Studies of Cultural Trait Transmission. *Evolutionary Anthropology*. In review.

Borgerhoff Mulder, M., M. George-Cramer, J. Eshelman, and A. Ortolani. 2001. A Study of East African Kinship and Marriage Using Phylogenetically Based Comparative Methods. *American Anthropologist* 103: 1059–1082.

Boyd, C. C. 1987. Interobserver Error in the Analysis of Nominal Attribute States. *Tennessee Anthropologist* 12: 88–95.

Boyd R., M. Borgerhoff Mulder, W. H. Durham, and P. J. Richerson. 1997. Are Cultural Phylogenies Possible? In *Human by Nature,* edited by P. Weingart, S. D. Mitchell, P. J. Richerson, and S. Maasen, pp. 355–386. Erlbaum, Mahwah, N.J.

Boyd, R., and P. J. Richerson. 1985. *Culture and the Evolutionary Process.* University of Chicago Press, Chicago.

Boyd, R., and P. J. Richerson. 1995. Why Does Culture Increase Human Adaptability? *Ethology and Sociobiology* 16: 125–143.

Brace, C. L. 1982. The Roots of the Race Concept in American Physical Anthropology. In *A History of American Physical Anthropology: 1930–1980,* edited by F. Spencer, pp. 11–29. Academic Press, New York.

Brace, C. L., and R. J. Hinton. 1981. Oceanic Tooth-Size Variation as a Reflection of Biological and Cultural Mixing. *Current Anthropology* 22: 549–569.

Bradley, B. A. 1997. Sloan Site Biface and Projectile Point Technology. In *Sloan: A Paleoindian Dalton Cemetery in Arkansas,* edited by D. F. Morse, pp. 53–57. Smithsonian Institution Press, Washington, D.C.

Brew, J. O. 1946. *Archaeology of Alkali Ridge, Southeastern Utah.* Peabody Museum of American Archaeology and Ethnology, Papers 21. Cambridge, Mass.

Brody, J. J. 1983. Mimbres Painting. In *Mimbres Pottery: Ancient Art of the American Southwest,* by J. J. Brody, C. J. Scott, and S. A. LeBlanc, pp. 69–127. Hudson Hill Press and the American Federation of the Arts, New York.

Brooks, D. R., and D. A. McLennan. 1991. *Phylogeny, Ecology, and Behavior: A Research Program in Comparative Biology.* University of Chicago Press, Chicago.

Brues, A. M. 1946. *The San Simon Branch: Excavations at Cave Creek and in the San Simon Valley II. Skeletal Material.* Medallion Papers, no. 35. Gila Pueblo, Globe, Ariz.

Bryant, D., F. Filimon, and R. D. Gray. 2005. Untangling Our Past: Languages, Trees, Splits and Networks. In *The Evolution of Cultural Diversity: A Phylogenetic Approach,* edited by R. Mace, C. J. Holden, and S. J. Shennan, pp. 67–83. University College London Press, London.

Bryant, D., and V. Moulton. 2002. NeighborNet: An Agglomerative Method for the Construction of Planar Phylogenetic Networks. *Workshop in Algorithms for Bioinformatics, Proceedings* 2002: 375–391.

Buikstra, J. E. 1980. Epigenetic Distance: A Study of Biological Variability in the Lower Illinois River Region. In *Early Native Americans,* edited by D. L. Browman, pp. 271–299. Mouton, Paris.

Buikstra, J. E., S. R. Frankenberg, and L. W. Konigsberg. 1990. Skeletal Biological Distance Studies in American Physical Anthropology: Recent Trends. *American Journal of Physical Anthropology* 82: 1–7.

Buikstra, J. E., and D. H. Ubelaker (editors). 1994. *Standards for Data Collection from Human Skeletal Remains.* Arkansas Archeological Survey, Fayetteville.

Bull, J. J. 1994. Virulence. *Evolution* 48: 1423–1437.

Burton, M. L., C. C. Moore, J. W. M. Whiting, A. K. Romney, D. F. Aberle, J. A. Barcelo, M. M. Dow, J. I. Guyer, D. B. Kronenfeld, J. E. Levy, and J. Linnekin. 1996. Regions Based on Social Structure. *Current Anthropology* 37: 87–123.

Buss, L. W. 1987. *The Evolution of Individuality.* Princeton University Press, Princeton, N.J.

Butler, B. H. 1971. T*he People of Casas Grandes: Cranial and Dental Morphology through Time.* Ph.D. dissertation, Department of Anthropology, Southern Methodist University, Dallas.

Campbell, J. 1955. *Pagan and Christian Mysteries.* Harper and Row, New York.

Campbell, L. 1997. *American Indian Languages.* Oxford University Press, Oxford.

Campbell, L. 1998. *Historical Linguistics: An Introduction.* Edinburgh University Press, Edinburgh.

Campbell, L. 1999. *Historical Linguistics: An Introduction.* MIT Press, Cambridge, Mass.

Caspari, R. 2003. From Types to Populations: A Century of Race, Physical Anthropology, and the American Anthropological Association. *American Anthropologist* 105: 65–76.

Cavalli-Sforza, L. L. 2000. *Genes, Peoples and Languages.* North Point Press, New York.

Cavalli-Sforza, L. L., and F. Cavalli-Sforza. 1995. *The Great Human Diasporas.* Addison-Wesley, Reading, Mass.

Cavalli-Sforza, L. L., and M. W. Feldman. 1981. *Cultural Transmission and Evolution: A Quantitative Approach.* Princeton University Press, Princeton, N.J.

Cavalli-Sforza, L. L., and M. W. Feldman. 2003. The Application of Molecular Genetic Approaches to the Study of Human Evolution. *Nature Genetics Supplement* 33: 266–275.

Cavalli-Sforza, L. L., P. Menozzi, and A. Piazza. 1994. *The History and Geography of Human Genes.* Princeton University Press, Princeton, N.J.

Cavalli-Sforza, L. L., E. Minch, and J. L. Mountain. 1992. Coevolution of Genes and Languages Revisited. *National Academy of Sciences, Proceedings* 89: 5620–5624.

Cavalli-Sforza, L. L., A. Piazza, P. Menozzi, and J. Mountain. 1988. Reconstruction of Human Evolution: Bringing Together Genetic, Archaeological, and Linguistic Data. *National Academy of Sciences, Proceedings* 85: 6002–6006.

Chakraborty, R. R., R. Blanco, F. Rothhammer, and E. Llop. 1976. Genetic Variability in Chilean Indian Populations and Its Association with Geography, Language, and Culture. *Social Biology* 23: 73–81.

Champion, T., C. Gamble, S. Shennan, and A. Whittle. 1984. *Prehistoric Europe.* Academic Press, New York.

Chapman, P. M. 1993. *Analysis of Non-Metric Cranial Traits from Prehistoric Easter Island with Comparisons to Peru.* M.A. thesis, Department of Anthropology, University of Wyoming. Laramie.

Chapman, P. M. 1997. A Biological Review of the Prehistoric Rapanui. *Journal of the Polynesian Society* 106: 161–174.

Chapman, P. M., and G. W. Gill. 1997. Easter Island Origins: Non-Metric Cranial Trait Comparison between Easter Island and Peru. *Rapa Nui Journal* 11: 58–63.

Chen, J., R. R. Sokal, and M. Ruhlen. 1995. Worldwide Analysis of Genetic and Linguistic Relationships of Human Populations. *Human Biology* 67: 595–612.

Cheverud, J. M., and J. E. Buikstra. 1978. A Study of Intragroup Biological Change Induced by Social Group Fission in *Maccaca mulatta* Using Discrete Cranial Traits. *American Journal of Physical Anthropology* 48: 41–46.

Cheverud, J. M., and J. E. Buikstra. 1981a. Quantitative Genetics of Skeletal Nonmetric Traits in the Rhesus Macaques on Cayo Santiago. I: Single Trait Heritabilities. *American Journal of Physical Anthropology* 54: 43–49.

Cheverud, J. M., and J. E. Buikstra. 1981b. Quantitative Genetics of Skeletal Nonmetric Traits in the Rhesus Macaques on Cayo Santiago. II: Phenotypic, Genetic, and Environmental Correlations between Traits. *American Journal of Physical Anthropology* 54: 51–58.

Cheverud, J. M., and J. E. Buikstra. 1982. Quantitative Genetics of Skeletal Nonmetric Traits in the Rhesus Macaques on Cayo Santiago. III: Relative Heritability of Skeletal Nonmetric and Metric Traits. *American Journal of Physical Anthropology* 59: 151–155.

Cheverud, J. M., J. E. Buikstra, and E. Twichell. 1979. Relationships between Non-Metric Skeletal Traits and Cranial Size and Shape. *American Journal of Physical Anthropology* 50: 191–198.

Chikhi, L., G. Destro-Bisol, G. Bertorelle, V. Pascalli, and G. Barbujani. 1998. Clines of Nuclear DNA Markers Suggest a Largely Neolithic Ancestry of the European Gene Pool. *National Academy of Sciences, Proceedings* 95: 9053–9058.

Chikhi, L., R. A. Nichols, G. Barbujani, and M. A. Beaumont. 2002. Y Genetic Data Support the Neolithic Demic Diffusion Model. *National Academy of Sciences, Proceedings* 99: 11008–11013.

Christenson, A. L. 1986. Projectile Point Size and Projectile Aerodynamics: An Exploratory Study. *Plains Anthropologist* 31: 109–128.

Clackson, J. 2000. Time Depth in Indo-European. In *Time Depth in Historical Linguistics,* edited by C. Renfrew, A. McMahon, and L. Trask, pp. 441–454. McDonald Institute for Archaeological Research, Cambridge.

Clarke, D. L. 1968. *Analytical Archaeology.* Methuen, London.

Clayton, D., S. Al-Tamimi, and K. Johnson. 2003. The Ecological Basis of Coevolutionary History. In *Tangled Trees: Phylogeny, Cospeciation and Coevolution,* edited by R. Page, pp. 310–342. University of Chicago Press, Chicago.

Clist, B. 1987. Early Bantu Settlements in West-Central Africa: A Review of Recent Research. *Current Anthropology* 28: 380–382.

Clist, B. 1989. Archaeology in Gabon, 1886–1988. *African Archaeological Review* 7: 59–95.

Cloak, F. T., Jr. 1973. Elementary Self-Replicating Instructions and Their Works: Toward a Radical Reconstruction of General Anthropology through a General Theory of Natural Selection. Paper presented at the Ninth International Congress of Anthropological and Ethnographical Sciences, Chicago.

Cloak, F. T., Jr. 1975. Is a Cultural Ethology Possible? *Human Ecology* 3: 161–182.

Coen, E. 2002. The Making of a Blossom. *Natural History* 11(4): 48–54

Collard, M., and B. A. Wood. 2000. How Reliable Are Human Phylogenetic Hypotheses? *National Academy of Sciences, Proceedings* 97: 5003–5006.

Collard, M., and B. A. Wood. 2001. Homoplasy and the Early Hominid Masticatory System: Inferences from Analyses of Living Hominoids and Papionins. *Journal of Human Evolution* 41: 167–194.

Collard, M., and S. J. Shennan. 2000. Ethnogenesis versus Phylogenesis in Prehistoric Culture Change: A Case-Study Using European Neolithic Pottery and Biological Phylogenetic Techniques. In *Archaeogenetics: DNA and the Population Prehistory of Europe,* edited by C. Renfrew and K. Boyle, pp. 89–97. McDonald Institute for Archaeological Research, Cambridge.

Cooper, R. A. 2002. Scientific Knowledge of the Past Is Possible. *American Biology Teacher* 64: 427–432.

Corruccini, R. S. 1972. The Biological Relationship of Some Prehistoric and Historic Pueblo Populations. *American Journal of Physical Anthropology* 37: 373–388.

Corruccini, R. S. 1998. On Hawikku Cemetery Kin Groups. *American Antiquity* 63: 161–163.

Cotterell, B., and J. Kamminga. 1990. *Mechanics of Pre-Industrial Technology.* Cambridge University Press, Cambridge.

Cowgill, G. 1972. Models, Methods and Techniques for Seriation. In *Models in Archaeology,* edited by D. L. Clarke, pp. 381–424. Methuen, London.

Cowlishaw, G., and R. Mace. 1996. Cross-Cultural Patterns of Marriage and Inheritance: A Phylogenetic Approach. *Ethology and Sociobiology* 17: 87–97.

Croft, W. 2000. *Explaining Language Change: An Evolutionary Approach.* Pearson, Singapore.

Cronk, L. 1999. *That Complex Whole: Culture and the Evolution of Human Behavior.* Westview, Boulder, Colo.

Crow, J. F., and M. Kimura. 1970. *An Introduction to Population Genetics Theory.* Harper and Row, New York.

Cuvier, G. B. 1829. *Le Règne Animal, Distribué d'après son Organisation, pour Servir de Base à l'Histoire Naturelle des Animaux et d'Introduction à l'Anatomie Comparée.* Déterville, Paris.

Darwin, C. 1859. *On the Origin of Species by Means of Natural Selection; or the Preservation of Favoured Races in the Struggle for Life.* Murray, London.

Darwin, C. 1871. *The Descent of Man, and Selection in Relation to Sex.* Murray, London.

Davis, C. O. 1995. *Treasured Earth: Hattie Cosgrove's Mimbres Archaeology in the American Southwest.* Sanpete, Tucson, Ariz.

Davis, J. I., and K. C. Nixon. 1992. Populations, Genetic Variation, and the Delimitation of Phylogenetic Species. *Systematic Biology* 41: 421–435.

Davison, J. 1997. *Gender, Lineage and Ethnicity in Southern Africa.* Westview, Boulder, Colo.

Dawkins, R. 1976. *The Selfish Gene.* Oxford University Press, New York.

de Munck, V., and A. V. Korotayev. 2000. Cultural Units in Cross-Cultural Research. *Ethnology* 39: 335–348.

Dean, B. 1915. An Explanatory Label for Helmets. *Metropolitan Museum of Art, Bulletin* 10: 173–177.

Demarest, A. A. 1986. *The Archaeology of Santa Leticia and the Rise of Maya Civilization.* Middle American Research Institute, Publication 52. New Orleans.

Demarest, A. A., and R. J. Sharer. 1982. The Origins and Evolution of Usulutan Ceramics. *American Antiquity* 47: 810–822.

Demarest, A. A., and R. J. Sharer. 1986. Late Preclassic Ceramic Spheres, Culture Areas, and Cultural Evolution in the Southeastern Highlands of Mesoamerica. In *The Southeast Maya Periphery*, edited by P. Urban and E. M. Schortman, pp. 194–223. University of Texas Press, Austin.

Dempsey, P., and M. Baumhoff. 1963. The Statistical Use of Artifact Distributions to Establish Chronological Sequence. *American Antiquity* 28: 496–509.

Denbow, J. 1990. Congo to Kalahari: Dates and Hypotheses about the Political Economy of the Western Stream of the Early Iron Age. *African Archaeological Review* 8: 139–176.

Dennett, D. C. 1995. *Darwin's Dangerous Idea: Evolution and the Meanings of Life.* Simon and Schuster, New York.

Derrida, J. 1976. *Of Grammatology* (translated by G. C. Spivak). Johns Hopkins University Press, Baltimore.

Devoto, G. 1962. *Origini Indeuropeo.* Instituto Italiano di Preistoria Italiana, Florence.

Dewar, R. E. 1995. Of Nets and Trees: Untangling the Reticulate and Dendritic in Madagascar's Prehistory. *World Archaeology* 26: 301–318.

Di Peso, C. C., J. B. Rinaldo, and G. J. Fenner (editors). 1974. *Casas Grandes: A Fallen Trading Center of the Gran Chichimeca,* vols. 4–7. Amerind Foundation, Dragoon, Ariz.

Diakonov, I. M. 1984. On the Original Home of the Speakers of Indo-European. *Soviet Anthropology and Archaeology* 23: 5–87.

Diamond, J. 1997. *Guns, Germs, and Steel.* Norton, New York.

Diamond, J., and P. Bellwood. 2003. Farmers and Their Languages: The First Expansions. *Science* 300: 597–603.

DiFiore, A., and D. Rendall. 1994. Evolution of Social Organization: A Reappraisal for Primates by Using Phylogenetic Methods. *National Academy of Sciences, Proceedings* 91: 9941–9945.

Doran, J. E., and F. R. Hodson. 1975. *Mathematics and Computers in Archaeology.* Harvard University Press, Cambridge, Mass.

Dow, M. M., and J. M. Cheverud. 1985. Comparison of Distance Matrices in Studies of Population Structure and Genetic Microdifferentiation: Quadratic Assignment. *American Journal of Physical Anthropology* 68: 367–373.

Driver, H. E., and A. L. Kroeber. 1932. Quantitative Expression of Cultural Relationships. *University of California Publications in American Archaeology and Ethnology* 31: 211–256.

Drucker, P. 1950. Culture Element Distributions: XXVI, Northwest Coast. *Anthropological Records* 9: 157–294.

Drucker, P. 1955. *Indians of the Northwest Coast.* Natural History Press, New York.

Drucker, P. 1965. *Cultures of the North Pacific Coast.* Chandler, New York.

Dunnell, R. C. 1971. *Systematics in Prehistory.* Free Press, New York.

Dunnell, R. C. 1978. Style and Function: A Fundamental Dichotomy. *American Antiquity* 43: 192–202.

Dunnell, R. C. 1980. Evolutionary Theory and Archaeology. *Advances in Archaeological Method and Theory* 3: 35-99.

Dunnell, R. C. 1981. Seriation, Groups, and Measurements. In *Manejos de Datos y Métodes Matematicos de Arqueologia,* edited by G. L. Cowgill, R. Whallon, and B. S. Ottaway, pp. 67–90. Union Internacional de Ciencias Prehistoricas y Protohistoricas, Mexico, D.F.

Dunnell, R. C. 1982. Science, Social Science and Common Sense: The Agonizing Dilemma of Modern Archaeology. *Journal of Anthropological Research* 38: 1–25.

Dunnell, R. C. 1986. Five Decades of American Archaeology. In *American Archaeology: Past and Future,* edited by D. J. Meltzer, D. D. Fowler, and J. A. Sabloff, pp. 23–49. Smithsonian Institution Press, Washington, D.C.

Dunnell, R. C. 1989. Aspects of the Application of Evolutionary Theory in Archaeology. In *Archaeological Thought in America,* edited by C. C. Lamberg-Karlovsky, pp. 35–49. Cambridge University Press, Cambridge.

Durham, W. H. 1990. Advances in Evolutionary Culture Theory. *Annual Review of Anthropology* 19: 187–210.

Durham, W. H. 1991. *Co-evolution: Genes, Culture, and Human Diversity.* Stanford University Press, Stanford, Calif.

Durham, W. H. 1992. Applications of Evolutionary Culture Theory. *Annual Review of Anthropology* 21: 331–355.

Dyen, I., J. B. Kruskal, and P. Black. 1992. *An Indoeuropean Classification: A Lexicostatistical Experiment.* American Philosophical Society, Transactions 82(5). Philadelphia.

Dyen, I., J. B. Kruskal, and P. Black. 1997. *FILE IE-DATA1.* Available at http://www.ntu.edu.au/education/langs/ielex/IE-DATA1.

Edgerton, R. B. 1971. *The Individual in Cultural Adaptation: A Study of Four East African Peoples.* University of California Press, Berkeley.

Efron, B., and R. Tibshirani. 1993. *An Introduction to the Bootstrap.* Chapman and Hall, New York.

Eggan, F. 1954. Social Anthropology and the Method of Controlled Comparison. *American Anthropologist* 56: 743–763.

Eggert, M. K. H. 1993. Central Africa and the Archaeology of the Equatorial Rainforest: Reflections on Some Major Topics. In *The Archaeology of Africa: Food, Metals and Towns,* edited by T. Shaw, P. Sinclair, A. Okpoko, and B. W. Andah, pp. 289–329. Routledge, London.

Ehret, C. 1971. *Southern Nilotic History: Linguistic Approaches to the Study of the Past.* Northwestern University Press, Evanston, Ill.

Ehret, C. 1998. *An African Classical Age: Eastern and Southern Africa in World History, 1000 B.C. to A.D. 400.* University Press of Virginia, Charlottesville.

Ehret, C. 2001. Bantu Expansions: Re-envisioning a Central Problem of Early African History. *International Journal of African Historical Studies* 34: 5–41.

Eizirik E., W. J. Murphy, and S. J. O'Brien. 2001. Molecular Dating and Biogeography of the Early Placental Mammal Radiation. *Journal of Heredity* 92: 212–219.

Eldredge, N. 2003. Mme. F. Besson and the Early History of the Périnet Valve. *The Galpin Society Journal* 56: 147–151.

Eldredge, N., and J. Cracraft. 1980. *Phylogenetic Patterns and the Evolutionary Process.* Columbia University Press, New York.

Eldredge, N., and S. J. Gould. 1972. Punctuated Equilibria: An Alternative to Phyletic Gradualism. In *Models in Paleobiology,* edited by T. J. M. Schopf, pp. 82–115. Freeman, Cooper, San Francisco.

El-Najjar, M. 1974. *People of Canyon de Chelly: A Study of Their Biology and Culture.* Ph.D. dissertation, Department of Anthropology, Arizona State University. Tempe.

Embleton, S. M. 1991. Mathematical Methods of Genetic Classification. In *Sprung from Some Common Source,* edited by S. L. Lamb and E. D. Mitchell, pp. 365–388. Stanford University Press, Stanford, Calif.

Ensminger, J. 1997. Transaction Costs and Islam: Explaining Conversion in Africa. *Journal of Institutional and Theoretical Economics* 153: 4–29.

Epperson, B. K. 2003. *Geographical Genetics.* Princeton University Press, Princeton, N.J.

Evans, J. 1850. On the Date of British Coins. *Numismatic Chronicle and Journal of the Numismatic Society* 12(4): 127–137.

Ewald, P. W. 1987. Transmission Modes and the Evolution of the Parasitism-Mutualism Continuum. *New York Academy of Sciences, Annals* 503: 295–306.

Excoffier, L., and Z. Yang. 1999. Substitution Rate Variation among Sites in Mitochondrial Hypervariable Region I of Humans and Chimpanzees. *Molecular Biology and Evolution* 16: 1357–1368.

Farris, J. S. 1989a. The Retention Index and Homoplasy Excess. *Systematic Zoology* 38: 406–407.

Farris, J. S. 1989b. The Retention Index and the Rescaled Consistency Index. *Cladistics* 5: 417–419.

Farris, J. S. 1991. Excess Homoplasy Ratios. *Cladistics* 7: 81–91.

Feierman, S. 1990. *Peasant Intellectuals.* University of Wisconsin Press, Madison.

Felsenstein, J. 1982. How Can We Infer Geography and History from Gene Frequencies? *Journal of Theoretical Biology* 96: 9–20.

Felsenstein, J. 1985. Phylogenies and the Comparative Method. *American Naturalist* 125: 1–15.

Felsenstein, J. 2004. *Inferring Phylogenies.* Sinauer, Sunderland, Mass.

Finney, B. 1993. Voyaging and Isolation in Rapa Nui Prehistory. *Rapa Nui Journal* 7: 1–6.

Fish, P. R. 1978. Consistency in Archaeological Measurement and Classification: A Pilot Study. *American Antiquity* 43: 86–89.

Fish, P. R., S. K. Fish, G. J. Gumerman, and J. J. Reid. 1994. Toward an Explanation for Southwestern Abandonments. In *Themes in Southwest Prehistory,* edited by G. J. Gumerman, pp. 135–165. School of American Research, Santa Fe, N.M.

Fisher, C., M. Foote, D. L. Fox, and L. R. Leighton. 2000. Stratigraphy in Phylogeny Reconstruction—Comment on Smith. *Journal of Paleontology* 76: 585–595.

Fisher, D. C. 1991. Phylogenetic Analysis and Its Application in Evolutionary Paleobiology. In *Analytical Paleobiology,* edited by N. L. Gilinsky and P. W. Signor, pp. 103–122. Paleontological Society, Short Courses in Paleobiology, no. 4. Washington, D.C.

Fisher, D. C. 1992. Stratigraphic Parsimony. In *MacClade: Analysis of Phylogeny and Character Evolution* (version 3), edited by W. P. Maddison and D. R. Maddison, pp. 124–129. Sinauer, Sunderland, Mass.

Fisher, D. C. 1994. Stratocladistics: Morphological and Temporal Patterns and Their Relation to Phylogenetic Process. In *Interpreting the Hierarchy of Nature,* edited by L. Grande and O. Rieppel, pp. 133–171. Academic Press, San Diego, Calif.

Fix, A. G. 1978. The Role of Kin-Structured Migration in Genetic Microdifferentiation. *Annals of Human Genetics* 41: 329–339.

Fix, A. G. 1999. *Migration and Colonization in Human Microevolution.* Cambridge University Press, Cambridge.

Flament, C. 1963. *Applications of Graph Theory to Group Structure.* Prentice-Hall, Englewood Cliffs, N.J.

Flenley, J. R., and P. G. Bahn. 2003. *Enigmas of Easter Island: Island on the Edge.* Oxford University Press, Oxford.

Flenniken, J. J., and A. W. Raymond. 1986. Morphological Projectile Point Typology: Replication Experimentation and Technological Analysis. *American Antiquity* 51: 603–614.

Flinn, M. V. 1981. Uterine vs. Agnatic Kinship Variability and Associated Cross-Cousin Marriage Preferences: An Evolutionary Biological Analysis. In *Natural Selection and Social Behavior,* edited by R. D. Alexander and D. W. Tinkle, pp. 439–475. Chiron Press, New York.

Flinn, M. V. 1997. Culture and the Evolution of Social Learning. *Evolution and Human Behavior* 18: 23–67.

Flinn, M. V., and B. S. Low. 1986. Resource Distribution, Social Competition, and Mating Patterns in Human Societies. In *Ecological Aspects of Social Evolution,* edited by D. I. Reubenstein and R. W. Wrangham, pp. 217–243. Princeton University Press, Princeton, N.J.

Foley, R. 1987. Hominid Species and Stone-Tool Assemblages: How Are They Related? *Antiquity* 61: 380–392.

Foley, R., and M. M. Lahr. 1997. Mode 3 Technologies and the Evolution of Modern Humans. *Cambridge Archaeological Journal* 7: 3–36.

Foley, R., and M. M. Lahr. 2003. On Stony Ground: Lithic Technology, Human Evolution, and the Emergence of Culture. *Evolutionary Anthropology* 12: 109–122.

Fontana, W. 2003. The Topology of the Possible. Unpublished working paper at the Santa Fe Institute: http://www.santafe.edu/sfi/publications/working-papers/03-03-017.pdf.

Ford, J. A. 1936. *Analysis of Indian Village Site Collections from Louisiana and Mississippi.* Louisiana State Geological Survey, Department of Conservation, Anthropological Study no. 2. Baton Rouge.

Ford, J. A. 1952. Measurements of Some Prehistoric Design Developments in the Southeastern States. *American Museum of Natural History, Anthropological Papers* 44: 313–384.

Ford, J. A. 1969. *A Comparison of Formative Cultures in the Americas: Diffusion or the Psychic Unity of Man.* Smithsonian Contributions to Anthropology 11. Washington, D.C.

Forey, P. L. 1990. Cladistics. In *Paleobiology: A Synthesis,* edited by D. E. G. Briggs and P. R. Crowther, pp. 430–434. Blackwell, Oxford.

Forey, P. L. 1992. Fossils and Cladistic Analysis. In *Cladistics: A Practical Course in Systematics,* edited by P. L. Forey, C. J. Humphries, I. J. Kitching, R. W. Scotland, D. J. Siebert, and D. M. Williams, pp. 124–136. Clarendon Press, Oxford.

Forster, P., and A. Toth. 2003. Toward a Phylogenetic Chronology of Ancient Gaulish, Celtic, and Indo-European. *National Academy of Sciences, Proceedings* 100: 9079–9084.

Foucault, M. 1966. *Les Mots et les Choses.* Gallimard, Paris.

Fox, D. L., D. C. Fisher, and L. R. Leighton. 1999. Reconstructing Phylogeny with and without Temporal Data. *Journal of Paleontology* 284: 1816–1819.

Freckleton, R. P., P. H. Harvey, and M. Pagel. 2002. Phylogenetic Analysis and Comparative Data: A Test and Review of Evidence. *American Naturalist* 160: 712–726.

Furst, P. T. 1998. Shamanic Symbolism, Transformation, and Deities in West Mexican Funerary Art. In *Ancient West Mexico: Art and Archaeology of the Unknown Past,* edited by R. F. Townsend, pp. 168–189. Thames and Hudson, London, and the Art Institute of Chicago, Chicago.

Gabora, L. 1996. A Day in the Life of a Meme. *Philosophical Psychology* 57: 901–938.

Gaffney, E. S., L. Dingus, and M. K. Smith. 1995. Why Cladistics? *Natural History* 104(6): 33–35.

Gamkrelidze, T. V., and V. V. Ivanov. 1995. *Indo-European and the Indo-Europeans: A Reconstruction and Historical Analysis of a Proto-Language and Proto-Culture.* Mouton de Gruyter, Berlin.

Garland, T., Jr., A. W. Dickerman, C. M. Janis, and J. A. Jones. 1993. Phylogenetic Analysis of Covariance by Computer Simulation. *Systematic Biology* 42: 265–292.

Geraghty, P. 2004. Borrowed Plants in Fiji and Polynesia: Some Linguistic Evidence. In *Borrowing: A Pacific Perspective,* edited by J. Tent and P. Geraghty, pp. 65–98. Pacific Linguistics, Canberra.

Gibbs, S., M. Collard, and B. A. Wood. 2002. Soft Tissue Anatomy of the Extant Hominoids: A Review and Phylogenetic Analysis. *Journal of Anatomy* 200: 3–49.

Giddens, A. 1984. *The Constitution of Society.* Cambridge University Press, Cambridge.

Gill, G. W. 1986. Final Report of Investigations of the 1981 Easter Island Anthropological Expedition. Manuscript on file, National Geographic Society, Washington, D.C.

Gill, G. W. 1990. Easter Island Rocker Jaws. *Rapa Nui Journal* 4: 21.

Gill, G. W., S. C. Haoa, and D. W. Owsley. 1997. Easter Island Origins: Implications of Osteological Findings. *Rapa Nui Journal* 11: 64–71.

Gill, G. W., and D. W. Owsley. 1993. Human Osteology of Rapanui. In *Easter Island Studies,* edited by S. R. Fischer, pp. 56–62. Oxbow Books, Oxford.

Gimbutas, M. 1973a. Old Europe c. 7000–3500 B.C., the Earliest European Cultures before the Infiltration of the Indo-European Peoples. *Journal of Indo-European Studies* 1: 1-20.

Gimbutas, M. 1973b. The Beginning of the Bronze Age in Europe and the Indo-Europeans 3500–2500 B.C. *Journal of Indo-European Studies* 1: 163–214.

Gingerich, P. D. 1985. Species in the Fossil Record: Concepts, Trends, and Transitions. *Paleobiology* 11: 27–41.

Gittleman, J. L., C. G. Anderson, M. Kot, and H.-K. Luh. 1996. Phylogenetic Lability and Rates of Evolution: A Comparison of Behavioral, Morphological and Life History Traits. In *Phylogenies and the Comparative Method in Animal Behavior,* edited by E. P. Martins, pp. 166–205. Oxford University Press, Oxford.

Gkiasta, M., T. Russell, S. Shennan, and J. Steele. 2003. Neolithic Transition in Europe: The Radiocarbon Record Revisited. *Antiquity* 77: 45–62.

Gladwin, H. S. 1936. Methodology in the Southwest. *American Antiquity* 1: 256–259.

Goldman, N., J. P. Anderson, and A. G. Rodrigo. 2000. Likelihood-Based Tests of Topologies in Phylogenetics. *Systematic Biology* 49: 652–670.

Goldschmidt, W. 1974. The Economics of Brideprice among the Sebei and in East Africa. *Ethnology* 13: 311–331.

Goodenough, W. H. 1957. Oceania and the Problem of Controls in the Study of Cultural and Human Evolution. *Journal of the Polynesian Society* 66: 146–155.

Goodenough, W. H. 1999. Outline of a Framework for a Theory of Cultural Evolution. *Cross-Cultural Research* 33: 84–107.

Goodyear, A. C. 1974. *The Brand Site: A Technofunctional Study of a Dalton Site in Northeastern Arkansas.* Arkansas Archeological Survey, Research Series, no. 7. Fayetteville.

Gould, S. J. 1986. Evolution and the Triumph of Homology, or Why History Matters. *American Scientist* 74: 60–69.

Gould, S. J., and R. C. Lewontin. 1979. The Spandrels of San Marco and the Panglossian Paradigm: A Critique of the Adaptationist Programme. *Royal Society London, Proceedings* B205: 581–598.

Grafen, A. 1989. The Phylogenetic Regression. *Royal Society London, Philosophical Transactions* B326: 119–157.

Graham, M. M. 1998. The Iconography of Rulership in Ancient West Mexico. In *Ancient West Mexico: Art and Archaeology of the Unknown Past,* edited by R. F. Townsend, pp. 190–203. Thames and Hudson, London, and the Art Institute of Chicago, Chicago.

Graham, R. W., C. V. Haynes, D. L. Johnson, and M. Kay. 1981. Kimmswick: A Clovis-Mastodon Association in Eastern Missouri. *Science* 213: 1115–1117.

Graves, M. W., and C. K. Cachola-Abad. 1996. Seriation as a Method of Chronologically Ordering Architectural Design Traits: An Example from Hawai'i. *Archaeology in Oceania* 31: 19–32.

Gray, R. D., and Q. D. Atkinson. 2003. Language Tree Divergence Times Support the Anatolian Theory of Indo-European Origin. *Nature* 426: 435–439.

Gray, R. D., and F. Jordan. 2000. Language Trees Support the Express-Train Sequence of Austronesian Expansion. *Nature* 405: 1052–1055.

Greenlee, D. 2002. *Accounting for Subsistence Variation among Maize Farmers in Ohio Valley Prehistory.* Ph.D. dissertation, Department of Anthropology, University of Washington. Seatle.

Griffin, J. B. 1967. Eastern North American Archaeology: A Summary. *Science* 156: 171–191.

Guglielmino, C. R., C. Viganotti, B. Hewlett, and L. L. Cavalli-Sforza. 1995. Cultural Variation in Africa: Role of Mechanisms of Transmission and Adaptation. *National Academy of Sciences, Proceedings* 92: 7585–7589.

Guthrie, M. 1967-1971. *Comparative Bantu: An Introduction to the Comparative Linguistics and Prehistory of the Bantu Languages, vols. 1-4.* Gregg, Farnborough, England.

Guyer, C., and J. M. Savage. 1986. Cladistic Relationships among Anoles (Sauria: Iguanidae). *Systematic Zoology* 35: 509–531.

Håkansson, T. 1988. *Bridewealth, Women, and Land: Social Change among the Gusii of Kenya.* Uppsala University, Stockholm.

Håkansson, T. 1989. Family Structure, Bridewealth, and Environment in Eastern Africa: A Comparative Study of House-Property Systems. *Ethnology* 28: 117–134.

Håkansson, T. 1990. Descent, Bridewealth, and Terms of Alliance in East African Societies. *Research in Economic Anthropology* 12: 149–173.

Halanych, K. M., and T. J. Robinson. 1999. The Utility of Cytochrome b and 12S rDNA Data for Phylogeny Reconstruction of Leporid (Lagomorpha) Genera. *Journal of Molecular Evolution* 48: 369–379.

Haldane, J. B. S. 1956. Can a Species Concept Be Justified? In *The Species Concept in Paleontology,* edited by P. C. Sylvester-Bradley, pp. 95–96. Systematics Association, London.

Hall, B. G. 2001. *Phylogenetic Trees Made Easy: A How-To Manual for Molecular Biologists.* Sinauer, Sunderland, Mass.

Hamming, R. 1980. *Coding and Information Theory.* Prentice-Hall, Upper Saddle River, N.J.

Handy, E. S., and M. K. Pukui. 1972. *The Polynesian Family System in Ka'u, Hawai'i.* Tuttle, Rutland, Vt.

Harary, F. 1969. *Graph Theory.* Addison-Wesley, Reading, Mass.

Harmon, M. J. 2000. Tracing the Styles of Electric Lighting: An "Illuminating" Look at the Cultural Transmission versus Independent Innovation Associated with Electric Lighting. Paper presented at the 33rd Annual Chacmool Conference, Calgary, Canada.

Harmon, M. J., R. D. Leonard, C. S. VanPool, and T. L. VanPool. 2000. Cultural Transmission: Shared Intellectual Traditions in Ceramics of the Prehistoric American Southwest and Northern Mexico. Paper presented at the 65th Annual Meeting of the Society for American Archaeology, Philadelphia.

Harpending, H. C., and E. Eller. 2004. Human Diversity and Its History. In *Biodiversity,* edited by M. Kato and N. Takahata, pp. 301–314. Springer-Verlag, Tokyo.

Harris, M. 1968. *The Rise of Anthropological Theory.* Crowell, New York.

Hartl, D. L., and A. G. Clark. 1997. *Principles of Population Genetics,* third ed. Sinauer, Sunderland, Mass.

Hartung, J. 1982. Polygyny and the Inheritance of Wealth. *Current Anthropology* 23: 1–12.

Harvey, P. H. 1996. Phylogenies for Ecologists. *Journal of Animal Ecology* 65: 255–263.

Harvey, P. H., and S. Nee. 1997. The Phylogenetic Foundations of Behavioural Ecology. In *Behavioural Ecology,* edited by J. R. Krebs and N. B. Davies, pp. 334–349. Blackwell, Oxford.

Harvey, P. H., and M. D. Pagel. 1991. *The Comparative Method in Evolutionary Biology.* Oxford University Press, Oxford.

Harvey, P. H., and A. Purvis. 1991. Comparative Methods for Explaining Adaptations. *Nature* 351: 619–623.

Harvey, P. H., and A. Rambaut. 1998. Phylogenetic Extinction Rates and Comparative Methodology. *Royal Society London, Proceedings* B265: 1691–1696.

Heglar, R. 1974. *The Prehistoric Population of Cochiti and Selected Inter-Population Biological Comparisons.* Ph.D. dissertation, Department of Anthropology, University of Michigan. Ann Arbor.

Heine, B. 1973. Zur Genetischen Gliederung der Bantu-Sprachen. *African Language Studies* 14: 82–104.

Hennig, W. 1950. *Grundzuge einer Theorie der phylogenetischen Systematik.* Deutscher Zentralverlag, Berlin.

Hennig, W. 1966. *Phylogenetic Systematics.* University of Illinois Press, Urbana.

Henrich, J. 2001. Cultural Transmission and the Diffusion of Innovations: Adoption Dynamics Indicate that Biased Cultural Transmission Is the Predominate Force in Behavioral Change. *American Anthropologist* 103: 992–1013.

Henrich, J., and F. J. Gil-White. 2001. The Evolution of Prestige: Freely Conferred Deference as a Mechanism for Enhancing the Benefits of Cultural Transmission. *Evolution and Human Behavior* 22: 165–196.

Henrich, J., and R. Boyd. 1998. The Evolution of Conformist Transmission and the Emergence of between-Group Differences. *Evolution and Human Behavior* 19: 215–242.

Henrich, J., and R. Boyd. 2001. Why People Punish Defectors: Weak Conformist Transmission Can Stabilize Costly Enforcement of Norms in Cooperative Dilemmas. *Journal of Theoretical Biology* 208: 79–89.

Henrici, A. 1973. Numerical Classification of the Bantu Languages. *African Language Studies* 14: 82–104.

Hewlett, B. S., and L. L. Cavalli-Sforza. 1986. Cultural Transmission among the Aka Pygmies. *American Anthropologist* 88: 922–934.

Hewlett, B. S., A. de Silvertri, and C. R. Guglielmino. 2002. Semes and Genes in Africa. *Current Anthropology* 43: 313–321.

Heyerdahl, T., and E. N. Ferdon, Jr. (editors). 1961. *Reports of the Norwegian Archaeological Expedition to Easter Island and the East Pacific, vol. 1: Archaeology of Easter Island.* Allen and Unwin, London.

Heyning, J. E., C. Thacker, D. C. Fisher, D. L. Fox, and L. R. Leighton. 1999. Phylogenies, Temporal Data, and Negative Evidence. *Science* 285: 1179.

Hillis, D. M. 1991. Discriminating between Phylogenetic Signal and Random Noise in DNA Sequences. In *Phylogenetic Analysis of DNA Sequences*, edited by M. M. Miyamoto and J. Cracraft, pp. 278–294. Oxford University Press, Oxford.

Hinnebusch, T. J. 1999. Contact and Lexicostatistics in Comparative Bantu Studies. In *Bantu Historical Linguistics: Theoretical and Empirical Perspectives,* edited by J.-M. Hombert and L. M. Hyman, pp. 173–205. Centre for the Study of Language and Information, Stanford, Calif.

Holden, C., and R. Mace. 1997. Phylogenetic Analysis of the Evolution of Lactose Digestion in Adults. *Human Biology* 69: 605–628.

Holden, C., and R. Mace. 1999. Sexual Dimorphism in Stature and Women's Work: A Phylogenetic Cross-Cultural Analysis. *American Journal of Physical Anthropology* 110: 27–45.

Holden, C. J. 2002. Bantu Language Trees Reflect the Spread of Farming across Sub-Saharan Africa: A Maximum-Parsimony Analysis. *Royal Society London, Proceedings* B269: 793–799.

Holden, C. J., and R. Mace. 1997. Phylogenetic Analysis of the Evolution of Lactose Digestion in Adults. *Human Biology* 69: 605–628.

Holden, C. J., and R. Mace. 1999. Sexual Dimorphism in Stature and Women's Work: A Phylogenetic Cross-Cultural Analysis. *American Journal of Physical Anthropology* 110: 27–45.

Holden, C. J., and R. Mace. 2002. Pastoralism and the Evolution of Lactase Persistence. In *Human Biology of Pastoral Populations,* edited by W. R. Leonard and M. H. Crawford, pp. 280–307. Cambridge University Press, Cambridge.

Holden, C. J., and R. Mace. 2003. Spread of Cattle Pastoralism Led to the Loss of Matriliny in Africa: A Co-Evolutionary Analysis. *Royal Society London, Proceedings* B270: 2425–2433.

Holden, C. J., R. Mace, and R. Sear. 2003. Matriliny as Daughter-Biased Investment. *Evolution and Human Behavior* 24: 99–112.

Holy, L. 1987. Introduction. Description, Generalization and Comparison: Two Paradigms. In *Comparative Anthropology,* edited by L. Holy, pp. 1–21. Blackwell, Oxford.

Hooton, E. A. 1930. *The Indians of Pecos Pueblo.* Papers of the Southwestern Exepedition, Phillips Academy, no. 4. Yale University Press, New Haven, Conn.

Horowitz, I., R. Zardoya, and A. Meyer. 1998. Platyrrhine Systematics: A Simultaneous Analysis of Molecular and Morphological Data. *American Journal of Physical Anthropology* 106: 261–281.

Howell, T. L., and K. W. Kintigh. 1996. Archaeological Identification of Kin Groups Using Mortuary and Biological Data: An Example from the American Southwest. *American Antiquity* 61: 537–554.

Howell, T. L., and K. W. Kintigh. 1998. Determining Gender and Kinship at Hawikku: A Reply to Corruccini. *American Antiquity* 63: 164–167.

Howells, W. W. 1973. *Cranial Variation in Man: A Study by Multivariate Analysis of Patterns of Difference among Recent Human Populations.* Peabody Museum of American Archaeology and Ethnology, Papers 67. Cambridge, Mass.

Hrdlička, A. 1931. Catalogue of Human Crania in the United States National Museum Collections. *United States National Museum, Proceedings* 78(2): 1–95.

Huelsenbeck, J. P., and J. Bollback. 2001. Application of the Likelihood Function in Phylogenetic Analysis. In *Handbook of Statistical Genetics*, edited by D. J. Balding, M. Bishop, and C. Cannings, pp. 415–439. Wiley, New York.

Huelsenbeck, J. P., and B. Rannala. 1997. Maximum Likelihood Estimation of Phylogeny Using Stratigraphic Data. *Paleobiology* 23: 174–180.

Huelsenbeck, J. P., and B. Rannala. 2000. Using Stratigraphic Information in Phylogenetics. In *Phylogenetics Analysis of Morphological Data,* edited by J. J. Wiens, pp. 165–191. Smithsonian Institution Press, Washington, D.C.

Huelsenbeck, J. P., and F. Ronquist. 2001. MRBAYES: Bayesian Inference of Phylogeny. *Bioinformatics* 17: 754–755.

Huelsenbeck, J. P., F. Ronquist, R. Nielsen, and J. P. Bollback. 2001. Bayesian Inference of Phylogeny and Its Impact on Evolutionary Biology. *Science* 294: 2310–2314.

Huffman, T. N. 1984. Expressive Space in the Zimbabwe Culture. *Man* 19: 593–612.

Huffman, T. N. 1989. *Iron Age Migrations.* Witwatersrand University Press, Johannesburg.

Hughes, S. S. 1998. Getting to the Point: Evolutionary Change in Prehistoric Weaponry. *Journal of Archaeological Method and Theory* 5: 345–408.

Hull, D. L. 1965. The Effect of Essentialism on Taxonomy–Two Thousand Years of Stasis (II). *British Journal of the Philosophy of Science* 16: 1–18.

Hull, D. L. 1988. *Science as a Process: An Evolutionary Account of the Social and Conceptual Development of Science*. University of Chicago Press, Chicago.

Hull, D. L. 2000. Taking Memetics Seriously: Memetics Will Be What We Make It. In *Darwinizing Culture: The Status of Memetics as a Science*, edited by R. Aunger, pp. 43–67. Oxford University Press, Oxford.

Hunt, T., C. P. Lipo, and S. Sterling. 2001. Posing Questions for a Scientific Archaeology. In *Posing Questions for a Scientific Archaeology,* edited by T. Hunt, C. P. Lipo, and S. Sterling, pp. 1–22. Bergin and Garvey, Westport, Conn.

Hurles, M. E., L. Matisoo-Smith, R. D. Gray, and D. Penny. 2003. Untangling Oceanic Settlement: The Edge of the Knowable. *Trends in Ecology and Evolution* 18: 531–540.

Hurt, T. D., and G. F. M. Rakita (editors). 2001. *Style and Function: Conceptual Issues in Evolutionary Archaeology*. Bergin and Garvey, Westport, Conn.

Hurt, T. D., G. F. M. Rakita, and R. D. Leonard. 2001. Models, Definitions, and Stylistic Variation: Comment on Ortman. *American Antiquity* 66: 745–746.

Hurt, T. D., T. L. VanPool, G. F. M. Rakita, and R. D. Leonard. 2001. Explaining the Co-occurrence of Traits in the Archaeological Record: A Further Consideration of Replicative Success. In *Style and Function: Conceptual Issues in Evolutionary Archaeology*, edited by T. D. Hurt and G. F. M. Rakita, pp. 51-67. Bergin and Garvey, Westport, Conn.

Huson, D. H. 1998. SplitsTree: Analyzing and Visualizing Evolutionary Data. *Bioinformatics* 14: 68–73.

Hutchison, D. W., and A. R. Templeton. 1999. Correlation of Pairwise Genetic and Geographic Distance Measures: Inferring the Relative Influences of Gene Flow and Drift on the Distribution of Genetic Variability. *Evolution* 53: 1894–1914.

Irwin, G. J. 1992. *The Prehistoric Exploration and Colonisation of the Pacific.* Cambridge University Press, Cambridge.

Jackman, T. R., A. Larson, K. de Queiroz, and J. B. Losos. 1999. Phylogenetic Relationships and Tempo of Early Diversification in Anolis Lizards. *Systematic Biology* 48: 254–285.

Jelinek, A. J. 1976. Form, Function and Style in Lithic Analysis. In *Cultural Change and Continuity,* edited by C. E. Cleland, pp. 19–34. Academic Press, New York.

Jobling, M. A., M. E. Hurles, and C. Tyler-Smith. 2004. *Human Evolutionary Genetics.* Garland Science, New York.

Johnson, J. A., and J. Crandall. 1990 *Classical Pa Kua Chang Fighting Systems and Weapons*. Ching Lung Martial Arts Association, Pacific Grove, Calif.

Jones, D. 2003. Kinship and Deep History: Exploring Connections between Culture Areas, Genes, and Languages. *American Anthropologist* 105: 501–514.

Jones, S. 2000. *Darwin's Ghost: The Origin of Species Updated*. Random House, New York.

Jones, W. 1807. Third Anniversary Discourse, 'On the Hindus.' In *The Collected Works of Sir William Jones,* vol. 3, pp. 24–46. Stockdale and Walker, London.

Jordan, F. M. 1999. *Nga Whakapapa o Nga Reo: Colonisation, Evolution and Interaction in Austronesian Languages.* Honors thesis, University of Auckland, Auckland.

Jordan, P., and S. J. Shennan. 2003. Cultural Transmission, Language and Basketry Traditions amongst the California Indians. *Journal of Anthropological Archaeology* 22: 42–74.

Jorgensen, J. G. 1969. *Salish Language and Culture.* Indiana University Press, Bloomington.

Justice, N. D. 1987. *Stone Age Spear and Arrow Points of the Midcontinental and Eastern United States: A Modern Survey and Reference.* Indiana University Press, Bloomington.

Keesing, R. M. 1974. Theories of Culture. *Annual Review of Anthropology* 3: 73–97.

Kennedy, M., and H. G. Spencer. 2000. Phylogeny, Biogeography, and Taxonomy of Australasian Teals. *Auk* 117: 154–163.

Kennedy, M., H. G. Spencer, and R. D. Gray. 1996. Hop, Step and Gape: Do the Social Displays of the Pelecaniformes Reflect Phylogeny? *Animal Behaviour* 51: 273–291.

Kennedy, M., R. D. Gray, and H. G. Spencer. 2000. The Phylogenetic Relationships of the Shags and Cormorants: Can Sequence Data Resolve a Disagreement between Behaviour and Morphology? *Molecular Phylogenetics and Evolution* 17: 345–359.

Kidder, A. V. 1917. A Design-Sequence from New Mexico. *National Academy of Sciences, Proceedings* 3: 369–370.

Kidder, A. V. 1924. *An Introduction to the Study of Southwestern Archaeology with a Preliminary Account of the Excavations at Pecos.* Papers of the Southwestern Expedition, Phillips Academy, No. 1. Yale University Press, New Haven, Conn.

Kidder, A. V. 1932. *The Artifacts of Pecos.* Papers of the Southwestern Expedition, Phillips Academy, no. 6. Yale University Press, New Haven, Conn.

Kimura, M., and G. H. Weiss. 1964. The Stepping Stone Model of Population Structure and the Decrease of Genetic Correlation with Distance. *Genetics* 49: 561–576.

Kirch, P. V. 1984. *The Evolution of the Polynesian Chiefdoms.* Cambridge University Press, Cambridge.

Kirch, P. V., and R. C. Green. 1987. History, Phylogeny, and Evolution in Polynesia. *Current Anthropology* 28: 431–456.

Kirch, P. V., and R. C. Green. 2001. *Hawaiki, Ancestral Polynesia: An Essay in Historical Anthropology.* Cambridge University Press, Cambridge.

Kirk, R. 1986. *Tradition and Change on the Northwest Coast: The Makah, Nuu-Chah-Nulth, Southern Kwakiutl, and Nuxalk.* University of Washington Press, Seattle.

Kishino, H., and M. Hasegawa. 1989. Evaluation of the Maximum Likelihood Estimate of the Evolutionary Tree Topologies from DNA Sequence Data, and the Branching Order in Hominoidea. *Journal of Molecular Evolution* 29: 170–179.

Kitching, I. J., P. L. Forey, C. J. Humphries, and D. M. Williams. 1998. *Cladistics: The Theory and Practice of Parsimony Analysis.* Oxford University Press, Oxford.

Klein, R. G. 1999. *The Human Career: Human Biological and Cultural Origins*, second ed. University of Chicago Press, Chicago.

Konigsberg, L. W. 1988. Migration Models of Prehistoric Postmarital Residence. *American Journal of Physical Anthropology* 77: 471–482.

Konigsberg, L. W. 1990. Analysis of Prehistoric Biological Variation under a Model of Isolation by Geographic and Temporal Distance. *Human Biology* 62: 49–70.

Konigsberg, L. W. 2000. Quantitative Variation and Genetics. In *Human Biology: An Evolutionary and Biocultural Perspective*, edited by S. Stinson, B. Bogin, R. Huss-Ashmore, and D. O'Rourke, pp. 135–162. Wiley-Liss, New York.

Konigsberg, L. W., and J. E. Buikstra. 1995. Regional Approaches to the Investigation of Past Human Biocultural Structure. In *Regional Approaches to Mortuary Analysis*, edited by L. A. Beck, pp. 191–219. Plenum, New York.

Kopytoff, I. 1987. The African Frontier: The Making of African Political Culture. In *The African Frontier: The Reproduction of Traditional African Societies*, edited by I. Kopytoff, pp. 3–84. Indiana University Press, Bloomington.

Kornbacher, K. D., and M. E. Madsen. 1999. Explaining the Evolution of Cultural Elaboration. *Journal of Anthropological Archaeology* 18: 241–242.

Kosakowsky, L. J., F. Estrada Belli, and H. Neff. 1999. Late Preclassic Ceramic Industries of Eastern Pacific Guatemala and Western El Salvador: The Pacific Coast as Core, Not Periphery. *Journal of Field Archaeology* 26: 377–390.

Kraus, B. S. 1954. Some Problems in the Physical Anthropology of the American Southwest: Comments. *American Anthropologist* 56: 620–623.

Krause, R. A. 1978. Toward a Formal Account of Bantu Ceramic Manufacture. In *Archaeological Essays in Honor of Irving B. Rouse*, edited by R. C. Dunnell and E. S. Hall, pp. 87–120. Mouton, New York.

Krieger, A. D. 1944. The Typological Concept. *American Antiquity* 9: 271–288.

Kroeber, A. L. 1916a. Zuñi Culture Sequences. *National Academy of Sciences, Proceedings* 2: 42–45.

Kroeber, A. L. 1916b. Zuñi Potsherds. *American Museum of Natural History, Anthropological Papers* 18(1): 1–37.

Kroeber, A. L. 1923. *Anthropology*. Harcourt, Brace, New York.

Kroeber, A. L. 1931. Historical Reconstruction of Cultural Growths and Organic Evolution. *American Anthropologist* 33: 149–156.

Kroeber, A. L. 1935. History and Science in Anthropology. *American Anthropologist* 37: 539–569.

Kroeber, A. L. 1945. Structure, Function and Pattern in Biology and Anthropology. *Scientific Monthly* 56: 105–113.

Kroeber, A. L. 1948. *Anthropology*, rev. ed. Harcourt Brace, New York.

Kroeber, A. L., and C. Kluckhohn. 1952. *Culture: A Critical Review of Concepts and Definitions*. Peabody Museum of American Archaeology and Ethnology, Papers 47. Cambridge, Mass.

Kuhner, M. K., and J. Felsenstein. 1994. A Simulation Comparison of Phylogeny Algorithms under Equal and Unequal Evolutionary Rates. *Molecular Biology and Evolution* 11: 459–468.

Kumar, V. K. 1999. Discovery of Dravidian as the Common Source of Indo-European. http://www.datanumeric.com/dravidian/

Ladefoged, T. N., and M. W. Graves. 2000. Evolutionary Theory and the Historical Development of Dry-Land Agriculture in North Kohala, Hawai'i. *American Antiquity* 65: 423–448.

Ladefoged, T. N., M. W. Graves, and R. P. Jennings. 1996. Dryland Agricultural Expansion and Intensification in Kohala, Hawai'i Island. *Antiquity* 70: 861–880.

Lake, M. W. 1996. Archaeological Inference and the Explanation of Hominid Evolution. In *The Archaeology of Human Ancestry: Power, Sex and Tradition*, edited by J. Steele and S. Shennan, pp. 184–206. Routledge, London.

Laland, K. N., J. Kumm, and M. W. Feldman. 1995. Gene-Culture Coevolutionary Theory: A Test Case. *Current Anthropology* 36: 131–156.

Lancaster, C. S. 1976. Women, Horticulture, and Society in Sub-Saharan Africa. *American Anthropologist* 78: 539–564.

Lang, A. 1885. *Custom and Myth,* second ed. Longmans, Green, London.

Lathrap, D. W. (editor). 1956. An Archaeological Classification of Culture Contact Situations. In *Seminars in Archaeology: 1955*, edited by R. Wauchope, pp. 1–30. Society for American Archaeology, Memoir, no. 11. Salt Lake City, Utah.

Lavachery, H. 1936. *Easter Island, Polynesia.* Smithsonian Institution, Washington, D.C.

Leonard, R. D., and G. T. Jones. 1987. Elements of an Inclusive Evolutionary Model for Archaeology. *Journal of Anthropological Archaeology* 6: 199–219.

Leonard, R. D., T. L. VanPool, C. S. VanPool, M. J. Harmon, T. Maxwell, R. Cruz Antillön, and G. Rakita. 2002. Casas Grandes Intellectual Traditions: Implications for Prehispanic Northern Mexico. Paper presented at the 8th Biennial Southwest Symposium, Tucson, Ariz.

Levin, D. A. 2002. Hybridization and Extinction. *American Scientist* 90: 254–261.

LeVine, R. A., and W. H. Sangree. 1962. The Diffusion of Age-Group Organization in East Africa: A Controlled Comparison. *Africa* 32: 97–110.

Lewis, P. O. 2001. A Likelihood Approach to Estimating Phylogeny from Discrete Morphological Character Data. *Systematic Biology* 50: 913–925.

Lewontin, R. C. 1974. *The Genetic Basis of Evolutionary Change*. Columbia University Press, New York.

Lieberman, D. E., B. A. Wood, and D. R. Pilbeam. 1996. Homoplasy and Early *Homo*: An Analysis of the Evolutionary Relationships of *H. habilis sensu stricto* and *H. rudolfensis. Journal of Human Evolution* 30: 97–120.

Lipo, C. P. 2001. *Science, Style and the Study of Community Structure: An Example from the Central Mississippi River Valley*. British Archaeological Reports, International Series, no. 918. Oxford.

Lipo, C. P., and M. Madsen. 2000. Neutrality, Style and Drift: Building Methods for Studying Cultural Transmission in the Archaeological Record. In *Style and Function in Archaeology,* edited by T. D. Hurt and G. F. M. Rakita, pp. 91–118. Bergin and Garvey, Westport, Conn.

Lipo, C. P., M. E. Madsen, T. Hunt, and R. C. Dunnell. 1997. Population Structure, Cultural Transmission, and Frequency Seriation. *Journal of Anthropological Archaeology* 16: 301–333.

Lockwood, C. A., and J. G. Fleagle. 1999. The Recognition and Evaluation of Homoplasy in Primate and Human Evolution. *Yearbook of Physical Anthropology* 42: 189–232.

Longyear, J. L., III. 1952. *Copán Ceramics: A Study of Southeastern Maya Pottery*. Carnegie Institution of Washington, Publication, no. 597. Washington, D.C.

Losos, J. B. 1999. Uncertainty in the Reconstruction of Ancestral Character States and Limitations on the Use of Phylogenetic Comparative Methods. *Behaviour* 58: 1319–1324.

Lumpkin, C. K. 1976. *A Multivariate Craniometric Analysis of Selected Southwestern Archaeological Populations*. Ph.D. dissertation, Department of Anthropology, University of New Mexico. Albuquerque.

Lumsden, C. J., and E. O. Wilson. 1981. *Genes, Mind, and Culture: The Co-Evolutionary Process.* Harvard University Press, Cambridge, Mass.

Lutzoni, F., M. Pagel, and V. Reeb. 2001. Major Fungal Lineages Are Derived from Lichen Symbiotic Ancestors. *Nature* 411: 937–940.

Lyman, R. L. 2001. Culture Historical and Biological Approaches to Identifying Homologous Traits. In *Style and Function: Conceptual Issues in Evolutionary Archaeology,* edited by T. D. Hurt and G. F. M. Rakita, pp. 69–89. Bergin and Garvey, Westport, Conn.

Lyman, R. L., and M. J. O'Brien. 1997. The Concept of Evolution in Early Twentieth-Century Americanist Archaeology. In *Rediscovering Darwin: Evolutionary Theory in Archeological Explanation,* edited by C. M. Barton and G. A. Clark, pp. 21–48. American Anthropological Association, Archeological Papers, no. 7. Washington, D.C.

Lyman, R. L., and M. J. O'Brien. 1998. The Goals of Evolutionary Archaeology: History and Explanation. *Current Anthropology* 39: 615–652.

Lyman, R. L., and M. J. O'Brien. 2000. Measuring and Explaining Change in Artifact Variation with Clade-Diversity Diagrams. *Journal of Anthropological Archaeology* 19: 39–74.

Lyman, R. L., and M. J. O'Brien. 2002. Classification. In *Darwin and Archaeology: A Handbook of Key Concepts*, edited by J. P. Hart and J. E. Terrell, pp. 69–88. Bergin and Garvey, Westport, Conn.

Lyman, R. L., and M. J. O'Brien. 2003a. Cultural Traits: Units of Analysis in Early Twentieth-Century Anthropology. *Journal of Anthropological Research* 59: 225–250.

Lyman, R. L., and M. J. O'Brien. 2003b. *W. C. McKern and the Midwestern Taxonomic Method.* University of Alabama Press, Tuscaloosa.

Lyman, R. L., and M. J. O'Brien. 2004. Nomothetic Science and Idiographic History in Twentieth-Century Americanist Anthropology. *Journal of the History of the Behavioral Sciences* 40: 77–96.

Lyman, R. L., M. J. O'Brien, and R. C. Dunnell. 1997. *The Rise and Fall of Culture History.* Plenum, New York.

Lyman, R. L., S. Wolverton, and M. J. O'Brien. 1998. Seriation, Superposition, and Interdigitation: A History of Americanist Graphic Depictions of Culture Change. *American Antiquity* 63: 239–261.

Mace, R. 1996. Biased Parental Investment and Reproductive Success in Gabbra Pastoralists. *Behavioral Ecology and Sociobiology* 38: 75–81.

Mace, R., and M. Pagel. 1994. The Comparative Method in Anthropology. *Current Anthropology* 35: 549–564.

Mace, R., and M. Pagel. 1997. Tips, Branches and Nodes. In *Human Nature: A Critical Reader,* edited by L. Betzig, pp. 297-310. Oxford University Press, New York.

Mace, T. K. 2003. *Cultural Transmission on the Northwest Pacific Coast.* M.A. thesis, Institute of Archaeology, University College London.

Mace, T. K., and P. Jordan. 2005. Regional Models for the Transmission of Culture: Cultural Diversity and Inheritance of Tradition on the NW Coast of North America. Manuscript on file, Department of Anthropology, University College London.

MacIntyre, F. 1999. 'Is Humanity Suicidal?' Are There Clues from Rapa Nui? *Rapa Nui Journal* 13: 35–41.

Maddison, D. R., and W. P. Maddison. 2000. *MacClade 4: Analysis of Phylogeny and Character Evolution.* Sinauer, Sunderland, Mass.

Maddison, W. P., and M. Slatkin. 1991. Null Models for the Number of Evolutionary Steps in a Character of a Phylogenetic Tree. *Evolution* 45: 1184–1197.

Madsen, M., C. Lipo, and M. Cannon. 1999. Fitness and Reproductive Trade-Offs in Uncertain Environments: Explaining the Evolution of Cultural Elaboration. *Journal of Anthropological Archaeology* 18: 251–281.

Malécot, G. 1950. Quelques Schemas Probabilistes sur la Variabilité des Populations Naturelles. *Annales de l'Universite de Lyon Science* 13: 37–60.

Mallory, J. P. 1989. *In Search of the Indo-Europeans: Languages, Archaeology and Myth.* Thames and Hudson, London.

Makarenkov, V. 2001. T-REX: Reconstructing and Visualizing Phylogenetic Trees and Reticulation Networks. *Bioinformatics Applications Note* 17(7): 664–668.

Martins, E. P., and T. Garland, Jr. 1991. Phylogenetic Analyses of the Correlated Evolution of Continuous Characters: A Simulation Study. *Evolution* 45: 534–557.

Martinsson-Wallin, H., and S. J. Crockford. 2001. Early Settlement of Rapa Nui (Easter Island). *Asian Perspectives* 40: 244–278.

Matthew, W. D. 1926. The Evolution of the Horse: A Record and Its Interpretation. *Quarterly Review of Biology* 1: 139–185.

Matthew, W. D. 1930. The Pattern of Evolution. *Scientific American* 143: 192–196.

Maynard Smith, J., and E. Szathmáry. 1997. *The Major Transitions in Evolution.* Oxford University Press, New York.

Mayr, E. 1969. *Principles of Systematic Zoology.* McGraw-Hill, New York.

Mayr, E., and P. D. Ashlock. 1991. *Principles of Systematic Zoology,* second ed. McGraw-Hill, New York.

McCall, G. 1979. Kinship and Environment on Easter Island: Some Observations and Speculations. *Mankind* 12: 119–137.

McCall, G. 1994. *Rapanui: Tradition and Survival on Easter Island.* University of Hawaii Press, Honolulu.

McCoy, P. 1976. *Easter Island Settlement Patterns in the Late Prehistoric and Protohistoric Periods.* Easter Island Committee, International Fund for Monuments, New York.

McElreath, R. 1997. *Iterated Parsimony: A Method for Reconstructing Cultural Histories.* M.A. thesis, Department of Anthropology, University of California, Los Angeles. http://www.anthro.ucdavis.edu/mcelreath/iteratedparsimony.pdf

McElreath, R., R. Boyd, and P. J. Richerson. 2003. Shared Norms and the Evolution of Ethnic Markers. *Current Anthropology* 44: 122–129.

McGrath, J. W., J. M. Cheverud, and J. E. Buikstra. 1984. Genetic Correlation between Sides and Heritability of Asymmetry for Nonmetric Traits in Rhesus Macaques on Cayo Santiago. *American Journal of Physical Anthropology* 64: 401–411.

McMahon, A. M. S., and R. McMahon. 1995. Linguistics, Genetics and Archaeology: Internal and External Evidence in the Amerind Controversy. *Philological Society, Transactions* 93: 125–225.

McMahon, A., and R. McMahon. 2003. Finding Families: Quantitative Methods in Language Classification. *Transactions of the Philological Society* 101: 7–55.

McWilliams, K. R. 1974. *Gran Quivira Pueblo and Biological Distance in the U.S. Southwest.* Ph.D. dissertation, Department of Anthropology, Arizona State University. Tempe.

Meggers, B. J., C. Evans, and E. Estrada. 1965. *Early Formative Period of Coastal Ecuador: The Valdivia and Machalilla Phases.* Smithsonian Contributions to Anthropology, no. 1. Washington, D.C.

Menozzi, P., A. Piazza, and L. L. Cavalli-Sforza. 1978. Synthetic Maps of Human Gene Frequencies in Europeans. *Science* 201: 786–792.

Mesoudi, A., A. Whiten, and K. N. Laland. 2004. Is Human Cultural Evolution Darwinian? Evidence Reviewed from the Perspective of *The Origin of Species. Evolution* 58: 1–11.

Métraux, A. 1940. *The Ethnology of Easter Island.* Bernice P. Bishop Museum, Honolulu.

Metropolis, N., A. W. Rosenbluth, M. N. Rosenbluth, A. H. Teller, and E. Teller. 1953. Equations of State Calculations by Fast Computing Machines. *Journal of Chemical Physics* 21: 1087–1091.

Middleton, J., and A. Rassam. 1995. *Encyclopaedia of World Cultures: Africa and the Middle East,* vol. 9. Hall, Boston.

Milgram, S. 1974. *Obedience to Authority: An Experimental View*. Harper and Row, New York.

Moore, C. C., and A. K. Romney. 1994. Material Culture, Geographic Propinquity, and Linguistic Affiliation on the North Coast of New Guinea: A Reanalysis of Welsch, Terrell & Nadolski (1992). *American Anthropologist* 96: 370–396.

Moore, C. C., and A. K. Romney. 1996. Will the 'Real' Data Please Stand up? Reply to Welsch (1996). *Journal of Quantitative Anthropology* 6: 235–261.

Moore, J. A. 2002. *From Genesis to Genetics: The Case of Evolution and Creationism*. University of California Press, Berkeley.

Moore, J. H. 1994a. Ethnogenetic Theory. *National Geographic Research and Exploration* 10: 10–23.

Moore, J. H. 1994b. Putting Anthropology Back Together Again: The Ethnogenetic Critique of Cladistic Theory. *American Anthropologist* 96: 370–396.

Moore, J. H. 2001. Ethnogenetic Patterns in Native North America. In *Archaeology, Language and History: Essays on Culture and Ethnicity,* edited by J. E. Terrell, pp. 30–56. Bergin and Garvey, Westport, Conn.

Morgan, L. H. 1877. *Ancient Society.* Holt, New York.

Morris, B. 1998. *The Power of Animals: An Ethnography*. Berg, Oxford.

Morris, S. A., B. Asnake, and G. Yen. 2003. Optimal Dendrogram Seriation Using Simulated Annealing. *Information Visualization* 2: 95–104.

Morris, S. A., G. Yen, Z. Wu, and B. Asnake. 2003. Timeline Visualization of Research Fronts. *Journal of the American Society for Information Science and Technology* 55: 413–422.

Moscovici, S. 1985. Social Influence and Conformity. In *Handbook of Social Psychology*, vol. 2, edited by G. Lindzey and E. Aronson, third ed., pp. 347–412. Random House, New York.

Murdock, G. P. 1949. *Social Structure.* Macmillan, New York.

Murdock, G. P. 1951. British Social Anthropology. *American Anthropologist* 53: 465–473.

Murdock, G. P. 1967. *Ethnographic Atlas.* University of Pittsburgh Press, Pittsburgh.

Murdock, G. P. 1971. Anthropology's Mythology. *Royal Anthropological Institute of Great Britain and Ireland, Proceedings* 1971: 17–24.

Murdock, G. P., and D. R. White. 1969. Standard Cross-Cultural Sample. *Ethnology* 8: 329–369.

Murray-McIntosh, R. P., B. J. Scrimshaw, P. J. Hatfield, and D. Penny. 1998. Testing Migration Patterns and Estimating Founding Population Size in Polynesia by Using Human mtDNA Sequences. *National Academy of Sciences, Proceedings* 95: 9047–9052.

Musil, R. R. 1988. Functional Efficiency and Technological Change: A Hafting Tradition Model for Prehistoric North America. In *Early Human Occupation in Far Western North America: The Clovis–Archaic Interface,* edited by J. A. Willig, C. M. Aikens, and J. L. Fagan, pp. 373–387. Nevada State Museum, Anthropological Papers, no. 21. Carson City.

Neel, J. V. 1967. The Genetic Structure of Primitive Human Populations. *Japanese Journal of Human Genetics* 12: 1–16.

Neel, J. V., and F. M. Salzano. 1967. Further Studies on the Xavante Indians. X. Some Hypotheses-Generalizations Resulting from These Studies. *American Journal of Human Genetics* 19: 554–574.

Neff, H. 1992. Ceramics and Evolution. *Archaeological Method and Theory* 4: 141–193.

Neff, H. 1993. Theory, Sampling, and Technical Studies in Archaeological Pottery Analysis. *American Antiquity* 58: 23–44.

Neff, H. 2002. Quantitative Techniques for Analyzing Ceramic Compositional Data. In *Ceramic Production and Circulation in the Greater Southwest: Source Determination by INAA and Complementary Mineralogical Investigations*, edited by D. M. Glowacki and H. Neff, pp. 15–36. Cotsen Institute of Archaeology, Los Angeles.

Neff, H., R. L. Bishop, and D. E. Arnold. 1990. Reexamination of the Compositional Affiliations of Formative Period Whiteware from Highland Guatemala. *Ancient Mesoamerica* 1: 171–180.

Neff, H., F. J. Bove, E. Robinson, and B. Arroyo. 1994. A Ceramic Compositional Perspective on the Formative to Classic Transition in Southern Mesoamerica. *Latin American Antiquity* 5: 333–358.

Neff, H., J. W. Cogswell, L. J. Kosakowsky, F. Estrada Belli, and F. J. Bove. 1999. A New Perspective on the Relationships among Cream Paste Ceramic Traditions of Southeastern Mesoamerica. *Latin American Antiquity* 10: 281–299.

Neff, H., J. W. Cogswell, and L. M. Ross, Jr. 2003. Microanalysis as a Supplement to Bulk Chemistry in Archaeological Ceramic Provenance Investigations. In *Patterns and Process: Essays in Honor of Dr. Edward V. Sayre*, edited by L. van Zelst and R. L. Bishop, pp. 201–234. Smithsonian Center for Materials Research and Education, Washington, D.C.

Neigel, J. E. 2002. Is FST Obsolete? *Conservation Genetics* 3: 167–173.

Neiman, F. 1995. Stylistic Variation in Evolutionary Perspective: Inferences from Decorative Diversity and Interassemblage Distance in Illinois Woodland Ceramic Assemblages. *American Antiquity* 60: 7–36.

Neiman, F. 1997. Conspicuous Consumption as Wasteful Advertising: A Darwinian Perspective on Spatial Patterns in Classic Maya Terminal Monument Dates. In *Rediscovering Darwin: Evolutionary Theory in Archeological Explanation,* edited by C. M. Barton and G. A. Clark, pp. 267–290. American Anthropological Association, Archeological Papers, no. 7. Washington, D.C.

Nelson, G., and N. I. Platnick. 1981. *Systematics and Biogeography: Cladistics and Vicariance.* Columbia University Press, New York.

Nelson, N. C. 1932. The Origin and Development of Material Culture. *Sigma Xi Quarterly* 20: 102–123.

Nettle, D. 2005. Human Genetic and Linguistic Diversity: Continental Patterns and Time Depth. Manuscript on file, University of Newcastle on Tyne, Newcastle, U.K.

Nettle, D., and L. Harriss. 2003. Genetic and Linguistic Affinities between Human Populations in Eurasia and West Africa. *Human Biology* 75: 331–344.

Nicholls, G., and R. D. Gray. 2005. Quantifying Uncertainty in a Stochastic Dollo Model of Vocabulary Evolutuion. In P*hylogenetic Methods and the Prehistory of Languages*, edited by J. Claekson, P. Forster, and C. Renfrew. MacDonald Institute for Archaeological Research, Cambridge. In press.

Nichols, J. 1997. Modeling Ancient Population Structures and Movement in Linguistics. *Annual Review of Anthropology* 26: 359–384.

Nielsen, R., J. L. Mountain, J. P. Huelsenbeck, and M. Slatkin. 1998. Maximum-Likelihood Estimation of Population Divergence Times and Population Phylogeny in Models without Mutation. *Evolution* 52: 669–677.

Nixon, K. C., and J. M. Carpenter. 1993. On Outgroups. *Cladistics* 9: 413–426.

Noll, F. B. 2002. Behavioral Phylogeny of Corbiculate Apidae (Hymenoptera; Apinae), with Special Reference to Social Behavior. *Cladistics* 18: 137–153.

Norell, M. A. 1992. Taxic Origin and Temporal Diversity: The Effect of Phylogeny. In *Extinction and Phylogeny,* edited by M. J. Novacek and Q. D. Wheeler, pp. 88–118. Columbia University Press, New York.

Norell, M. A. 1993. Tree-Based Approaches to Understanding History: Comments on Ranks, Rules, and the Quality of the Fossil Record. *American Journal of Science* 293: 407–417.

North, D. C. 1990. *Institutions, Institutional Change and Economic Performance*. Cambridge University Press, Cambridge.

Nunn C. L., M. Borgerhoff Mulder, and S. Langley. 2005. Comparative Methods for Studying Cultural Trait Evolution: A Simulation Study. *Cross-Cultural Research.* In press.

Nunn, C. L., M. Borgerhoff Mulder, and S. Langley. n.d. Comparative Methods for Studying Cultural Trait Evolution: A Simulation Study. Manuscript in possession of the authors.

Nurse, D. 1996. Historical Classifications of the Bantu Languages. *Azania* 29: 65–75.

Nurse, D. 1997. The Contributions of Linguistics to the Study of History in Africa. *Journal of African History* 38: 359–391.

Obler, R. S. 1985. *Women, Power, and Economic Change*. Stanford University Press, Stanford, Calif.

O'Brien, M. J. 1985. Archaeology of the Central Salt River Valley: An Overview of the Prehistoric Occupation. *Missouri Archaeologist* 46. Columbia.

O'Brien, M. J. (editor). 1996. *Evolutionary Archaeology: Theory and Application*. University of Utah Press, Salt Lake City.

O'Brien, M. J., J. Darwent, and R. L. Lyman. 2001. Cladistics Is Useful for Reconstructing Archaeological Phylogenies: Palaeoindian Points from the Southeastern United States. *Journal of Archaeological Science* 28: 1115–1136.

O'Brien, M. J., and T. D. Holland. 1990. Variation, Selection, and the Archaeological Record. *Archaeological Method and Theory* 2: 31–79.

O'Brien, M. J., T. D. Holland, R. J. Hoard, and G. L. Fox. 1994. Evolutionary Implications of Design and Performance Characteristics of Prehistoric Pottery. *Journal of Archaeological Method and Theory* 1: 259–304.

O'Brien, M. J., and R. D. Leonard. 2001. Style and Function: An Introduction. In *Style and Function: Conceptual Issues in Evolutionary Archaeology,* edited by T. D. Hurt and G. F. M. Rakita, pp. 1–23. Bergin and Garvey, Westport, Conn.

O'Brien, M. J., and R. L. Lyman. 1998. *James A. Ford and the Growth of Americanist Archaeology*. University of Missouri Press, Columbia.

O'Brien, M. J., and R. L. Lyman. 1999. *Seriation, Stratigraphy, and Index Fossils: The Backbone of Archaeological Dating*. Kluwer Academic/Plenum, New York.

O'Brien, M. J., and R. L. Lyman. 2000a. *Applying Evolutionary Archaeology: A Systematic Approach*. Kluwer Academic/Plenum, New York.

O'Brien, M. J., and R. L. Lyman. 2000b. Evolutionary Archaeology: Reconstructing and Explaining Historical Lineages. In *Social Theory in Archaeology,* edited by M. B. Schiffer, pp. 126–142. University of Utah Press, Salt Lake City.

O'Brien, M. J., and R. L. Lyman. 2002a. Evolutionary Archaeology: Current Status and Future Prospects. *Evolutionary Anthropology* 11: 26–36.

O'Brien, M. J., and R. L. Lyman. 2002b. The Epistemological Nature of Archaeological Units. *Anthropological Theory* 2: 37–56.

O'Brien, M. J., and R. L. Lyman. 2003a. *Cladistics and Archaeology*. University of Utah Press, Salt Lake City.

O'Brien, M. J., and R. L. Lyman. 2003b. Resolving Phylogeny: Evolutionary Archaeology's Fundamental Issue. In *Essential Tensions in Archaeological Method and Theory,* edited by T. L. VanPool and C. S. VanPool, pp. 115–135. University of Utah Press, Salt Lake City.

O'Brien, M. J., R. L. Lyman, Y. Saab, E. Saab, J. Darwent, and D. S. Glover. 2002. Two Issues in Archaeological Phylogenetics: Taxon Construction and Outgroup Selection. *Journal of Theoretical Biology* 215: 133–150.

O'Brien, M. J., and R. E. Warren. 1983. An Archaic Projectile Point Sequence from the Southern Prairie Peninsula: The Pigeon Roost Creek Site. In *Archaic Hunters and Gatherers in the American Midwest,* edited by J. L. Phillips and J. A. Brown, pp. 71–98. Academic Press, New York.

O'Brien, M. J., and W. R. Wood. 1998. *The Prehistory of Missouri.* University of Missouri Press, Columbia.

O'Hara, R. J. 1988. Homage to Clio, or, Towards an Historical Philosophy for Evolutionary Biology. *Systematic Zoology* 37: 142–155.

O'Leary, M. A., and J. H. Geisler. 1999. The Position of Cetacea within Mammalia: Phylogenetic Analysis of Morphological Data from Extinct and Extant Taxa. *Systematic Biology* 48: 455–490.

Orians, G. 1969. On the Evolution of Mating Systems in Birds and Mammals. *American Naturalist* 103: 589–603.

O'Rourke, D. H. 2003. Anthropological Genetics in the Genomic Era: A Look Back and Ahead. *American Anthropologist* 105: 101–109.

O'Rourke, D. H., M. G. Hayes, and S. W. Carlyle. 2000. Ancient DNA Studies in Physical Anthropology. *Annual Review of Anthropology* 29: 217–242.

Otte, M. 1997. The Diffusion of Modern Languages in Prehistoric Eurasia. In *Archaeology and Language,* edited by R. Blench and M. Spriggs, pp. 74–81. Routledge, London.

Pääbo, S. 2000. Of Bears, Conservation Genetics, and the Value of Time Travel. *National Academy of Sciences, Proceedings* 97: 1320–1321.

Paciotti, B., and M. Borgerhoff Mulder. 2004. Sungusungu: The Role of Preexisting and Evolving Social Institutions among Tanzanian Vigilante Organizations. *Human Organization.* 63: 113–125.

Page, R. 1993. *COMPONENT (version 2.0).* Natural History Museum, London.

Page, R. 2003. Introduction. In *Tangled Trees: Phylogeny, Cospeciation and Coevolution,* edited by R. Page, pp. 1–21. University of Chicago Press, Chicago.

Page, R. D. M. 2001a. *Nexus Data Editor (NDE) for Windows*, Version 0.5.0. http://taxonomy.zoology.gla.ac.uk/rod/NDE/nde.html

Page, R. D. M. 2001b. *TreeView*, Version 1.6.6. http://taxonomy.zoology.gla.ac.uk/rod/treeview.html

Pagel, M. 1994. Detecting Correlated Evolution on Phylogenies: A General Method for the Comparative Analysis of Discrete Characters. *Royal Society London, Proceedings* B255: 37–45.

Pagel, M. 1997. Inferring Evolutionary Processes from Phylogenies. *Zoologica Scripta* 26: 331–348.

Pagel, M. 2000. Maximum-Likelihood Models for Glottochronology and for Reconstructing Linguistic Phylogenies. In *Time Depth in Historical Linguistics,* edited by C. Renfrew, A. McMahon, and L. Trask, pp. 189–207. McDonald Institute for Archaeological Research, Cambridge.

Pagel, M. n.d. *DISCRETE.* www.ams.reading.ac.uk/zoology/pagel

Palmer, C. T., B. E. Fredrickson, and C. F. Tilley. 1997. Categories and Gatherings: Group Selection and the Mythology of Cultural Anthropology. *Evolution and Human Behavior* 18: 291–308.

Parsons, L. A. 1967. *Bilbao, Guatemala: An Archaeological Study of the Pacific Coast Cotzumalguapa Region,* vol. 1. Milwaukee Public Museum, Publications in Anthropology 11. Milwaukee, Wis.

Penny, D. 1982. Towards a Basis for Classification: The Incompleteness of Distance Measures, Incompatibility Analysis and Phenetic Classification. *Journal of Theoretical Biology.* 96: 129–142.

Petrie, W. M. F. 1899. Sequences in Prehistoric Remains. *Royal Anthropological Institute of Great Britain and Ireland, Journal* 29: 295–301.

Petrie, W. M. F. 1901. *Diospolis Parva.* Egypt Exploration Fund, Memoir 20, London.

Phillips, P., J. A. Ford, and J. B. Griffin. 1951. *Archaeological Survey in the Lower Mississippi Alluvial Valley, 1940–1947.* Peabody Museum of Archaeology and Ethnology, Papers 25. Cambridge, Mass.

Phillipson, D. W. 1993. *African Archaeology.* Cambridge University Press, Cambridge.

Pietrusewsky, M. 2000. Metric Analysis of Skeletal Remains: Methods and Applications. In *Biological Anthropology of the Human Skeleton*, edited by M. A. Katzenberg and S. R. Saunders, pp. 375–415. Wiley-Liss, New York.

Pitt Rivers, A. H. (Lane Fox). 1874a. On the Principles of Classification Adopted in the Arrangement of His Anthropological Collection, Now Exhibited in the Bethnal Green Museum. *Royal Anthropological Institute, Journal* 4: 293–308.

Pitt Rivers, A. H. (Lane Fox). 1874b. *Catalogue of the Anthropological Collection Lent by Colonel Lane Fox for Exhibition in the Bethnal Green Branch of the South Kensington Museum, June 1874, parts I and II.* Science and Art Department, Committee of Council on Education, London.

Pitt Rivers, A. H. (Lane Fox). 1875. The Evolution of Culture. *Royal Institution of Great Britain, Proceedings* 7: 496–520.

Pitt Rivers, A. H. (Lane Fox). 1891. Typological Museums, as Exemplified by the Pitt Rivers Museum in Oxford and His Provincial Museum in Farnham Dorset. *Society of Arts, Journal* 40: 115–122.

Platnick, N. I., and D. Cameron. 1977. Cladistic Methods in Textual, Linguistic, and Phylogenetic Analysis. *Systematic Zoology* 26: 380–385.

Pocklington, R. 1996. *Population Genetics and Cultural History.* M.A. thesis, Department of Anthropology, Simon Fraser University. Burnaby, British Columbia.

Pocklington, R. 2001. Memes and Cultural Viruses. In *International Encyclopedia of the Behavioral Sciences,* edited by N. J. Smelser and P. B. Bates, pp. 9554–9556. Elsevier, Amsterdam.

Pocklington, R., and M. L. Best. 1997. Cultural Evolution and Units of Selection in Replicating Text. *Journal of Theoretical Biology* 188: 79–87.

Pocklington, R., and W. H. Durham. 2005. The Myth of Homology in the Americas. Manuscript on file, Stanford University, Palo Alto, Calif.

Poloni, E. S., O. Semino, G. Passarino, A. S. Santachiara-Benerecetti, I. Dupanloup, A. Langaney, and L. Excoffier. 1997. Human Genetic Affinities for Y-chromosome P49a,f/ TaqI Haplotypes Show Strong Correspondence with Linguistics. *American Journal of Human Genetics* 61: 1015–1035.

Powell, V. 1995. Bifaces of the Calf Creek Horizon: A Collection from Cedar Canyon, Oklahoma. *Oklahoma Anthropological Society, Bulletin* 42: 145–165.

Purvis, A., J. L. Gittleman, and H.-K. Luh. 1994. Truth or Consequences: Effects of Phylogenetic Accuracy on Two Comparative Methods. *Journal of Theoretical Biology* 167: 293–300.

Read, D. W. 1974. Some Comments on Typologies in Archaeology and an Outline of a Methodology. *American Antiquity* 39: 216–242.

Read, D., and S. A. LeBlanc. 2003. Population Growth, Carrying Capacity, and Conflict. *Current Anthropology* 44: 59–85.

Reeve, J., and E. Abouheif. 2003. *Phylogenetic Independence.* Version 2.0, http://www.biology.mcgill.ca/faculty/abouheif/programs.html

Renfrew, C. 1987. *Archaeology and Language: The Puzzle of Indo-European Origins.* Cape, London.

Renfrew, C. 1992. Archaeology, Genetics and Linguistic Diversity. *Man* 27: 445–478.

Renfrew, C. 2000a. 10,000 or 5000 Years Ago? Questions of Time Depth. In *Time Depth in Historical Linguistics,* edited by C. Renfrew, A. McMahon, and L. Trask, pp. 413–439. McDonald Institute for Archaeological Research, Cambridge.

Renfrew, C. 2000b. Archaeogenetics: Towards a Population Prehistory of Europe. In *Archaeogenetics: DNA and the Population Prehistory of Europe,* edited by C. Renfrew and K. Boyle, pp. 89–97. McDonald Institute for Archaeological Research, Cambridge.

Renfrew, C. 2001. From Molecular Genetics to Archaeogenetics. *National Academy of Sciences, Proceedings* 98: 4830–4832.

Renfrew, C., and K. Boyle (editors). 2000. *Archaeogenetics: DNA and the Population Prehistory of Europe.* McDonald Institute for Archaeological Research, Cambridge.

Rexová, K., D. Frynta, and J. Zrzavý. 2003. Cladistic Analysis of Languages: Indo-European Classification Based on Lexicostatistical Data. *Cladistics* 19: 120–127.

Rheindt, F. E., T. U. Grafe, and E. Abouheif. 2004. Rapidly Evolving Traits and the Comparative Method: How Important is Testing for Phylogenetic Signal? *Evolutionary Ecology Research* 6:377–396.

Rhymer, J. M., and D. Simberloff. 1996. Extinction by Hybridization and Introgression. *Annual Review of Ecology and Systematics* 27: 83–109.

Rice, W. R. 1989. Analyzing Tables of Statistical Tests. *Evolution* 43: 223–225.

Richards, M., V. Macaulay, E. Hickey, E. Vega, B. Sykes, V. Guida, C. Rengo, D. Sellitto, F. Cruciani, T. Kivisild, R. Villems, M. Thomas, S. Rychkov, O. Rychkov, Y. Rychkov, M. Golge, D. Dimitrov, E. Hill, D. Bradley, V. Romano, F. Cali, G. Vona, A. Demaine, S. Papiha, C. Triantaphyllidis, G. Stefanescu, J. Hatina, M. Belledi, A. Di Rienzo, A. Novelletto, A. Oppenheim, S. Norby, N. Al-Zaheri, S. Santachiara-Benerecetti, R. Scozari, A. Torroni, and H. J. Bandelt. 2000. Tracing European Founder Lineages in the Near Eastern mtDNA Pool. *American Journal of Human Genetics* 67: 1251–1276.

Richerson, P. J., and R. Boyd. 2000. Built for Speed: Pleistocene Climate Variation and the Origin of Human Culture. *Perspectives in Ethology* 13: 1–45.

Richtsmeier, J. T., J. M. Cheverud, and J. E. Buikstra. 1984. The Relationship between Cranial Metric and Nonmetric Traits in the Rhesus Macaques From Cayo Santiago. *American Journal of Physical Anthropology* 64: 213–222.

Ringe, D., T. Warnow, A. Taylor. 2002. Indo-European and Computational Cladistics. *Philological Society, Transactions* 100: 59–129.

Ringe, D., T. Warnow, A. Taylor, A. Michailov, and L. Levinson. 1998. Computational Cladistics and the Position of Tocharian. *Journal of Indo-European Studies* 26: 391–414.

Roberts, F. H. H. 1939. *Archaeological Remains in the Whitewater District Eastern Arizona,* Part I: *House Types.* Bureau of American Ethnology Bulletin, no. 121. Washington, D.C.

Roberts, F. H. H. 1940. *Archaeological Remains in the Whitewater District Eastern Arizona,* Part II: *Artifacts and Burials.* Bureau of American Ethnology Bulletin, no. 121. Washington, D.C.

Roberts, J. M., C. C. Moore, and A. K. Romney. 1995. Predicting Similarity in Material Culture among New Guinea Villages from Propinquity and Language: A Log-Linear Approach. *Current Anthropology* 36: 769–788.

Robson Brown, K. A. 1995. *A Phylogenetic Systematic Analysis of Hominid Behaviour.* Ph.D. dissertation, University of Cambridge. Cambridge.

Robson Brown, K. A. 1996. Systematics and Integrated Methods for the Modelling of the Pre-Modern Human Mind. In *Modelling the Early Human Mind,* edited by P. Mellars and K. Gibson, pp. 103–117. McDonald Institute for Archaeological Research, Cambridge.

Rock, I. (editor). 1990. *The Legacy of Solomon Asch: Essays in Cognition and Social Psychology.* Erlbaum, Hillsdale, N.J.

Rodseth, L. 1998. Distributive Models of Culture: A Saparian Alternative to Essentialism. *American Anthropologist* 100: 55–69.

Rogers, A. P., and E. Cashdan. 1997. The Phylogenetic Approach to Comparing Human Populations. *Evolution and Human Behavior* 18: 353–358.

Rogers, A. R. 1987. A Model of Kin-Structured Migration. *Evolution* 41: 417–426.

Rogers, A. R. 1988. Does Biology Constrain Culture? *American Anthropologist* 90: 819–831.

Romney, A. K. 1957. The Genetic Model and Uto-Aztecan Time Perspective. *Davidson Journal of Anthropology* 3: 35–41.

Ross, M. 1997. Comment on "The Dimensions of Social Life in the Pacific: Human Diversity and the Myth of the Primitive Isolate" by J. E. Terrell, T. L. Hunt, and C. Gosden. *Current Anthropology* 38: 182–184.

Rosser, Z. H., T. Zerjal, M. E. Hurles, M. Adojaan, D. Alavantic, A. Amorim, W. Amos, M. Armenteros, E. Arroyo, G. Barbujani, G. Beckman, L. Beckman, J. Bertranpetit, E. Bosch, D. G. Bradley, G. Brede, G. Cooper, H. B. Corte-Real, P. de Knijff, R. Decorte, Y. E. Dubrova, O. Evgrafov, A. Gilissen, S. Glisic, M. Golge, E. W. Hill, A. Jeziorowska, L. Kalaydjieva, M. Kayser, T. Kivisild, S. A. Kravchenko, A. Krumina, V. Kucinskas, J. Lavinha, L. A. Livshits, P. Malaspina, S. Maria, K. McElreavey, T. A. Meitinger, A. V. Mikelsaar, R. J. Mitchell, K. Nafa, J. Nicholson, S. Norby, A. Pandya, J. Parik, P. C. Patsalis, L. Pereira, B. Peterlin, G. Pielberg, M. J. Prata, C. Previdere, L. Roewer, S. Rootsi, D. C. Rubinsztein, J. Saillard, F. R. Santos, G. Stefanescu, B. C. Sykes, A. Tolun, R. Villems, C. Tyler-Smith, and M. A. Jobling. 2000. Y-Chromosomal Diversity in Europe Is Clinal and Influenced Primarily by Geography, Rather than by Language. *American Journal of Human Genetics* 67: 1526–1543.

Routledge, K. 1919. *The Mystery of Easter Island.* Sifton, Praed, London.

Rowe, J. H. 1959. Archaeological Dating and Cultural Process. *Southwestern Journal of Anthropology* 15: 317–324.

Ruhlen, M. 1991. *A Guide to the World's Languages*, vol. 1, *Classification.* Arnold, London.

Rushforth, S., and J. S. Chisholm. 1991. *Cultural Persistence: Continuity in Meaning and Moral Responsibility among the Bearlake Athapaskans.* University Arizona Press, Tucson.

Sahlins, M. D. 1955. Esoteric Efflorescence in Easter Island. *American Anthropologist* 57: 1045–1052.

Sahlins, M. D. 1999. Two or Three Things That I Know about Culture. *Royal Anthropological Institute, Journal* 5: 399–421.

Sanderson, M. 2002a. R8s, *Analysis of Rates of Evolution*, version 1.50. http://ginger.ucdavis.edu/r8s

Sanderson, M. 2002b. Estimating Absolute Rates of Evolution and Divergence Times: A Penalized Likelihood Approach. *Molecular Biology and Evolution* 19: 101–109.

Sanderson, M. J., and M. J. Donoghue. 1989. Patterns of Variation in Levels of Homoplasy. *Evolution* 43: 1781–1795.

Sanderson, M. J., M. J. Donoghue, W. Piel, and T. Eriksson. 1994. TreeBASE: A Prototype Database of Phylogenetic Analyses and an Interactive Tool for Browsing the Phylogeny of Life. *American Journal of Botany* 81: 183.

Sanderson, M. J., and L. Hufford. 1996. Homoplasy and the Evolutionary Process: An Afterword. In *Homoplasy: The Recurrence of Similarity in Evolution,* edited by M. J. Sanderson and L. Hufford, pp. 271–301. Academic Press, San Diego, Calif.

Santley, R. S., T. W. Killion, and M. T. Lycett. 1986. On the Maya Collapse. *Journal of Anthropological Research* 42: 123–159.

Saunders, S. R. 1989. Nonmetric Skeletal Variation. In *Reconstruction of Life from the Skeleton*, edited by M. Y. Iscan and K. A. R. Kennedy, pp. 95–108. Wiley-Liss, New York.

Sayles, E. B. 1937. Stone: Implements and Bowls. In *Excavations at Snaketown:* I. *Material Culture,* edited by H. S. Gladwin, E. W. Haury, E. B. Sayles, and N. Gladwin, pp. 101–120. Medallion Papers, no. 25. Globe, Ariz.

Schiffer, M. B. 1999. Behavioral Archaeology: Some Clarifications. *American Antiquity* 64: 166–168.

Schiffer, M. B., and J. M. Skibo. 1987. Theory and Experiment in the Study of Technological Change. *Current Anthropology* 28: 595–622.

Schiffer, M. B., and J. M. Skibo. 1997. The Explanation of Artifact Variability. *American Antiquity* 62: 27–50.

Schiffer, M. B., J. M. Skibo, J. L. Griffitts, K. Hollenback, and W. A. Longacre. 2001. Behavioral Archaeology and the Study of Technology. *American Antiquity* 66: 729–737.

Schillaci, M. A., and C. M. Stojanowski. 2000. Postmarital Residence and Population Structure at Pueblo Bonito. *American Journal of Physical Anthropology, Supplement* 30: 271.

Schillaci, M. A., and C. M. Stojanowski. 2002. A Reassessment of Matrilocality in Chacoan Culture. *American Antiquity* 67: 343–356.

Schleicher, A. A. 1863. *Die Darwinische Theorie und die Sprachwissenschaft.* Bohlau, Weimar, Germany.

Schmidt, J. 1872. *Die Verwantschaftsverhaltnisse der Indogermanischen Sprachen.* Bohlau, Weimar, Germany.

Schmidt, P. 1978. *Historical Archaeology: A Structural Approach in an African Culture.* Greenwood, Westport, Conn.

Schmidt, P. R. 1975. A New Look at Interpretations of the Early Iron Age in East Africa. *History of Africa* 2: 127–136.

Schneider, D. M., and K. Gough. 1961. *Matrilineal Kinship.* University of California Press, Berkeley.

Schneider, H. K. 1964. A Model of African Indigenous Economy and Society. *Comparative Studies in Society and History* 7: 37–55.

Schöndube, O. 1998. Natural Resources and Human Settlements in Ancient West Mexico. In *Ancient West Mexico: Art and Archaeology of the Unknown Past,* edited by R. F. Townsend, pp. 204–215. Thames and Hudson, London, and the Art Institute of Chicago, Chicago.

Schrage, L. 1979. A More Portable FORTRAN Random Number Generator. *ACM Transactions on Mathematical Software* 5: 132–138.

Sellen, D. W., and R. Mace. 1997. Fertility and Mode of Subsistence: A Phylogenetic Analysis. *Current Anthropology* 38: 878–889.

Sellen, D. W., and R. Mace. 1999. A Phylogenetic Analysis of the Relationship between Sub-adult Mortality and Mode of Subsistence. *Journal of Biosocial Science* 31: 1–16.

Seltzer, C. C. 1944. *Racial Prehistory in the Southwest and the Hawikuh Zunis*. Peabody Museum of American Archaeology and Ethnology, Papers 23. Cambridge, Mass.

Semino, O., G. Passarino, P. J. Oefner, A. A. Lin, S. Arbuzova, L. E. Beckman, G. De Benedictis, P. Francalacci, A. Kouvatsi, S. Limborska, M. Marcikiæ, A. Mika, B. Mika, D. Primorac, A. S. Santachiara-Benerecetti, L. L. Cavalli-Sforza, and P. A. Underhill. 2000. The Genetic Legacy of Palaeolithic *Homo sapiens sapiens* in Extant Europeans: A Y Chromosome Perspective. *Science* 290: 1155–1159.

Service, E. R. 1964. Archaeological Theory and Ethnological Fact. In *Process and Pattern in Culture: Essays in Honor of Julian H. Steward,* edited by R. Manners, pp. 364–375. Aldine, Chicago.

Sharer, R. J. 1978. Pottery and Conclusions. In *The Prehistory of Chalchuapa, El Salvador*, vol. 3, edited by R. J. Sharer, pp. 1–226. University of Pennsylvania Press, Philadelphia.

Shaw, L. C. 1996. The Use of Caves as Burial Chambers on Easter Island. *Rapa Nui Journal* 10: 101–103.

Shaw, L. C. 2000. Human Burials in the Coastal Caves of Easter Island. In *Easter Island Archaeology: Research on Early Rapa Nui Culture,* edited by C. M. Stevenson and W. S. Ayers, pp. 59–80. Easter Island Foundation, New York.

Shennan, S. J. 1991. Tradition, Rationality, and Cultural Transmission. In *Processual and Postprocessual Archaeologies: Multiple Ways of Knowing the Past,* edited by R. W. Preucel, pp. 197–208. Center for Archaeological Investigations, Southern Illinois University at Carbondale, Occasional Paper no. 10.

Shennan, S. J. 2000. Population, Culture History, and the Dynamics of Culture Change. *Current Anthropology* 41: 811–835.

Shennan, S. J. 2001. Demography and Cultural Innovation: A Model and Some Implications for the Emergence of Modern Human Culture. *Cambridge Archaeological Journal* 11: 5–16.

Shennan, S. J. 2002. *Genes, Memes and Human History: Darwinian Archaeology and Cultural Evolution*. Thames and Hudson, London.

Shennan, S. J., and M. Collard. 2005. Investigating Processes of Cultural Evolution on the North Coast of New Guinea with Multivariate and Cladistic Analyses. In *The Evolution of Cultural Diversity: A Phylogenetic Approach,* edited by R. Mace, C. J. Holden, and S. J. Shennan. pp. 133–164. University College London Press, London.

Shennan, S. J., and J. R. Wilkinson. 2001. Ceramic Style Change and Neutral Evolution: A Case Study from Neolithic Europe. *American Antiquity* 66: 577–594.

Shepard, A. O. 1936. The Technology of Pecos Pottery. In *The Pottery of Pecos,* vol. 2, edited by A. V. Kidder and A. O. Shepard, pp. 389–587. Phillips Academy, Southwestern Expedition Papers, no. 7. Andover, Mass.

Shepard, A. O. 1948. *Plumbate: A Mesoamerican Tradeware*. Carnegie Institution of Washington, Publication 573. Washington, D.C.

Shillington, K. 1995. *History of Africa,* rev. ed. Macmillan, London.

Shimodaira, H., and M. Hasegawa. 1999. Multiple Comparisons of Log-Likelihoods with Applications to Phylogenetic Inference. *Molecular Biological Evolution* 16: 1114–1116.

Shweder, R. A. 2002. Culture: Contemporary Views. *International Encyclopedia of the Social and Behavioral Sciences*, pp. 3151–3158. Elsevier, New York.

Simpson, G. G. 1953. *The Major Features of Evolution*. Columbia University Press, New York.

Simpson, G. G. 1963. Historical Science. In *The Fabric of Geology*, edited by C. C. Albritton, Jr., pp. 24–48. Freeman, Cooper, Stanford, Calif.

Simpson, G. G. 1970. Uniformitarianism: An Inquiry into Principle, Theory, and Method in Geohistory and Biohistory. In *Essays in Evolution and Genetics in Honor of Theodosius Dobzhansky,* edited by M. K. Hecht and W. C. Steere, pp. 43–96. Appleton, New York.

Skála, Z., and J. Zrzavý. 1994. Phylogenetic Reticulations and Cladistics: Discussion of Methodological Concepts. *Cladistics* 10: 305–313.

Smith, A. B. 2000. Stratigraphy in Phylogeny Reconstruction. *Journal of Paleontology* 74: 763–766.

Smith, E. A. 2001. On the Coevolution of Cultural, Linguistic and Biological Diversity. In *On Biocultural Diversity: Linking Language, Knowledge, and the Environment,* edited by L. Maffi, pp. 95–117. Smithsonian Institution Press, Washington, D.C.

Smouse, P. E., and J. C. Long. 1992. Matrix Correlation Analysis in Anthropology and Genetics. *Yearbook of Physical Anthropology* 35: 187–213.

Smouse, P. E., J. C. Long, and R. R. Sokal. 1986. Multiple Regression and Correlation Extensions of the Mantel Test of Matrix Correspondence. *Systematic Zoology* 35: 627–632.

Sober, E. 1984. *The Nature of Selection: Evolutionary Theory in Philosophical Focus.* University of Chicago Press, Chicago.

Sober, E. 1988. *Reconstructing the Past: Parsimony, Evolution, and Inference.* MIT Press, Cambridge, Mass.

Sokal, R. R. 1988. Genetic, Geographic and Linguistic Distances in Europe. *National Academy of Sciences, Proceedings* 85: 1722–1726.

Sokal, R. R., J. H. Camin, F. J. Rohlf, and P. H. A. Sneath. 1965. Numerical Taxonomy: Some Points of View. *Systematic Zoology* 14: 237–243.

Sokal, R. R., R. M. Harding, and N. L. Oden. 1989. Spatial Patterns of Human Gene Frequencies in Europe. *American Journal of Physical Anthropology* 80: 267–294.

Sokal, R. R., N. L. Oden, and C. Wilson. 1991. Genetic Evidence for the Spread of Agriculture in Europe by Demic Diffusion. *Nature* 351: 143–145.

Sokal, R. R., and F. J. Rohlf. 1995. *Biometry,* third ed. Freeman, San Francisco.

Sokal, R. R., and P. H. A. Sneath. 1963. *Principles of Numerical Taxonomy.* Freeman, San Francisco.

Soper, R. 1971. A General Review of the Early Iron Age of the Southern Half of Africa. *Azania* 6: 5–37.

Spaulding, A. C. 1953. Statistical Techniques for the Discovery of Artifact Types. *American Antiquity* 18: 305–313.

Spaulding, A. C. 1955. Prehistoric Cultural Development in the Eastern United States. In *New Interpretations of Aboriginal American Culture History*, edited by B. J. Meggers and C. Evans, pp. 12–27. Anthropological Society of Washington, Washington, D.C.

Spaulding, A. C. 1960. Statistical Description and Comparison of Artifact Assemblages. In *The Application of Quantitative Methods in Archaeology,* edited by R. F. Heizer and S. F. Cook, pp. 60–83. Viking Fund Publication in Anthropology, no. 28. Wenner-Gren Foundation for Anthropological Research, New York.

Spear, T. T. 1997. *Mountain Farmers: Moral Economies of Land & Agricultural Development in Arusha & Meru.* University of California Press, Berkeley.

Spencer, P. 1997. *The Pastoral Continuum.* Oxford University Press, Oxford.

Spencer, M., E. A. Davidson, A. C. Barbrook, and C. J. Howe. 2004. Phylogenetics of Artificial Manuscripts. *Journal of Theoretical Biology* 227: 503–511.

Sperber, D. 1996. *Explaining Culture: a Naturalistic Approach*. Blackwell, Cambridge.

Spier, L. 1917. An Outline for a Chronology of Zuni Ruins. *American Museum of Natural History, Anthropological Papers* 18: 207–331.

Spriggs, M., and A. Anderson. 1993. Late Colonization of East Polynesia. *Antiquity* 67: 200–217.

Spuhler, J. N. 1954. Some Problems in the Physical Anthropology of the American Southwest. *American Anthropologist* 56: 604–619.

Stadler, B. M. R., P. F. Stadler, G. Wagner, and W. Fontana. 2001. The Topology of the Possible: Formal Spaces Underlying Patterns of Evolutionary Change. *Journal of Theoretical Biology* 213: 241–274.

Stafleu, F. A. 1969. A Historical Review of Systematic Biology. In *Systematic Biology,* edited by C. G. Sibley, pp. 16–44. National Academy of Sciences, Washington, D.C.

Stanhope, M. J., V. G. Waddell, O. Madsen, W. de Jong, S. B. Hedges, G. C. Cleven, D. Kao, and M. S. Springer. 1998. Molecular Evidence for Multiple Origins of Insectivora and for a New Order of Endemic African Insectivore Mammals. *National Academy of Sciences, Proceedings* 95: 9967–9972.

Steel, M. A., M. D. Hendy, and D. Penny. 1988. Loss of Information in Genetic Distances. *Nature* 333: 494–495.

Stefan, V. H. 1999. Craniometric Variation and Homogeneity in Prehistoric/Protohistoric Rapa Nui (Easter Island) Regional Populations. *American Journal of Physical Anthropology* 110: 407–419.

Stefan, V. H. 2000. *Craniometric Variation and Biological Affinity of the Prehistoric Rapanui (Easter Islanders): Their Origin, Evolution, and Place in Polynesian Prehistory.* Ph.D. dissertation, Department of Anthropology, University of New Mexico. Albuquerque.

Stevenson, C. M. 1984. *Corporate Descent Group Structure in Easter Island Prehistory.* Ph.D. dissertation, Department of Anthropology, Pennsylvania State University. University Park.

Stevenson, C. M. 1986. The Socio-Political Structure of the Southern Coastal Area of Easter Island. In *The Evolution of Island Societies,* edited by P. V. Kirch, pp. 69–77. Cambridge University Press, Cambridge.

Stevenson, C. M. 2002. Territorial Divisions on Easter Island in the Sixteenth Century: Evidence from the Distribution of Ceremonial Architecture. In *Pacific Landscapes: Archaeological Approaches,* edited by T. N. Ladefoged and M. W. Graves, pp. 211–229. Bearsville Press, Los Osos, Calif.

Stevenson, C. M., T. N. Ladefoged, and S. Haoa. 2002. Productive Strategies in an Uncertain Environment: Prehistoric Agriculture on Easter Island. *Rapa Nui Journal* 16: 17–22.

Steward, J. H. 1929. Diffusion and Independent Invention: A Critique of Logic. *American Anthropologist* 31: 491–495.

Steward, J. H. 1944. Re: Archaeological Tools and Jobs. *American Antiquity* 10: 99–100.

Steward, J. H. 1954. Types of Types. *American Antiquity* 56: 54–57.

Stewart, T. D. 1940. Skeletal Remains from the Whitewater District, Eastern Arizona. In *Archaeological Remains in the Whitewater District Eastern Arizona,* Part II: *Artifacts and Burials,* edited by F. H. H. Roberts, pp. 153–166. Bureau of American Ethnology Bulletin, no. 121. Washington, D.C.

Stewart, T. D. 1954. Some Problems in the Physical Anthropology of the American Southwest: Comments. *American Anthropologist* 56: 619–620.

Stojanowski, C. M. 2003. Matrix Decomposition Model for Investigating Prehistoric Intracemetery Biological Variation. *American Journal of Physical Anthropology* 122: 216–231.

Suttles, W. 1990. Introduction. In *Handbook of North American Indians,* vol. 7, *The Northwest Coast,* edited by W. Suttles, pp. 1–15. Smithsonian Institution Press, Washington, D.C.

Sutton, J. E. G. 1972. New Radiocarbon Dates for Eastern and Southern Africa. *Journal of African History* 13: 1–24.

Swadesh, M. 1952. Lexico-Statistic Dating of Prehistoric Ethnic Contacts. *American Philosophical Society, Proceedings* 96: 453–463.

Swadesh, M. 1955. Towards Greater Accuracy in Lexicostatistic Dating. *International Journal of American Linguistics* 21: 121–137.

Swadesh, M. 1971. What Is Glottochronology? In *The Origin and Diversification of Language,* edited by J. Sherzer, pp. 271–284. Aldine, Chicago.

Swinscow T. D. V. 1977. *Statistics at Square One,* second ed. British Medical Association, London.

Swofford, D. L. 1991. When Are Phylogeny Estimates from Molecular and Morphological Data Incongruent? In *Phylogenetic Analysis of DNA Sequences,* edited by M. M. Miyamoto and J. Cracraft, pp. 295–333. Oxford University Press, New York.

Swofford, D. L. 1998. PAUP*: *Phylogenetic Analysis Using Parsimony (*and Other Methods*)* (version 4). Sinauer, Sunderland, Mass.

Swofford, D. L., G. J. Olsen, P. J. Waddell, and D. M. Hillis. 1996. Phylogenetic Inference. In *Molecular Systematics,* second ed., edited by D. M. Hillis, C. Moritz, and B. K. Mable, pp. 407–514. Sinauer, Sunderland, Mass.

Tehrani, J. J., and M. Collard. 2002. Investigating Cultural Evolution through Biological Phylogenetic Analyses of Turkmen Textiles. *Journal of Anthropological Archaeology* 21: 443–463.

Teltser, P. A. 1995. Culture History, Evolutionary Theory, and Frequency Seriation. In *Evolutionary Archaeology: Methodological Issues,* edited by P. A. Teltser, pp. 51–68. University of Arizona Press, Tucson.

Temkin, I. 2004. The Evolution of the Baltic Psaltery. *The Galpin Society Journal* LVII: 219–230.

Templeton, A. R. 1998. Nested Clade Analyses of Phylogeographic Data: Testing Hypotheses about Gene Flow and Population History. *Molecular Ecology* 7: 381–397.

Templeton, A. R., E. Routman, and C. A. Phillips. 1995. Separating Population Structure from Population History: A Cladistic Analysis of the Geographical Distribution of Mitochondrial DNA Haplotypes in the Tiger Salamander, *Ambystoma tigrinurn. Genetics* 140: 767–782.

Terrell, J. E. 1986. Causal Pathways and Causal Processes: Studying the Evolutionary Prehistory of Human Diversity in Language, Customs, and Biology. *Journal of Anthropological Archaeology* 5: 187–198.

Terrell, J. E. 1987. Comment on "History, Phylogeny, and Evolution in Polynesia" by P. V. Kirch and R. C. Green. *Current Anthropology* 28: 447–448.

Terrell, J. E. 1988. History as a Family Tree, History as an Entangled Bank: Constructing Images and Interpretations of Prehistory in the South Pacific. *Antiquity* 62: 642–657.

Terrell, J. E. 2001. Introduction. In *Archaeology, Language, and History: Essays on Culture and Ethnicity,* edited by J. E. Terrell, pp. 1–10. Bergin and Garvey, Westport, Conn.

Terrell, J. E., T. L. Hunt, and C. Gosden. 1997. The Dimensions of Social Life in the Pacific: Human Diversity and the Myth of the Primitive Isolate. *Current Anthropology* 38: 155–195.

Terrell, J. E., K. M. Kelly, and P. Rainbird. 2001. Foregone Conclusions? In Search of "Papuans" and "Austronesians." *Current Anthropology* 42: 97–124.

Thieme, M., and H. Neff. 1993. Examination and Analysis of Clay Materials in a Pottery Producing Town in Oaxaca, Mexico. Paper presented at the 92nd Annual Meeting of the American Anthropological Association, Washington, D.C.

Thompson, L. C., and M. D. Kinkade. 1990. Languages. In *Handbook of North American Indians,* vol. 7, *The Northwest Coast,* edited by W. Suttles, pp. 30–51. Smithsonian Institution Press, Washington, D.C.

Thompson, R. H. 1956. An Archaeological Approach to Cultural Stability. In *Seminars in Archaeology: 1955,* edited by R. Wauchope, pp. 31–57. Society for American Archaeology, Memoir, no. 11. Salt Lake City, Utah.

Thompson, R. H. (editor) 1958. *Migrations in New World Culture History.* University of Arizona, Social Science Bulletin 27.

Thompson, W. J. 1889. *Te Pito de Henua, or Easter Island.* Smithsonian Institution, Washington, D.C.

Tobisson, E. 1986. *Family Dynamics among the Kuria.* University of Gothenburg Press, Gothenburg, Sweden.

Tomczak, P. D., and J. F. Powell. 2003. Postmarital Residence Practices in the Windover Population: Sex-Based Dental Variation as an Indicator of Patrilocality. *American Antiquity* 68: 93–108.

Trask, R. L. 1996. *Historical Linguistics.* Arnold, New York.

Trask, R. L. 2003a. Re: *Language Tree Rooted in Turkey.* http://groups.yahoo.com/group/evolutionary-psychology/message/28240

Trask, R. L. 2003b. Re: *Language Tree Rooted in Turkey.* http://groups.yahoo.com/group/evolutionary-psychology/message/28291

Trimingham, J. S. 1970. *A History of Islam in West Africa.* Oxford University Press, Oxford.

Tschauner, H. 1994. Archaeological Systematics and Cultural Evolution: Retrieving the Honour of Culture History. *Man* 29: 77–93.

Turchin, P. 2003. *Historical Dynamics.* Princeton University Press, Princeton, N.J.

Turner, C. G., II. 1999. The Dentition of Casas Grandes with Suggestions on Epigenetic Relationships among Mexican and Southwestern U.S. Populations. In *The Casas Grandes World,* edited by C. F. Schaafsma and C. L. Riley, pp. 229–233. University of Utah Press, Salt Lake City.

Tylor, E. B. 1871. *Primitive Culture.* Murray, London.

Tylor, E. B. 1889. On a Method of Investigating the Development of Institutions. *Royal Anthropological Institute of Great Britain and Ireland, Journal* 18: 245–272.

Underhill, P. A. 2003. Inference of Neolithic Population Histories Using Y-Chromosome Haplotypes. In *Examining the Farming/Language Dispersal Hypothesis,* edited by P. Bellwood and C. Renfrew, pp. 65–78. McDonald Institute for Archaeological Research, Cambridge.

Van Buren, G. E. 1974. *Arrowheads and Projectile Points.* Arrowhead, Garden Grove, Calif.

Van Neer, W. 2000. Domestic Animals from Archaeological Sites in Central and West-Central Africa. In *The Origins and Development of African Livestock: Archaeology, Genetics, Linguistics and Ethnography,* edited by R. M. Blench and K. C. MacDonald, pp. 163–190. University College London Press, London.

VanPool, C. S., T. L. VanPool, D. A. Phillips, Jr., and M. J. Harmon. 2000. The Changing Faces of Horned/Plumed Serpents in the Greater North American Southwest. Paper presented at the 33rd Annual Chacmool Conference, Calgary, Canada.

Vansina, J. 1984. West Bantu Expansion. *Journal of African History* 25: 129–145.

Vansina, J. 1990. *Paths in the Rainforests: Toward a History of the Political Tradition in Equatorial Africa.* University of Wisconsin Press, Madison.

Voeghlin, C. F., and F. M. Voeghlin. 1977. *Classification and Index of the World's Languages.* Elsevier, New York.

Vogt, E. Z. 1964. The Genetic Model and Maya Cultural Development. In *Desarollo Cultural de los Mayos,* edited by E. Z. Vogt and A. Ruz, pp. 9–48. Universidad Nacional Autonoma de Mexico, Mexico, D.F.

Wake, D. B. 1991. Homoplasy: The Result of Natural Selection, or Evidence of Design Limitations? *American Naturalist* 138: 543–567.

Washburn, S. L. 1951. The New Physical Anthropology. *New York Academy of Sciences, Transactions* 13: 298–304.

Wasserman, S., and K. Faust. 1994. *Social Network Analysis: Methods and Applications*. Cambridge University Press, Cambridge.

Watkins, C. 1969. *Indogermanische Grammatik III/1. Geschichte der Indogermanischen Verbalflexion*. Verlag, Heidelberg, Germany.

Wayne, R. K., E. Geffen, D. J. Girman, K. P. Koepfli, L. M. Lau, and C. R. Marshall. 1997. Molecular Systematics of the Canidae. *Systematic Biology* 46: 622–653.

Welsch, R. L. 1996. Language, Culture and Data on the North Coast of New Guinea. *Journal of Quantitative Anthropology* 6: 209–234.

Welsch, R. L., J. A. Nadolski, and J. E. Terrell. 1992. Language and Culture on the North Coast of New Guinea. *American Anthropologist* 94: 568–600.

West, G. B., J. H. Brown, and B. J. Enquist. 1997. A General Model for the Origin of Allometric Scaling Laws in Biology. *Science* 276: 122–126.

Wetherington, R. K. 1978. Descriptive Taxonomy of Kaminaljuyú Ceramics. In *The Ceramics of Kaminaljuyú, Guatemala*, edited by R. K. Wetherington, pp. 3–50. Pennsylvania State University Monograph Series on Kaminaljuyú, University Park.

Whaley, L. J. 2001. Manchu-Tungusic Culture Change among Manchu-Tungusic Peoples. In *Archaeology, Language, and History: Essays on Culture and Ethnicity*, edited by J. E. Terrell, pp. 103–124. Bergin and Garvey, Westport, Conn.

Whallon, R. J. 1972. A New Approach to Pottery Typology. *American Antiquity* 37: 13–33.

Whallon, R. J., and J. A. Brown (editors). 1982. *Essays on Archaeological Typology*. Center for American Archeology, Evanston, Ill.

Wheat, J. B., J. C. Gifford, and W. W. Wasley. 1958. Ceramic Variety, Type Cluster, and Ceramic System in Southwestern Pottery Analysis. *American Antiquity* 24: 34–47.

Whittaker, J. C., D. Caulkins, and K. A. Kamp. 1998. Evaluating Consistency in Typology and Classification. *Journal of Archaeological Method and Theory* 5: 129–164.

Wilder, D. A. 1977. Perception of Groups, Size of Opposition, and Social Influence. *Journal of Experimental Social Psychology* 13: 253–268.

Wiley, E. O. 1981. *Phylogenetics: The Theory and Practice of Phylogenetic Systematics*. Wiley-InterScience, New York.

Wiley, E. O., D. J. Siegel-Causey, D. R. Brooks, and V. A. Funk. 1991. *The Compleat Cladist: A Primer of Phylogenetic Procedures*. University of Kansas, Museum of Natural History, Special Publication, no. 19. Lawrence. (available online at http://www.amnh.org/learn/pd/fish_2/pdf/compleat_cladist.pdf)

Wilhelmsen, K. H. 1993. The Potential of Evolutionary Theory for Explaining Relationships between Culture and Environment. In *Culture and Environment: A Fragile Coexistence*, edited by R. W. Jamieson, S. Abonyi, and N. A. Mirau, pp. 155–163. University of Calgary Archaeological Association, Calgary.

Wilhelmsen, K. H., and T. Miles. 2005. The Application of Thermoluminescence Dating to Catastrophically Heated Chert Artifacts. In *New Methods of Lithic Analysis,* edited by M. Shott and N. Maloney. Institute of Archaeology, University College London. London. In press.

Willer, D., and J. Willer. 1973. *Systematic Empiricism: A Critique of a Pseudoscience*. Prentice-Hall, Englewood Cliffs, N.J.

Willey, G. R. 1953. Archaeological Theories and Interpretation: New World. In *Anthropology Today,* edited by A. L. Kroeber, pp. 361–385. University of Chicago Press, Chicago.

Willey, G. R., R. M. Leventhal, A. A. Demarest, and W. L. Fash. 1994. *Ceramics and Artifacts from Excavations in the Copán Residential Zone.* Peabody Museum of Archaeology and Ethnology, Papers 80. Cambridge, Mass.

Willey, G. R., and P. Phillips. 1958. *Method and Theory in American Archaeology.* University of Chicago Press, Chicago.

Williams-Blangero, S., and J. Blangero. 1989. Anthropometric Variation and the Genetic Structure of the Jirels of Nepal. *Human Biology* 61: 1–12.

Williamson, K., and R. M. Blench. 2000. Niger-Congo. In *African Languages: An Introduction,* edited by B. Heine and D. Nurse, pp. 11–42. Cambridge University Press, Cambridge.

Wilson, T. 1898. Class A, Beveled Edges. *American Archaeologist* 2: 141–143.

Woese, C. R. 2000. Interpreting the Universal Phylogenetic Tree. *National Academy of Sciences, Proceedings* 97: 8392–8396.

Wolf, E. 1982. *Europe and the People without History.* University of California Press, Berkeley.

Wolpoff, M. H. 1999. *Paleoanthropology.* McGraw-Hill, Boston.

Wright, S. 1931. Evolution in Mendelian Populations. *Genetics* 16: 97–159.

Wright, S. 1943. Isolation by Distance. *Genetics* 28: 114–138.

Wright, S. 1951. The Genetical Structure of Populations. *Annals of Eugenics* 15: 323–354.

Wu, C. I., and W. H. Li. 1985. Evidence for Higher Rates of Nucleotide Substitution in Rodents than in Man. *National Academy of Sciences, Proceedings* 82: 1741–1745.

Yang, Z., and A. D. Yoder. 2003. Comparison of Likelihood and Bayesian Methods for Estimating Divergence Times Using Multiple Gene Loci and Calibration Points, with Application to a Radiation of Cute-Looking Mouse Lemur Species. *Systematic Biology* 52: 705–716.

Yoder, A. D. 1994. The Relative Position of the Cheirogaleidae in Strepsirhine Phylogeny: A Comparison of Morphological and Molecular Methods and Results. *American Journal of Physical Anthropology* 94: 25–46.

Yoder, A. D., M. M. Burns, S. Zehr, T. Delefosse, G. Veron, S. M. Goodman, and J. J. Flynn. 2003. Single Origin of Malagasy Carnivora from an African Ancestor. *Nature* 421: 734–737.

Yoder, A. D., and Z. Yang. 2000. Estimation of Primate Speciation Dates Using Local Molecular Clocks. *Molecular Biology and Evolution* 17: 1081–1090.

Zimmerman, W. 1931. Arbeitsweise der Botanischen Plylogenetik under Anderer Gruppierungswissenshaften. In *Handbuch der Biologischen Arbeitsmethoden*, edited by E. Aberhalden, pp. 941–1053. Urban and Schwarzenberg, Berlin.

Zimple, C., and G. W. Gill. 1986. A Comparison of Discrete Cranial Traits among Late Prehistoric Easter Islanders. *American Journal of Physical Anthropology* 69: 283.

Zvelebil, M. 1995. At the Interface of Archaeology, Linguistics and Genetics: Indo-European Dispersals and the Agricultural Transition in Europe. *Journal of European Archaeology* 3: 33–70.

Contributors

Quentin Atkinson
Department of Psychology
University of Auckland
Auckland 1020 New Zealand

Robert L. Bettinger
Department of Anthropology
University of California, Davis
Davis, California 95616

Monique Borgerhoff Mulder
Department of Anthropology
University of California, Davis
Davis, California 95616

Mark Collard
Department of Anthropology and
Sociology
University of British Columbia
Vancouver, Canada V6T 1Z1.

John Darwent
Department of Anthropology
University of California, Davis
Davis, California 95616

John Dudgeon
Department of Anthropology
University of Hawaii at Manoa
Honolulu, Hawai'i 96822

Robert C. Dunnell
21 Pruett Road
Natchez, Mississippi 39120

Jelmer Eerkens
Department of Anthropology
University of California, Davis
Davis, California 95616

Niles Eldredge
Division of Paleontology
The American Museum of Natural
History
New York, New York 10024

Corine M. Graham
Department of Anthropology
University of California, Davis
Davis, California 95616

Russell D. Gray
Department of Psychology
University of Auckland
Auckland 1020 New Zealand

N. Thomas Håkansson
Department of Anthropology
University of Kentucky
Lexington, Kentucky

Marcel J. Harmon
Department of Anthropology
University of New Mexico
Albuquerque, NM 87131

Clare J. Holden
Department of Anthropology
University College London
London WC1H 0PY England

Peter Jordan
Institute of Archaeology
University College London
London WC1H 0PY England

Robert D. Leonard
Department of Anthropology
University of New Mexico
Albuquerque, NM 87131

Carl P. Lipo
Department of Anthropology
California State University,
Long Beach
Long Beach, California 90840

R. Lee Lyman
Department of Anthropology
University of Missouri
Columbia, Missouri 65203

Thomas Mace
Institute of Archaeology
University College London
London WC1H 0PY England

Richard McElreath
Department of Anthropology
University of California, Davis
Davis, California 95616

Jennifer W. Moylan
Department of Anthropology
University of California, Davis
Davis, California 95616

Hector Neff
Department of Anthropology
California State University,
Long Beach
Long Beach, California 90840

Charles L. Nunn
Department of Anthropology
University of California, Davis
Davis, California 95616

Michael J. O'Brien
Department of Anthropology
University of Missouri
Columbia, Missouri 65203

Richard Pocklington
Department of Anthropological
Sciences
Stanford University
Stanford, CA 94305

Gordon F. M. Rakita
Department of Sociology, Anthro-
pology, and Criminal Justice
University of North Florida
Jacksonville, Florida 32224

Laura A. Salter
Department of Mathematics and
Statistics
University of New Mexico
Albuquerque, NM 87131

Stephen J. Shennan
Institute of Archaeology
University College London
London WC1H 0PY England

Jamshid J. Tehrani
Department of Anthropology
University College London
London WC1H 0PY England

Christine S. VanPool
Department of Anthropology
University of New Mexico
Albuquerque, NM 87131

Todd L. VanPool
Department of Anthropology
University of New Mexico
Albuquerque, NM 87131

Index